Word and Paradigm Morphology

Word and Paradigm Morphology

JAMES P. BLEVINS

OXFORD
UNIVERSITY PRESS

OXFORD

UNIVERSITY PRESS

Great Clarendon Street, Oxford, OX2 6DP,
United Kingdom

Oxford University Press is a department of the University of Oxford.
It furthers the University's objective of excellence in research, scholarship,
and education by publishing worldwide. Oxford is a registered trade mark of
Oxford University Press in the UK and in certain other countries

© James P. Blevins 2016

The moral rights of the author have been asserted

First Edition published in 2016
Impression: 1

Published in the United States of America by Oxford University Press
198 Madison Avenue, New York, NY 10016, United States of America

British Library Cataloguing in Publication Data
Data available

Library of Congress Control Number: 2016933521

ISBN 978-0-19-959354-5 (hbk)
ISBN 978-0-19-959355-2 (pbk)

Printed in Great Britain by
Clays Ltd, St Ives plc

To my teachers
Emmon, Roger and Edwin

Contents

Acknowledgments

This volume has been over 15 years in preparation, which has allowed it to benefit from advances in the field of morphology during this prolonged gestation. The volume initially grew out of a concise introduction to realizational models, compiled in advance of a morphology meeting in Cambridge. At the suggestion of Farrell Ackerman, this study guide was extended to a more general synthesis of realizational approaches. Before the completion of this version could see the light of day, it was superseded by a number of disruptive developments. In 2001, a special issue of the *Transactions of the Philological Society* devoted to morphological paradigms reprinted Robins's 'In defense of WP' from 1959, together with a group of contemporary studies. Although the intent of the issue had been to trace continuity within the modern WP tradition, it instead underscored differences between the role that words and paradigms played in classical WP models and in current realizational models.

This prompted an expansion of the original project to include a consideration of the classical model. The expansion coincided with a number of convergent developments. One was the appearance of a series of papers, including Kostić *et al.* (2003) and Moscoso del Prado Martín *et al.* (2004*b*), presenting an information-theoretic approach to morphological processing. It soon become clear that information theory provided the best available tool for formalizing at the classical WP of perspective. Very shortly afterwards, the development of the general discriminative perspective in Ramscar and Yarlett (2007); Ramscar *et al.* (2010, 2013*a*), among others, and the Naive Discriminative Learner model in Baayen *et al.* (2011) identified the sources of uncertainty in morphological systems that were estimated by global entropy measures.

A 15-year project is bound to incur a wide range of intellectual debts, and apologies are offered in advance for any lapses in acknowledging contributions or influences. The greatest debts are owed to Farrell Ackerman, who has read and commented on nearly every version of the volume, and to Olivier Bonami and Hans-Heinrich Lieb, who have provided extremely detailed critical remarks. I am also grateful to Juliette Blevins for a very close reading of the final version, and to Richard Sproat and Greg Stump for their rather more skeptical comments on drafts of much earlier versions. At the outset of the project, the perspective on realizational approaches reflected interactions with members of a UK morphology network whose members included Harald Clahsen, Gerald Gazdar, Andrew Spencer and Greville Corbett and his colleagues in the Surrey Morphology Group. As the focus of the volume shifted to implicational approaches, it showed a greater influence from interactions with Alice Harris, Aleksandar Kostić, Rob Malouf, Fermín Moscoso del Prado Martín and Andrea Sims. The perspective adopted in the final chapters of the volume owes a conspicuous debt to ongoing collaborations with Harald Baayen, Michael Ramscar, Petar Milin, Jeroen Geertzen, and Emmanuel Keuleers.

At various points during during the writing of the volume my understanding of morphological issues has been clarified by discussions with Peter Matthews, William Marslen-Wilson and Michele Miozzo at Cambridge, with Anna Morpurgo Davies and Martin Maiden in meetings of the Philological Society, and with Mark Aronoff (among others) in wider forums. It should be stressed that the usual proviso about acknowledgment not implying agreement applies with particular force here. Nearly all of those mentioned above will disagree with at least some of the content of the volume and most will take exception to the way in which many of the issues are presented.

It gives me particular pleasure to thank Alain Peyraube, director of the Collegium de Lyon, for providing a supportive and—in large part due to interactions with fellow resident Csaba Pléh—highly stimulating environment in which to connect the dots between the classical WP models in Chapters 3–5 and their discriminative information-theoretic counterparts in Chapters 7 and 8. I am also grateful to Principal Geoffrey Ward and Homerton College for providing a quiet scholarly setting in which to bring the project to completion.

On a personal note, I would also like to offer heartfelt thanks to those who provided intervals of social sanctuary during an often eventful 15 years.

Preface

It has often been observed that academic disciplines are social constructs. This lends a measure of iconicity to a field like linguistics, whose object of study is itself shaped by social and historical forces. In much the same way that the patterns in a language cannot be fully understood without some knowledge of their origins and development, the principles of modern linguistics cannot be explicated without at least some clarification of the intellectual context in which they arose and the factors that guided their evolution. These types of considerations are particularly relevant to the study of morphology. The principles that define approaches to morphological analysis can rarely be understood in isolation from a more general conception of the structure of language and the 'place' that morphology occupies within that structure.

To provide this kind of context, the present study incorporates a discussion of the history and development of ideas that have exerted a decisive influence on word and paradigm models. The largest stock of ideas have their origins in the classical grammatical tradition. Others derive from refinements of that tradition, notably during the Neogrammarian period. Still others reflect the direct or indirect influence of the alternative 'morpheme-based' conception, particularly in the form that this approach has assumed in generative accounts.

The resulting volume combines a snapshot of current word and paradigm models with an overview of the intellectual lineages they represent, and highlights key points of divergence from morpheme-based accounts. The treatment of these approaches and alternatives is meant to be reasonably self-contained, and Chapters 2, 3–5, 6 and 7–8 can all be read more or less independently. The discussion should be accessible to non-specialists with at least some prior training in linguistics or philology. For these readers, the volume can serve as an introduction to morphology and morphological theory from the perspective of word and paradigm models. For readers with a more specific interest in morphology, the volume can be read more as a research monograph that traces the history of ideas that underlie these models, contrasting the intuitions and implementations that define classical and contemporary variants.

These pedagogical and research goals are to a large degree complementary. Students, as well as researchers in neighbouring fields, are often unacquainted with traditional approaches and particularly unaware of the continuity between these older models and guiding assumptions of 'construction-based', 'usage-based' and other 'examplar-based' perspectives. The degree to which information theory provides a natural metatheory for classical models is also not widely appreciated. It can be hoped that an accessible introduction to this tradition will spur interest in exploring it beyond its current boundaries.

List of figures

List of tables

List of abbreviations

Ø	zero plural marker
I/II/III	first/second/third conjugation, declension, series (see p.116), classes (see p.147), or blocks (see p.249)
1sg	1st person singular
1p	1st person
1pl	1st person plural
2sg	2nd person singular
2p	2nd person
2pl	2nd person plural
3	3rd person
3p	3rd person
3sg	3rd person singular
3pl	3rd person plural
Abes	Abessive
A(cc)	accusative
Ades	Adessive
Act	active
AMM	A-Morphous Morphology (see p.202)
Cond	conditional
Dat	dative
DC1	1st declension
DM	Distributed Morphology
Fem	feminine
Fut	future
G(en)	genitive
IA model	item and arrangement model
Imp	imperative
Impf	imperfective
Infin	infinitive
Illa	illative
Illa2	second or short illative
Iobj	indirect object
IP model	item and process model

Indic	indicative
Ines	Inessive
Inst	instrumental
Loc	locative
N	noun
N(om)	nominative
Masc	masculine
NBP	'No Blur Principle' (see p.323)
Neg	negative
Neut	neuter
Obj	object
P1–5	plural noun patterns (see p.140)
PEP	'Paradigm Economy Principle' (see. p.312)
Part	partitive
Part2	second or stem partitive
Pass	passive
Perf	perfective
PF(M)	paradigm function (morphology) (see pp.216–17)
Pl	plural
Plu	plural
Poss	possessive
Prtl	participle
PSC	Paradigm Structure Condition (see p.134)
Q1/Q2/Q3	'first/second/third quantity' (see p.134)
S1–3	singular noun patterns (see p.140)
Sg	singular
Sbjv	subjunctive
Subj	subject
WP model	word and paradigm model

Part I
The classical WP model

1

Revival of the WP model

The modern revival of the word and paradigm model dates, for all intents and purposes, from the publication of Hockett's *Two models of grammatical description* in 1954. This revival is something of an unintended consequence, given that Hockett's study is mainly an extended comparison of two variants of morphemic analysis and, in many ways, represents the high-water mark of the morpheme-based tradition. Bloomfield (1933) had earlier provided the foundation for models of morphemic analysis by decomposing words into minimal units of lexical form (morphemes) and minimal features of 'arrangement' (taxemes). But Bloomfield's proposals seemed programmatic and obscure in many respects, and it fell to his successors to develop his approach into a general model of morphemic analysis. The most influential line of development led to what Hockett (1954) termed the 'item and arrangement' (IA) model. By reducing Bloomfield's diverse features of arrangement to features of 'order' and 'selection', Harris (1942) and Hockett (1947) arrived at a simple model in which word structure could be represented by linear sequences of morphemes. The remaining features of arrangement were relegated to other levels of analysis, notably to a 'morphophonemic' level that mediated between sequences of morphemes and surface forms (consisting of sequences of phonemes).

Much of the appeal of the IA model derived from its compatibility with item-based approaches in other domains. The analysis of sound systems into minimal distinctive units had inspired a search for parallels in the grammatical system. In this context, the analysis of words into arrangements of morphemes appeared to converge with the phrase-structure descriptions assigned by models of Immediate Constituent analysis (Wells 1947) and to offer a uniform item-based treatment of grammatical structure. Even more generally, the IA model fit well with a conception of linguistic analysis as a general process of segmentation and classification, one in which the minimal units at a given level were composed of arrangements of units at the next level down. The basic hierarchy, in which phrases consist of arrangements of words, and words consist of arrangements of morphemes, had again been set out earlier, in Bloomfield (1926: §III), but it was only later that Bloomfield's schematic postulates were elaborated into a uniform system of levels based on part-whole relations.

1.1 From segmentation to classification

From the outset, the Post-Bloomfieldians were aware of the challenges that faced the IA model. The segmentation of words into arrangements of formatives

Word and Paradigm Morphology. First edition. James P. Blevins
© James P. Blevins 2016. First published 2016 by Oxford University Press

sometimes produced analyses in which there appeared to be a shortfall of meaning-bearing segments, and at other times produced analyses in which there seemed to be an excess of segments. In yet other cases, analyses contained segments whose status as 'items' seemed highly dubious. Many of the inventive solutions that the Post-Bloomfieldians developed to meet these challenges remain with us, in the form of the 'zero', 'empty' and 'portmanteau' morphs that still populate morphological analyses. The use of 'replacive' and 'subtractive' morphs to describe stem alternations and truncations also survives in modern accounts, in the guise of elements that trigger 'readjustment rules' (Halle and Marantz 1993) or other 'morphophonemic' devices.

The typological biases of the IA model were also evident to at least some Post-Bloomfieldians. In later reflections on the development of the IA model, Hockett (1987: 81f.) remarks that, "We seemed to be convinced that, whatever might superficially appear to be the case, every language is 'really' agglutinative". As noted with particular clarity by Lounsbury (1953), the attempt to impose an agglutinative analysis on the forms of a fusional (or 'flectional') language often led to a type of indeterminacy that the model could not resolve:

In a fusional language, if one seeks to arrive at constant segments . . . conflicts arise in the placing of the cuts. One comparison of forms suggests one placement, while another comparison suggests another. Often, in fact, no constant segment can be isolated at all which corresponds to a given constant meaning. Situations of this kind often permit of more than one solution according to different manners of selecting and grouping environments. (Lounsbury 1953: 172)

Significantly, cases with "more than one solution" presented as much of a challenge as those in which "no constant segment can be isolated at all". The reason for this was that multiple solutions tended to reflect the multiple ways in which forms were organized into patterns in a language. Imposing a fixed segmentation on these cases was not only arbitrary but destructive, since isolating one pattern would disassemble a form in ways that disrupted other patterns. Given that any segmentation would privilege some patterns while disrupting others, it followed that the problem of assigning "constant segments" could not be overcome by imposing a segmentation strategy by fiat.

The issues raised by Lounsbury (1953) were not resolved or even directly addressed in subsequent developments of the IA model, which consisted mainly of technical solutions to fundamental problems of analysis. The primacy of technical elaborations in turn reflected a general reorientation of linguistics during the Post-Bloomfieldian period, as the study of the structure (and history) of languages gave way to the study of the methods and techniques employed in the description and analysis of languages (Blevins 2013). In this intellectual setting, the appearance of *Two models of linguistic description* marked a first, tentative, step in the shift from the exploration of narrow technical refinements to a broader assessment of the subversive effect of admitting elements like 'subtractive' or 'replacive' morphs. After acknowledging that these 'items' were really processes masquerading as forms, Hockett proceeded to outline a uniformly process-based alternative. Hockett termed this model the 'item and process' (IP) model, recognizing an intellectual debt to the process-based perspective of Sapir (1921), which he, like other Post-Bloomfieldians, had previously regarded with considerable suspicion.

The two models that Hockett articulated are still in current use, as are the terms 'IA' and 'IP', and his 1954 paper remains a landmark of morphemic analysis. But the explicit formulation of IA and IP models had brought larger issues into sharper focus.[1] By 1951, when, as Hockett notes, "most of the paper was written" (p. 386), he had to come to realize that the IA and IP models shared fundamental idealizations, and that his exclusion of the 'word and paradigm' (WP) model reflected the somewhat parochial conception of morphological analysis that he shared with fellow Post-Bloomfieldians. After noting that this "defect in the paper" (ibid.) had initially led him to withhold publication, Hockett offers, by way of mitigation, a plea for equal treatment:

Quite apart from minor variants of IP or IA, or models that might be invented tomorrow, there is one model which is clearly distinct from either IA or IP, and which is older and more respectable than either. This is the WORD AND PARADIGM (WP) model, the traditional framework for the discussion of Latin, Greek, Sanskrit, and a good many more modern familiar languages. It will not do to shrug this frame of reference off with the comment that it is obviously insufficiently general, incapable of organizing efficiently the facts of a language like Chinese. As yet we have NO completely adequate model: WP deserves the same consideration here given to IP and IA. (Hockett 1954: 386)

Hockett did not attempt a general reappraisal until much later, in the context of a 'Resonance Theory' that, as he noted, "in surprising measure harks back to Saussure" (Hockett 1987: 96). By this time, Hockett's direct influence on the field had waned and his attempts to place the Bloomfieldian programme in a broader historical context had less impact than his earlier development of morphemic analysis. But his "apologies for not having worked [a] consideration of WP into the present paper" (Hockett 1954: 386) provoked a reaction that would ultimately lead to the rehabilitation of the ancient model.

Sections 1.2 and 1.3 now trace this rehabilitation, focussing on developments within the dominant intellectual lineages that fall within the WP framework. The point of departure for this morphological tradition is the CLASSICAL WP model, which Hockett describes above as "the traditional framework for the discussion of Latin, Greek, Sanskrit, and a good many more modern familiar languages". The following summary focusses primarily on two traditions. Models that formalize the classical model in terms of interpretive rule or constraint systems are collectively designated as REALIZATIONAL models. Models that adopt a complex system perspective and emphasize patterns of interdependency, recently formalized in terms of information theory and discriminative learning, are grouped together as IMPLICATIONAL models.[2]

---

[1] As Hockett (1968: 29) remarked later "It is interesting to note that we no sooner achieved a pure item-and-arrangement model (not yet called that) than we began to wonder whether it was really what we wanted".

[2] Models such as Lexeme-Morpheme Base Morphology (Beard 1995) or Whole Word Morphology (Ford *et al.* 1997; Singh and Starosta 2003) can be viewed as variants of realizational models. Bochner (1993) is likewise a precursor of implicational approaches. Other paradigmatic models, such as Seiler

1.2 The ancient model and its adaptations

The most immediate reaction to Hockett's mea culpa was the 'defence' of WP offered in Robins (1959). Prompted by the fact that "neither Hockett nor anyone else seems as yet to have taken up the suggestion" that WP should be given the same consideration as IA and IP (pp. 116f.), Robins set out some of the empirical considerations that had led earlier proponents of the WP model to regard it as a general theoretical model, rather than as a practical framework for language description. Robins stresses particularly the distinctive role played by words and collections of words in a classical WP approach:

The main distinctive characteristics of a formalized WP model of grammatical description would then be the following: the word is taken as the basic unit of both syntax and morphology, and variable words are grouped into paradigms for the statement of their morphological forms and the listing of their various syntactic functions. (Robins 1959: 127)

Significantly, when Robins turns to the advantages of WP analyses, he, like Hockett, defines the WP model largely in opposition to IA and IP models. Whereas classical models had no unit intervening between words and sounds (or letters), Robins (1959: 127) acknowledges that "the morpheme must be recognized as the minimal element of grammatical structure". He then clarifies that these 'morphemes' are essentially units of form (corresponding to what Hockett (1947) had termed 'morphs') and that meaning and grammatical functions are primarily associated with words in WP approaches:

Some entities that are clearly to be assigned morphemic status may be seen in several languages to bear conflicting and even contradictory grammatical functions when considered in isolation . . . On the other hand words anchored, as it were, in the paradigms of which they form a part usually bear a consistent, relatively simple and statable grammatical function. The word is a more stable and solid focus of grammatical relations than the component morpheme by itself. Put another way, grammatical statements are abstractions, but they are more profitably abstracted from words as wholes than from individual morphemes. (Robins 1959: 128)

In the course of identifying "the characteristics of a formalized WP model of grammatical description", Robins offers a modern reinterpretation of the classical model that introduces a number of substantive assumptions. By distinguishing the minimal 'units of form' in a morphological system from the minimal units that can be assigned a stable meaning or function, he arrives at a theoretical hybrid that combines what he sees as the descriptive strengths of WP and IA/IP models. The resulting hybrid grafts an IA view of morphotactics, which recognizes sub-word units, onto a WP view of morphosyntax/morphosemantics,

(1965), Carstairs (1983), or the axiomatic approach to morphology in Integrational Linguistics (Lieb 1976, 1980, 1983, 1992, 2005, 2013), represent independent developments of the classical model.

which associates grammatical properties and meanings with whole words. Other aspects of Robins's reinterpretation are more subtle, though their effects on the development of the WP tradition are just as far reaching. By focussing on the role of words in a classical model, rather than on the analogical relations that bind words to paradigms, Robins reinforces the impression that the primary contrast between WP and IA/IP concerns units of analysis. The idea that models are distinguished by the units they recognize more than by the relations they establish between units had been fostered by Hockett's terminology and would frame the terms of subsequent debates between advocates of 'word-based' and 'morpheme-based' models. By treating " 'derivation' and 'inflection' . . . as covering approximately the comparable situations" (p. 136), Robins further de-emphasizes the implicational properties that had placed paradigms at the centre of the classical WP model. What is mainly carried forward from the classical WP model in this formalization is the assumption that words are the primary locus of grammatical meaning.

The rehabilitation of the WP model continued in the work of Matthews (1965, 1972, 1991), which also provided a bridge between theoretical linguistics and classical and philological traditions, in which the WP model had never entirely fallen out of favour. Although Robins (1959) had sketched out the architecture of a WP model and described a range of patterns that seemed particularly amenable to analysis in WP terms, he stopped short of formalizing these patterns explicitly. Matthews (1965) takes up this challenge by showing how the inflectional component of a grammar can be described in terms of sets of morphosyntactic properties and rules that 'realize' them:

On the positive side, the word-and-paradigm model appears to have some specific advantages. A *prima facie* case, in the field of inflectional and 'derivational' morphology, has been established by Robins (1959): the patterning of overt 'morphemic segments', within the word, may often be described in a way which is quite at variance with the patterning of the relevant 'morphemes'. But it is, of course, no more than a *prima facie* case. The discussion can be carried no further until the word-and-paradigm approach has been characterized at least as clearly as current versions of morphemics.

The present paper is intended to supply a part of this formulation. It is restricted to inflectional problems alone: to be more precise, it deals with that subsection of the grammar (we will call it the INFLECTIONAL COMPONENT) which assigns a realization, or various alternative realizations, to each grammatical word. (Matthews 1965: 142)

The model that Matthews proposes is strikingly simple in its basic conception. The PARADIGM of an item is represented by sets of properties (what in other traditions are termed 'features'), each corresponding to a cell of the paradigm. The LEXICAL ENTRY of the item specifies a root or stem form on which the forms of the paradigm are based. The REALIZATION RULES of a grammar 'interpret' properties by applying operations to a form. A set of such rules realize or 'spell out' the inflected surface form that is associated with a paradigm cell of an item by interpreting the properties of the cell and successively modifying the base form of the item.

This approach is elaborated in detail in Matthews (1972), where it is applied to the analysis of aspects of Latin conjugation.[3]

To a large extent, the precise formalization developed in Matthews (1965, 1972) served more as a 'proof of concept' than as an explicit model for subsequent analyses. Nevertheless, the basic conception of morphological analysis was both appealing and influential. Because property sets were specified independently of forms, these sets could be interpreted by property-preserving rules that defined surface forms. Correspondences between properties and forms could be stated where they obtained, but dissociations could also be accommodated. This conception of morphological analysis-as-interpretation is what unites the class of contemporary realizational models. In some ways the most direct descendant of initial realizational accounts is the model of Autonomous Morphology (Aronoff 1994), which expands the role of 'stem indices' and exploits the distinction between morphological rules and the operations they apply but does not add any new rule types. Network Morphology (Corbett and Fraser 1993; Brown and Hippisley 2012) also represents a conservative extension of a basic realizational model in which generalizations are expressed by means of inheritance hierarchies. The Extended WP model (Anderson 1982)—subsequently A-Morphous Morphology (Anderson 1992)—shows the greatest influence of the generative tradition, as it assembles the property bundles that define paradigm cells at the preterminal nodes of syntactic representations, and invokes a rule of lexical insertion to introduce lexical stems. The use of paradigm functions and other devices in Paradigm Function Morphology (Stump 2001) reduce the role of realization rules to the point that the model can perhaps only residually be characterized as realizational.

A larger group of approaches exploit the descriptive potential of dissociating 'units of content' and 'units of form', which Beard (1995) terms the Separation Hypothesis. These include 'lexeme-based' models (Zwicky 1985; Beard 1995), along with approaches that mediate realization via 'stem spaces' (Bonami and Boyé 2006, 2007) or other types of articulated lexical structures (Sagot and Walther 2013). A version of the Separation Hypothesis is also adopted by morphemic models such as Distributed Morphology, when they "endorse the separation of the terminal elements involved in the syntax from the phonological realization of these elements" (Halle and Marantz 1993: 111).

Although initial formalizations of WP models principally explored realizational strategies, the exemplar-based perspective of classical WP models found a more direct resonance in the approach to derivational and syntactic constructions in Construction Grammar and Morphology (Booij 2010). Some of the leading ideas of classical WP models were also developed in different ways in other theoretical traditions. The notion of an inflectional paradigm is central to the Paradigm Economy Principle of Carstairs (1983) and to the descendant No Blur Principle of Carstairs-

---

[3] For the sake of clarity, the following descriptions adapt Matthews' conventions. Grammatical attributes such as CASE are designated as 'features', specifications such as *genitive* as 'values', and the term 'properties' is reserved for feature-value pairs.

McCarthy (1994). The economy effects measured in these studies suggest the relevance of paradigmatic organization to affix-based models. Integrational models (Lieb 1976, 2013) likewise extend the classical notion of inflectional paradigm by organizing word forms into syntactic word paradigms, and sub-word units into morphological stem and affix paradigms. This extension has the effect of projecting the Separation Hypothesis onto parallel syntactic and morphological paradigm spaces, which are much like the linked form and content paradigms proposed in Stump (2006).

1.3 Word-based morphology

The first stage in the rehabilitation of the WP model was essentially complete by the reprinting of Robins (1959) in 2001, nearly a half century after the plea for equal treatment in Hockett (1954). The realizational approaches developed during this time were, as Hockett had anticipated, "clearly distinct from either IA or IP" and had decisively corrected "the erroneous impression that there were principally just two archetypes" (386). But other issues remained unresolved. One issue concerned how faithfully realizational models represented the "traditional framework for the discussion of Latin, Greek, Sanskrit" that Hockett had originally had in mind. Another concerned the applicability of realizational WP models to isolating or agglutinative patterns or, indeed, to derivational processes. These issues had been set aside to some degree while the viability of WP approaches was being established in the inflectional domain, where classical models had been most successfully applied. It was only by reexamining the model underlying these approaches that the rejuvenated WP tradition could begin to assess the suitability of WP as a general model of morphological analysis, and to address the types of objections that had led proponents of IA and IP models initially to neglect WP approaches.

   It is worth recalling that Hockett's initial endorsement of the WP model had not been unqualified. Instead, it had carried the caveat "that it is obviously insufficiently general, incapable of organizing efficiently the facts of a language like Chinese", voicing one of the primary concerns about the model. The response offered by Robins (1959) sets the tone for much of the subsequent literature. Rather than addressing the objection directly, Robins deflects it by shifting the terms of debate onto the question of whether WP analyses of isolating languages might be correct in identifying words as minimal units:

To say that paradigms are not part of a model applied to a language whose words do not exhibit grammatical paradigms is labouring the obvious, but it may still be urged that the word as formally established is the most profitable unit to be taken as basic in the statement of the sentence structures of such languages . . . (Robins 1959: 123)

This retreat to an essentially word-based perspective reflects Robins' general view that the descriptive success of the WP model derives principally from the treatment of words as minimally meaningful units. However, Robins appears to regard even the status of words as negotiable, and leaves open the possibility of assigning morphemic analyses to genuinely agglutinative languages:

The segmentation into morphemes need not take into account any need for a parallel representation of the grammatical categories applicable in every word in any class (though, of course, IT MAY DO SO IF A CLEAR STATEMENT ON THESE LINES IS POSSIBLE). (Robins 1959: 133, emphasis added)

Behind this theoretical pragmatism lay a deeper agnosticism. Early proponents of the modern WP model began with the modest goal of establishing the model on the same footing as IA and IP models. Having achieved that goal, they saw no point in replacing overblown universalist claims for IA or IP models with similar claims for the WP model. Robins (1959) and Matthews (1972), in particular, were openly skeptical about whether any single model of morphology could be applied with equal success to all types of languages:

It may also be that while each of the models discussed in this paper is feasible with every language, one of them is more appropriate with certain languages; possibly Mixteco, at least on Pike's analysis, is not a 'WP language', and certainly on the evidence we have considered some languages are less suitably 'IA' or 'IP languages'. (Robins 1959: 144)

In particular, there is no reason to assume (*pace* Hockett, 1954, and others) that the same model of description must be equally applicable to all languages. The opposite view may be more illuminating. (Matthews 1965: 141)

Finally, it has become clear at least that different languages raise quite different problems in morphological analysis. It is therefore possible that they also require quite different sorts of description. (Matthews 1972: 156)

Hockett's original admission that "we have NO completely adequate model" had reflected dissatisfaction with technical solutions to problems of analysis created by IA and IP models, especially when applied to languages of the flectional type. The caution expressed by Robins and Matthews acknowledged the complementary obstacles that the WP model faced in analyzing the types of languages that IA and IP models had been expressly designed to describe. The most immediate empirical challenges lay in showing how the WP model could avoid imposing inflectional paradigms on isolating languages like Chinese, or avoid treating words as basic in agglutinating languages like Turkish.

To a large extent, these challenges grew out of the strategy of retrofitting a formal model onto an established descriptive tradition. The problem is present from the outset of the modern revival when Hockett (1954) characterizes ancient grammatical descriptions as embodying a 'word and paradigm' model. This designation accurately emphasizes the role that words and inflectional paradigms play in classical WP approaches. However, it begs the question whether these components define the WP model, or merely specify the units and structures to which the model has been most fruitfully applied.

Although this question arises in a particularly acute form for the WP model, it reflects a more general source of unclarity in Hockett's classification. The detailed elaboration of IA and IP approaches in Hockett (1954) never explicitly distinguishes between general FRAMEWORKS of analysis and the MODELS that instantiate frameworks by specifying substantive assumptions, including assumptions about units of analysis. The IA framework that emerges from Hockett's description is fundamentally concatenative in nature, representing word structure by means of combinations of sub-word units. The models that instantiate IA frameworks are typically 'atomistic' in that they operate with segmentally minimal units. However, these models could just as well concatenate larger units, such as stems, or even sequences of affixes that frequently collocate and pattern like units. The defining property is that word structure (and word meaning) arises through the concatenation of units.

The central innovation in the IP framework is the introduction of processes that apply operations other than concatenation to a base. Unlike realization rules, processes do not 'spell out' previously specified features. Rather they are feature-modifying or 'incremental' in the sense of Stump (2001). Just as the concatenation of a morpheme to a base yields a unit that augments the features and form of the base, the application of a process may alter the features and modify the form associated with an input to which it applies. However, models that instantiate IP frameworks are again free to specify different types of inputs (roots, stems or other units), along with different formal operations.

1.3.1 The 'item and pattern' model

The designations 'IA' and 'IP' both classify frameworks in terms of combinatoric strategies (involving arrangements or processes) and leave models to specify the types of units that are concatenated or modified. In contrast, Hockett (1954) does not characterize a 'WP' in terms of general combinatorial strategies, but in terms of a pair of specific units: words and (inflectional) paradigms. Hence the 'WP model' described by Hockett and Robins is indeed a model in the sense proposed above, instantiating a more abstract framework. This underlying framework is based on implicational relations, often between properties and forms or between pairings of properties and forms. The most accurate designation for this framework in Hockett's terms would be ITEM AND PATTERN. In realizational models that instantiate this framework, the distinctive patterns are defined by the features in abstract paradigm cells (or property bundles) that trigger realization rules. Items correspond in turn to the output of those rules. More conservative implicational models formalize counterparts of the exemplary paradigms and principal parts of a classical grammar. In this variant, it is possible to identify patterns by reference to paradigms whose cells contain properties and forms, items consist of a single pairing of properties and forms, and the comparison of items against patterns may be used to sanction the deduction of items via processes of analogical extension or, more generally, on the basis of correlations. A distinctive property of this second approach is that it defines implicational structure over networks of interrelated 'units as wholes', and abstracts smaller units from these networks. In treating parts as 'abstractions' over larger wholes, the resulting neo-Saussurean conception inverts the Bloomfieldian view that wholes are 'constructed' from smaller parts.

From this perspective, WP models, both realizational and implicational, can be seen as instantiations of an item and pattern framework that is 'tuned' to the structure of a flexional language. A highly salient morphological feature of these languages is the grammatical role and predictive value of words and paradigms. The privileged status of words reflects the fact that, as Robins (1959: 128) puts it, "the word is a more stable and solid focus of grammatical relations than the component morpheme by itself". Hence it is often possible to associate determinate properties with words, even when they are composed of grammatically or semantically indeterminate parts. The role of paradigms derives likewise from the fact that the feature space of an inflectional paradigm is essentially closed and uniform. This allows a realizational model to define the abstract cells of an inflectional system independently of the forms that realize those cells. The closed and uniform structure of inflectional paradigms also provides a maximally reliable analogical base for deducing new forms based on previously encountered forms. Taken together, the informativeness of words and the interdependence of cells in a paradigm determine "the . . . general insight . . . that one inflection tends to predict another" (Matthews 1991: 197).

Recognizing WP models as specific instantiations of a more general implicational framework helps to clarify how item and pattern approaches can be applied to languages in which words and paradigms play a less significant role. Consider first isolating patterns and derivational formations. In an isolating language, standard inflectional paradigms will not guide deductions about novel forms. Yet other sets of word forms may still establish patterns that are of predictive value. 'Morphological families' consisting of sets of derivationally-related forms exhibit their own patterns of interpredictability, which in some cases are as reliable as the expectations generated by inflectional paradigms.[4] Both in size and composition, these 'families' show far more item-specific variation than inflectional paradigms. Whereas inflectional paradigms are broadly uniform within a given word or inflection class, families of derivational formations can vary in size by orders of magnitude.[5] The 'lexical neighbours' of an item may also be of deductive value, as may be other word classes. The idea that an inflectional paradigm is the extreme case of a predictive pattern is implicit in the way that the notion 'paradigm' is extended to broader classes of related forms in Robins (1959: 121) and Moscoso del Prado Martín (2003).[6]

---

[4] These families have well-attested effects on language processing, and it is hard to imagine that these effects do not in some way reflect the organization of a speaker's lexicon. See, among others, Schreuder and Baayen (1997), de Jong (2002), Kostić et al. (2003), Moscoso del Prado Martín et al. (2004b), and the discussion in Chapter 7.

[5] The fact that members of a given word or inflection class tend to have a comparable number of forms helps to account for the observation that the processing of inflectional forms is more sensitive to token frequency whereas the processing of derivational formations is more sensitive to the type frequency of related items (Baayen et al. 1997).

[6] See Pounder (2000) for a similar extension of 'paradigm' to derivational families. Models of integrational linguistics (fn. 2 above) propose more general paradigmatic extensions. Until Lieb (1980),

Identifying implicational relations as the cornerstone of WP models also avoids the need to impose a uniform analysis on all languages at the level of units. Although it is reasonably well established that most languages do not conform to the 'agglutinative ideal' of a morpheme-based model, there is no reason in principle why some languages could not approach this ideal.[7] In a perfectly morphemic language, grammatical properties would reliably predict the formatives that realize them (modulo regular phonological processes), and formatives would reliably signal the properties that they realize. In such a language, implication would retain a central role, but shift its locus from relations between words to relations between formatives and grammatical properties.

An implicational model also integrates the patterns that Aronoff (1994) classes as 'morphomic'. Much of the contemporary discussion of 'morphomes' focusses on the descriptive problems that they pose for analyses that attempt to assign them a determinate analysis in isolation. From an implicational perspective, it is not the patterns themselves that are problematic but the assumption that the components of the patterns can be analyzed separately. Implicit in classical and philological treatments of morphomic patterns is the view that they serve a predictive or diagnostic function (Maiden 2005). This relational view is most clearly expressed in the description of the patterns that Matthews (1972) terms 'Priscianic' or 'parasitic'. In these patterns, a form in one part of an inflectional paradigm sanctions reliable predictions about the shape of another. The fact that systematic correspondences that are orthogonal to the distinctive grammatical properties of the synchronic system may be maintained—and extended (Maiden 2005)—calls into question the role of shared properties in more 'normative' cases of exponence. From an implicational standpoint, it is the 'structuralist morpheme' rather than the 'Priscianic morphome' that is the special case, as this pattern abstracts away from the larger systems to which a form belongs and establishes a fixed relation between properties and forms strictly at the level of the formative.[8] Hence whereas morphomes do not fit well into a morphemic account, an account that treats morphomes as units of predictive value subsumes morphemes as morphomes that encapsulate a biunique prediction between properties and forms.

In sum, the pivotal role of words and paradigms in WP approaches reflects the high information load that words carry within the implicational networks defined by paradigms and other morphological 'families'. The stable grammatical information associated with a word not only serves to identify its own function

paradigms were treated as sets of word-categorization pairs; from Lieb (1983) lexical words are treated as paradigm-meaning pairs, with 'meaning' a psychological concept. By allowing 'improper paradigms', this approach extends a paradigmatic treatment to arbitrary parts of speech in arbitrary languages, including Chinese (Sackman 2000; Su 2011). A paradigmatic treatment is not extended to derivational families which are treated as 'word families' or sets of lexical words (Lieb 2013).

[7] See Hockett (1987: §7.4) for discussion of the origins of the agglutinative ideal.

[8] Morphological patterns of this type can be described solely by 'rules of exponence' (Zwicky 1985) which spell out the features of a single paradigm cell or feature bundle 'locally' by units of form, without the need for 'rules of referral' or other strategies that relate the realization of multiple forms. However, as discussed in Chapters 5–7, there is little empirical evidence that morphological uncertainty can in general be resolved effectively at the formative level, and considerable experimental evidence that speakers do not in fact process individual words in isolation from other words.

but also locates it within an inflectional paradigm and within the larger morpho-logical system. In this way, the grammatical information associated with a form facilitates deductions about other forms, based on systematic correspondences and interdependencies within a language. Aspects of form that sanction implications likewise express a type of information, information which can be modelled by notions developed within information theory (Shannon 1948). In the case of an inflectional paradigm, the informativeness of a form correlates with the degree to which knowledge of that form reduces uncertainty about other forms in the same paradigm. The notion of uncertainty reduction is implicit in the use of 'diagnostic' principal parts in classical accounts, though from a more explicit information-theoretic perspective, nearly all forms are informative to some degree about others.

An item and pattern model is thus well-adapted to exploiting the stable informa-tion content of word-sized units and the tight implicational structure determined by inflectional paradigms in languages where these units and patterns are both present. However, these units and structures are best regarded not as parts of the model *per se* but as recurrent elements in language that facilitate the application of an item and pattern model. Maintaining a clear distinction between frameworks and their instantiations offers a useful perspective on the intrinsic properties of item and pattern models as well as on the scope and limits of WP approaches, classical as well as modern, that instantiate them.

1.3.2 Morphological units and relations

Shifting the basis of classification from units of analysis to the relations between units also determines a general taxonomy of morphological models. The contrast between what has been termed 'constructive' and 'abstractive' perspectives (Blevins 2006b) is a version of a split that reflects the the contemporary influence of two ancient Indo-European grammatical traditions.[9]

The Eastern tradition is represented by CONSTRUCTIVE (or 'atomistic') frame-works, which can be traced, via Bloomfield, to the Sanskrit grammarians. These frameworks describe patterns in a morphological system in terms of relations between minimal units within individual forms. The main variants of this approach are the concatenative ('item and arrangement' or 'IA') models, which disassem-ble forms into sequences of minimal units and operational ('item and process' or 'IP') models, which encapsulate units of form in processes. There are near-contemporary variants of both models. Lieber (1992) presents a IA account, while Steele (1995) outlines an IP approach.

The Western tradition is represented by ABSTRACTIVE frameworks, which describe the patterns within a morphological system in terms of relations abstracted from forms and associated properties. Different approaches abstract different types of patterns and relations. The realizational model described in Section 1.2 above abstracts individual associations between grammatical properties and form variants and expresses them via 'spell out' rules. The implicational models

---

[9] See Matthews (1994) and Cordona (1994) for surveys of these traditions.

Constructive		Abstractive (WP)	
Concatenative (IA)	Operational (IP)	Realizational	Implicational

FIGURE 1.1   General classification of morphological models

proposed or assumed within the grammatical tradition that includes Paul (1920), Saussure (1916) and Kuryłowicz (1949) exhibit a network organization. The structure of a language is defined by an association between a system of contrasts at the level of grammatical meaning and a system of contrasts at the level of form, but there need not be any correspondence between individual form contrasts and meaning contrasts. This conception was not formalized until the modern period. An axiomatic WP model is proposed in Lieb (1992, 2005). The approach initially outlined in Ackerman *et al.* (2009) uses information theory to represent implicational structure and discriminative learning models to associate systems of contrasts. The development of these models is summarized in Chapters 7 and 8.

The contrasts outlined above determine the classification in Figure 1.1, in which the two abstractive models subdivide the 'WP archetype' from Hockett (1954). Realigning Hockett's taxonomy so that it classifies models in terms of relations helps to avoid some of the confusions and oversimplifications that can arise on unit-based classifications. The fundamental problem is that there is often a degree of ambiguity between morphosyntactic and morphotatic interpretations of morphological units. This problem is clearly illustrated by the familiar and, in many ways, useful contrast between 'morpheme-based' and 'word-based' accounts. IA and IP models are both morphosyntactically 'morpheme-based', given that processes encapsulate the same grammatical information as morphemes. But unlike IA models, IP models are not morphotactically formative- or morph-based, since processes can apply to an input without any mediating segmental unit. Likewise, classical WP models and realization-based approaches are both morphosyntactically 'word-based', since they treat the word as the smallest grammatically meaningful unit of a grammar. Classical models are also morphotactically word-based, in that they treat surface word forms as the basic form units of a system, and regard roots, stems and exponents as abstractions over a lexicon of full word forms. However, the morphotactic assumptions of realizational approaches pattern more with those of IA and IP models, in which surface word forms are assembled from smaller elements. Realization-based models assume a model of the lexicon in which open-class items are represented by minimal roots or stems, and surface word forms are defined in terms of these units through the application of realization rules. This places realizational approaches between classical WP models and constructive accounts, at least with respect to their ontological assumptions. Whereas realization-based approaches agree with classical WP approaches about the morphosyntactic status of words, they agree with constructive models in treating surface words as derived units.

Underlying the development of these morphological models (and theories) is the assumption that the word stock of a language is not an unstructured form inventory. Words are taken to exhibit various types of systematic patterns and interdependencies, reflected in their assignment to morphological 'families', 'paradigms', 'classes' and 'series'. The models outlined in Figure 1.1 differ in what they identify as the locus of this organization, and in the strategies that they deploy to express patterns. It is instructive to isolate these strategies and accompanying notions of locality before examining the more technical form in which they are incorporated into contemporary accounts.

The information-theoretic approach developed within the implicational WP tradition offers a useful perspective on the common goals shared by these models, and clarifies how the strategies employed in different models serve to reduce the uncertainty involved in associating properties and forms. Abstractive models express the structuralist view that languages form "un système où tout se tient" in which the correspondence between properties and forms is established in the context of a larger network of associations. The structuralist morpheme encapsulates a much more local conception, in which this correspondence is defined between individual properties and the smallest isolable units of form in a system, so that uncertainty can be fully resolved without reference to other formatives, words, or any type of paradigmatic structure.

These differences between abstractive and constructive perspectives are reflected in the 'granularity' of lexical units. As one moves from left to right in Figure 1.1, the morphotactic and morphosyntactic components of lexical entries become progressively larger. At one extreme lie the fundamentally 'atomistic' lexicons of constructive accounts, which associate minimal collections of lexical properties with (segmentally minimal) root morphemes. In concatenative accounts, minimal sets of grammatical features are also associated with grammatical morphemes, whereas in operational approaches these features are encapsulated within processes. The lexicon of an abstractive model is, by comparison, more 'molecular'. Realizational models associate intrinsic lexical features with root (or stem) entries, but treat the paradigm cell—or 'morphosyntactic representation' (Anderson 1992)—as the smallest unit containing lexical and grammatical features. Hence realizational models are morphosyntactically molecular but morphotactically atomistic. Implicational models lie at the opposite extreme from concatenative accounts, as they assume a lexicon consisting mainly of (partially) instantiated paradigms.

Although the WP tradition is united by a common origin and a stock of core assumptions, individual WP models embody different and at least partly complementary conceptions of 'language', 'grammar' and 'morphological analysis'. The exemplar-based format of classical WP models reflects their pedagogical heritage. Pedagogical goals or idealizations also underlie many of the properties of these models, from their appeal to effective but unspecified processes of analogy, to the completeness and uniformity of the exemplary paradigms and principal part inventories that they exhibit. The language described by a classical grammar corresponds to the set of forms jointly defined by the exemplary paradigms and principal parts of the grammar. Realizational and implicational models generalize this conception in characteristically different ways.

Realizational models adopt the perspective of formal language theory, in which a 'language' is a set of expressions or structures and a 'grammar' is a device for enumerating these sets. Realizational approaches thus extract the generalizations exhibited by the exemplary analyses of a classical WP model and encapsulate these patterns within an explicit system of rules and constraints. The network-based conception developed by implicational models expresses the patterns exhibited by systems of contrasts in terms of information theoretic measures (Shannon 1948) and discriminative learning models (Rescorla and Wagner 1972; Rescorla 1988). These formal differences reflect fundamentally divergent perspectives on the nature of 'grammatical knowledge'. Whereas a realizational perspective expresses a speaker's knowledge of a morphological system in terms of a symbolic rule system, an implicational perspective expresses this knowledge in terms of the state of a learning model.

These alternative conceptions of 'grammar' and 'knowledge' lend themselves to different types of implementation. The symbolic rule systems of realizational models are particularly amenable to NLP implementation. Models of Network Morphology (Corbett and Fraser 1993) adopt a general purpose, cognitively neutral, knowledge representation language, DATR, for the formulation and implementation of analyses. Work within the finite state morphological tradition has likewise shown that the descriptions assigned by models of Paradigm Function Morphology (Stump 2001) can be compiled into finite state transducers (Karttunen 2003). In contrast, network-based implicational models fall within a cognitive tradition that includes 'emergentist' (Bybee 1985, 2010), 'usage-based' (Tomasello 2003; Diessel 2015) and 'construction-based' (Goldberg 2005; Booij 2010) branches. This conception is more compatible with cognitively motivated models of comprehension, production and learning such as Baayen *et al.* (2011) and Ramscar *et al.* (2013*a*).

1.4 Overview

Given the influence that constructive and abstractive traditions have had on each other, a study of the modern development of WP approaches must take into account the origin, motivation and evolution of models of morphemic analysis. On the one hand, the constructive model elaborated by Bloomfield and his successors was in certain respects a reaction against classical accounts, as the Bloomfieldians sought to base a new science of linguistics on notions that were both more abstract and also more clearly the output of 'objective' distributional analysis than the words and paradigms that underpinned more practical descriptive and pedagogical grammars.[10] On the other hand, the modern rehabilitation of WP models took place in the shadow of the Bloomfieldian tradition. A constructivist influence is particularly evident in the theoretical hybridization of realizational models, but is also reflected in the reorientation of the goals and the methods of morphological analysis.

---

[10] As Hockett (1987: 81) later reminiscences, "We specialists were sophisticated enough to know that words are not the minimum units, but the chief modification needed to render the lay statement correct was just to replace 'word' by 'morpheme' ".

To place modern WP models in the intellectual context in which they evolved, Chapter 2 reviews the constructive perspective developed within the Post-Bloomfieldian tradition, highlighting some of the ideas about theoretical uniformity and parsimony that guided this tradition. Chapters 3–5 then set out the components of a classical WP model and identify some of the idealizations that reflect the use of this model in pedagogical and descriptive traditions. The second part of the monograph traces the development of modern WP approaches in detail, comparing realizational and implicational models, and assessing their suitability as the basis for a general morphological theory.

2

The Post-Bloomfieldian legacy

Arguably the most influential claim expounded within the Bloomfieldian tradition is the idea that morphological (and, indeed, linguistic) analysis is fundamentally a process of identifying and classifying minimal recurrent units, and that the classification of larger units is derivative of the analysis of these minimal units. Procedures of segmentation and classification are so deeply embedded in current linguistic practice that they are often perceived as intrinsic to linguistic analysis rather than as embodying specific assumptions about the grammatical role of part-whole structures. In the same way that phonemic and phrase structure analysis consists largely of parsing a string into component phonemes or phrases, morphological analysis is taken to involve breaking words down into minimal, individually meaningful, units, or 'morphemes'.

The practice of parsing words into morphemes is so well established that introductory textbooks often present the identification of morphemes as the core task—or even as the sole task—of morphological analysis. To take just two examples, O'Grady and Dobrovolsky (1996: 112) state:

The most important component of word structure is the MORPHEME, the smallest unit of language which carries information about meaning or word structure.

In a section titled 'Morphemes: The Minimal Units of Meaning', Fromkin *et al.* (2010: 81) likewise assert that "the linguistic term for the most elemental unit of linguistic form is MORPHEME". What is noteworthy about these passages is that they are presented by their authors as uncontroversial statements of fact. Morphological analysis is construed solely in terms of processes of segmentation and classification that parse words into their ultimate constituents.

The idea that morphemes provide the basis for morphological analysis is also assumed in the problem sets that follow in the tradition of workbooks and textbooks such as Nida (1949) or Gleason (1955). These typically require the reader to identify and classify the morphemes and allomorphs that occur within a set of complex forms. Exercises of this type reinforce the impression that morphological analysis consists essentially of segmenting words into morphemes, and that other tasks, such as assigning words to paradigms or other larger classes, are merely convenient ways of presenting data or organizing it for pedagogical purposes. The primacy of morphemes is further reinforced by other practices, such as the convention of assigning 'morpheme glosses' to complex forms in linguistic examples. What is again striking about these descriptive practices and conventions is how they tacitly treat the morpheme as an indispensable component of morphological analysis in general, rather than as an element of a particular model of analysis.

Word and Paradigm Morphology. First edition. James P. Blevins
© James P. Blevins 2016. First published 2016 by Oxford University Press

The appeal of this kind of constructive approach owes much to the initial simplicity of a purely syntagmatic approach, particularly one in which individual features determine the forms that express them, and forms signal the features that they express. This conception is particularly well suited to introductory presentations of morphology and to the formulation of problem sets that isolate a single alternation or pattern within a language.[1] But these practical tasks also reflect a more general view of linguistic structure, encapsulated in the hypothesis that the application of principles of segmentation and classification can reveal a biunique correspondence between 'minimal units of meaning' and 'minimal units of form'. Classical WP accounts also adopt a version of feature-form biuniqueness but assume, based in part on the tangled patterns of exponence exhibited by classical languages, that words and paradigm cells are the smallest units that can be brought into this correspondence.

The cardinal achievement of the Bloomfieldian model was to reorient morphological analysis away from a classical word-based perspective towards a more atomistic approach, in which meanings were associated with sub-word formatives. From a contemporary standpoint, the most striking aspect of this reorientation is its persistence, long after morphemic analysis was repudiated or simply abandoned by initial proponents and redefined beyond all recognition in later accounts. This apparent conundrum can be resolved by the observation that the morphemic tradition is united by the use of the term 'morpheme' rather than any substantive claim about morphological analysis.

2.1 Bloomfieldian analysis

The proximate origins of morphemic analysis lie in the work of Leonard Bloomfield, though Bloomfield's approach served more as a source of inspiration than as an explicit model of analysis. The two most consequential aspects of Bloomfield's model are the dissociation of lexical form from grammatical arrangement and the recognition of a separate component, termed the 'lexicon', which consists, at least for the most part, of minimal lexical forms:[2]

A linguistic form which bears no partial phonetic-semantic resemblance to any other form, is a SIMPLE form or MORPHEME... The total stock of morphemes in a language is its LEXICON. (Bloomfield 1933: 161f.)

It is natural for a contemporary reader to interpret this passage in the context of a hierarchy of linguistic levels, one in which phonemes are combined to form

---

[1] The creeping tendency to conflate 'morphs' (units of form) with 'morphemes' (units of meaning) reinforces the impression that the identification of morphemes is essential to an analysis of the distribution and variation exhibited by morphs.

[2] The postulation of a separate lexicon was accompanied by the claim that this lexical repository was largely free of patterns or 'redundancy', i.e., that "the lexicon is really an appendix of the grammar, a list of basic irregularities" (Bloomfield 1933: 274).

morphemes, morphemes are combined to form words, words are combined to form phrases, and so on. However, this construal is anachronistic, anticipating revisions that would appear later, in the work of Bloomfield's successors. The initial Bloomfieldian conception is more intricate and, in many ways, closer in character to contemporary construction-based and discriminative approaches.

The most novel—and difficult—aspect of this model involves the relation between 'forms' and 'arrangements'. Arrangements are the more transparent notion, corresponding to something like 'dimensions of grammatically distinctive variation'. Of the four types of arrangement that Bloomfield distinguished, three ('order', 'modulation' and 'modification') are relatively straightforward:

The meaningful arrangements of forms in a language constitute its grammar. In general, there seem to be four ways of arranging linguistic forms. (1) ORDER is the succession in which the constituents of a complex form are spoken . . . (2) MODULATION is the use of phonemes which do not appear in any morpheme, but only in grammatical arrangements of morphemes . . . (3) PHONETIC MODIFICATION is a change in the primary phonemes of a form . . . (4) SELECTION of forms contributes a factor of meaning because different forms in what is otherwise the same grammatical arrangement, will result in different meanings. (Bloomfield 1933: 163f.)

The linear order of formatives is an obvious dimension of variation, as are the suprasegmental properties (such as stress or intonation) that Bloomfield subsumes under modulation. His notion of phonetic modification likewise encompasses a range of contextually-conditioned phenomena, including devoicing or sandhi patterns. It is the notion of 'selection' that gives Bloomfield's model its distinctive character. The basic idea is simple, and even familiar to those accustomed to thinking in construction-based terms. Rather than treating forms solely as the sum of independently assembled parts, the Bloomfieldian model integrates a 'top-down' perspective in which constructions are described in terms of characteristic choices of components. The reason that this is not merely a different perspective on the 'bottom-up' assembly of forms from minimal elements is that selection is associated with a meaning component (what Bloomfield calls an 'episememe') which is in addition to the meanings contributed by the parts selected (which he terms 'sememes'):

The features of grammatical arrangement appear in various combinations, but can usually be singled out and separately described. A simple feature of grammatical arrangement is a GRAMMATICAL FEATURE or TAXEME. A taxeme is in grammar what a phoneme is in the lexicon—namely, the smallest unit of form. Like a phoneme, a taxeme, taken by itself, in the abstract, is meaningless. Just as combinations of phonemes or, less commonly, single phonemes, occur as actual lexical signals (phonetic forms), so combinations of taxemes, or, quite frequently, single taxemes, occur as conventional grammatical arrangements, TACTIC FORMS. A phonetic form with its meaning is a linguistic form; a tactic form with its meaning is a GRAMMATICAL FORM. When we have occasion to contrast the purely lexical character of a linguistic form with the habits of arrangement to which it is subject, we shall speak of it as a LEXICAL FORM. In the case of lexical forms we have defined the smallest meaningful units as morphemes, and their meanings as sememes; in the same way, the smallest meaningful units of grammatical form may be spoken of as tagmemes, and their meanings as EPISEMEMES. (Bloomfield 1933: 166)

Bloomfield's obscure terminology makes an already difficult conception even more challenging. However, the key feature of this conception is that meaningful 'units of form' are not just 'chunks' of segmental material, but include any distinctive characteristics that can be ABSTRACTED from a form. It is of course possible to think of minimal lexical forms, i.e. 'morphemes' as being represented (and, possibly, stored) independently of the larger forms from which they are abstracted. But it is not possible to conceive of minimal units of grammatical form, i.e. 'tagmemes', in the same way. In later Post-Bloomfieldian accounts, the notion of selection is encapsulated in rules or complex lexical entries. But Bloomfield describes selectional taxemes with reference to forms or construction types that exhibit them. It is therefore misleading to think of Bloomfieldian analysis as consisting of the disassembly of complex forms into minimal units of lexical and grammatical form, and the assignment of these units to separate lexical and grammatical inventories. Analysis is more a process of classification in which complex forms perform a dual function, providing the data to which procedures of analysis are applied, and at the same time serving as the repository of units of grammatical form.

2.1.1 Bloomfieldian semiotics

Within the Bloomfieldian model, morphemic analysis isolates a lexical relation between meaning and form. Morphemes were 'lexical forms' with meanings, which Bloomfield termed 'sememes'. This position is clearly expressed in Postulate 9 in Bloomfield (1926) and repeated in Bloomfield's *Language*:

In the case of lexical forms, we have defined the smallest meaningful units as morphemes and their meanings as sememes . . . (Bloomfield 1933: 166)

In the semiotic terms proposed by Saussure (1916), morphemes represent the *signifiants* of a minimal lexical sign and sememes represent the *signifiés*. There is no Bloomfieldian term for the sign, encompassing *signifiant* and *signifié*.

As emphasized by Bloomfield's 'lexical' qualification, morphemic analysis represents one dimension of analysis, at the level of form as well as at the level of meaning. Although it is now conventional to apply the term 'form' to segmental units of various sizes, this is not the usage that Bloomfield adopts. Instead, Bloomfield treats ARRANGEMENTS as minimal units of grammatical form, parallel to minimal units of lexical form. Each type of form is paired with a characteristic meaning. Sememes are associated with morphemes and episememes with grammatical arrangements. This leads, as Matthews (1993: 75) remarks, to analyses in which a notion such as plurality is multiply expressed. A plural sememe is associated with the English plural marker in regular formations. A plural episememe is likewise associated with the plural construction that selects a basic stem and plural marker in regular formations, and other combinations in irregulars. Hence a regular form such as *books* is associated with the plural sememe from the ending -*s* and with the plural episememe associated with the taxeme of selection that defines the plural construction.

The Bloomfieldian model is of interest in its own right, not least because of the points of contact between Bloomfieldian 'arrangements' and the discriminative contrasts discussed in Chapter 8. However in the context of the development of morphemic analysis, the atomistic perspective of the Bloomfieldian model is its main legacy. The reduction of morphological analysis to morphemic analysis came later, as did notions of feature-form biuniqueness.

2.1.2 Bloomfieldian exegesis

Faced with the convolutions of this model, it is perhaps not surprising that Bloomfield's successors concluded that it contained "contradictions" (Harris 1942: 169) or "didn't make sense" (Hockett 1968: 20), and proceeded to develop those aspects that seemed most transparent.[3] Consequently, as Matthews (1993) observes, the issues addressed by Bloomfield's followers are not intrinsic to the model itself but appear to rest on their reinterpretations of Bloomfield's position. The central assumption introduced by the Post-Bloomfieldians was the idea that units at one level of analysis were directly COMPOSED OF units at the next lower level of analysis, so that morphemes were composed of phonemes, complex forms composed of morphemes, etc. The source of this assumption is set out explicitly in Hockett (1961):

The simplest and earliest assumption about the relation between morphemes and phonemes was that a morpheme is COMPOSED OF phonemes: the morpheme *cat* is composed of the phonemes /k/, /æ/, and /t/ in that arrangement. This put phonemes and morphemes in line with words, phrases, and sentences, since it was also assumed that a word consists of one or more morphemes (in a specified arrangement), a phrase of one or more words, and so on.

This assumption is either explicit, or implicit but very close to the surface, in much of the early Prague discussion and in Bloomfield's postulates [Bloomfield (1926)]. In the latter, for example, morphemes are defined first (§9), and phonemes later (§15, §16). The wording of the two sections last cited, together with §18, clearly implies that morphemes are composed of phonemes. While Bloomfield does not say quite this, he does say, in the commentary on Assumption 6 (§18), that 'The morphemes of a language can thus be analyzed into a small number of meaningless phonemes.' (Hockett 1961: 29)

As Hockett acknowledges, Bloomfield does not directly assert that morphemes are composed of phonemes; this claim is merely an inference that Hockett and his contemporaries drew from Bloomfield's sometimes opaque discussions of morphology. Bloomfield characteristically spoke of larger units being "described by" smaller parts, as in the claim that "[a]ny utterance can be fully described in terms of lexical and grammatical forms" (Bloomfield 1933: 167). Description in this sense involves, as noted above, a general process of classification. The shift

---

[3] Pike (1943: 65) similarly remarks that "part of the difficulty of Bloomfield's material for the beginning student was the lack of clarity in his statements of the relationship between taxemes and tagmemes, and the actual operation with these principles".

to a more decompositional part-whole perspective is clear in Hockett's discussion of Bloomfield's postulates and in his restatement of 'full description' as a general principle of TOTAL ACCOUNTABILITY:

Every morph, and every bit of phonemic material, must be determined by (i.e. predictable from) the morphemes and the tagmemes (if any) of which the utterance is composed. (Hockett 1947: 235)

This shift was the decisive step in the development of what Hockett (1954) termed the 'item and arrangement' (IA) model. Reinterpreting Bloomfield's model in terms of relations between utterances and the items out of which they were "composed" achieved the same formal clarity that could be obtained by simplifying Bloomfieldian constituency analysis to phrase structure analysis:

The origin of phrase structure grammar was, in short, Bloomfieldian constituency analysis, and the origin of that, in turn, was what remained of Bloomfield's model when, first, grammatical arrangement is reduced to selection and order and, secondly, all reference to meaning is taken out. (Matthews 1993: 148)

2.2 The Concatenative (IA) model

By reducing Bloomfield's intricate taxonomy of forms and arrangements to a single hierarchy of part-whole relations, his successors arrived at a conception that was strikingly simple and transparent. At each linguistic level, elements could be organized into sequences that formed the primes for the next higher level.[4] The lowest, phonemic, level assigned classes of phones to phonemes. The morphemic level organized sequences of phonemes into morphemes. The syntactic level organized sequences of morphemes into larger constituents (Wells 1947). In this way, a uniform part-whole analysis could be extended from phone to utterance. Uniformity was not regarded solely as an end in itself, but reflected the Descriptivists' practical and methodological interest in general procedures of analysis. A model in which levels differ solely in the nature of the elements they contain can obtain a complete analysis by applying general procedures of segmentation and classification. The morpheme lies squarely at the heart of this model. By combining sequences of sub-meaningful elements into meaningful units, morphemes provide the point of entry for meaning.

The resulting 'Russian doll' model is appealing in its sheer simplicity, so much so that it is still widely assumed in informal presentations of grammar and morphology, particularly in introductory textbooks.[5] However, in its most basic form, this model was immediately shown to be inadequate. A central problem arose in

---

[4] This conception is carried over into transformational models (Chomsky 1975).

[5] A good recent example is Bloomer *et al.* (2004: 180), who explain that "each sentence consists of clauses, each clause consists of phrases, each phrase consists of words, each word consists of morphemes and each morpheme consists of phonemes".

connection with even simple cases of stem allomorphy. An example considered by both Harris (1942) and Hockett (1961) involves English singular-plural pairs such as *knife~knives* and *calf~calves*. The relevant feature of these pairs is just that the singular form ends in a voiceless fricative, /f/, whereas the stem of the plural ends in the voiced counterpart, /v/. The alternation cannot be treated as purely phonological, given pairs such as *fife~fifes* and *gaff~gaffs*, which represent the productive pattern. This pattern does not raise difficulties for Bloomfield, because he did not assume that morphemes were composed directly of phonemes. But in any model that does make this assumption, the fact that *knife* (/naif/) and *kniv-* (/naiv/) end in different phonemes means that they cannot be treated as the same morpheme, and hence that *knife* and *knives* share no morphemes in common. Bloomfield's successors understandably regarded this outcome as unsatisfactory and realized that it called for a refinement of their initial assumptions.

Fortunately, a solution was near at hand. Hockett (1942) had earlier formulated principles of phonemic analysis that treated phonemes as abstract units, representing classes of phones with a non-contrastive distribution. Morphemic analysis could be established on exactly the same basis. A MORPHEME could be treated as an abstract unit, which represented classes of MORPHS with a non-contrastive distribution. Defining morphs as sequences of phonemes forged a more indirect link between morphemes and phonemes in a way that avoided the problems posed by morphologically conditioned allomorphy. To return to the earlier example, the morpheme {KNIFE} would represent the two ALLOMORPHS /naif/ and /naiv/, whereas {FIFE} would represent just /faif/. Hence the morpheme {KNIFE} could be a common element in the analyses of *knife* and *knives*, realized as /naif/ in the singular and as /naiv/ in the plural.[6]

The introduction of an abstract level mediating between morphological and phonological levels removed the main obstacle to the development of a general model of analysis based on simple classes and sequences. The removal of meaning from the grammar proper eliminated 'sememes' and 'episememes' from grammatical analyses. This led in turn to the collapse of Bloomfield's distinction between meaning-bearing tagmemes and sub-meaningful taxemes. What remained then were just two fundamental elements: morphemes, representing classes of morphs, and phonemes, representing classes of phones:

Most linguists agree on the existence, or at least on the inescapable utility, of two kinds of basic elements in a language: morphemes and phonemes. (Hockett 1961: 29)

---

[6] This was not the only solution proposed at the time. An alternative discussed by Harris (1942) and Hockett (1961) represented the final consonant in *knife~knives* by a 'morphophoneme' /F/ (though see Hockett (1987: §7.4) on 'morphophonemes'):

We therefore create a morphophonemic symbol, say /F/, which represents /v/ before /-z/ 'plural' and /f/ elsewhere, and say that there is but one English morpheme /najF/. (Harris 1942: 170)

Other alternatives include an item-specific "morphophonemic formula" that would ensure that "/f/ is replaced by /v/ before /-z/ 'plural' in the following morphemes—*knife, wife, ...*" (Harris 1942: 170). Although the specific mechanisms vary, all of these proposals introduce an abstract level mediating between morphemes and phonemes.

Given the reduction of syntax to selectional and ordering relations (Matthews 1993: 148), words and larger syntactic constructions could be composed of sequences of morphemes. The model of grammar that emerges from these revisions is a recognizably modern, constituency-based model:

We summarize this by asserting that every language has its own GRAMMAR. The grammar, or grammatical system, of a language is (1) THE MORPHEMES USED IN THE LANGUAGE, and (2) THE ARRANGEMENTS IN WHICH THESE MORPHEMES OCCUR RELATIVE TO EACH OTHER IN UTTERANCES. (Hockett 1958: 129)

Within this model, morphological analysis reduces to the syntagmatic arrangement of morphemes. The general method of morphemic analysis is outlined in Harris (1942) and refined in Hockett (1947). This method proceeds in three steps. The first step examines the utterances of a language to identify "recurrent partials with constant meaning" (Hockett 1947: 322). Those recurrent partials that are not composed of smaller forms are classified as morphs, or "morpheme alternants" in the terminology proposed by Harris (1942):

We divide each expression in the given language into the smallest sequences of phonemes which have what we consider the same meaning when they occur in other expressions, or which are left over when all other parts of the expression have been divided off... The resultant minimum parts we call not morphemes, but MORPHEME ALTERNANTS. (Harris 1942: 170)

The second step assigns morphs to a common morpheme if they satisfy the semantic and distributional criteria outlined in Section 2.2.3. The final step sets up the morphophonemic conventions that regulate the selection and shape of the allomorphs that realize a given morpheme in a particular context. In effect, these steps trace a loop that extracts morphemes from surface forms and then invokes rules to reassociate these abstract representations with their surface realization. At each step in this procedure the IA model is confronted with problems created by the disassembly and reassembly of forms.

2.2.1 Problems of segmentation

By associating meaning with formatives, the IA model enhances the significance of word-internal structure. The issues that arise in segmenting utterances into words had been instrumental in Bloomfield's (1914) arguments against classical word-based conceptions. Yet segmenting utterances into morphs did not solve any outstanding problems that arose in identifying word-sized units. On the contrary, segmenting utterances into formatives created a range of new issues, as the analyst was now faced with the challenge of arriving at a principled basis for factoring complex forms into stems and inflections, and isolating the root from derivational exponents and stem formatives. The treatment of 'thematic vowels' illustrated the types of choices: should these vowels be treated as part of a stem, as part of an ending, or as separate from both? And what segmentation should be assigned in cases where a thematic vowel is fused or absent in specific forms or, as in Spanish preterites described by Green (1997) below, where segmentation leaves a 'residue'?

The order of morphemes is fixed: (derivational prefix(es)) + lexical stem + theme vowel + tense marker (sometimes including an empty morph) + person marker. Some forms, however, have fused in the course of history and a neat segmentation is not always possible. The preterit is the most difficult paradigm to analyse, since the theme vowel is sometimes indistinguishable, and segmenting the second and third person plural markers in the regular way, /-is, -n/, leaves an awkward residue that occurs nowhere else in the system. (Green 1997: 99)

Problems of this sort arose even in very simple systems. For example, neither Harris (1942) nor Hockett (1947) was able to decide on the segmentation of English *children*. Harris (1942: 113) contrasts the alternatives *child + ren* and *childr + en* and concludes only that "each of the points of division has advantages and disadvantages". Returning to this "recalcitrant" problem, Hockett (1947: 240) considers three further analyses: *child + r + en*, *child* with vowel change + *en*, and no division, and again reaches no firm conclusions, suggesting that "this is one of the cases in which all of our preferential criteria . . . fail and nothing remains but a resort to convenience". As these examples illustrate, the challenge that faced the IA model model was not one of merely deciding on a consistent segmentation but of arriving at a principled segmentation.

Non-contiguous arrangements of morphs presented a separate problem, as they required a departure from the simplest procedures of segmentation. The 'long components' introduced in Harris (1941, 1951) provided the most general description of infixed and circumfixed morphs. Infixation is illustrated by the Tagalog 'actor focus' marker *um* in (2.1a) and by the Lezgian repetitive marker *x* in (2.1b). Circumfixation is illustrated by the Georgian superlative marker *u. . . esi* in (2.2a) and the Chuckchee negative marker *e. . . ke* in (2.2b).

(2.1) Infixation in Tagalog and Lezgian
       a. *bása* ~ *bumása* 'to read' (Aspillera 1981: 46)
       b. *akun* 'see' ~ *axkun* 'see again' (Haspelmath 1993: 175)

(2.2) Circumfixation in Georgian and Chuckchee
       a. *q'ru* 'deaf' ~ *u-q'ru-esi* 'the most deaf' (Tschenkéli 1958: 225)
       b. *tejkev-ək* 'fight' ~ *e-tejkev-ke-it-ək* 'not to fight' (Comrie 1981: 247)

The principal difficulty presented by thematic vowels and discontinuous arrangements was, in a sense, methodological. In the case of theme vowels, it was possible to cut forms into contiguous parts and even to impose a consistent segmentation. The challenge arose in justifying one split over another. Infixes and circumfixes could also be isolated, though at the cost of departing from procedures that divided utterances into successively smaller sequences.

Yet as acknowledged in the quotation from Lounsbury (1953) on p. 4 above, the search for a principled basis for assigning (or evaluating) segmentations may turn

TABLE 2.1   Competing motivation for genitive plural forms in -*te*

	Sg	Plu	Sg	Plu	Sg	Plu
Nominative	sikk	sikud	raamat	raamatud	auto	autot
Genitive	siku	*sikkude*	raamatu	**raamatute**	auto	*autode*
Partitive	sikku	sikkusid	raamatut	raamatuid	autot	autosid
		'goat'		'book'		'car'

out to be misconceived in cases where cuts are motivated by separate, mutually incompatible, patterns. Matthews (1972) returns to this point in his discussion of the theoretical implications of Latin conjugation. Matthews stresses at the outset of his study that the main challenge faced by segmentation-based models of analysis does not arise in imposing cuts but in evaluating alternatives. In the simple case of the infinitive FERRE 'to bring', as he notes, there is language-internal motivation for each of the segmentations *fer-r-e* and *fer-re*. Selection of either of these choices disrupts the other pattern.

Genitive plural forms in Estonian present an instructive case in which "one comparison of forms suggests one placement, while another comparison suggests another". There are two genitive plural patterns in Estonian, partly conditioned by the metrical structure of the stem. Nouns with non-trochaic stems form genitive plurals in -*te*; nouns with trochaic stems, along with loans and other members of a defective 'fourth' declension, form genitive plurals in the default -*de*.[7] This variation is illustrated in Table 2.1 by the grammatical case forms of the basic Estonian nouns SIKK and RAAMAT and the loan AUTO.

A comparison of the forms in Table 2.1 determines an unambiguous segmentation of the forms *sikkude* and *autode* into the vowel-final stems *sikku* and *auto* and the genitive plural ending -*de*. Assigning a similar analysis to *raamatute*, as proposed by Tuldava (1994: 195), reinforces the cross-class parallel between the stems *raamatu*, *sikku* and *auto*, and establishes a paradigmatic contrast between -*te* and -*de*. Yet, as noted by Mürk (1997: 13), nouns with genitive plurals in -*te* also exhibit a distinctive class-internal pattern. Comparison of the genitive plural with the partitive singular motivates a segmentation into a consonant-final base *raamatut* and a genitive plural marker -*e*.

The choice between the cuts of *raamatute* illustrate two problems for a segmentation-based analysis. The first is that the competing motivation comes from different parts of the morphological system: *raamatu/te* is motivated by cross-class comparisons and *raamatut/e* by a class-internal comparison. It may be possible to assign priority to one source by fiat, but there is no principled basis for this decision. The second, and more fundamental, problem is that segmentation forces a choice between two convergent analyses. In fact, *raamatute* contrasts SIMULTANEOUSLY with the partitive singular in its own class and with the genitive plurals in other classes. Yet expressing either pattern via segmentation treats one pattern as significant and disrupts the other.

---

[7] Where *d* is a short voiceless stop and *t* a long counterpart. See also Erelt *et al.* (1995, 2013) and Blevins (2008a) for more discussion of noun classes in Estonian.

Conundrums of this type call into question the usefulness of segmentation even as a tool for describing morphological structure. From a classical WP perspective, the problems that arise in segmenting forms reflect the intrinsically destructive character of decompositional analysis. The procedure that Lounsbury (1953) outlines starts from a comparison of a set of forms, which identifies patterns of overlap and alternation. Abstractive generalizations stated over these forms can capture the full range of variation, including any convergent patterns. In contrast, the use of decompositional strategies tends to disrupt at least some of the patterns, and isolates 'recurrent' units, which, on closer analysis, often exhibit patterns of subphonemic variation.[8]

2.2.2 Special morphs

Other fundamental challenges arose in cases where no analysis could be made to conform to the strictures of the IA model. From the earliest formulations of this model, it was clear that the notion of 'morph' would have to be more abstract than just a sequence of segmental phonemes. Harris (1942) identifies three initial classes of non-segmental morphs, (or, again, "morpheme alternants"):

It is useful to generalize this definition of morpheme alternant by taking sequence to mean not only additive sequence (the addition of phonemes), but also zero (the addition of no phoneme), negative sequence (the dropping of a phoneme), and phonemic component sequence (the addition of a physiological feature of phonemes). (Harris 1942: 170)

The introduction of 'zeros' is the most conservative of these generalizations, as it just extends a uniform morphotactic analysis to forms in which a morpheme has no segmental realization. The notion of a 'phonetically null' morph appears to originate with the Post-Bloomfiedians, as it contrasts with the interpretation of zeros as literal absence in Bloomfield:

His [Bloomfield's JPB] use of zero is apparently the classic use found in Sanskrit grammar, namely the removal of something, and its replacement by nothing, rather than the distributionalist version, in which a 'zero element' is present. (Fought 1999: 13)

The most restrictive treatment of zero elements was suggested by Bloch (1947: 402), who proposed that "no morpheme has zero as its only alternant". This constraint disallows zero MORPHEMES, such as the zero singular sometimes posited in analyses of English nouns. However, it allows zero MORPHS as one of the realizations of a morpheme. Hence it is compatible with an analysis of plural *sheep* in terms of a stem *sheep* and a zero plural marker 'Ø'.

Reinterpreting zeros as 'phonetically null segments' also creates the challenge of arranging these 'segments'. As Anderson (1992) notes, the large number of possible arrangements of zeros leads to pervasive indeterminacy:

---

[8] As discussed in Kemps *et al.* (2005); Plag *et al.* (2016) and Chapter 8.3.

the assumption that any information which is not overtly signalled nonetheless corresponds to some zero morpheme leads to the formal problem of assigning a place in the structure (and linear order) to all of those zeros. (Anderson 1992: 61)

The other generalizations create even more vexing difficulties. Under "phonemic component sequences", Harris subsumed the suprasegmental properties that Bloomfield (1933) had treated as 'modulation' (and which Firth (1948) termed 'prosodies'). Classifying these properties as extended types of morphs is merely the first tentative step away from a method based on 'dividing expressions into sequences of phonemes'. Treating 'subtraction' as another type of 'alternant' is a more decisive step in the same direction. To illustrate a subtractive pattern, Harris (1942: 110) cites the formation of Hidatsa imperatives in (2.3a). The Papago forms in (2.3b) provide another familiar case, in which perfectives lack the final *-m* of the corresponding imperfectives.[9]

(2.3)   Truncation in Hidatsa and Papago
     a.   *cicic* 'he jumped' ~ *cic* 'jump!', *ika·c* 'he looked' ~ *ika* 'look!'
     b.   *him* ~ *hi* 'walking', *hihim* ~ *hihi* 'walking.PL' (Zepeda 1983)

However, it is the treatment of ablaut and other stem alternations as 'replacements' that signals the abandonment of a general method of analysis based on dividing expressions into segmental material. To extend an IA analysis to ablaut patterns in English, Harris (1942) proposes a complex "negative-additive" element that 'drops' one vowel and 'adds' another:[10]

In *took* we have two morphemes: *take*, and /ej/~/u/ 'past time'. The latter occurs also in *shook* as compared with *shake*. It is a combination of negative and additive sequences: dropping /ej/ and adding /u/. Another negative-additive morpheme is /a/~/e/ 'plural', which occurs in *men* as compared with *man*. (Harris 1942: 171)

The use of subtractive and replacive morphs introduces non-segmental 'items' that cannot be brought into a linear 'arrangement' with segmental material. As Matthews (1972: 59) emphasizes, "the attempt to disguise 'replacement' as a segment" merely confounds segments and processes:

The notion of 'replacement' . . . is one which is quite foreign to the Item and Arrangement view of language. What is involved is not a certain segment in a certain position . . . but the process by which the segment arrived in such a position; to speak of this process as a

---

  [9] Subtraction tends to be invoked in cases in which the truncated or remnant unit can be defined prosodically but not segmentally, so that a single subtraction process describes an alternation requiring multiple, segmentally distinct, affixal patterns.

  [10] Although Harris (1942) refers to this element as a 'morpheme' he seems to mean 'morpheme alternant', corresponding to what Hockett (1947) calls 'replacive' morphs.

'morph', or as the 'allomorph' of a particular morpheme, would be a blatant conceptual error. (Matthews 1972: 59)

Process morphs also create seemingly intractable difficulties for the notion of 'arrangement', as reflected in the deliberations of Hockett (1947):

Men is therefore morphemically {MAN} + {s}. But—so runs the argument that would set up alternation morphs—*men* and *man* resemble each other in phonemic shape, both containing *m-n*...One morph in *men* is *man*. The other is the alternation *a~e*. Or – arguing now for a zero morph – *men*...consists of an alternant *men* of {MAN} plus an alternant /Ø/ of {s}. (Hockett 1947: 340)

On an analysis on which "[o]ne morph in *men* is *man*. The other is the alternation *a~e*", it is unclear how to order the morphs *man* and *a~e*. The second alternative considered by Hockett adopts the solution that Bernard Bloch had developed in his analysis of stem allomorphy in English verbs. Bloch (1947: 404) treated ablauted preterites such as *took* as consisting of a tense-neutral stem allomorph *took* and a zero inflectional marker. The plural *men* could be handled similarly in terms of a number-neutral stem allomorph of the morpheme {MAN}, followed by a zero allomorph of plural {s}.

The indirect treatments of truncation and stem ablaut were necessitated by the agglutinative bias of the IA model. The model reduced all form variation to affixation by encapsulating alternations in 'items' that could be concatenated. The 'primary' items consisted, as expected, of segmental material. Non-affixal alternations were expressed by 'secondary' (or 'trojan horse') items that could induce changes in morphotactic structure. Yet the unification achieved by treating these items as 'morphs' was never more than terminological:

the new definition of 'morph' is no longer that with which we began; perhaps, therefore, it would be advisable to distinguish terminologically between, say, 'primary morphs' (those of overt phonemic content) and 'extended morphs' (including primary ones and morphs of the zero, replacement, or subtraction types). (Hockett 1947: 240)

2.2.3 Classification

Once an utterance is divided syntagmatically into a sequence of recurrent partials, primary as well as secondary, these elements must be grouped paradigmatically into abstract morphemes. The three basic criteria that guide this classification are set out in Harris (1942):

A morpheme unit is thus a group of one or more alternants which have the same meaning and complementary distribution.

In units consisting of more than one alternant, the total distribution of all the alternants (i.e. the combined range of environments in which each of them occurs) must equal the range of environments in which some unit with but a single alternant occurs. (Harris 1942: 171)

This combination of semantic and distributional criteria were largely carried forward in subsequent versions of Post-Bloomfieldian morphemic analysis. The principal revision introduced in Hockett (1947) replaces the requirement that morphs must occur in "complementary" distribution by the weaker condition that their distribution must merely be "non-contrastive":

Two or more morphs are grouped into a single morpheme if they fit the following grouping requirements: (a) they have the same meaning; (b) they are in non-contrastive distribution; and (c) the range of the resultant morpheme is not unique. (Hockett 1947: 322f.)

The first criterion imposed by Harris (1942) and Hockett (1947) characterizes morphemes as semantically (rather than formally) coherent classes of elements. Hence although meaning is not part of a grammatical description *per se* in the IA model, meaning (or at least a contrast between sameness and difference of meaning) is fundamental to morphemic analysis. The second criterion in Harris (1942) requires that two realizations of a common morpheme must be in complementary distribution. The revision in Hockett (1947) reflects his view that this condition is too strong in cases where alternatives occur with no obvious difference in meaning or function. English noun plurals provide a simple illustration. Hockett notes that the exponent [s] and the exponent that consists of final segment voicing together with [z] occur in non-complementary distribution in pairs such as *hoofs~hooves*. Pairs such as *oxen~oxes* show a similarly non-complementary distribution for [ən] and [əz] To account for these cases, Hockett weakens Harris's second criterion to the requirement that morphs need only occur in non-contrastive distribution.

The third criterion is the most subtle. Its most direct effect is to prevent synonymous forms from being coerced into morphemes. Harris (1942) illustrates this effect by contrasting the morphemic status of the forms of English BE with the synonyms TWENTY and (somewhat archaic) SCORE:

Thus the combined environments of *am, are, be* are included in the environments in which *walk* occurs: *I am, they are, to be*, as compared with *I walk, they walk, to walk*. The case is different with *twenty* and *score*, even though they have the same meaning and never occur in the same environment. For there is no morpheme unit in English which consists of only one alternant and which occurs in the combined distribution of twenty and score. Therefore, we consider the alternants *am, are, be* as being members of a single morpheme unit; but of the alternants *twenty* and *score*, each constitutes a morpheme unit by itself. (Harris 1942: 172)

The third criterion has a similar, though less obvious, effect on the grouping of inflectional exponents. On any morphemic analysis, the English plural morpheme {s} will contain the phonologically conditioned allomorphs [z], [əz] and [s]. However, the status of the [ən] in *oxen* or the 'Ø' associated with *sheep* is less straightforward. These allomorphs are clearly morphologically conditioned, given that phonologically similar nouns take the regular plural by default, as in the case of *box~boxes* and *heap~heaps*. The treatment of these elements ultimately distinguishes two different conceptions of the morpheme. If [ən] and 'Ø' are not assigned to the morpheme {s}, then its realizations will retain a similarity in form.

	hoof	*hoofs*		*hooves*	
Morphemes	{HOOF}	{HOOF}	{s}	{HOOF}	{s}
Morphs	/huf/	/huf/	/z/	/huv/	/z/
Alternants	[huf]	[huf]	[s]	[huv]	[z]

FIGURE 2.1   Morphological and phonological allomorphy

If formally heterogeneous allomorphs such as [ən] and 'Ø' are included, then {s} will merely enumerate all of the strategies for expressing plural number in English. All of the candidate allomorphs of {s} satisfy the first two conditions specified by Harris (1942) and Hockett (1947): they all have the same meaning and occur in a non-contrastive distribution.

It is the third criterion that is decisive here. If {s} is to have a non-unique range, then some morpheme must have the same distribution as the plural allomorphs do collectively. Harris (1942: 111) suggests that "the range of environments" of {s} "equals that of zero 'singular', the suffix *-ful* and other single-alternant morpheme units". Yet neither of Harris's examples is persuasive. As Hockett (1947: 230) notes, "[t]he zero element with meaning 'noun singular'... has a very dubious status, having no alternant of other than zero shape". Likewise even if one accepts that *-ful* or some other derivational affix combines as productively with noun stems as plural exponents do, it is unclear why the distribution of a derivational ending should be relevant to the identification of an inflectional morpheme. Later refinements of morphemic analysis do not improve on Harris's third criterion. For example, the far more elaborate conditions in Nida (1948: 421) reintroduce a version of this criterion as a restriction on the grouping of "[f]orms which possess a common semantic distinctiveness, but which differ in their phonemic form".

The issues that arise in determining whether [ən] is an allomorph of {s} illustrate the kinds of problems created by morphemic analysis, even when applied to extremely simple patterns. Moreover, the genuine ambiguity present in the notions 'morph' and 'allomorphy' remains largely unresolved in later accounts. For the sake of clarity, it is therefore useful to reserve the term 'morph' for morphologically conditioned allomorphs, and apply Harris' term '(morpheme) alternant' to phonologically conditioned variants. This refinement of the Descriptivist terms is illustrated by the description of the English singular *hoof*, and the plurals *hoofs* and *hooves* in Figure 2.1. The lexical morpheme {HOOF} has two lexically-conditioned morphs. The 'default' stem allomorph /huf/ realizes the singular *hoof* and underlies the regular plural formation *hoofs*. The voiced stem allomorph /huv/ occurs only in the alternative plural *hooves*. The grammatical plural morpheme {s} is realized in both plural forms by the allomorph /z/. This allomorph is in turn realized by the alternants [z] and [s] in the surface word forms *hoofs* and *hooves*.

2.2.4 'An agglutinating system gone wrong'

Much of the appeal of the IA model derived from the apparently simple and intuitive treatment that it offered for concatenative patterns. A regular plural like *hoofs* could be broken down into a stem form, *hoof*, which realizes lexical meaning, and an inflectional form, *-s*, that realizes plurality. Yet complications' arise in extending this type of analysis even to the full range of inflectional patterns of English. More complex inflectional systems raised further challenges. To preserve the letter of the IA model, the Descriptivists explored a variety of mainly technical solutions. Mismatches between 'units of meaning' and 'units of form' are repaired through the postulation of more "special kinds of morphs":

> The alteration [of Harris (1942)] by which the number of morphemes in an utterance fails in some cases to coincide with the number of morphs consists of recognizing two special kinds of morphs: EMPTY MORPHS, which have no meaning and belong to no morpheme; and PORTMANTEAU MORPHS, which belong simultaneously to two (or, theoretically, more) morphemes, and have simultaneously the meaning of both. (Hockett 1947: 236)

As examples of empty morphs, Hockett (1947) cites theme vowels in Spanish conjugations. To illustrate portmanteau morphs, he gives the example of the French contraction *au*, which occurs in place of the preposition and article sequence *à le*. Yet these additional morphs merely created greater analytical indeterminacy, without addressing the source of meaning–form mismatches.

Portmanteau morphs provide an alternative analysis of patterns that can be described in terms of zeros. In the comments that precede the discussion of *men* on p. 31 above, Hockett (1947: 339) acknowledges that "one solution, and certainly the most obvious one, is to regard *men* as a single portmanteau morph, representing the morpheme sequence {MAN} + {s}". Thus the IA model makes available at least the three analyses in Figure 2.2: (i) *man* and a replacive plural allomorph, (ii) *men* and a zero plural allomorph, and (iii) portmanteau *men*, without providing criteria for choosing between them.

More generally, allowing empty and portmanteau morphs largely rescinds the 'principle of total accountability' on page 24 above. Whenever there are more morphs than morphemes, the excess morphs can be treated as 'empty'; if there are more morphemes than morphs, the shortfall can be made up by invoking portmanteau (or zero) morphs. Taken together, these refinements amount to the abandonment of the central empirical claims of the IA model. Worse yet, the strategy of introducing a special morph to handle each type of mismatch between a 'unit of meaning' and a 'unit of form' did not address the source of these mismatches, so much as treat their symptoms.

Languages of the 'flectional' type, expose the severe limitations of this strategy. As Matthews (1972: 132ff.) shows, the Latin verb *re:ksisti:* 'you had ruled' (*rēxistī* in the standard pedagogical orthography) exhibits the many-many feature-form

	Replacement		Zero		Portmanteau	
Morphemes	{MAN}	{s}	{MAN}	{s}	{MAN}	{s}
Morphs	/mæn/	/æ/ ~ /ɛ/	/mæn/	Ø	/mɛ n/	

FIGURE 2.2   Candidate IA analyses of English *men*

re:k	s	is	ti:
(STEM)			2ND sg
			PERFECTIVE

FIGURE 2.3   Morphological analysis of Latin *re:ksisti* (Matthews 1972: 132)

re:k	REGO	
s		
is	PERFECTIVE	
ti:		2ND sg

FIGURE 2.4   Many-to-many feature-form associations

relations displayed in Figure 2.3. The ending *-ti:* exhibits what is usually termed a 'fusional' pattern, in which a single formative realizes the features perfective aspect, 2nd person and singular number. At the same time, the perfective feature exhibits a converse 'fissional' pattern, as it is realized by each of the formatives *-s-*, *-is-*, and *-ti:*.

From the standpoint of a classical grammar, Figure 2.3 is a case of 'overextraction', in which meaning is associated with sub-meaningful units of form. In the conjugational paradigm of REGO, there is a unique (in this case, biunique) correspondence between the second person perfective active cell and the word form *re:ksisti:*. However, no such correspondence can be established between the features contained in the cell and the formatives that make up the word form.[11] Instead, further decomposition of the features of the cell and further disassembly of the form produce the non-binunique pattern in Figure 2.4.

As in the simpler patterns discussed by Harris and Hockett, there are technical solutions for the challenges posed by flectional languages. The 'extended exponence' (Matthews 1972) illustrated by the multiple perfective markers in Figure 2.4 can be accommodated by designating one formative as 'primary' and excluding any other, 'secondary' exponents in the determination of morphemic biuniqueness.[12] Indeed, as the subsequent history of the IA model shows, an item-based analysis can be extended to nearly any recalcitrant pattern through the introduction of special morphs or construction-specific conventions. However, the original goal of the IA model was not solely to maximize the use of items, but to bring out the correspondence between items and units of meaning. If, as Matthews (1972) notes,

[11] Parallel remarks apply to more 'morphological' relations. The perfect indicative active is one of the four 'principal parts' of a Latin verb identified by pedagogical descriptions such as Hale and Buck (1903). Although it is conventional to cite the perfect indicative in the 1sg, the 2sg form *re:ksisti:* is equally 'diagnostic' of a third conjugation verb like REGO. As it happens, the consonant-final stem *re:k* is also diagnostic of the third conjugation, though this reflects the fact that inflections in the perfect active series do not exhibit class-specific variation in Latin and is not true of stems in general.

[12] See Carstairs (1987) and Noyer (1992) for accounts that develop this contrast, and Harris (2009) for a comprehensive discussion of extended exponence.

this correspondence does not obtain, the central motivation for items and for the IA model itself is undermined:

One motive for the post-Bloomfieldian model consisted, that is to say, in a genuinely factual assertion about language: namely, that there is some sort of matching between minimal 'sames' of 'form' (morphs) and 'meaning' (morphemes). *Qua* factual assertion this has subsequently proved false: for certain languages, such as Latin, the correspondence which was envisaged apparently does not exist . . . One is bound to suspect, in the light of such a conclusion, that the model is in some sense wrong. (Matthews 1972: 124)

2.3 The Operational (IP) model

From a classical perspective, what was most wrong about the IA model was the attempt to associate meaning with units of form which, at least in the case of flectional patterns, could not be assigned meanings in isolation. This foundational issue was not revisited by the architects of the IA model until later. Instead, their initial responses explored modest revisions of assumptions about the disassembly of forms.[13] The decomposition of meanings raised parallel issues, but these were largely passed over. In his discussion of Harris's criteria for grouping morphs into morphemes, Hockett (1947) declares:

The first of them, involving meaning, is obviously the most difficult to handle . . . The second and third requirements are purely distributional, and more easily subject to analysis and modification. (Hockett 1947: 327f.)

The definition of "a morpheme unit" as "a group of one or more alternants which have the same meaning" (Harris 1942: 171) is carried over in the notion of "recurrent partials with constant meaning" (Hockett 1947: 322). Yet 'sameness of meaning' was only ever formulated operationally, via the 'paired utterance test' (Harris 1951: 32). Hence the 'units of meaning' in an IA model depended on a purely operational notion of 'sameness' or 'constancy' of meaning.

Procedures of morphotactic analysis were articulated more explicitly. But this explicitness only served to highlight the biases built into the IA model. By reducing Bloomfield's diverse 'arrangements' to a single property of linear order, the Post-Bloomfieldians had, whether by accident or design, arrived at a model that was optimized for the analysis of agglutinative patterns. Deviations from an agglutinative ideal could only be described indirectly, by constructing an abstract agglutinative arrangement that is subsequently converted to an observable surface form, as Hockett (1987) later acknowledges:

We were providing for alternations by devising an "agglutinative analog" of the language and formulating rules that would convert expressions in that analog into the shapes in which they are actually uttered. Of course, even such an agglutinative analog, with its accompanying

---

[13] As shown later by Roark and Sproat (2007: §3), IA and IP models are in fact computationally equivalent and can both be implemented by finite state transducers.

conversion rules, could be interpreted merely as a descriptive device. But it was not in general taken that way; instead it was taken as a direct reflection of reality. (Hockett 1987: 83)

The highly abstract conception of grammatical structure implied by this practice (what Hockett (1987: 184) termed 'the transducer fallacy') was again not reconsidered until much later. It was the problems that derived from the treatment of 'units of form' as "sequences of phonemes" (Harris 1942: 170) that were of most immediate concern. By the early 1950s, Hockett had come to realize that the initial solutions, which coerced form variation into types of special morphs, merely subverted the nature of the original IA model:

> Could we not modify our definition of 'morph' in such a way as to allow subtractives and replacives in those circumstances where they seem so clearly convenient? Of course we can do so. But such action seems to be equivalent—perhaps rather unexpectedly—to removing the keystone of the whole IA arch; the model begins to collapse . . . When we pick up the pieces and try to fit them together, again—without restoring the keystone—we find that we are no longer dealing with anything that looks like IA; we have a new model on our hands. (Hockett 1954: 394)

Hockett terms the new model 'item and process' (IP), in recognition of its debt to the process-based view of Sapir (1921), which Bloomfield and his successors had regarded with suspicion. To clarify how this model differs from the IA model, it is useful to begin with the Bloomfieldian notion of a LINGUISTIC FORM as "a phonetic form which has a meaning" (Bloomfield 1933: 138). A form in this sense has two components, a 'meaning', which can be represented by a set B of grammatical and semantic properties, and a 'phonetic form' X. As a minimal linguistic form, a morpheme {M} is a pair $\langle B, X \rangle$, where B is a minimal property set and X is a single morph. In an IA model, non-minimal morphological units are built up from adjacent morphemes by combining the feature sets and concatenating the morphs of the morphemes. An IP model retains a set of basic stem or root morphemes but represents affixal morphemes by processes. Like morphemes, a process has two components, a grammatical FUNCTION f that maps one property set B onto an augmented set B' and an OPERATION o that maps a phonetic form X onto a modified form X'.[14] In an IP model, non-minimal morphological units are built up by applying a process $\mathbb{P}$ to a morphemic pair $\langle B, X \rangle$ to define a new 'output' pair $\langle f(B), o(X) \rangle$.

The derivation of *hoofs* and *men* in Figure 2.5 illustrates this process-based perspective. Since processes, like segmental morphemes, have constant meaning and variable form, the function f adds the feature 'PLU' to the property set of *hoofs* and *men*. However, whereas /hufz/ is formed by suffixation of /z/, /mɛn/ is defined by an ablauting operation that substitutes ɛ for æ in /mæn/.

These analyses highlight the central insight that affixal and nonaffixal alternations can be treated more naturally as types of processes than as types of segments. In the case of ablaut alternations, an operation (whether stated in terms

---

[14] The separation between processes and operations anticipates a similar distinction between rules and operations in models of Montague Grammar (Bach 1979, 1980).

$\mathbb{P}$	*hoofs*	*men*
$\langle f, o \rangle$	$\langle \{\text{NOUN}\}, /\text{huf}/ \rangle$	$\langle \{\text{NOUN}\}, /\text{mæn}/ \rangle$
$f(B) = B \cup \{\text{PLU}\}$	$f(\{\text{NOUN}\}) = \{\text{NOUN}, \text{PLU}\}$	$f(\{\text{NOUN}\}) = \{\text{NOUN}, \text{PLU}\}$
$/X/ \rightarrow /Xz/$	$/\text{huf}/ \rightarrow /\text{hufz}/$	—
$/X\text{æ}Y/ \rightarrow /X\varepsilon Y/$	—	$/\text{mæn}/ \rightarrow /\text{mɛn}/$
Output	$\langle \{\text{NOUN}, \text{PLU}\}, [\text{hufs}] \rangle$	$\langle \{\text{NOUN}, \text{PLU}\}, [\text{mɛn}] \rangle$

FIGURE 2.5   IP analyses of affixal and ablauting plurals in English

of segment replacement or phonological feature change) can replace /æ/ by /ɛ/ in /mæn/. Including this operation among those available to the plural process avoids the artificiality of introducing a 'replacive' morph to trigger replacement. Similar analyses apply to 'subtraction' and other process morphs, all of which can be described directly as operations on items, rather than as special, operation-inducing items. From an IP perspective, affixal patterns reflect simple types of operations which tend to preserve their inputs. For example, the regular ending /z/ can be encapsulated in the operation '/X/ → /Xz/'. The morphotactic effect is the same in these cases, but the new model drops the pretense that 'replacement' or 'subtraction' are special kinds of item that must therefore somehow be brought into a linear arrangement with other items.

In other respects, the new model represents a modest revision of the IA model. Like IA approaches, IP models assume a lexicon consisting of an inventory of minimal elements, stems or roots, from which complex forms are derived. The derivation of complex forms involves adding grammatical properties to those associated with the root, in parallel with the modification of the root form.[15] Although no longer uniformly item-based, the resulting IP model remains firmly morpheme-based. Whereas the IA model associates all meaning with segmental morphemes, the IP model associates lexical meaning with root morphemes, and grammatical meaning with morphemic processes.

As in the IA model, the morphophonemic level plays a vital role mediating between morphemes and surface forms. Morphologically conditioned allomorphy is not eliminated, but relocated, expressed by variation in the operations associated with a process. The selectional relation between a noun and plural exponent is expressed in the IP model by the CHOICE of the operation that either suffixes /z/, ablauts the stem vowel, or else effects some other change.

Hockett (1954) also suggests that the IA strategies for dealing with violations of total accountability remain available in an IP model, should the analyst wish to invoke them. Yet despite the close correspondence between the models, it is not entirely clear that these strategies are directly transferable:

Empty root-alternants [and] portmanteau root-alternants . . . are definable and allowable as in IA, should there be any need for them. Zero alternant roots and zero markers of processes are likewise allowable, under similar limitations. (Hockett 1954: 396)

---

[15] In the terms of Stump (2001), both IA and IP are 'incremental' models that increment the properties of underspecified roots in the course of constructing words.

To begin with, the shift to a process-based perspective greatly weakens the internal motivation for zero morphs. There is no obvious need for zero exponents in models that can contain processes that apply no operation.[16] For example, the 'zero marking' of plural *sheep* can be described by a process that applies no operation to the noun stem (though a plural process is still required to add plural features to the underspecified properties of the stem).[17]

Empty morphs raise more fundamental difficulties. An 'empty' strategy that modifies forms while preserving features can be formulated as a process with a feature-preserving function and a form-altering operation. Yet the interaction of processes in an IP model is largely governed by the 'feeding' and 'bleeding' relations determined by the successive addition of features to an initially underspecified stem entry. Thus the interaction of feature-preserving processes must be regulated in some other way. The applicability of such processes can be restricted if the feature-preserving function is specified for features that must be present (or absent) in the input, like the 'constraining equations' of LFG (Kaplan and Bresnan 1982) and repeated application is barred in some way. However, this extension amounts to introducing a class of realization rules into an IP model, since standard exponence rules preserve the features and (potentially) modify the form of their inputs. Hence the 'realizational processes' required to accommodate empty morphs within an IP model are no less artificial than process morphs are within IA models.

To a large extent, the IP model reassigns the complexity of an IA analysis from the morphotactic structure of individual forms onto the derivational structure defined by the successive application of processes to a root entry. This shift in the direction of a realization-based perspective is reflected in Hockett's suggestion that the material present in a form need not be either morphemic or 'empty', but may serve merely as a marker of a process that has applied:

Some of the phonemic material in a derived form may be, not part of any underlying form, but rather a REPRESENTATION or MARKER of the process. (Hockett 1954: 396)

The recognition of non-morphemic 'markers' again subverts the conception of morphological analysis as the association of minimal 'units of meaning' with minimal 'units of form'. In some cases a process may add (or modify) a single feature, and/or introduce a single marker. But there is no principled grounds within this scheme of analysis for regarding a biunique relation between features and exponents as normative or canonical.[18]

In sum, the introduction of processes eliminates some of the artifactual problems created by the IA model, by allowing a description to incorporate non-segmental

---

[16] Equivalently, processes can apply inert 'identity' operations which preserve the input form, thereby achieving the same effect as the 'identity function default' of Paradigm Function Morphology (Stump 2001).

[17] Requiring that every process must contain at least some operation captures the condition that "no morpheme has zero as its only alternant" (Bloch 1947: 402).

[18] The notion that processes must represent a simple property by a single exponent thus has no place in later approaches that adopt an IP perspective, such as Articulated Morphology (Steele 1995) or early models of HPSG (Pollard and Sag 1987).

phonetic alternations that have been co-opted to express morphological contrasts. In particular, by interposing processes between properties and forms, the IP model avoids the artificiality of treating process morphs as 'change-inducing' items. The resulting model is, however, less uniform than a pure IA model. Items no longer occupy the central role that they have within a system based on procedures of segmentation and classification, but they are not eliminated altogether in favour of processes. Instead, roots constitute a residual class of morphemic items in the new model, even as exponents are recast as 'markers' of processes. In some cases, the appeal to processes shifts the problems posed by feature-form mismatches from the morphotactic to the derivational structure of a form. Process-based analyses simplify the morphotactic structure of elements like plural *sheep*, or singular nouns in English in general, since they avoid the need to introduce zeros bearing number features. However, the derivational structure of *sheep* is no simpler, since a form-preserving process must still apply to derive the plural, and a separate process must apply to derive the singular. A model that constructs inflected forms 'incrementally' from stems—whether by concatenating morphs or by applying processes—has no straightforward way to declare that singular number is realized by the basic noun stem in English. The fundamental obstacle to expressing this kind of generalization is not the role of items in the IA model but the role of morphemes; the problem is intrinsic to morphemic analysis. The challenges posed by cumulative and overlapping exponence derive similarly from the nature of the relation between features and forms, not from assumptions about the representation of forms or form variation.

2.4 The Decade of the Morpheme

Ultimately, the problems that occupied the Post-Bloomfieldians during what Hockett (1987: 81) later termed "the Decade of the Morpheme" derived from their attempt to associate grammatical meaning with sub-word units rather than from the particular morphotactic assumptions they adopted or the specific techniques they employed. This orientation was part of Bloomfield's morphological legacy, reflecting the influence of Pāṇini and the Sanskrit grammarians on Bloomfield's thought (Emeneau 1988). Bloomfield had famously regarded Pāṇini's concise description of Sanskrit as "an indispensable model for the description of languages" (Bloomfield 1929) and even appears to have attached theoretical importance to the economy of presentation achieved by Pāṇini.

However, by the end of the decade Hockett had begun to distinguish the properties of languages from the properties of language descriptions. This led him to question whether techniques for achieving economy of exposition in a written morphemic analysis had any genuine status within the grammar of a language, or any relevance to the use or acquisition of language by speakers:

Morphophonemes, morphs, phones, and acoustic phones are ARTIFACTS OF ANALYSIS or CONVENIENCES FOR DESCRIPTION, not elements in a language. (Hockett 1961: 42)

By 1967, Hockett had ceased to see morphemic analysis as anything other than a linguist's concise shorthand for more psychologically plausible descriptions. For a more 'realistic' alternative, Hockett offers a description that conforms to a classical WP model, consisting of sets of word forms organized into paradigms and extended by processes of analogy:

To cover the complex alternations of Yawelmani by principal-parts-and-paradigms would take much more space than is occupied in the first sections of this paper by the morphophoneme-and-rewrite-rule presentation. But there would be a net gain in realism, for the student of the language would now be required to produce new forms in exactly the way the native user of the language produces or recognizes them—by analogy . . . A correct principal-parts-and-paradigms statement and a correct morphophoneme-and-rule statement subsume the same actual facts of an alternation, the former more directly, the latter more succinctly. We ought therefore to be free to use the latter, provided we specify that it is to be understood only as convenient shorthand for the former. (Hockett 1967: 221f.)

Hockett's endorsement of the WP model in part reflected his view that the problems that had arisen in elaborating morphemic analysis were artifacts of the Post-Bloomfieldians' narrow frame of reference (Hockett 1987: 82ff.).[19]

Within this frame of reference, the status of the morpheme was reinforced by parallels with the phoneme and by the fact that morphemes could be identified on the basis of procedures of distributional analysis. Indeed, the morpheme can be seen more as a product of a motivated method than as a motivated unit in its own right. Hence when examined outside this methodological context, the morpheme may strike the modern reader as a somewhat peculiar morphological unit. A description of a grammatical system must identify the properties that are distinctive within that system. But there is no clear reason for treating each individual property as a kind of 'unit'. The strategy of parcelling individual properties into morphemes just appears to reflect the fact that the Post-Bloomfieldians had only rudimentary techniques at their disposal for representing feature information. A model that incorporates even simple feature 'bundles' (as nearly all contemporary models do) can represent individual distinctive properties within a larger set or structure. In such a model, there is no need to assume that every distinctive property has some discrete realization. Instead, it can be left as an empirical question which feature combinations are realized in a given language, and HOW they are realized: singly, cumulatively, multiply, etc. The observation that individual person and number properties have discrete realizations in a language such as

---

[19] This position is echoed in the perspective that Matthews (1991) attributes to a proponent of a classical WP model who encounters a modern IA analysis:

An apologist for ancient grammar would answer that these elements [morphemes] are fictions. They are created by the modern method; and, if we foist them on a flectional system, we are bound to describe it as an agglutinating system that has somehow gone wrong. (Matthews 1991: 204)

Turkish does not entail that the same features must have discrete realizations in, say, Russian any more than the fusional realization of person and number features in Russian determine an 'underlyingly fusional' structure for Turkish.

In a contemporary setting, there is neither formal nor empirical motivation for the assumption that individual properties should be parcelled into 'units'. The idea that properties should be realized exactly once in a form seems even more out of place in a model of linguistic systems that serve a communicative function. It is well known that distinctive phonological contrasts tend to be multiply cued: an obstruent voicing contrast, for example, may be cued by voice onset time differences at consonant release, by durational differences in consonant closure, and by durational differences in preceding vowels. The same advantages accrue in the morphological domain, where multiple exponents of a grammatical property enhance communication over a noisy channel and contribute to robustness in general. It is unclear why one would make the *a priori* assumption that each distinctive property should be uniquely realized, let alone build such an assumption into the architecture of a morphological model. It is thus unsurprising that this assumption is falsified by patterns of extended exponence in various languages, and enigmatic that it was ever seriously entertained.

2.4.1 'A remarkable tribute to the inertia of ideas'

In short, for all its familiarity, the structuralist morpheme represents a particular and, in many respects, extreme view of the way that grammatical information is organized and packaged within a language. The morpheme is not something that is 'in' a language or which can reasonably be said to have been discovered, or otherwise established, except with reference to methods that themselves stand in need of validation. Unlike words, morphemes do not in general occur in isolation and are rarely demarcated in the speech stream by phonetic cues or other language-internal evidence. Hence, the procedures of analysis developed for identifying morphemes do not refine some 'pretheoretical notion of morpheme', for there is no such notion. Instead, like the morphophoneme, the morpheme is a purely theoretical construct within the specific model of distributional analysis developed by the Post-Bloomfieldians.

Given that the careful formulation of principles of morphemic analysis led many of its initial proponents to abandon a morpheme-based model, one might have expected the structuralist morpheme to suffer the same fate as the structuralist phoneme. But even though the notion of the morpheme had been modelled on and supported by the phoneme in Post-Bloomfieldian approaches, their paths diverged with the eclipse of these approaches. Early generative accounts (Halle 1959; Chomsky and Halle 1965) led a determined attack against the phoneme, or at least against a level of phonemic representation. In contrast, the morpheme successfully jumped hosts and enjoyed a new lease of life within the emerging generative paradigm. This was not because any of the outstanding problems with morphemic analysis had been solved in the meantime. The procedures and definitions in Harris (1942), Hockett (1947) and Nida (1948) remained the most explicit statements of morphemic analysis, as indeed they do today. Later versions of the IA model simply took morphemes for granted and focused on technical refinements of morphemic analysis.[20]

Many of the problems and solutions associated with the original IA model persist in its modern variants and derivatives. For example, the analysis of verbal inflection in Halle and Marantz (1993: 126f.) is essentially an amalgam of the analyses of Harris (1942) and Bloch (1947). A strong preterite form such as *took* is analyzed as consisting of a zero tense marker preceded by a stem in which the effect of a replacive morph is shifted onto an item-specific 'readjustment rule'. This type of analysis preserves the most problematic features of Post-Bloomfieldian accounts. The tense features of *took* are 'marked' by a covert element, while the vowel change that actually distinguishes the preterite form is treated as a case of 'stem allomorphy' that serves no signalling function. The problems posed by zeros are, if anything, even more acute in modern accounts, given the expanded role that zeros play in generative approaches, as Pullum and Zwicky (1992) point out. The morphotactic problems posed by non-segmental alternations are intrinsic to the IA model because they derive from the basic agglutinative bias of this model.

As Chomsky (1965) acknowledges in one of the early generative treatments of inflectional morphology, the problems with morphemic analysis identified in the 1940s survive intact in transformational accounts that attempt to impose an agglutinative IA analysis onto fusional patterns. After enumerating the complications that arise in representing German declensions in terms of discrete case, number and gender morphemes, he concludes:

I know of no compensating advantage for the modern descriptivist reanalysis of traditional paradigmatic formulations in terms of morpheme sequences. This seems, therefore to be an ill-advised theoretical innovation. (Chomsky 1965: 174)

As Chomsky clearly appreciated at the time, there was no principled reason why standard transformational models should be morpheme-based rather than word-based. Much the same remains true into the contemporary period, as the modern WP approaches of Aronoff (1994), Beard (1995), Stump (2001) and, especially, Anderson (1992) are all broadly compatible with subsequent transformational models. Nevertheless, in what Matthews (1993: 92f.) characterizes as "a remarkable tribute to the inertia of ideas", the adoption of a morpheme-based model in Chomsky and Halle (1968) set a decisive precedent. The influence exercised by 'analytical precedents' and 'exemplary analyses' within the transformational paradigm (Blevins 2008*b*) discouraged the reevaluation of the status of the morpheme, so that morphemic analysis became part of the transformationalist toolkit. The alternative approaches that split off like tributaries from the transformational tradition were largely preoccupied with syntax and simply carried the morpheme-based model with them. There is no obvious internal motivation for morpheme-based analysis within models such as Lexical Functional Grammar (Kaplan and Bresnan 1982; Dalrymple 2001), Generalized Phrase Structure Grammar (Gazdar

---

[20] In accounts such as Lieber (1992) morphemes are regarded as so firmly established that there is no need for an index entry for 'morpheme', much less a definition.

et al. 1985) or Head-driven Phrase Structure Grammar (Pollard and Sag 1994). Yet each of these models adopted, at least initially, a mainly morpheme-based model of morphology, in practice if not necessarily in principle. In time, morpheme-based analyses became established in textbook presentations of these models and in general introductions to the study of language and linguistics.

Yet this period of consolidation coincided with a retreat from the substantive claims of morphemic analysis within descendants of morphemic models. Although models such as D[istributed] M[orphology] (Halle and Marantz 1993) retain the term 'morpheme', the notion in DM has at most a historical connection to the original 'morpheme-as-sign' conception. The term 'morpheme' is applied to various constructs that mostly lack a specific label in other approaches but are in any case devoid of semiotic content. In initial models of DM, the term 'morpheme' is used to refer ambiguously to (i) a grammatical feature bundle, which occurs as the terminal element of a syntactic tree, or (ii) a grammatical feature bundle, together with a phonological feature bundle:

The terminal elements of [syntax] trees consist of complexes of grammatical features. These terminal elements are supplied with phonological features only after Vocabulary insertion at MS [morphological structure]. Although nothing hinges on this terminology in what follows, we have chosen to call the terminal elements "morphemes" both before and after Vocabulary insertion, that is, both before and after they are supplied with phonological features. (Halle and Marantz 1993: 114)

On the first of these conceptions, the DM 'morpheme' is closest to the Bloomfieldian sememe, or the *signifié* of a Saussurean sign. On the second, it appears to encompass the whole sign. In neither case does it correspond to the morphemes defined by Bloomfield (1933), Harris (1942) or Hockett (1947).

The break from the Bloomfieldian tradition of morphemic analysis is complete when later versions of DM apply 'morpheme' to an "abstract unit":

A morpheme is an abstract syntactic unit that finds an interpretation in form and in meaning . . . The notion of "abstract" when applied to morphemes characterizes not only the independence of a particular morpheme from a specific realization in form but also its independence from a specific semantic value. For example, the "plural" morpheme in English is the same morpheme, appearing in the same syntactic position with respect to the noun stem, whether it conveys a meaning associated with "more than one" (as in "cats" and "oxen") or whether it does not (as in "(eye-)glasses" or "pants"). More generally, the features associated with morphemes by linguists, while connected to their syntactic and semantic properties, find their grammatical import (their role in the syntax in particular) independent of their possible semantic (or phonological) interpretations. (Marantz 2013: 1f.)

On this view, the "plural" morpheme need not be associated with a constant 'unit of form', since it the 'same' morpheme in *cats* and *oxen*. It also need not be associated with any stable 'unit of meaning' since it may or may not convey a notion of plurality. Whatever the function of such an "abstract" unit within the theoretical frame of reference assumed by DM, it preserves no part of the original conception of the morpheme as a Saussurian sign linking minimal 'units of form' and 'units of meaning'. On the contrary, DM adopts an extreme anti-morphemic position, given that it eliminates all of the components of the traditional Bloomfieldian morpheme (meaning, form and linkage) and simply reassigns the term 'morpheme' to an abstract 'unit' dictated by the syntax.

In sum, to paraphrase Matthews (1993: 92), current models of morphemic analysis, at least as represented by DM, provide a remarkable tribute to the inertia of nomenclature, insofar as they preserve the term 'morpheme' while abandoning all of the substantive claims originally associated with the notion.

2.4.2 Words, paradigms and analogy

This chapter has summarized how a model whose limitations were well understood a half-century ago came for a while to occupy a dominant role within modern approaches to the analysis of word structure. To overcome these limitations, we now shift our focus outside the narrow frame of reference provided by the Post-Bloomfieldian tradition, to models that offer a more flexible analysis of the diversity of patterns exhibited by morphological systems.

The development of these models must be set against the backdrop of the ideas inherited from the classical model. This model is, as Hockett (1954: 386) stresses, of more than purely historical interest. As "the traditional framework for the discussion of Latin, Greek, Sanskrit, and a good many more modern familiar languages", the classical WP model survives largely intact in current pedagogical and reference grammars and dictionaries. Even for the time that it was eclipsed theoretically by morphemic models, the WP model remained the primary framework for broad-coverage grammars, and it is in the pedagogical and descriptive traditions that the assumptions of the classical WP model are perhaps most faithfully represented, albeit with idealizations.

The pivotal role that words and paradigms play in comprehensive descriptions naturally leads one to ask why pedagogical and reference materials should be organized in terms of words and exemplary sets of words, and whether this organization is of any general theoretical relevance. One possible answer is, of course, that the structure of descriptive grammars again reflects sheer intellectual inertia. Grammars of classical languages are organized into paradigms and principal parts, and the Western grammatical tradition merely perpetuates an established practice. While there may be some truth to this view, the continued relevance of the WP model points to the descriptive value of words and exemplary patterns. Pedagogical and reference grammars are driven more by considerations of utility than by theoretical commitments. As Matthews (1991: 187f.) remarks, with regards to flectional languages at least, neither the Bloomfieldian model nor any theoretical approach developed since Bloomfield's time organizes the facts of a language more transparently than the classical WP model. This organizational scheme contains three interacting sets of assumptions: assumptions about units, assumptions about grammatically significant patterns and assumptions about the mechanisms that relate the two. Chapters 3–5 now consider each set of assumptions in turn.

3

Words

As discussed in Chapter 1.2, the primacy of grammatical words in WP models is not due to any *a priori* preference for words over smaller (or larger) units of form but reflects the view that there is a sharply diminishing return from pushing morphological analysis below the word level. This utilitarian perspective is expressed succinctly by Robins (1959: 128) when he acknowledges that "grammatical statements are abstractions" before continuing "but they are more profitably abstracted from words as wholes than from individual morphemes". At a practical level, the descriptive utility of words is mostly taken for granted in teaching grammars, dictionaries and reference grammars. Even Bloomfield (1933) freely concedes the advantages that words enjoy over sub-word units for the preparation of these types of practical materials:

For the purposes of ordinary life, the word is the smallest unit of speech. Our dictionaries list the words of a language; for all purposes except the systematic study of language, this procedure is doubtless more useful than would be a list of morphemes. (Bloomfield 1933: 178)

It is indisputable that written grammars and dictionaries impose constraints and introduce idealizations that have no counterparts in a speaker's linguistic system. Nevertheless, it is not clear that the main distortion arises at the level of units, rather than in the correspondence between the organization of a description and the structure of a linguistic system. In particular, there appears to be no compelling reason to believe that the notions of compactness and complexity that apply to written descriptions have any direct relevance to the linguistic system described. The Bloomfieldian attempt to remove redundancy from the lexicon, like the classical goal of identifying unique principal parts for any word or inflection class, conforms to a grammar 'design aesthetic' that has advantages for written descriptions but no established linguistic or psycholinguistic motivation. Hence, as argued in more detail in Chapter 4.4, it is not the recognition of words as basic units that makes dictionaries unsuitable for "the systematic study of language". Instead, the primary discrepancies lie in the idealizations that have been tacitly incorporated into the notions of the 'lexicon' or 'mental lexicon' since Bloomfield's time. Foremost among these is the conception of a lexicon as a static, redundancy-free repository of discrete items, with no encoding of frequency or distribution.

3.1 The psychological status of words

Whereas Bloomfield and his successors regarded the practical utility of words as evidence that they were not suitable objects of scientific study (Hockett

Word and Paradigm Morphology. First edition. James P. Blevins
© James P. Blevins 2016. First published 2016 by Oxford University Press

1987: 81), proponents of word-based approaches drew the opposite conclusion, and attributed the pre-theoretical salience and practical usefulness of words to their 'psychological reality' in the minds of speakers. In a familiar discussion of this point, Sapir (1921) begins by considering the difference between abstracting words from sentences and abstracting roots from words:

But is not the word, one may object, as much of an abstraction as the radical element? Is it not as arbitrarily lifted out of the living sentence as the minimum conceptual element out of the word? (Sapir 1921: 32f.)

In the continuation of this passage, Sapir suggests that it is the "psychological reality" of words that distinguishes them from roots and exponents:

Linguistic experience, both as expressed in standardized, written form and as tested in daily usage, indicates overwhelmingly that there is not, as a rule, the slightest difficulty in bringing the word to consciousness as a psychological reality. No more convincing test could be desired than this, that the naïve Indian, quite unaccustomed to the concept of the written word, has nevertheless no serious difficulty in dictating a text to a linguistic student word by word; he tends, of course, to run his words together as in actual speech, but if he is called to a halt and is made to understand what is desired, he can readily isolate the words as such, repeating them as units. He regularly refuses, on the other hand, to isolate the radical or grammatical element, on the ground that it "makes no sense". (Sapir 1921: 33)

Hockett (1967) appeals similarly to the psychological status of words and paradigms in his comparison of WP and morphemic analyses of the verbal system of Yawelmani on p. 41 above. After acknowledging that a description of "the complex alternations of Yawelmani" in terms of paradigms and principal parts "would take much more space" in a written grammatical description than a morphemic analysis (221f.), he goes on to add that the loss of economy would be compensated by "a net gain in realism" on the grounds that "the student of the language would now be required to produce new forms in exactly the way that the native speaker produces or recognizes them—by analogy".

For proponents of classical WP models, words are as central to first language acquisition as they are to explicit language instruction. Following on from a discussion of the pedagogical usefulness of words and paradigms (cited in the discussion of paradigms on p. 69 below), Matthews (1991: 188) suggests that "it is not clear that, when native speakers learn a flexional language, they do not themselves learn words as wholes". For Hermann Paul, the learning of paradigms and principal parts is merely a more explicit means of acquiring the knowledge of a native speaker, so that "the relation of the speaker to inflected forms in the moment of use"[1] is "much the same as that which is gained through the natural acquisition of a first language"[2] (Paul 1920: 112).

---

[1] "das Verhältnis des Sprechenden zu den Flexionsformen in Augenblicke der Anwendung".
[2] "ungefähr das nämliche wie dasjenige, welches bei der natürlichen Erlernung der Muttersprache gewonnen wird".

From the 'learning-based' perspective outlined in Chapter 8, the pedagogical usefulness of words reflects the same formal and interpretive stability that determines the relevance of words to "the systematic study of language". Within an approach that conceptualizes a speaker's knowledge of a language in terms of a learning state, the optimal pedagogical description would be one that isolates the structure and patterns that learners must extract from input.

3.1.1 Experimental evidence

Classical claims about the psychological reality of words (and paradigms) mostly predate the advent of experimental methodologies for probing the psychological status of theoretical constructs. But the classical perspective receives a measure of confirmation from contemporary experimental studies. One source of empirical support for a word-based conception of the mental lexicon comes from studies of frequency effects on lexical processing. To describe a lexicon as 'word-based' does not necessarily entail a literal repository of word forms. A word-based lexicon might be represented instead as a network structure in which paths or sequences corresponding to words have a particular salience or integrity. Frequency effects also need not (and almost certainly should not) be thought of in terms of what Baayen (2010) terms a 'counter in the head', based on pure repetition, but are more likely to reflect local syntactic and morphological co-occurrence probabilities. Thus although many initial studies and results are framed in terms of frequency effects, a discussion of these effects does not carry a commitment to a repetition-based explanation.

A number of these studies showed that the frequency of inflected forms and the size of derivational 'families' have a robust effect on lexical processing. One line of research investigated correlations between response latencies in visual decision tasks and various frequency measures related to inflected forms. The earliest studies established that the surface frequency of an inflected form in a corpus was negatively correlated with response latencies (Taft 1979). The base frequency of a word (the summed frequency of its inflected variants) was later found to exhibit a positive correlation with response latencies (Baayen *et al.* 1997). The logarithm of the ratio between these measures (surface frequency and base frequency) again exhibited a negative correlation (Hay 2001). These and other studies served to confirm the effect of token frequencies on the processing of inflected forms. A second line of research has demonstrated that the processing of an item is influenced by the size of its 'morphological family'. Following Schreuder and Baayen (1997), this research investigated the effect of type frequency on response latencies in visual decision. A range of studies found that an increase in number of semantically transparent items in the morphological family of a form facilitated processing of the form (de Jong 2002; Moscoso del Prado Martín 2003; Moscoso del Prado Martín *et al.* 2004a).

A third line of research grew out of attempts to measure the 'inflectional information' or 'morphological information' expressed by a form. A series of initial studies measured the information carried by inflected noun forms in Serbian (Kostić 1991, 1995; Kostić *et al.* 2003). These studies developed a surprisal-based perspective in which the information carried by an item corresponds to the negative log of its probability (i.e., the less likely, the more informative an item is). This general measure was refined by weighting the probabilities of items for the number of functions and meanings they express. Kostić *et al.* (2003) showed that the resulting notion of inflectional information correlates positively with response latencies and that the processing cost of an inflected variant is predicted by its frequency and functional load.

These studies of information load led in turn to efforts to obtain a unified measure of the effects attributed to token frequency counts in the inflectional domain and type frequency counts in the derivation domain. In the process of pursuing this goal, Moscoso del Prado Martín *et al.* (2004*b*) adopt a notion of 'paradigm' that encompassed derivational families as well as inflectional paradigms and employ a standard entropy measure (Shannon 1948) to calculate a frequency-weighted measure of morphological information. These refinements permit Moscoso del Prado Martín *et al.* (2004*b*) to subsume the family size information that correlates with type-frequency effects and the inflectional information that correlates with token-frequency effects under a single measure, which they term the 'information residual' of a word.

Subsequent studies, including Baayen *et al.* (2006) and Baayen *et al.* (2008), suggested that inflectional and derivation effects should in fact be kept apart. However, the usefulness of an information-theoretic perspective was strikingly confirmed in the investigation of paradigmatic effects in Serbian declensions. As initially reported in Milin *et al.* (2009*a*), response latencies in a visual decision task were positively correlated with the degree of divergence between the probability distribution of an inflected variant in the paradigm of an item and the distribution of the variant within the inflection class to which the item belongs. The greater the divergence between these distributions, the longer the response latencies and the higher the error rates in lexical decision tasks. The models under current development within this tradition define a unified perspective on language processing by combining information theory and discriminative learning without consolidating separate morphological domains. The study of Balling and Baayen (2012) demonstrates the relevance of information theory to the study of 'uniquenenss points' in auditory comprehension, Mulder *et al.* (2014) provide an analysis of derivational family effects in terms of discriminative learning, and Baayen *et al.* (2011) and Baayen *et al.* (2013) outline a general model of paradigmatic and frequency effects.

The design of these studies was not guided by the assumptions of a classical model, though the results are explicable within this model. From a classical WP perspective, it is not altogether surprising that token frequency effects would be more significant for inflection, and type frequency more significant for derivation. Given the relatively uniform structure of inflectional systems, the type count of inflected variants should be comparable for (non-defective) items belonging to a given word or inflection class. Hence token frequency is expected to be the primary locus of variation. In contrast, as shown by resources such as CELEX (Baayen *et al.* 1995), the 'families' of forms associated with distinct derivational bases can vary by orders of magnitude. Hence type frequency effects are expected to be stronger for derivation.

Yet the same sources that highlight the contrast between inflectional paradigms and derivational families also reveal critical idealizations in the classical WP perspective. The productivity of regular inflectional processes is traditionally assumed to determine uniform paradigms for items within a given word or inflection class. Paradigm size is thus not expected to vary, except where forms are unavailable due to paradigm 'gaps' or 'defectiveness'. However, as discussed in more detail in Chapter 8, this *a priori* expectation is not borne out. Many potentially available inflected forms are unattested in corpora, because corpora do not converge on uniformly populated paradigms as they increase in size. Instead, the forms of a corpus obey Zipf's law at all sample sizes and exhibit a distribution in which the frequency of a form is inversely proportional to its rank. Hence larger corpora reinforce patterns exhibited in smaller corpora, while introducing progressively fewer new forms.

Insofar as corpora provide the best available descriptions of the input encountered by speakers they indicate that speakers are not, as often assumed, exposed to full paradigms for all relatively frequent open-class items. Rather, as Hockett (1967) suggests, the speaker's lexicon comprises a collection of partial paradigms that collectively exhaust the form variation in the language:

in his analogizing . . . [t]he native user of the language . . . operates in terms of all sorts of internally stored paradigms, many of them doubtless only partial and he may first encounter a new basic verb in any of its inflected forms. (Hockett 1967: 221)

The discussion in Chapter 8 proposes that lexical neighbourhoods are a central part of the creative engine of the morphological system, permitting the extrapolation of the full system of variants from partially attested patterns.

3.1.2 A statistical inferencing engine

This general research tradition raises two points of particular relevance to classical WP models. The first is that a range of current studies suggests that speakers are sensitive to frequency and distributional relations involving word-sized units. This information is almost completely absent from theoretical models of the lexicon, which are inexplicably preoccupied with redundancy avoidance. The second is that the processing of a word form appears to be influenced (whether facilitated or inhibited) by related forms. This effect conflicts with the constructivist idealization that individual forms are defined in isolation. Morphological family effects seem to indicate that related word forms are not only represented in a speaker's mental lexicon but that they are 'co-activated' in the processing of a given form. These effects appear especially compatible with models that link families of word forms into networks of elements with shared formal, grammatical, and semantic properties.

In a contemporary setting, this type of network architecture was initially associated with the linguistic models proposed by Bybee (1985, 2001) and with 'associationist' computational models. The general-purpose connectionist or neural net models (Rumelhart and McClelland 1986; Plunkett and Marchman 1993) are the most familiar of these approaches, though networks have been developed more recently to model aspects of complex morphological systems, as in Pirrelli *et al.*

(2011) and Marzi *et al.* (2014). A fundamentally similar conception underlies the sort of classical model outlined by Paul (1920). In a formal reconstruction of this model, the lexicon is represented not as a static collection of minimal units but as a statistical inferencing engine, in which frequent forms and patterns support deductions about the shape and properties of unencountered (or infrequently encountered) forms. Within inflectional systems in particular, clusters of cells will define expectations about missing forms of a paradigm, with confidence levels that correspond to the informativeness of the predictive cells.[3] The patterns exhibited by families of derivational forms will also define a space of analogical extensions. There is recent evidence that family size and analogical pressures influence the stress patterns in noun compounds (Plag 2010), complementing earlier studies that found analogy to play a role in the interpretation of new compounds (van Jaarsveld *et al.* 1994).

A network architecture is combined with an inferencing (or uncertainty reducing) mechanism in the naive discriminative model outlined in Chapter 8.

3.1.3 Word structure

From a classical WP perspective, the practical benefits of word-based descriptions carry over to the use of words for "the systematic study of language" because the same properties that make words useful for practical descriptions, notably stable relations between forms and grammatical features, are also of theoretical value. The WP model does not exclude the possibility that 'atomic' units of grammatical meaning might be brought into correspondence with minimal units of form in some languages or patterns. However, WP approaches proceed from the assumption that a morphemic correspondence is certainly not normative, and frequently cannot be established in cases where a stable relation exists between words and grammatical properties.

Classical languages provide paradigm examples in which a relatively stable property-form relation at the word level cannot be projected downwards onto subword units. Latin *rēxistī* on p. 35 above shows some of the types of many-many relations that arise between putative units of meaning and units of form. This case is by no means the most extreme example of its kind; classical Greek exhibits even more tangled patterns. To illustrate the range of relations that can hold between properties and forms, Matthews (1991) considers the classical Greek verb form *elelýkete* 'you had unfastened' in Figure 3.1.

As Matthews observes, the realization of aspect and voice confounds any attempt to establish a biunique property-formative correspondence:

e	le	lý	k	e	te
		PERF		PAST INDIC	2ND PLU
PAST				ACTIVE	

FIGURE 3.1   Exponence relations in Ancient Greek *elelýkete* (Matthews 1991: 173)

---

[3] Other patterns, such as phonological similarity with phonological 'neighbours' may generate separate and even opposing expectations, as discussed in Pertsova (2004).

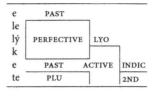

FIGURE 3.2   Many-to-many feature-form associations

But categories and formatives are in nothing like a one-to-one relation. That the word is Perfective is in part identified by the reduplication *le-* but also by the suffix *-k-*. At the same time, *-k-* is one of the formatives that help to identify the word as Active; another is *-te* which, however, also marks it as '2nd Plural'. (Matthews 1991: 173)

More generally, Figure 3.2 shows how systematically properties and formatives are multiply associated. On one side, the properties past, perfective and active are realized by multiple exponents. On the other, all of the formatives other than the first pair, *e-* and *-le-*, realize two, and sometimes three, properties. There is nothing exceptional about *elelýkete* within the inflectional system of Greek. On the contrary, the paradigm of LYO 'to unfasten' is treated as exemplary in standard grammars such as Goodwin (1894). Matthews (1991: 174) notes that this paradigm does not show "any crucial irregularity" and "is in fact the first that generations of schoolchildren used to commit to memory". Yet since the properties of *elelýkete* are realized at multiple points within this form, individual features cannot be correlated with single formatives.

3.1.4 Exponence relations

Examples of this kind do not show that formatives cannot be associated with properties, nor that a biunique property-form correspondence cannot be established. What they do show is that these positions cannot be maintained simultaneously. No conflict arises in classical models, which preserve biuniqueness but do not associate properties with formatives.[4] As with Latin *rēxistī* above, there is a biunique relation between the word form *elelýkete* and the SET of properties associated with the '2nd person plural past perfective indicative active' paradigm cell of the verb LYO. Although the relation between individual properties and formatives is not similarly biunique, there is still a correlation between these elements. Following Matthews (1972, 1991), this looser property-form correlation is termed (MORPHOLOGICAL) EXPONENCE. The principal types of exponence relations are depicted in Figure 3.3.

The 'Morphemic' pattern in Figure 3.3 exhibits the biunique property-formative correspondence associated with the Post-Bloomfieldian morpheme. There is nothing to exclude this pattern within a WP account, and the analyses of the formatives *e-* and *-le-* in Figure 3.2 conform to the morphemic ideal. However, there is

---

[4] Indeed, classical variants of the WP model do not even recognize morphological units between words and phonemes/graphemes (Matthews 1994; Law 1998).

Pattern	Morphemic	Cumulative	Extended	Empty	Zero
Properties	P	$P_I \ldots P_n$	P	—	P
	|	|	|		
Morphs	μ	μ	$\mu_1 \cdots \mu_n$	μ	—

FIGURE 3.3   Types of exponence (cf. Matthews 1991: 170ff)

TABLE 3.1   Regular conjugation classes in Spanish

	I	II	III
Infinitive	amar	vender	partir
1sg Future	amaré	venderé	partiré
	'love'	'sell'	'leave'

also nothing normative about this configuration, and the remaining patterns in Figure 3.3 all deviate from it in one way or another. The fusional or 'Cumulative' pattern in Figure 3.3 is illustrated by each of the remaining exponents in Figure 3.2, from the root *lý* through the agreement suffix *-te*. The fissional or 'Extended' pattern in Figure 3.3 is illustrated by the spell-out of the perfective, active and past features in Figure 3.2.

The 'Empty' and 'Zero' patterns represent the two extremes in which there is no exponence relation. A formative is empty when it is not associated with any properties and properties are realized by zero when they are not associated with any formatives. These patterns are symmetrical in that they both involve a complete dissociation of properties and morphs. However they are also very different in character. Incontrovertibly empty morphs appear to be comparatively rare, whereas zero exponence is a pervasive and systematic phenomenon. Theme vowels in Romance are among the most commonly-cited examples of empty morphs (Hockett 1947: 337, Anderson 1992: 54). In Spanish, verbs are normally assigned to conjugations based on the final vowel in the infinitive. The first conjugation contains regular verbs with infinitives in *-ar*, the second conjugation contains verbs with infinitives in *-er*, and the third conjugation contains verbs with infinitives in *-ir*. Verbs preserve the conjugation vowel in future (and conditional) forms, which consist of an infinitive stem and an ending corresponding to a reduced present (or conditional) form of the auxiliary HABER 'to have'. Table 3.1 illustrates these patterns.

Although these elements do not carry any clear 'denotative' meaning, they nevertheless serve as markers of 'conjugational class' and thereby convey morphological information about the inflectional patterns followed by other forms of an item.[5] Thus the variation in infinitive endings in Table 3.1 is largely preserved in the present indicative paradigms in Table 3.2.

---

[5] It is worth bearing in mind that ostensibly 'pure' morphological classes may show statistical tendencies to align with syntactic or semantic classes.

TABLE 3.2   Present indicative paradigms in Spanish

	I		II		III	
	Sg	Plu	Sg	Plu	Sg	Plu
1st	amo	amamos	vendo	vendemos	parto	partimos
2nd	amas	amáis	vendes	vendéis	partes	partimos
3rd	ama	aman	vende	venden	parte	parten

TABLE 3.3   Linking elements in German (Duden 2005)

	-n-		-s-	
Nom Sg	Spinne	Rakete	Arbeit	Liebe
Nom Plu	Spinnen	Rakaten	—	—
Compound	Spinnennetz	Rakatenstufe	Arbeitsamt	Liebesbrief
	'spider (web)'	'rocket (stage)'	'job (center)'	'love (letter)'

Formatives that occur in derived forms and compounds are also frequently regarded as empty morphs (or, equivalently, as unanalyzed parts of 'stem allomorphs'). This type of account goes back at least as far as the treatment of ancient Greek in Bloomfield (1933: 225). Bloomfield analyzes Greek nouns as having a "kernel" that underlies their inflectional paradigm and a 'stem allomorph' that functions as a "deriving form" and as a "compounding form". On this analysis, the noun HIPPOS 'horse' has the kernel *hipp* and the stem allomorph *hippo*, which occurs in *hippote:s* 'horseman' and *hippokantharos* 'horse-beetle'. Significantly, the Bloomfieldian account contrasts whole stems without assigning any individual properties to the formative *-o-*:

Thus, we distinguish between the *kernel* [hipp-], which actually... appears in all the [inflected JPB] forms and the stem [hipp-o-], which underlies the further derivation. (Bloomfield 1933: 225f.)

The *Fugenelemente* 'linking elements' that occur in West Germanic compounds are also commonly treated as empty formatives (Wiese 1996, Booij 1997). Table 3.3 illustrates two patterns involving feminine nouns in German. Regular feminine nouns ending in schwa form their plural in *-n*, as illustrated by the pairs *Spinne~Spinnen* and *Rakete~Raketen*. When nouns of this class occur as the first element of a compound, they also take the *n*-form, almost always obligatorily, and irrespective of the number features of the compound.

Compound bases in *-n* thus represent a simple case of 'parasitic' (Matthews 1972) or 'morphomic' (Aronoff 1994) syncretism, as they share the form but not the features of the corresponding plural.[6] The compounds based on ARBEIT and LIEBE in Table 3.3 illustrate the opposite pattern, in which the linking element *-s-*

---

[6] Morphomic patterns are discussed in more detail in Chapter 5.

is fully dissociated from the inflectional paradigms of these nouns. The formative *s* occurs in two places in common noun declensions, as a general plural form, and as a genitive singular marker for strong masculines. The linking element *-s-* cannot be assigned either analysis in Table 3.3. Both nouns are abstract here and have no real plural, though the the plurals of corresponding count-noun senses would in any case be be formed in *-(e)n*. As feminines, these nouns are also uninflected in the singular (as described in more detail in Table 4.9). Hence *-s-* is a pure 'linking element' in these compounds and has at most an analogical connection to plural or genitive markers.

As with conjugation vowels, the classification of linking elements as 'empty' reflects what may just be an excessively narrow conception of 'meaning'. As Carstairs-McCarthy (1994) argues in a different context, class affiliation can be regarded as the meaning of a conjugation vowel. Realizational models adopt this expanded notion of meaning when they treat theme vowels (or other types of elements) as the 'spell-out' of class 'features'. From a classical WP perspective, the same basic idea can be expressed in terms of the implicational relations between theme elements and class-specific patterns of form variation. In either case, the 'meaning' carried by these elements is system-internal, providing information about other forms or patterns within the system. Bloomfield's 'deriving' and 'compounding' forms can be viewed in a similar light, as conveying information about 'construction type'.

In some systems, elements may occur in a range of contexts, inflectional and derivational. Whitney (1889) describes a pattern of this kind in Sanskrit:

All the simple vowels come to assume in certain cases the aspect of union-vowels, or insertions between root or stem and ending of inflection or of derivation.

   a. That character belongs oftenest to *i*, which is very widely used: 1. before the *s* of aorist and future and desiderative stems ... 2. in tense-inflection, especially perfect ... 3. in derivation ... (Whitney 1889: 86)

These types of cases present acute difficulties for an analysis that seeks to assign a common meaning that spans the contexts in which elements like "union-vowels" occur. It is of course conceivable that these formatives are separate elements, with only a residual diachronic connection. However, it is also possible that the choice of union vowels, or their patterns of alternation and distribution, may play a role in identifying lexical or morphological classes in a language. Because a classical account does not treat formatives as SIGNS in the sense of Saussure (1916), there is no expectation that they will be associated with discrete meanings. Hence where the analysis of words into smaller units isolates elements that cannot be associated with any discernible meaning or function, this can be regarded as a symptom of morphological 'overextraction', i.e., the attempt to associate properties with sub-meaningful units.

Anderson (1992: 89) identifies the /t/ in Menominee *ke-t-ōs* 'your canoe' as a genuinely empty formative, which he characterizes as a "morphologically con-ditioned concomitant of the addition of a possessive marker to a vowel-initial stem". However, even 'conditioned' formatives of this kind will not be entirely 'empty' if they serve to discriminate possessive constructions from other forms that begin with the same initial sequences of phonemes. More generally, the communicative function of language leads one to expect that 'morphological noise' will be comparatively rare and unstable, as speakers and learners assign some kind of interpretation to patterns of form variation. In many cases, an understanding of the function of 'empty' elements will also require statistical analysis of paradigmatic or syntagmatic distribution.

The pervasive phenomenon of 'zero exponence' can be regarded as an extreme case of pattern-based meaning, in which speakers assign interpretations based on the absence of elements that occur elsewhere in a system. Noun paradigms in English provide a simple example. Plural nouns in English are marked by the suffix /z/ (represented orthographically as -s). There is, however, no marking of singular number, and none is needed, given that a singular noun is unambiguously identified by the lack of a plural marker. A zero morph adds no information to what speakers can already deduce from the absence of any realized exponent.[7] Similar patterns are even more typical of more intricate paradigms. As Anderson (1992) notes, Georgian verbal paradigms provide a striking illustration of the fact that that "information may sometimes be conveyed not by constituents that are present in the structure of a given word, but precisely by the fact that certain other material is ABSENT":

Consider the Georgian Verb form *mogk'lav* in [Table 3.4], for example, . . . This form represents agreement with a first-person singular Subject and a second-person singular Direct Object . . . But while an overt affix (/g/) is present to signal agreement with the second-person Object, no affix marks the fact that the Subject of this Verb is (and must necessarily be) first-person singular. This agreement can be inferred from the following information. The Subject cannot be second person, because if it were, the sentence would be reflexive— but reflexive forms in Georgian are grammatically third person, and this Verb has a second-person Object. Similarly, the Subject cannot be third person, since, if it were, there would be a suffix (/-s/) at the end of the Verb. Thus . . . the Subject must be first person. But it must be singular, rather than plural, since a first-person plural Subject would trigger the introduction of a suffix /t/ at the end of the Verb. We know therefore that the Subject of this Verb must be first-person singular, but this fact is not signaled by the presence of any overt affix in the word. (Anderson 1992: 87)

The interpretation of an unmarked form need not invoke this kind of 'process of elimination' deduction each time that the form is encountered. Instead, a classical model can treat this deduction as part of an acquisition process in which speakers place or locate forms within the paradigm of an item. It is the lack of this larger

---

[7] As noted in Chapter 2, some Post-Bloomfieldian accounts introduced a 'zero' singular marker in such cases (Harris 1942: 110), and the practice survives in contemporary work. Hockett (1947: 230) recognized that this type of element had "a very dubious status", and the coherence of a 'zero marker' is questioned by Matthews (1991: 124). From a classical WP perspective, the appeal to 'zeros' can be seen as a means of compensating for the rigidly syntagmatic character of the Post-Bloomfieldian model, which has no provision for any type of paradigmatic comparison or deduction.

TABLE 3.4   Future indicative paradigm of K'VLA 'kill' (Tschenkéli 1958: §31)

Subject	1 Sg	1 Pl	Object 2 Sg	2 Pl	3
1 Sg	–	–	**mogk'lav**	mogk'lavt	movk'lav
1 Pl	–	–	mogk'lavt	mogk'lavt	movk'lavt
2 Sg	momk'lav	mogvk'lav	–	–	mok'lav
2 Pl	momk'lavt	mogvk'lavt	–	–	mok'lavt
3 Sg	momk'lavs	mogvk'lavs	mogk'lavs	mogk'lavt	mok'lavs
3 Pl	momk'laven	mogvk'laven	mogk'laven	mogk'laven	mok'laven

paradigmatic context in Post-Bloomfieldian models that creates the need for 'zero morphs' to record the properties of unmarked forms.

In sum, words may be divided into formatives in a WP model, but this division does not in general yield individually meaningful parts. Words remain the smallest Saussurean 'signs' of a language. As the passage from Robins (1959) on p. 6 above makes clear, this treatment of words rests on the empirical claim that grammatical properties are more reliably associated with whole words (or larger expressions), than with component formatives.[8] A WP approach is still able to represent the internal structure of word forms and even, via exponence relations, express any systematic correlations between this structure and grammatical properties. The use of analogical strategies to interpret or extend morphological patterns in WP approaches also attributes a measure of internal structure to the words that define patterns. This structure may remain implicit, as in the "patterns of modification" given in classical grammars (Matthews 1991: 191), or it may be expressed more explicitly, as in proportional analogies (Paul 1920). But in either case, analogical strategies exploit the predictive value of word structure without mediating those predictions through the assignment of properties to individual formatives.

3.2 Types of 'words'

The idea that words are minimal signs does not rest on the claim that the grammatical properties of words are always fully determinate, but merely that they are, cross-linguistically, more determinate than any smaller unit. The words in a periphrastic construction are often grammatically indeterminate in isolation. Yet whereas this indeterminacy is an exceptional property of periphrasis, it is highly typical of sub-word units. A similar claim applies to morphotactic constancy. Although words may not always be demarcated in the speech stream, they are more clearly and consistently demarcated than any smaller unit.

---

[8] Some word-based accounts do in fact treat words as unstructured wholes (Singh and Starosta 2003), while others (Anderson 1992; Aronoff 1994; Stump 2001) represent morphological structure more in terms of the 'derivational history' defined by spell-out rules than in terms of morphotactic arrangement. Yet even in these accounts the claim that words are grammatically basic remains logically independent of the claim that they exhibit no structure above the phonological level.

3.2.1 Grammatical and phonological words

These claims can be clarified by distinguishing two of the established senses of the notion 'word'. Phonological words (or WORD FORMS) are sequences of phonemes (or graphemes). Grammatical words (or WORDS) are phonological words (or sequences of phonological words, in the case of multi-word expressions) with a morphosyntactic interpretation. It is the second of these senses that is of primary relevance to 'word-based' models. Bloomfield's notion of "a minimum free form" provides the classic definition of the 'grammatical' word:

A minimum free form is a WORD.
A word is thus a form which may be uttered alone (with meaning) but cannot be analyzed into parts that may (all of them) be uttered alone (with meaning). (Bloomfield 1926: 156)

On this interpretation, the three homophonous occurrences of *hit* in (3.1) are different words, realizing the preterite, past participle and infinitive forms of the verb HIT. This is the notion of word that is most relevant to measures of token frequency, which treat each occurrence of a form as a separate 'token'.

(3.1)   a. She *hit* the target.   (PRETERITE)
         b. She has *hit* the target.   (PAST PARTICIPLE)
         c. She will *hit* the target.   (INFINITIVE)

A "minimum free form . . . (with meaning)" also corresponds to the unit from which Robins (1959: 128) claims "grammatical statements . . . are more profitably abstracted . . . than from individual morphemes". In most languages, the abstraction of words is facilitated by cues that enhance their perceptual salience. Open-class items are often subject to a minimum word constraint, whether measured in terms of moras, syllables or metrical feet, and there is experimental evidence that speakers exploit these constraints in the segmentation of continuous speech (Norris *et al.* 1997). Words often define the positions at which stress, pitch or other suprasegmental features are realized, and word edges may be marked by processes such as boundary lengthening (Bybee 2001). The perceptual salience of words is enhanced by the fact that words (unlike sub-word units such as phonemes or morphemes) may stand on their own as independent utterances. In addition, if there is any content to notions like 'the one-word stage' (Dromi 1987), it would appear that the word is the basic utterance during early stages of language acquisition.

As one might expect, the functional load of individual cues varies across languages, reflecting general differences in phonological systems, so that no single cue identifies words cross-linguistically. Moreover, it is often word FORMS that are most clearly demarcated in the speech stream by phonetic cues. Word forms in this sense are sequences of phonemes (or graphemes) without a fixed meaning or function. In (3.1), the single word form *hit* realizes the preterite, past participle and infinitive forms of the verb HIT. The same word form realizes other forms of HIT, as well as the corresponding noun in *They took a hit*, etc. Such simple forms do not ordinarily play a significant grammatical role, though they are central to recent frequency-based models.[9]

Although grammatical words often correspond to single word forms, the correlation between these units may be imperfect, disrupted by phonological or syntactic processes. Cliticization of prosodically light elements creates sequences in which multiple grammatical words correspond to a single phonological word. In (3.2a), the contracted phonological word *she's* corresponds to the grammatical words *she* and *has*. Separable particles illustrate a converse mismatch, in which a single grammatical word such as German *wegwerfen* 'throw out' is realized by the word forms *werfen* and *weg* in (3.2b).

(3.2)   a. *She's* hit the flowers.

    b. Sie   *werfen* die Werbung einfach *weg*.
       they throw the flyers   simply out
       'They simply throw the flyers out.'

As Robins (1959) acknowledges, these processes introduce discrepancies between the notion of 'word' relevant for the description of grammatical relations, and the sense of 'word' that is marked phonetically. This divergence has led some scholars to question the status and even the usefulness of the notion 'word' as a unit of analysis, within individual systems and across languages. Matthews (2002: 266) summarizes the collection of typological studies in Dixon and Aikhenvald (2002) by observing that they "make clear not just that criteria conflict, but that different linguists may resolve some kinds of conflict very differently". Haspelmath (2011: 70) echoes this assessment in acknowledging " 'Words' as language-specific units are often unproblematic . . . but the criteria employed in different languages are often very different." Following a comprehensive cross-linguistic survey of prosodic domains, Schiering *et al.* (2010: 657) likewise conclude that "the 'word' has no privileged or universal status in phonology, but only emerges through frequent reference of sound patterns to a given construction type in a given language".

Although they bring new data and methods to bear on questions regarding the status of words, these studies essentially reprise a longstanding criticism of word-based approaches. The difficulty of demarcating words is taken by Bloomfield (1914) as evidence for the primacy of the sentence:

> It has long been recognized that the first and original datum of language is the sentence,—that the individual word is the product of a theoretical reflection which ought not to be taken for granted, and, further, that the grouping of derived and inflected words into paradigms, and the abstraction of roots, stems, affixes, or other formative processes, is again the result of an even more refined analysis. (Bloomfield 1914: 65)

The epistemological priority that Bloomfield assigns to utterances is particularly compatible with exemplary construction-based approaches, such as Booij (2010),

---

[9] In accounts such as Bybee (2010) that treat phonetic reduction as a frequency effect, word form frequency is often taken to determine the rate or extent of reduction.

as well as with a more utterance-based model of the lexicon. But the "abstraction" of units that Bloomfield mentions is entirely parallel to "abstractions" in the passage on p. 6 above, where Robins (1959: 128) notes that "grammatical statements are abstractions, but they are more profitably abstracted from words as wholes than from individual morphemes". At every level below the utterance (or even discourse), the units of a linguistic analysis are subject to exactly the same type of cost-benefit analysis.

Hence, while it is true that discrepancies arise between phonological and grammatical words, within and across languages, these discrepancies arise precisely because there ARE cues which, with varying degrees of reliability, mark word boundaries or otherwise guide the segmentation of utterances into words. The existence of mismatches should not obscure the fact that the two notions of 'word' overlap, at least partially, in many languages, and that this overlap permits speakers to isolate grammatical words. Although grammatical words may be imperfectly demarcated, sub-word units—including, significantly, roots—are rarely if ever cued at all by phonetic properties. There is no discrepancy between the 'grammatical morpheme' and the 'phonological morpheme' for the simple reason that there is no such thing as a 'phonological morpheme'. Hence the objection that grammatical words are not reliably and invariantly cued in the speech stream provides no motivation for shifting the focus of morphological analysis onto units smaller than the word (such as stems, roots or morphemes), since these units require an even greater degree of abstraction from the speech signal. The observation that words are abstractions just falls under the broader generalization that ALL linguistic units smaller than utterances are abstracted from larger sequences of connected speech.

It is also worth bearing in mind the possibility that much of the debate about the alignment of grammatical and phonological words may be misconceived at a more fundamental level. Nearly all linguistic approaches to this issue frame the problem in terms of specifying reliable and cross-linguistically valid cues for demarcating grammatical words. Underlying these approaches is the assumption that there should be some set of necessary and sufficient conditions for defining words in a given language, or across languages.

From an abstractive perspective, the cross-linguistic variability of phonetic cues does not necessarily call into question the status of words as units but may instead reflect the fact that the cues serve a secondary function, reinforcing boundaries that are principally of PREDICTIVE value. From this standpoint, what unites the units that 'emerge' in different languages is the fact that they reflect common statistical patterns. The 'words' of a given language will have two characteristic properties. The first is that they correspond to sequences that occur between peaks of uncertainty about following phonetic material. The second is that they reduce uncertainty about following words. Statistical units abstracted in this way from larger forms will be 'emergent' in essentially the sense of Schiering et al. (2010: 657). Phonetic cues will then tend to reinforce these units in ways that reflect the sound patterns of individual languages.

This perspective has mainly been developed in the large and diverse psycholinguistic and computational literature on word segmentation and recognition.[10] This

---

[10] See Geertzen et al. (2016) for an exploration of this idea in a linguistic context.

literature includes work on identifying 'uniqueness points' in Marslen-Wilson and Welsh (1978), Marslen-Wilson and Tyler (1980) and Balling and Baayen (2012), neural network-based predictive models (Elman 1990), and statistical models of word segmentation (Goldwater *et al.* 2009). The models of word segmentation developed in these studies are based on the observation that entropy (roughly, uncertainty about the segments that follow) declines as more of a word is processed, then peaks again at word boundaries. The treatment of 'words' as statistically emergent units of predictive value is expressed directly in the second assumption below:

Observations about predictability at word boundaries are consistent with two different kinds of assumptions about what constitutes a word: either a word is a unit that is statistically independent of other units, or it is a unit that helps to predict other units (but to a lesser degree than the beginning of a word predicts its end). (Goldwater *et al.* 2009: 22)

From this perspective, the phonological word would correspond to phonetic sequences between entropy 'peaks', with phonetic cues representing one source of entropy reduction. The correlation between phonological and grammatical words could be similarly probabilistic rather than defined by discrete criteria.

On this type of approach, the absence of invariant linguistic cues does not call into question the status of the units that are cued. Rather, it is the idea that these cues are DEFINITIONAL that stands in need of revision. A predictive perspective also helps to account for the intractability of what Spencer (2012) terms 'The Segmentation Problem'. Given that uncertainty is continuous, not discrete, it is only by smoothing that we obtain discrete boundaries and units. Generalizing over these units lends a measure of support to the traditional claim that words are "a more stable and solid focus of grammatical relations than the component morpheme". But this does not necessarily determine a unique segmentation of the speech stream, least of all at the sub-word level.

3.2.2 Lexemes and lemmas

Both grammatical and phonological words are kinds of word tokens. In examples (3.1) and (3.2), there are four occurrences of the word form *hit*, corresponding to two occurrences of the past participle *hit*, and one occurrence each of the preterite and infinitive. Given that grammatical words are defined as word forms with fixed meanings, their identification depends on assumptions about the parts of speech and morphosyntactic properties in a language.

Insofar as occurrences of grammatical words are tokens of a common word 'type', they imply another, more abstract notion of 'word'. This notion of 'word type' usu-ally goes under the name LEXEME. Matthews (1972: 160) characterizes the lexeme in this sense as "the lexical element ... to which the forms in [a] paradigm as a whole ... can be said to belong".[11] In a later discussion of the same point, Matthews

---

[11] This usage is more restricted than the notion of 'lexeme' as a minimal unit of syntactic analysis in Lyons (1963: 11f.), which also encompasses idiomatic phrases. An even earlier use of 'lexeme' is found

Phonological Word	Grammatical Word	Lexeme
phonological form	form-feature pair	set of form-feature pairs
/hɪt/	⟨/hɪt/, [v, PAST, ...]⟩	{⟨/hɪt/, [v, PAST, ...]⟩,...}

FIGURE 3.4   Varieties of 'words' (cf. Matthews 1972, 1991)

(1991: 26) suggests that a lexeme is "a lexical unit and is entered in dictionaries as the fundamental element in the lexicon of language". Lexemes are thus reminiscent of the lexicographer's notion of a LEMMA, which is the citation form of an item or the headword under which it is listed in a dictionary.[12] The connection between these notions is reinforced by the fact that lexemes are conventionally represented by the citation form of an item in small caps, i.e., by the lemma of the item. However, whereas a lemma is a distinguished form, a lexeme is normally construed as a set of grammatical words. The fundamental contrast between phonological words (word forms), grammatical words (words) and lexemes is summarized in Figure 3.4.

The fact that lexical meanings do not enter into this opposition reflects the discriminative approach to meaning outlined in Chapter 8.4. The three-way contrast between word forms, grammatical words and lexemes resolves a systematic ambiguity in the use of the term 'word' as applied to the form *hit*, the preterite *hit* and the lexeme HIT. Not all items give rise to a full ternary split, since different notions of word may coincide in particular cases. There is usually at least a partial correlation between grammatical words and word forms. For closed-class categories, the distinction between lexeme and grammatical word may not be especially relevant or useful, since a preposition or conjunction will usually be associated with a single grammatical word. The same may be true of open-class categories in an isolating language such as Vietnamese if nouns and verbs are represented by single grammatical words.

Despite the fact that a lexeme may contain just a single grammatical word, treating lexemes as sets of words provides a coherent interpretation for an intuitive but otherwise formally obscure notion. By characterizing a lexeme as "the lexical unit that grammatical words are forms of", Matthews (1972, 1991) invites questions about the nature of lexical units. Subsequent refinements tend to preserve the same attractive intuition and formal unclarity. Aronoff (1994) summarizes the properties of lexemes in the following terms:

To recapitulate, a lexeme is a (potential or actual) member of a major lexical category, having both form and meaning but being neither, and existing outside of any particular syntactic context. (Aronoff 1994: 11)

in Hockett (1958: 169ff.), who uses the term to designate sequences that always occur as grammatical forms in a context where they are not part of any larger unit which also invariably occurs as a grammatical form.

[12] There is also an alternative interpretation of the term 'lemma' still in circulation. In psycholinguistic models of speech production, lemmas are often construed as abstract conceptual entries that represent "the nonphonological part of an item's lexical information" (Levelt 1989).

Stump (2001: 277) likewise states that "[t]he notion of lexeme assumed here is that of e.g. Matthews 1972, Aronoff 1994" and repeats the quotation from Aronoff (1994) above. Other works in this tradition, such as Beard (1995), construe 'lexeme' in a way that tacitly adopts these definitions.

The characterization offered by Aronoff (1994) does not readily apply to any kind of conventional lexical 'unit' or 'item'. However, it does accurately describe the properties of a set of grammatical words. If each grammatical word is construed as a pairing of features with a form, the set of pairs comprising a lexeme will share 'a major lexical category' and 'meaning', along with common elements of 'form', and a distributional range that is not coextensive with the 'particular syntactic context' in which any one of the grammatical words occurs.

Interpreting lexemes as sets of forms is also compatible with the disambiguating function of 'lexemic indices' in realizational accounts such as Stump (2001). The members of a given lexeme λ can, if desired, be assigned an index i_λ. This index will then serve to distinguish grammatical words from different lexemes that happen to be realized by homophonous phonological words:[13]

In general, it is necessary to regard a root X as being indexed for its association with a particular lexeme, since phonologically identical roots associated with distinct lexemes may exhibit distinct morphological behavior; in English, for example the root *lie* of the lexeme LIE$_1$ 'recline' must be distinguished from the root *lie* of the lexeme LIE$_2$ 'prevaricate', since their paradigms are different (e.g. past tense *lay* vs. *lied*). I shall treat this indexing as covert, but shall use a function 'L-index' to make overt reference to it when necessary; thus *lie* 'recline' carries a covert index LIE$_1$ (so that L-index(*lie*) = LIE$_1$), while *lie* 'prevaricate' carries a covert index LIE$_2$ (so that L-index(*lie*) = LIE$_2$). (Stump 2001: 43)

On a classical conception in which the main morphological part-whole relation holds between words and larger collections of forms, lexemes will be a significant unit of organization within a speaker's mental lexicon. Lexemes will intervene between inflectional paradigms and morphological families. However, it is lemmas, not lexemes, that are 'entered into dictionaries'. The conventional lemma form of an item represents the lexeme, and it is only in cases of irregularity that additional members of the lexeme are listed as well.

3.2.3 Paradigms and families

Distinguishing grammatical words from lexemes introduces many of the same kinds of issues that confront lexicographers when they attempt to distinguish primary 'word entries' from 'word senses'. These issues bear in a direct way on the delineation of inflectional and derivational processes. From a classical WP perspective, inflectional processes are said to define (or, more generally, relate) forms of a lexeme (i.e., grammatical words), whereas derivation derives (or relates) lexemes. It is typically assumed that the grammatical words that comprise a lexeme

---

[13] Similar remarks apply to the use of lexeme indices to guide the application of realization rules in accounts such as Blevins (2003) and Spencer (2003).

must belong to the same word class, preserve a core lexical semantics and argument structure, and even share a set of 'intrinsic' features that are invariant for a given item. Inflectional processes are regarded as monotonic processes that add features to the invariant properties that can be associated with stems. In contrast, processes that alter class or argument structure are treated as derivational, since these changes create new lexemes.

Classical descriptive practices are not fully consistent with this split, as noted in recent works such as Haspelmath (1996) and Spencer (1999). In particular, conjugational paradigms often include categorial hybrids, such as participles, which exhibit adjectival properties, and gerunds or masdars, which exhibit nominal properties. The inclusion of passive participles also introduces argument structure variation into conjugational paradigms. This inconsistency would appear to undermine the coherence of the notion 'lexeme', along with associated conceptions of the inflection/derivation divide, if, as these authors assume, the notions 'lexeme' and 'inflectional paradigm' are taken to coincide.

However, it is also possible to interpret classical descriptions more charitably, as inexplicit rather than inconsistent. Pursuing the line of analysis outlined above, lexemes can be reconstructed as sets that occupy a position between inflectional paradigms and morphological families, as in Figure 3.5.

This interpretation also resolves a systematic ambiguity in the use of the term 'paradigm'. Nouns typically have a unified set of forms, inflected for case, number, definiteness, etc., which can be consolidated in a single declensional paradigm. Hence the lexeme MRÈŽA 'network' contains the single paradigm in Table 3.5, and there is no real harm in conflating paradigm with lexeme.

In contrast, the inflected forms of verbs often exhibit a sub-organization into sets of forms that share the same tense/aspect/mood features and vary in their agreement features. This is illustrated by the conventional classification of the

Inflectional paradigm	Lexeme	Morphological family
set of grammatical words	union of paradigms	union of lexemes

FIGURE 3.5   Lexical organization of grammatical words

TABLE 3.5   Paradigm of Croatian MRÈŽA 'network' (Barić *et al.* 2005: 157)

	Sg	Plu
Nom(inative)	mrȅža	mrȅže
Gen(itive)	mrȅžē	mrêžā
Dat(ive)	mrȅži	mrȅžama
Acc(usative)	mrȅžu	mrȅže
Inst(rumental)	mrȅžōm	mrȅžama
Loc(ative)	mrȅži	mrȅžama
Voc(ative)	mrȅžo	mrȅže

TABLE 3.6   Synthetic forms of Croatian ŽÈLETI 'want' (Barić *et al.* 2005: 257)

	Present		Aorist		Imperfect	
	Sg	Plu	Sg	Plu	Sg	Plu
1st	žèlīm	žèlīmo	žèljeh	žèljesmo	žèljāh	žèljāsmo
2nd	žèlīš	žèlīte	žèljē	žèljeste	žèljāše	žèljāste
3rd	žèlī	žèlē	žèlje	žèljēšē	žèljāše	žèljāhū

forms of ŽÈLETI 'want' in Table 3.6 into present, aorist or imperfect sets. The term 'paradigm' is applied to these smaller sets of forms in references to 'the present indicative paradigm of ŽÈLETI' but to the full set of inflected forms in references to 'the (conjugational) paradigm of ŽÈLETI'. The distinction between paradigm and lexeme in Figure 3.5 provides a simple resolution. The term 'paradigm' is reserved for the first, smaller, set of forms, and 'lexeme' is applied to the complete set of forms in the paradigms. With this clarification, the 'present indicative paradigm of ŽÈLETI' is a subset of the 'the lexeme ŽÈLETI'.

A general characteristic feature of Slavic verbs is that they come in imperfective/perfective pairs. Corresponding to the forms of imperfective ŽÈLETI there is a parallel series of forms of perfective POŽÈLETI. The relation between imperfective and perfective verbs is standardly regarded as 'word formation' or, following Aronoff (1994) and Beard (1995), 'lexeme formation'. Processes that relate distinct lexemes define the third member in the classification in Figure 3.5, the 'morphological family'. In the present case, the morphological family of ŽÈLETI will contain the imperfective lexeme ŽÈLETI itself, the perfective lexeme POŽÈLETI, and other lexemes derivationally related to ŽÈLETI.

This organization provides a structure within which to reconstruct standard classifications without inconsistency, and also without prejudging answers to the questions of analysis that arise. Reconciling grammatical descriptions with WP models and other 'lexeme-based' approaches involves determining, for any set of related forms, at what level they are related, whether internal to the paradigm, lexeme or family. Traditional grammatical descriptions tend to draw a primary split between inflectional processes, which relate grammatical words belonging to the same lexeme, from derivation, which relates distinct lexemes. Over time, the terms 'inflection' and 'derivation' have become overloaded with other associations and assumptions, to the point that accounts such as Haspelmath (1996) appear to identify inflectional with productive processes. Although it might be best to replace these terms altogether, it will suffice if inflection is understood as applying to 'endocentric', within-lexeme processes and derivation to 'exocentric', cross-lexeme processes.[14]

---

[14] Classical WP accounts do not distinguish processes that apply within single paradigms from those that apply across paradigms, though this distinction corresponds to the contrast between 'contextual' and 'inherent' inflection in Booij (1993, 1996).

This formulation in turn requires a classification of processes based on the nature of the relations they establish rather than on their productivity or transparency. Usually, this classification is framed in terms of the properties shared by the members of a lexeme. Traditionally, inflectional processes relate forms that share a set of 'intrinsic' properties of a lexeme, whereas derivational processes relate forms that may have different intrinsic properties. As mentioned directly above, these shared properties are normally taken to include aspects of meaning, recurrent units of form, a set of 'inherent' features and a common or similar argument structure. There is nothing theory-specific about this choice of 'constant' properties; essentially the same set of attributes are associated with a 'lexical entry' in a Post-Bloomfieldian approach.[15]

A coherent split between inflection and derivation can then be maintained by imposing a consistent classification on the problematic elements discussed by Haspelmath (1996) and Spencer (1999). Consider categorial hybrids, beginning with participles. One type of analysis avoids the problem of classifying verbal participles altogether by treating them not as forms of a paradigm, but as components of a larger periphrastic form. The idea that synthetic and periphrastic forms both realize the paradigm cells of a morphological system underlies the comprehensive descriptions of Curme (1922, 1935), and is developed in a more formal setting in Ackerman and Stump (2004). On this account, verbal participles are no more members of a paradigm than the stem of a synthetic form is.[16] Alternatively, active participles can be included in the lexeme of a verb if, as has often been suggested, participles are treated not as a distinct word class but as a word class that neutralizes the categorial distinction between verbs and adjectives. On this analysis, active participles can be included in the lexeme of a verb, provided that the lexeme is defined as a set of grammatical words with NONCONTRASTIVE (rather than identical) values for word class and other intrinsic features. A similar analysis extends to other 'hybrids' that are analyzable as neutralizing rather than altering word class.

However, one might also want to reconsider the inflectional status of participles. Although participles are sometimes included in 'paradigms', they tend to be associated more with whole lexemes than with specific subsets of inflected forms. This association can also be expressed at the level of the morphological family. In languages where participles inflect exactly like adjectives, an analysis at the level of the family removes a source of morphological heterogeneity from verb lexemes. Active participles are thereby assimilated to 'masdars' and other varieties of derived nominals which, irrespective of their productivity, comprise separate lexemes in the morphological family of a verb. The regular and predictable members of this family can even be regarded as forming a kind of 'derivational paradigm', along the lines suggested in the treatment of 'paradigmatic derivation' in Austerlitz (1966) and Blevins (2001).

---

[15] This correspondence reflects the fact that the Post-Bloomfieldian lexical entry is, from a classical WP perspective, an abstraction over a set of grammatical words.

[16] On this analysis, the participial forms that do not occur as parts of complex tenses would, wherever possible, be assigned to determinate verbal or adjectival categories.

TABLE 3.7   Classification of Georgian screeves (Aronson 1990: 462)

Series	'Tense'	Nonpast	Past	Subjunctive
I	Present	Present Indicative	Imperfect	Conjunctive Present
I	Future	Future Indicative	Conditional	Conjunctive Future
II	Aorist	Aorist Indicative		Optative
III	Perfect	Present perfect	Pluperfect	

The classification of passive participles and other forms depends on the treatment of argument structure. Passive forms can be included in the lexeme of a verb if the forms in a lexeme need only share a common logical (or thematic) argument structure. This assumption underlies standard descriptions of a language like Georgian that organize the ten paradigms of the language into three inflectional 'series', each with distinctive surface valence demands.[17]

If, however, the words that make up a lexeme are required to have common surface valence (subcategorization) demands, then active and passive words will belong to different lexemes but again to a common morphological family. On this alternative, Series I and II in Table 3.7 would belong to a different lexeme from Series III but fall within a common family. Either choice restores coherence to a standard perspective in which lexemes occupy a position between inflectional paradigms and morphological families.[18]

3.3 Summary

In assessing the status of words in a WP model, it is worth bearing in mind the essentially utilitarian view articulated by Robins (1959):

In many ways, and quite apart from any phonological markers, the word is a unique entity in grammar, and not just a stage in the progression 'from morpheme to utterance'. As a grammatical element the word is unique in its relative fixity of internal morphemic structure, its focal status in relation to syntactically relevant categories, and, in inflected words, the stability of its paradigms. All of these factors make it a strong basis for grammatical description, both morphological and syntactic. The assumption of a simple ascent in order of size from single morpheme to complete sentence, ignoring or blurring the distinction of morphological structuring and syntactic structuring, achieves its apparent simplicity at the cost of neglecting or distorting patent structural features of languages. (Robins 1959: 137)

---

[17] Briefly, in Series I the logical subject is nominative and the logical object is 'dative'; in Series II the logical subject is 'narrative' and the logical object is nominative; and in Series III the logical subject is dative and the logical indirect object is nominative. For discussion and analysis of these patterns, see, among others, Tschenkéli (1958), Harris (1981), Anderson (1986) and Blevins (2015*b*).

[18] On either alternative, 'morphosemantic' alternations (Sadler and Spencer 1998) like causativization will relate distinct lexemes within a larger morphological family.

Word-based analyses confront genuine challenges in demarcating word forms, in determining their grammatical properties, in assigning them to larger form classes and in establishing the structure of those classes. But these are the kinds of descriptive issues that arise on any explicit grammatical analysis and, as the discussion of morphemic models in Chapter 2 suggests, few if any of these tasks are facilitated by a shift in focus to units smaller than words.

4

Paradigms

As with words, it is the practical usefulness of paradigms that accounts for their role in descriptions of grammatical systems. Comprehensive descriptions of languages with intricate morphological systems tend to enumerate exemplary paradigms and patterns at different levels of generality. This is particularly true of grammars prepared for pedagogical purposes, as Matthews (1991) observes:

Pupils begin by memorising paradigms. These are sets of words as wholes, arranged according to grammatical categories. This is not only traditional, it is also effective. They learn that different members of a paradigm are distinguished by their endings . . . They can then transfer these endings to other lexemes, whose paradigms they have not memorised . . . It seems unlikely that, if a structuralist method or a method derived from structuralism were employed instead, pupils learning Ancient Greek or Latin—or, for that matter, Russian, Modern Greek or Italian—would be served nearly so well. (Matthews 1991: 187f.)

No practical alternative has been devised that replaces exemplary patterns by a more theoretical description in which, e.g., abstract underlying representations were related to surface realizations by general rules or constraints.[1] In part, this is due to the fact that theoretical models since Bloomfield's time have not been designed with practical (or comprehensive) description in mind, so that the output of an analysis may range from nontransparent to indeterminate (Karttunen 2006). The same general suspicion of practical notions that coloured Bloomfieldian attitudes towards the use of words for "the systematic study of language" also plays a role in the attitude towards exemplary patterns.

The Bloomfieldian scepticism towards words and paradigms also derives from more fundamental assumptions. By reducing words to independent aggregates of smaller parts, Bloomfieldian models disrupt any properties of words and any relations between words that cannot be recast in terms of properties of their parts, or in terms of relations between their parts. The organization of words into classes, or the definition of relations over these classes clearly falls outside the purview of this type of model. Yet this 'atomistic' perspective rests ultimately on little more than a theoretical aesthetic that places a premium on what Bloomfield terms "scientific compactness":

---

[1] There have been occasional attempts to establish descriptive grammars on a more 'theoretical' basis. An instructive example is provided by the use of Tagmemics (Pike 1943, 1967) as the foundation for descriptive grammars published by the Summer Institute of Linguistics. The success of this effort can be gauged from the assessment that "Tagmemics chokes on its own terminological complexity" (Hockett 1968: 33).

Word and Paradigm Morphology. First edition. James P. Blevins
© James P. Blevins 2016. First published 2016 by Oxford University Press

The inflectional forms are relatively easy to describe, since they occur in parallel paradigmatic sets; the traditional grammar of familiar languages gives us a picture of their inflectional systems. It may be worth noticing, however, that our traditional grammars fall short
of scientific compactness by dealing with an identical feature over and over again as it occurs
in different paradigmatic types. Thus, in a Latin grammar, we find the nominative-singular
sign -s noted separately for each of the types *amīcus* 'friend', *lapis* 'stone', *dux* 'leader', *tussis*
'cough', *manus* 'hand', *faciēs* 'face', when, of course, it should be noted only once, with a full
statement as to where it is and where it is not used. (Bloomfield 1933: 238)

For Bloomfield, as for many of his successors, it is self-evident that the distribution of an inflectional exponent such as nominative singular -s should be expressed
declaratively, by means of "a full statement", rather than exhibited in traditional
paradigm tables. Whatever the merits of this notion of 'compactness' for the
preparation of written grammars (or for the transmission of an oral grammatical
tradition), it has no established relevance to language acquisition or use. There is at
present no evidence that the language faculty imposes memory demands that strain
the storage capacity of the human brain, or that linguistic notions of 'compactness'
would be relevant to reducing this load.[2]

4.1 Recurrence and redundancy

From a classical WP perspective, the entire Bloomfieldian notion of 'compactness'
rests on a conflation of recurrent and redundant structure. A classical description of
an inflectional system will exhibit a network of recurrent patterns. The same stem
or stems will tend to recur in the inflected forms that make up the paradigm of
an item. The distribution of exponents will also exhibit systematic patterns across
the paradigms of distinct items. Yet these recurrent patterns are only redundant if
they are predictable from their components or from other aspects of the system.
An atomistic description that disassembles an inflectional system into inventories
of basic stems and exponents will eliminate any recurrent morphological structure.
But it will not reduce redundancy unless the decomposition satisfies each of the
preconditions in (4.1).

(4.1)   PRECONDITIONS FOR LOSSLESS DECOMPOSITION
        a. The parts identified as recurrent must be genuinely identical.
        b. Properties of the wholes can be reconstituted from their parts.
        c. The original wholes can be recovered from their simple parts.

Neither of the first two preconditions is met by any decompositional model.
As discussed in Chapter 8.3, the Bloomfieldian model of "scientific compactness"
operates with imprecise notions of orthographic and phonemic 'identity' that
obscure sub-phonemic contrasts that are systematically produced and discriminated by speakers. The distributional properties of whole forms are also not

---

[2] Or, as Bolinger (1979: 110) puts it, "The human brain is not a vestigial organ".

determinable from the distribution of their parts. In fact, the relationship between these distributions is grammatically significant, exerting an influence on everything from the processing strategies applied to the wholes to the productivity of their parts (Hay 2001; Hay and Baayen 2002, 2006).

It is, however, the third precondition in (4.1) that is most directly relevant to the status of paradigms. The reassembly of forms from their minimal parts is exactly what is NOT in principle possible in an inflection class system. The need to assign items to inflection classes only arises when the co-occurrence of base and exponent is not determined by substantive properties of the whole or those of its parts. An inflection class system is thus defined by distributional patterns over bases and exponents that cannot be reduced to independent selectional properties. The qualification 'independent' is of course critical here, since any unit can be represented as 'parts' that explicitly encode their affiliation with a larger unit. To a large extent, this strategy merely provides a distributed representation of the original unit. In contemporary morphemic and realizational approaches, these types of distributed representations tend to be expressed in terms of 'indexical' features of various kinds. The proliferation of diacritic features has a subtly subversive effect on morphological analysis. Rather than exhibiting the structure and organization of a morphological system, analyses formalize a process of reassembling units from parts that were explicitly encoded to mark the forms from which they were initially obtained. Even when this procedure is successfully implemented, it is unclear what it achieves.

4.1.1 Paradigmatic allomorphy

Regular plurals in English illustrate the kinds of conditions that would have to be met for recurrent structure to be genuinely redundant. There is no need to appeal to inflection classes in English to describe regular plurals, which appear to be decomposable into noun stems and plural suffixes with no loss of information. The properties of the plural form are the sum of the lexical properties of the noun stem and the number properties of the plural suffix /z/. The surface form of the suffix, [s], [z], or [əz], is likewise conditioned by the final segment of the noun stem. Let us also provisionally assume that, unlike in Dutch (Baayen *et al.* 2003; Kemps *et al.* 2005), the phonetic properties of a noun stem in isolation do not contrast systematically with its properties in a plural form.[3] Although differences in frequency are known to influence duration and patterns of reduction (Bybee and Hopper 2001; Gahl 2008), let us assume that the variation between individual singular and plural forms does not determine discriminative contrasts. Under these conditions, the stem+affix structure in *vans* and *boxes* is recurrent and redundant, and the plural forms can be reconstituted from the stems *van* and *box* and the plural suffix.

---

[3] The apparent redundancy exhibited by English plural forms may just reflect the fact that phonemic (and orthographic) transcriptions are too coarse-grained to capture distinctive sub-phonemic contrasts, or that they generalize over realizations of these contrasts that vary across populations, individuals and/or across lifespans (Ramscar *et al.* 2013*b*).

TABLE 4.1   Inanimate 'soft stem' declensions in Russian (Timberlake 2004)

	I (Masculine)		II (Feminine)		III (Feminine)	
	Sg	Pl	Sg	Pl	Sg	Pl
Nom	slovar'	slovari	nedelja	nedeli	tetrad'	tetradi
Gen	slovarja	slovarej	nedeli	nedel'	tetradi	tetradej
Dat	**slovarju**	slovarjam	nedele	nedeljam	tetradi	tetradjam
Acc	slovar'	slovari	**nedelju**	nedeli	tetrad'	tetradi
Inst	slovarëm	slovarjami	nedelej	nedeljami	**tetradju**	tetradjami
Loc	slovare	slovarjax	nedele	nedeljax	tetradi	tetradjax
	'dictionary'		'week'		'notebook'	

Yet what is not predictable is the fact that these noun stems occur with the regular marker, rather than following the irregular patterns exhibited by *men* or *oxen*. The 'morphologically conditioned allomorphy' involved in the selection of an irregular plural marker is not redundant, since it is not predictable from the properties or the form of the noun stems *man* or *ox* in isolation.

Given that relatively few nouns follow these irregular patterns in English, a speaker can learn them as exceptions and assume that other nouns follow the regular pattern in general. However, 'morphologically conditioned allomorphy' has a more central role in languages with inflection classes because this type of 'allomorphy' is what essentially defines inflection class morphology. The Russian noun declensions in Table 4.1 provide an illustrative example.

The three declensions in Table 4.1 are not defined by class-specific endings, but by class-specific DISTRIBUTIONS of a set of common endings. The dative plural *-am*, instrumental plural *-ami* and locative plural *-ax* can all be assigned the same meaning in all declensions. But the interpretation of the endings Ø, *-a*, *-u*, *-e*, and *-ej* is context dependent. For example, each declension contains a form in *-u* (marked in bold in Table 4.1). It is possible to eliminate this recurrent structure by separating the stems *slovar'*, *nedel'* and *tetrad'* from three homophonous *-u* endings: a dative singular ending in the first declension, an accusative singular ending in the second and an instrumental singular ending in the third. Yet this analysis does not eliminate any redundancy, because there is then no principled basis for deciding which ending occurs with each of the stems. The choice is not phonologically conditioned (as in English), given that all of the stem forms end in a 'soft' palatalized consonant. The exponent is also not predictable from gender (or any other features), as the interpretation of forms in *-u* differs for feminine nouns in the second and third declensions.[4]

There are of course technical strategies for restoring the information lost in disassembling the forms in Table 4.1. Following Chomsky (1965: 171) and Matthews (1965, 1972), inflection class is frequently expressed by 'class features'. In the present

---

[4] Moreover, although the second declension consists mainly of feminines (and is sometimes referred to as a 'feminine' class), it also contains animate masculine nouns such as MUŽČINA 'man' and masculine hypochoristics such as VANJA or VOLOLDYA, all of which follow the same inflectional pattern as animate second declension feminines.

TABLE 4.2   Class-indexed stem, exponent, and word entries

Stem	Exponent	Word Form
⟨slovar', [N, I]⟩	⟨u, [I, DAT SG]⟩	⟨slovarju, [N, I, DAT SG]⟩
⟨nedel', [N, II]⟩	⟨u, [II, ACC SG]⟩	⟨nedelju, [N, II, ACC SG]⟩
⟨tetrad', [N, III]⟩	⟨u, [III, INST SG]⟩	⟨tetradju, [N, III, INST SG]⟩

example, declension class features can be used to associate stems with exponents. As in Table 4.2, the entries for each of the stems are annotated with the features 'I', 'II' and 'III', and the exponents are marked for the same features. If the features of a stem and exponent must match, these entries will define just the three forms in -u in Tables 4.1 and 4.2.[5]

The status of class features and other types of indexical features is considered in more detail Chapter 6, in the discussion of the realizational models that make the most systematic use of these devices. However, in the present context, the key point illustrated by 'morphologically conditioned class allomorphy' is the way that it brings out the contrast between recurrent and redundant structure. Russian nouns exhibit a recurrent stem+suffix structure. But this structure is not redundant because it is not predictable from the parts of the structure in isolation. Hence an analysis that reduces recurrent structure by separating out minimal parts must be augmented by 'assembly instructions' that restore information about the co-occurrence of stems and exponents.

4.1.2 Constructional or 'gestalt' exponence

From a classical WP perspective, the difference between recurrence and redundancy reflects the constructional character of morphology. An inflected form is a lexical construction that is interpreted in a paradigmatic context. The declensional system of Estonian illustrates one kind of intrinsically constructional pattern. Table 4.3 lists partial paradigms of four first declension nouns in Estonian. The forms in bold, *kukke*, *lukku*, *pukki* and *sukka*, exhibit the variation characteristic of grade-alternating nouns. Each form contains a lexically-specific theme vowel that distinguishes the partitive from the consonant-final nominative singular. Each form also contains a 'strong' stem (marked here by consonant gemination) that distinguishes the partitive from the 'weak' genitive singular form. As with the Russian forms in -u in Tables 4.1, the stem+vowel structure of the partitive and genitive case forms in Table 4.3 is fully regular.

Also as in Russian, the recurrent structure in Estonian declensions is not redundant. Each of the forms *kukke*, *lukku*, *pukki* and *sukka* realizes partitive singular, and each is composed of a strong stem and theme vowel. Yet it is precisely because these parts recur in the paradigms in Table 4.3 that neither can be associated in

---

[5] The 'matching' requirement can be regulated by a 'destructive' unification operation (Shieber 1986), by a 'nondestructive' nondistinctness check (Ingria 1990) or by a 'semi-destructive' subsumption requirement (Blevins 2011).

TABLE 4.3   First declension partitives in Estonian (Erelt 2006; Blevins 2008a)

Nom Sg	kukk	lukk	pukk	sukk
Part(itive) Sg	**kukke**	**lukku**	**pukki**	**sukka**
Gen Sg	kuke	luku	puki	suka
Illa(tive)2 Sg	kukke	lukku	pukki	sukka
	'rooster'	'lock'	'trestle'	'stocking'

isolation with partitive case. Partitive cannot be associated with the strong stems *kukk, lukk, pukk* and *sukk*, since strong stems also realize the nominative. Partitive also cannot be associated with the theme vowels *-a, -e, -i* and *-u*, since these vowels occur in the genitive singular. Both strong stem and theme vowel also occur in the 'short' illative singular forms in Table 4.3.

Moreover, neither stem nor vowel is predictable from the other. A strong stem can be followed by any of the four theme vowels in Estonian. Conversely, each theme vowel occurs with both the strong and the weak stem in these paradigms. Unlike in Russian, theme vowels are lexical and cut across declension classes. As a result, there is no principled means of reassembling the partitive singular from its parts, based either on the substantive properties that can be associated with these parts or even with indexical class features.

Partitive case is an irreducibly word-level feature that is realized by the combination of a strong stem and a theme vowel. This type of GESTALT EXPONENCE (Ackerman *et al.* 2009) is difficult to describe if stems and theme vowels are disassembled and represented separately in the lexicon.[6] Together, strong stems and theme vowels realize partitive singular, but individually, they cannot be assigned discrete meanings that 'add up' to partitive singular. The constructional character of grammatical meaning in a language like Estonian raises a fundamental challenge, one that cannot be met by invoking a more abstract notion of meaning or by any other purely technical maneuver.[7]

4.2 Paradigm structure

The constructional character of inflectional forms underscores an important difference between 'analyzability' and morphemic 'decomposition'. An individual word form is often analyzable into parts that recur elsewhere in its inflectional paradigm or in the morphological system at large. But the 'recurrent partials' that distinguish a pair of word forms need not function as signs that are directly associated with the

---

[6] See Bickel (1994) for a discussion of morphological gestalts in the context of a perspective that also develops Hockett's (1987) notion of morphological 'resonances'.

[7] As discussed in Blevins (2008a), a strategy of decomposing case into abstract 'features' will not work in Estonian. The nominative and genitive forms of the nouns in Table 4.3 are each based on different stems in the singular and plural, so that no consistent feature decomposition can be assigned to the nominative or genitive case.

difference in grammatical meaning between the word forms. Instead, the variation exhibited by parts may serve to differentiate larger forms in ways that identify their place within a larger set of forms. The idea that variation is not individually meaningful but "locates" a form "in a paradigm" reflects a classical WP conception in which, as Matthews (1991) remarks, paradigms are the primary locus of part-whole relations:

In the ancient model the primary insight is not that words can be split into roots and formatives, but that they can be located in paradigms. They are not wholes composed of simple parts, but are themselves the parts within a complex whole. In that way, we discover different kinds of relation, and, perhaps, a different kind of simplicity. (Matthews 1991: 204)

Treating paradigms as fundamental units of grammatical organization conveys the same kinds of advantages as treating words as the basic grammatical signs. Just as words may have properties that cannot be assigned to their parts, sets of words may express information that cannot be associated with individual words. The forms in Table 4.3 illustrate both patterns. Recall from Section 4.1.2 that a partitive singular can be analyzed into a stem and theme vowel, but partitive case cannot be assigned to either part. A comparison of the forms in Table 4.3 likewise identifies the stem and vowels in Table 4.4.

The inventories in Table 4.4 imply the existence of the pairs *kukke/kuke*, *lukku/luku*, *pukki/puki* and *sukka/suka*. But they do not supply the interpretation of these pairs, given that nouns with a strong and weak stem may follow either of two gradation patterns (Erelt *et al.* 2000). In the 'weakening' pattern in Table 4.3, the partitive is strong and the genitive is weak. In the 'strengthening' pattern in Table 4.5, the genitive is strong and the nominative is weak.

A comparison of the forms of a paradigm will usually identify a set of stems and exponents. But in isolation these elements often do not provide enough information to reconstitute the original forms. As noted in Section 4.1, the forms in the Russian paradigms in Table 4.1 can be reduced to three stems and three partially overlapping sets of case endings. However, from these parts alone, there is no principled means of reassociating stems and endings. Because class is marked

TABLE 4.4 First declension stems and theme vowels

Strong Stem	kukk	lukk	pukk	sukk
Weak Stem	kuk	luk	puk	suk
Theme Vowel	e	u	i	a

TABLE 4.5 Strengthening patterns in Estonian (Mürk 1997)

Nom Sg	hape	kate	lõke	sete
Gen Sg	happe	katte	lõkke	sette
Part Sg	hapet	katet	lõket	setet
	'acid'	'covering'	'bonfire'	'sediment'

TABLE 4.6 Qualitative weakening gradation (Mürk 1997)

Nom Sg	lugu	suga
Gen Sg	loo	soa
Part Sg	lugu	suga
Illa2 Sg	lukku	sukka
	'tale'	'sley'

by the distribution of endings, removal of the endings leaves formally indistinguishable stems. The Estonian paradigms in Tables 4.3 and 4.5 can likewise be reduced to stems and theme vowels, which can be recombined to recover strong and weak forms. Yet the distribution of these forms in the paradigm of an item is not recoverable from the parts.[8]

Even the contrast between strong and weak stems depends on their distribution in a paradigm rather than on morphosyntactic or phonetic properties. The partial paradigms for LUGU and SUGA in Table 4.6, like those for LUKK and SUKK in Table 4.3, contain the forms *lukka* and *sukka*. Yet whereas *lukk* and *sukk* function as strong stems in Table 4.3, they occur solely within the short illative singular forms in Table 4.6. Gradation in the nouns in Table 4.6 follows a 'qualitative' pattern, in which the strong forms *lugu* and *suga* differ segmentally from the weak forms *loo* and *soa*. The contrast between the homophones *lukku* 'lock' and 'tale' and *sukka* 'stocking' and 'sley' does not lie in their internal structure, as each pair is composed of a common stem form and theme vowel. Instead, the difference reflects their external relations to larger sets of forms, relations that are not preserved in an inventory of stems and theme vowels.

In sum, words (or sets of words) may exhibit patterns and relations that are difficult to express declaratively in terms of general principles that govern the combination of sub-word units. Regular nouns in English can be described in terms of a set of stems and a regular plural suffix that exhibits phonologically predictable allomorphy. In Russian, the stems and endings require additional class features. In Estonian, the contribution made by COMBINATIONS of elements makes it difficult to apportion the properties of a form to sub-word units and general combinatorial principles, even if guided by features. This 'informational asymmetry' between sets of words and their recurrent parts motivates the perspective of Kuryłowicz (1949), on which words are basic units, and stems and exponents are abstractions "founded on" words:

---

[8] In fact, the theme vowels in Tables 4.3 and 4.5 do provide some information about gradation. Apart from isolated examples such as LÕUNA 'south, noon', strengthening gradation is confined to nouns with the theme vowel *-e*. Hence a noun with a strong and weak stem and a theme vowel other than *-e* will almost always follow the weakening pattern. However, this deduction is again not attributable to the properties of individual formatives but to the distribution of theme vowels over the paradigms of the language.

TABLE 4.7 Grammatical case forms of PUKK 'trestle'

	Sg	Plu
Nom	pukk	pukid
Gen	puki	pukkide
Part	pukki	pukkisid
Illa2/Part2	pukki	pukke

For the notion of the stem is dependent on the concrete forms composing the paradigm: one finds the stem in disengaging the elements that are common to all the case forms of a paradigm (when dealing with declension).[9] (Kuryłowicz 1949: 159)

In addition to predicting a common stem and the variation in exponents, the forms of a paradigm also imply information about each other. The paradigms in Table 4.1 illustrate a number of general dependencies in Russian declensions. A nominative singular in -*a* identifies a second declension noun. A nominative singular that ends in a soft consonant identifies a first declension noun if the noun is masculine and a third declension noun if the noun is feminine. It is conventional to assign items to classes based on the forms that realize a given paradigm cell. However, the opposite deduction, which classifies items based on the meaning they associate with a given form, is equally effective. In the paradigms in Table 4.1 the forms in -*u* are diagnostic. A form in -*u* that realizes dative singular identifies a first declension noun, one that realizes accusative singular identifies a second declension noun, and one that realizes instrumental singular identifies a third declension noun.

The effectiveness of these deductive procedures is not a quirk of Russian but reflects the general implicational structure of inflectional systems. Even tighter patterns of mutual implication operate over Estonian declensions. For example, each of the partitive singular forms in Table 4.3 implies the rest of the forms in its paradigm. This striking pattern of deductions can be illustrated with reference to the paradigm of PUKK 'trestle'. The full set of grammatical case forms, given in Table 4.7, is directly implied by the partitive singular form.

In a paradigm containing a strong vowel-final partitive singular such as *pukki*, the remaining singular forms are fully predictable. The short illative singular *pukki* is identical to the partitive, the nominative singular *pukk* is related by truncation, and the genitive singular *puki* is a weak variant of the partitive singular. The 'stem partitive plural' *pukki* also reflects the default *i↔e* 'exchange pattern' for nouns with theme vowel -*i* (or -*e*). The long partitive plural *pukkisid* and genitive plural *pukkide* follow the general first declension patterns, adding -*sid* and -*de* to the partitive singular base. The nominative plural *pukid* exhibits a class-neutral pattern in which -*d* is added to the genitive singular base. Furthermore, all of the remaining

---

[9] Car la notion du thème est postérieure aux formes concrètes composant le paradigme: on trouve le thème en dégageant les éléments communs à toutes les formes casuelles du paradigme (quand il s'agit de la déclinaison).

TABLE 4.8   Semantic case forms of PUKK 'trestle'

	Sg	Plu
Illative	pukisse	pukkidesse
Inessive	pukis	pukkides
Elative	pukist	pukkidest
Allative	pukile	pukkidele
Adessive	pukil	pukkidel
Ablative	pukilt	pukkidelt
Translative	pukiks	pukkideks
Terminative	pukini	pukkideni
Essive	pukina	pukkidena
Abessive	pukita	pukkideta
Comitative	pukiga	pukkidega

'semantic' (or 'local') case forms are predictable from the genitive singular and plural forms in Table 4.7. As the forms in Table 4.8 show, the semantic case endings do not inflect for number, so that stem selection represents the only variation in these forms.

A strong genitive singular such as *happe* in Table 4.5 licenses comparable deductions within the paradigms of nouns that exhibit strengthening gradation. Other classes exhibit other characteristic patterns of interdependency, which are recognized in nearly all descriptions of Estonian.[10] In keying these deductions to the informativeness of the partitive singular, the present description follows the classical practice of identifying class based on a distinguished 'diagnostic form'. However, this overstates the informational asymmetry between partitive singulars and other forms. A genitive singular such as *puki* is also diagnostic of a weakening declension. Although morphologically weak, the stem *puk* is phonetically long (or 'second quantity' Q2). A Q2 genitive singular can only occur in a paradigm with an overlong ('third quantity' Q3) nominative and partitive singular.[11] The genitive plural is also diagnostic, since the removal of the ending *-de* identifies the partitive singular base. Moreover, since all of the semantic case endings are invariant, each of the semantic case forms identifies the corresponding genitives. Hence, nearly every form is either diagnostic of class or identifies a form that is diagnostic.

The informativeness of individual words and the symmetry of interdependencies give rise to particularly efficient deductions in Estonian. However, an implicational structure defined by interdependent alternations is characteristic and even definitive of inflection class systems. It is these patterns of mutual prediction that act as the primary force binding inflected forms into the "complex whole" that Matthews

---

[10] One model of the structure of the Estonian inflectional system is outlined in Blevins (2007, 2008a). More traditional classifications, which differ mainly in where they draw the line between classes and subclasses, are presented in Erelt *et al.* (1995), Mürk (1997), Saagpakk (2000), Erelt *et al.* (2000), Erelt (2003) and Erelt (2006).

[11] Stops do not contrast in voicing in Estonian, and the orthographic pairs associated with voicing contrasts in English are used to express length contrasts. The series *b/d/g* is short (Q1), the series *p/t/k* is long (Q2), and *pp/tt/kk* are all overlong (Q3).

specifies on p. 75 above. Individual patterns are frequently noted in descriptions of inflectional systems and often serve as the basis for assigning items to classes. Yet because these patterns are so transparently represented by exemplary paradigms, there have been comparatively few attempts to express implicational relations symbolically (or sub-symbolically, via networks), in a format that abstracts away from the sets of forms that exhibit those relations. The Paradigm Structure Conditions of Wurzel (1984) represent the most systematic attempt to capture mutual interdependency:[12]

Observation of complicated paradigms shows that implicative relations do not only obtain between one basic inflexional form, either lexical (*sobaka* [Russian 'dog' JPB]) or non-lexical (*Männer* [German 'men' JPB]), and all the other inflexional forms, but exist throughout the whole paradigm: all paradigms (apart from suppletive cases) are structured on the basis of implicative patterns which go beyond the individual word, patterns of varying complexity. Of particular complexity in this respect is, for example, the implicative pattern of the *i*-declension in Latin: /im/ in the A.Sg. ⊃ /ī/ in the Abl.Sg. ⊃ /īs/ in the A.Pl. ⊃ /ium/ in the G.Pl. ⊃ ... From the A.Sg. form we can derive, via a number of steps, all other forms, but not vice-versa. Since the implicative patterns determine the structure of the paradigms of a language we call them implicative PARADIGM STRUCTURE CONDITIONS (PSCs). (Wurzel 1984: 208)

Although this passage is phrased in terms of a process that "can derive, via a number of steps, all other forms", PSCs can also be interpreted non-derivationally, as wellformedness constraints, or 'paradigm admissibility conditions'. This interpretation is highly compatible with a classical WP perspective in which part-whole analysis largely involves determining whether a particular set of forms comprises a paradigm or whether a particular form belongs to a given paradigm. Yet PSCs are also fundamentally limited by their use of the material conditional '⊃' to model implicational relations. This restricts the application of PSCs to exceptionless patterns, and excludes any statistical patterns involving strongly but not invariably correlated dependencies. The challenge of modelling probabilistic dependencies was not met in any general way until the development of modern implicational WP models, and it is in the context of discriminative, information-theoretic approaches (discussed in Chapters 7 and 8) that the most promising solutions appear to lie.

4.3 Principal parts

The predictive structure of inflectional systems is also what allows classical WP accounts to factor them into exemplary 'patterns' and lexical 'identifiers'. Given the interdependence of inflectional 'choices', a system can be described by exemplary

---

[12] In much the same way that the Unaccusativity Hypothesis of Relational Grammar (Perlmutter 1978) provides a general statement of the descriptive generalizations about argument structure offered in descriptive grammars, PSCs provide a formalized statement of the form correspondences noted in reference and pedagogical grammars.

paradigms that exhibit the morphological patterns in the system, together with principal parts that identify the patterns followed by non-exemplary items. As Matthews notes, this organization lends cohesion to individual paradigms and underlies the efficiency of inflectional systems:

The most general insight is that one inflection tends to predict another . . . This insight can be incorporated into any model. Traditionally, it is the basis for the method of exemplary paradigms. If the alternations were independent, these would have to be numerous . . . But since they are interdependent, their number can be very small . . . It is more attractive to learn paradigms as wholes than each alternation separately. (Matthews 1991: 197f.)

The leading idea developed in the "method of exemplary paradigms" is that form variation in a grammatical system can be exhibited by exemplary patterns that serve a dual role. On the one hand, exemplary paradigms specify the forms of particular lexical items. On the other hand, they provide a model for the inflection of non-exemplary items. Hence one and the same paradigm exhibits the forms of an actual lexical item while representing morphological patterns characteristic of the class to which that item belongs. In the same way that stems are not basic units in a classical WP model, but are instead abstracted from a set of forms, classes are not 'properties' of items but are abstractions over sets of paradigms that exhibit congruent patterns of form variation. The class of an item is exhibited via characteristic patterns of form alternation. Unlike Bloomfieldian approaches, classical WP models do not dissociate lexis or 'form' from grammar or 'combinatorics'. Also unlike realizational models, they do not radically separate properties from forms. The notion of a set of abstract paradigm cells (or morphosyntactic representatations) that are 'filled in' by spell-out rules arises later, in the models developed by Matthews (1972), Anderson (1992), Aronoff (1994) and Stump (2001). Instead, classical WP models embody a distinctively 'integrative' exemplar-based conception.

The patterns exhibited by exemplary paradigms are extended by matching 'principal parts' against cells in exemplary paradigms, and deducing additional forms by analogy to the forms that realize other exemplary cells. The diagnostic value of principal parts is not due to the features that they realize or to any aspect of their own form, such as the presence or absence of a particular exponent, or whether they serve as a 'base' for other forms, etc. Rather, a form is of diagnostic value to the extent that it has a distinctive (morphologically conditioned) shape corresponding to each class. In Russian, as in many Slavic languages, the nominative singular can be regarded as "the basic case [form]" (Corbett 1991: 35) from which other forms can be deduced. As noted in Section 4.2, the form of the nominative singulars in Table 4.1 is informative about the declension class of the corresponding nouns. A nominative singular in -*a* identifies a second declension noun. A nominative singular that ends in a soft consonant identifies a first declension noun if the noun is masculine and a third declension noun if the noun is feminine. Alternatively, the class of a noun can be identified from a nominative singular that ends in a soft consonant, together with any other singular case form.

It is conventional to assign items to classes by holding a paradigm cell constant and comparing the forms that realize that cell. However, the opposite deduction, which classifies items based on the properties they associate with a given form, is equally effective and, in fact, more economical in Russian. As again remarked in Section 4.1.1, the forms in -*u* are fully diagnostic. A form in -*u* that realizes dative singular identifies a first declension noun, one that realizes accusative singular identifies a second declension noun, and one that realizes instrumental singular identifies a third declension noun.

Russian declensions thus approach a kind of pedagogical ideal, in which one principal part can identify the class of a noun and sanction reliable inferences about other forms of the noun. The paradigms in Table 4.1 also illustrate the pedagogical insight that not all forms are equally informative in the same way. In particular, the shape of the dative, instrumental and locative plural is so uniform across the paradigms in Table 4.1 that these forms merely serve to identify a soft stem noun (a hard stem noun would end in unpalatalized -*am*, -*ami* and -*ax*). The diagnostic (and morphosyntactic) value of other case forms in Table 4.1 lies between these extremes. The lack of any general metric for measuring diagnostic values between 'fully informative' and 'fully uninformative' is an acknowledged limitation of classical WP approaches, one which is again addressed by information-theoretic formalizations of these models.

Variation in the diagnostic value of cells and forms may reflect a range of factors, including how recently the forms have been morphologized, whether they have been subject to levelling, and other aspects of their origins and history. In Russian, as in many flectional systems, this variation also exhibits a fundamental trade-off between different types of information. For example, the diagnostic value of a form such as *nedelja* is offset by the fact that it is a highly ambiguous marker of grammatical features. The shape of *nedelja* does not immediately identify it as a nominative singular, but once it has been classified as a nominative singular form, it unambiguously identifies class. In contrast, a form such as *nedeljami* unambiguously realizes the instrumental plural but is of no direct value in identifying class. Contemporary morphological descriptions often recognize only one dimension of this information matrix, representing grammatical information, such as case, number and gender, while neglecting class-identifying aspects of form or leaving them implicit in the structure of exemplary paradigms and the choice of principal parts. Part of the problem lies in the fact that predictive value is not a property of a form in the same way that case is and hence cannot readily be expressed as a 'feature', even if one accepts the use of diacritic features for expressing class affiliation.

4.3.1 Paradigm uniformity and cohesion

In the Russian noun paradigms in Table 4.1, the class of a noun and its full 12-cell paradigm can be deduced from a small number of forms, and often from the nominative singular alone. The economy of this declensional system rests in large part on its uniformity. One can, for example, speak of 'the paradigm' of a regular Russian noun, rather than of 'the singular (sub)paradigm', 'the plural (sub)paradigm', etc. Uniformity in this sense is independent of complexity, as one can see by contrasting Russian and German declensions. Noun paradigms

TABLE 4.9 Singular declensional patterns in
German (cf. Duden 2005: 197)

| | Masc | | Neut | Fem |
	S1	S2	S1	S3
Nom	Pegel	Prinz	Segel	Regel
Acc	Pegel	Prinzen	Segel	Regel
Dat	Pegel	Prinzen	Segel	Regel
Gen	**Pegels**	**Prinzen**	**Segels**	**Regel**
	'level'	'prince'	'sail'	'rule'

in German are inflectionally simpler than in Russian, with fewer cases and less
form variation in general. However, they are also less uniform, due to a partial
dissociation between singular and plural patterns. This dissociation leads to a
comparatively large number of 'word types' which exhibit very weak implicational
relations between singular and plural forms.

The three regular singular patterns are illustrated in Table 4.9. The diagnostic
genitive forms are set in bold.[13] Pattern S3 characterizes feminine nouns, which
are invariant in the singular. Neuters likewise follow just the 'strong' pattern S1, in
which the genitive singular is marked by -(e)s. Masculine nouns exhibit the only
variation, as they may follow either the strong pattern S1, marked by -(e)s, or the
'weak' pattern S2, marked by -(e)n.

The corresponding plural formations are illustrated in Table 4.10.[14] Each of the
patterns P1–P5 is classified by the shape of its ending and whether it is, or can be,
based on an umlauted variant of the singular stem. A comparison of the forms in
the first two blocks of rows shows that masculine and neuter nouns both follow all
five patterns, although comparatively fewer neuter nouns follow the weak pattern
P2 and only a very few exhibit umlaut in P3. The bottom block of rows shows that
feminine nouns do not form plurals in -er and that they tend to require umlauted
stems in patterns P3 and P5.

There are various correlations between the gender and stem form of a noun and
the plural pattern that it follows. These subgeneralizations are discussed in detail in
reference and pedagogical grammars such as Duden (2005), as well as in theoretical
studies such as Köpke (1988) and Neef (1998). Of the patterns in Table 4.10, only
plurals in -s are productive across all genders.[15] Unlike English, in which the default

---

[13] This table omits the proper name class listed in Duden (2005: 197), which patterns with S1 nouns.
It also excludes the pattern exhibited by NAME 'name' and a handful of other nouns, which have
accusatives and datives in -en and genitives in -ens.

[14] The nominative, accusative and genitive forms are always identical, so these forms are listed just
once, in the rows labelled 'N/A/G'.

[15] The ending -s is often regarded as the default plural marker in German because it is associated
with a large and diverse class of elements (Clahsen et al. 1992; Marcus et al. 1995). This class includes
loans, such as Büros 'offices' or Tabus 'taboos', abbreviations, such as LKWs (Lastkraftwagens) 'trucks',
proper names such as die Müllers and hypochoristics such as Omas 'grandmothers'. An alternative is
that -s marks non-native nouns that do not conform to usual nominal phonotactics or are otherwise
anomalous in the context of the German noun system (Rettig 1972; Wunderlich 1999).

TABLE 4.10   Plural patterns in German (cf. Duden 2005: 226)

	P1	P2	P3		P4	P5	
Ending	-s	-(e)n	-e	-e	-er	Ø	Ø
Stem	–uml	–uml	–uml	+uml	+uml	–uml	+uml
N/A/G	Uhus	Prinzen	Hunde	Bünde	Münder	Balken	Gärten
Dat	Uhus	Prinzen	Hunden	Bünden	Mündern	Balken	Gärten
(Masc)	'owls'	'princes'	'dogs'	'waistbands'	'mouths'	'beams'	'gardens'
N/A/G	Autos	Ohren	Jahre	Flöße	Länder	Muster	Klöster
Dat	Autos	Ohren	Jahren	Flößen	Ländern	Mustern	Klöstern
(Neut)	'cars'	'ears'	'years'	'rafts'	'countries'	'patterns'	'cloisters'
N/A/G	Bars	Regeln	—	Hände	—	—	Töchter
Dat	Bars	Regeln	—	Händen	—	—	Töchtern
(Fem)	'bars'	'rules'	—	'hands'	—	—	'daughters'

-s marker is statistically predominant, plurals in -s are relatively infrequent and the vast majority of plural nouns in German follow one of the patterns P2–P5. The applicability of these remaining patterns is conditioned by gender and stem shape. The apparent generality of pattern P2 reflects the fact that it almost certainly collapses two synchronically distinct plural strategies. Plurals in -(e)n are the default for 'native' feminine nouns, as well as for feminine nouns formed with productive endings such as -ung and -heit, as expressed in the second 'basic rule' (*Grundregel*) in Duden (2005: 193). The formation of masculine and neuter plurals in -(e)n is much more restricted and cannot be regarded as productive in the modern language.[16]

Laaha *et al.* (2006: 282f.) further subclassify the patterns in table 4.10 and rank the expanded set of combinations on a four-point productivity scale: 'fully productive', 'productive', 'weakly productive', and 'nonproductive'. They suggest in particular that P3 is weakly productive for masculine and neuter nouns with consonant-final stems, and is the default for those ending in a sibilant, such as *Fax~Faxe*. They likewise classify P5 as productive for masculine and neuter nouns whose stems end in a schwa followed by -n or -r and as weakly productive for those whose stems end in -l. The graded notion of productivity applied to these patterns is defined in terms of competition between alternatives. A plural strategy is 'fully productive' if it is the only strategy that applies to a given gender/stem combination, 'productive' if it is opposed by a second strategy and 'weakly productive' if it is opposed by two other strategies. Although formulated in terms of plural strategies, this scale provides a rough measure of the morphological information that a gender/stem combination provides about the plural form of a noun. In a system in which each plural strategy is equiprobable, the morphological information expressed by a given combination will be inversely proportional to

[16] There is sound psychological and neurolinguistic support for distinguishing feminines in -(e)n from masculines and neuters (Penke *et al.* 1999; Clahsen 1999).

the number of applicable plural strategies. If only one strategy can apply, then there is no uncertainty and knowing the gender/stem combination identifies the basic plural form. If two equiprobable strategies are applicable, the gender/stem combination reduces the uncertainty to two alternatives; if three strategies are applicable, the uncertainty is reduced to three alternatives. However, the number of alternative strategies only provides a meaningful measure of relative uncertainty or productivity if each of the alternatives is equally likely. A cell with three alternative realizations but a strong bias in favour of one has considerably less uncertainty than a cell with two equiprobable realizations. The same concerns arise for any productivity scale that correlates the 'strength' or 'degree' of productivity with the number of alternatives without considering their distributional properties.

To extend the classification proposed in Laaha *et al.* (2006) to a probabilistic model of correlations between gender/stem patterns and plural strategies, it would be useful to adopt an information-theoretic perspective that provides a frequency-weighted measure of uncertainty.[17] Yet what would still be absent from this picture would be a correlation between the factors that condition inflectional patterns in the singular and plural. The declensional system contains exactly one case of this kind, which is cited by Laaha *et al.* (2006):

In reality, the choice of plural formation depends largely on gender and/or inflection class as manifested also in the expression of the four German cases in the singular. Thus if a masculine has the suffix *-en* in the Gen.Sg., it must also have it for the plural, e.g. *der Fürst* 'prince, sovereign', Gen.Sg. *des Fürst-en* implies the plural *Fürst-en*. (Laaha *et al.* 2006: 279)

The broader claim that "the choice of plural formation depends largely on gender and/or inflection class as manifested . . . in the singular" is unfounded, as Table 4.11 shows. Matching the singular patterns in Table 4.9 with the plural patterns in Table 4.10 defines 19 combinations, which highlight the almost complete dissociation of singular and plural sub-paradigms in German. A particularly clear

TABLE 4.11   Combinations of singular and plural patterns in German

	uml	S1 Masc	S1 Neut	S2 Masc	S3 Fem
P1	–	UHU	AUTO	—	KAMERA
P2	–	STAAT	OHR	PRINZ	REGEL
P3	–	HUND	JAHR	—	—
P3	+	BUND	(FLOSS)	—	HAND
P4	+	MUND	LAND	—	—
P5	–	BALKEN	MUSTER	—	—
P5	+	GARTEN	(KLOSTER)	—	TOCHTER

[17] Though these statistical generalizations do not not always suffice to predict the plural reliably from gender/stem patterns, as illustrated by the contrast between the masculine pairs *Hund~Hunde*, *Bund~Bünde* and *Mund~Münder* in Table 4.10.

reflex of this dissociation is the existence of nouns that are traditionally described as belonging to 'mixed declensions'. For example, the masculine noun STAAT 'state' follows the 'strong' pattern S1 in the singular and the 'weak' pattern P2 in the plural. As Laaha *et al.* (2006) note, the converse mixture does not occur, as masculine nouns that follow the weak pattern S1 in the singular always follow the corresponding weak pattern P2 in the plural. However, this is the only inflectional restriction on masculine or neuter nouns, since a strong masculine or neuter can in principle follow any plural pattern. Feminine nouns are all invariant in the singular and thus do not exhibit ANY inflectional variation that can correlate with the choice of plural patterns.

In sum, there is a weaker integration of singulars and plurals into cohesive form sets in German than in Russian. The genitive singular of a German noun identifies the remaining singular forms. The nominative, accusative and genitive forms are all equally diagnostic within the plural sub-paradigm.[18] Except in the case of the weak masculine pattern S2, singulars are not reliable predictors of plural patterns. In contrast, the singular class is predictable from the plural and stem form of a noun, apart from mixed declensions that pattern like STAAT. The full range of patterns is predictable from a plural and genitive singular form. Hence, the best account of this type of fractured system is one that recognizes separate singular and plural principal parts for each noun.

4.3.2 Implicational structure of inflectional series

German declensions illustrate a simple type of multiple-part system in which each of the principal parts is of high diagnostic value within a sub-network and a weaker implicational relation holds across networks and between principal parts. Conjugational systems are often structured in this way, comprising multiple sub-paradigms, organized around larger inventories of principal parts.[19] If a system is extremely simple or highly uniform, a single principal part may still suffice. For example, Bonami and Boyé (2003) propose that regular verbs in French are based on a single principal part. In a subsequent study (Bonami and Boyé 2007), they argue that irregular verbs can also be based on a single principal part, provided that the part may be chosen 'dynamically' (Finkel and Stump 2007), that is, not necessarily the same principal part for each verb.

Languages in which regular items can be represented by a single diagnostic form conform to a pedagogical ideal of inflectional economy. A similar conception underlies more theoretical principles, such as the Single Base Hypothesis of Albright (2002). However, the variation within conjugational systems is often not

---

[18] Even the dative plural is highly informative, since it unambiguously identifies the basic plural form except when it ends in an *-n* following a schwa or liquid.

[19] Items with a purely etymological connection can also function as models for the deduction of inflected forms. Like the 'pseudo-plural' compound bases in German in Section 3.1.4 and the grammatical case form bases in Estonian in Section 4.2, this is a 'morphomic' (Aronoff 1994) relation between items at the level of form. As Spencer (2013) notes, this type of pattern is characteristic of prefixed Indo-European verbs.

predictable from a single form. Instead, the paradigms of a verb cluster into groups, usually termed 'series', based on a common or similar stem. Descriptions of these types of systems specify a principal part for each sub-paradigm or series. Latin conjugations provide a familiar illustration:

Certain forms of the verbs are known as the Principal Parts, because they furnish the key to the inflection of any given verb, showing, as they do, the Present Stem and thereby the Conjugation, and the Perfect and Participial Stems. These are: 1. THE PRESENT INDICATIVE ACTIVE, cited in the First Person Singular. 2. THE PRESENT INFINITIVE. 3. THE PERFECT INDICATIVE ACTIVE, cited in the First Person Singular. 4. THE PERFECT PASSIVE PARTICIPLE, cited in the Nominative Singular Neuter. (Hale and Buck 1903: 77)

Principal parts representing the four basic Latin conjugations are given in Table 4.12. Each class is represented by four forms of an exemplary verb. The first pair, the indicative active and infinitive, are drawn from the present series. Standard grammars represent the present indicative by the 1sg form, given in parentheses in Table 4.12. However, the uniform ending of this form makes it an unsuitable principal part. In particular, the 1sg present indicative neutralizes the contrasts between classes I and II and between classes III_{io} and IV. These contrasts are preserved in the 2sg forms in Table 4.12.[20] The second pair, the indicative active and passive participle, are drawn from the perfect series. The need for four forms of each verb reflects the fact that no two rows of forms exhibit congruent inflectional patterns. For example, inspection of the present series shows why the classes in Table 4.12 cannot be represented by a single principal part. Selecting just present indicative forms would not distinguish third conjugation *capiō* from fourth conjugation *audiō*. Selecting present infinitive forms would distinguish *capere* from *audīre* but at the cost of losing the contrast within the third conjugation between TEGŌ and CAPIŌ. Similar considerations justify each of the standard principal parts. But even an inventory of four principal parts achieves considerable economy, given that Latin verbs may have up to 150 inflected forms and periphrases.

Although the present forms in Table 4.12 "show . . . the Present Stem and thereby the Conjugation", the present Stem is not itself a principal part, but rather a 'recurrent partial' that is exhibited by the word forms that do serve as principal

TABLE 4.12   Principal parts of Latin verbs (Hale and Buck 1903: 82ff.)

	Present		Perfect		
	Indic Act	Infin	Indic Act	Pass Prtl	
I	amās (amō)	amāre	amāvī	amātum	'to love'
II	monēs (moneō)	monēre	monuī	monitum	'to advise'
III	tegis (tegō)	tegere	tēxī	tēctum	'to cover'
III_{io}	capis (capiō)	capere	cēpī	captum	'to take'
IV	audīs (audiō)	audīre	audīvī	audītum	'to hear'

[20] I am grateful to Olivier Bonami for drawing these points to my attention.

parts. A classical WP model is consistently word-based, at the level of grammar and lexicon. Like the exemplary paradigms that instantiate the morphological patterns of a language, the principal part inventories that represent the lexicon consist of whole word forms that realize specific paradigm cells.

As this description of Latin illustrates, a highly diagnostic principal part may become established as a citation form within a grammatical tradition. However, it is important to bear in mind that the value of a principal part is determined by its informativeness with respect to other forms, not by its status in terms of notions like morphosyntactic or morphotactic 'markedness'. Forms whose unmarked status is due to the neutralization of within-item variation are often among the least useful principal parts, since they tend to neutralize class-defining variation. At the other extreme, highly infrequent or even archaic forms may preserve diagnostic phonetic characteristics that have been reduced or otherwise obscured in more frequent forms. This type of diagnostic value is of limited relevance to any analysis that is meant to underlie a model of naturalistic language acquisition or use. The essential prerequisites for principal parts are that they occur above a nominal frequency threshold (i.e., be in active circulation) and that they exhibit class-identifying variation.

The first of these conditions is distributional and the second is implicational. Both are independent of morphosyntactic or morphotactic considerations. Hence principal parts may be found in nearly any cell of an inflectional system. This point is illustrated by the principal parts of the Russian conjugational system. Russian verbs can be assigned to two basic conjugations based on the stem-final vowels in present paradigms.[21] In all present paradigms, the 1sg ends in -*u*. In the first conjugation (or '*e*-conjugation'), the vowel -*u* also occurs in the 3pl, and -*e* occurs elsewhere. The second conjugation (or '*i*-conjugation') exhibits a contrast between -*a* in the 3pl, and -*i* elsewhere. These patterns are displayed by the present paradigms in Table 4.13.

The lexemes DELAT' and GOVORIT' exhibit regular inflectional endings and show no stem allomorphy, as illustrated by the first rows of forms in Table 4.14. Hence a single principal part could identify both the stem and conjugation vowel of these items, if all verbs were equally uniform. Yet they are not, as the forms in the second row in Table 4.14 show. Hence one needs to know that the stems of a verb do

TABLE 4.13 Exemplary present paradigms in Russian (Wade 1992: 230ff.)

	I		II	
	Sg	Plu	Sg	Plu
1st	delaju	delaem	govorju	govorim
2nd	delaeš'	delaete	govoriš'	govorite
3rd	delaet	delajut	govorit	govorjat
	'to do'		'to speak'	

---

[21] And further subdivided based on stem patterns (Timberlake 2004: 99ff.).

TABLE 4.14   Standard conjugational series in Russian (Unbegaun 1957: 166)

	Present Series			Past/Infinitive Series		
	1sg	3sg	3pl	Infinitive	Past Masc	Past Prtl
I	delaju	delaet	delajut	delat'	delal	delavšij
II	govorju	govorit	govorjat	govorit'	govoril	govorivšij
I	išču	iščet	iščut	iskat'	iskal	iskavšij
II	smotrju	smotrit	smotrjat	smotret'	smotrel	smotrevšij
II	vižu	vidit	vidjat	videt'	videl	videvšij

not alternate, information that is most efficiently expressed by a second principal part. So a single principal part does not suffice, even for fully regular verbs. The general patterns exhibited by verbs with alternating stems are illustrated by the forms of ISKAT' 'to find', SMOTRET' 'to look at' and VIDET' 'to see' in Table 4.14. The lexeme ISKAT' shows the characteristic first conjugation pattern, in which stems in the present series exhibit consonant mutation. The lexeme SMOTRET' 'to look at' exhibits a similar series-level split, in which the stem-final vowel -*i* in the present series alternates with -*e* in the past series. The lexeme VIDET' combines both patterns. Consonant mutation occurs just in the 1sg, as is characteristic of alternating second conjugation verbs, and there is a series-level contrast between -*i* and -*e*.

The Russian conjugational system exhibits much additional variation, though the patterns in Table 4.14 suffice to clarify the usual motivation for distinguishing a present stem, which underlies the present series, from an infinitive stem, which underlies the past series. A fundamentally similar analysis is preserved in more theoretical accounts, such as Brown (1998):

It follows therefore that there are two main variants of the stem, or two allostems. These are the stem used in the infinitive and the past tense and the stem used in the present tense. (Brown 1998: 199)

Since most forms of an item tend to be at least partially informative about class, selecting a specific form again reflects the essentially pedagogical goal of assigning a maximally economical and uniform description. Forms in the past series are mutually predictable, so the infinitive is as good a choice as any. However, there is greater variation in the relative informativeness of present forms. As noted already, the 1sg is the least informative, so it is a poor choice of principal part (much as in the Latin paradigms in Table 4.12). For the purposes of identifying class, the stem vowels in 3pl forms are as informative as the stem vowel in the remaining present forms. However, some verbs exhibit further consonant mutations in all forms but the 1sg and 3pl. This pattern is illustrated by the forms of MOČ' 'be able to' in Table 4.15.

Hence the most informative present form is the 3pl form, as it preserves a class-identifying vowel and unmutated stem. The diagnostic value of this form is of course frequently noted in descriptive and pedagogical grammars. Wade

TABLE 4.15 Present and Past Series forms of моč 'be able to'

	1sg	3sg	3pl	Infinitive	Past Masc	Past Prtl
I	mogu	možet	mogut	moč'	mog	mogšij

(1992: 228) uses the 3pl as the reference form for the present series in proposing that "[t]he present-future stem of a verb is derived by removing the last two letters [i.e. segments] of the third-person plural of the verb". Levin *et al.* (1979: 195) goes even further in suggesting that "[t]he 3rd Person plural implies the entire conjugation membership", at least for regular verbs.[22]

In sum, the variation in the Russian conjugation system motivates multiple principal parts. The past series can be represented by the infinitive citation form or, equivalently, by a past form or past participle. But the best representative of the present series is the 3pl present form (or any form, including the present Active participle, which predicts the 3pl present form). This choice reflects the fact that the value of a principal part correlates with its relative informativeness, not with its status as a citation or reference form. In one sense this is unsurprising. Given that all forms are at least partially informative, there is no obvious reason why a specific form should invariably be the most informative. As with other properties of linguistic systems, informativeness will tend to reflect various interacting and even counteracting factors. For example, any general tendency to align inflectional patterns with highly frequent forms may be disrupted by the influence that frequency appears to exert in inducing or accelerating sound changes. As Bybee (2010) notes:

A robust finding that has emerged recently in quantitative studies of phonetic reduction is that high-frequency words undergo more change or change at a faster rate than low-frequency words. (Bybee 2010: 20)

Individual forms may likewise exhibit characteristic distributional profiles across languages, reflecting differences in paradigm size, syntactic construction inventories, and general patterns of use. Hence the principal parts of a morphological system will, in effect, emerge from the language model that a speaker constructs based on frequency and patterns of co-occurrence. As discussed in greater detail in Chapter 7, the task of 'choosing' principal parts is one that arises in describing languages, rather than in acquiring and using them. A formal reconstruction of a classical WP model should provide an effective means of measuring the mutual information between forms. This measure should identify fully diagnostic forms (and sets of forms). But the task of 'justifying' the choice of 'correct' principal parts is essentially a pseudo-problem that reflects pedagogical idealizations about 'compact' grammatical descriptions.

From a classical WP perspective, one can also see stem-based descriptions of inflection systems as something of a pseudo-solution to this pseudo-problem. Representing lexical items by stems or stem sets avoids the need to select particular

---

[22] The diagnostic value of the 3pl is reinforced by the fact that it also predicts other present forms, notably the present Active participle, discussed in Section 5.1.

forms that display the stems. In the simpler Russian nouns in Section 4.1, the isolation of stems removes diagnostic endings. In verbs, the distinctive stem vowels and consonantal variation occur inside inflections, so stems retain information about class membership. For single-stem verbs like DELAT' and GOVORIT', one stem form can both identify class and also underlie the full set of inflected forms.[23] However, the stems of multiple-stem verbs must be associated with appropriate sets of forms. Hence a stem-based description replaces the problem of principal part selection by a problem of stem selection. As in the description of Russian conjugations, the class-specific (or subclass-specific) distribution stems can be expressed by indexical features that associate stems and endings with paradigm cells or inflected forms.

Stem selection principles might appear to be less stipulative than the diacritic class features introduced to associate nouns and case endings. In particular, the fact that variation occurs within present and past series might suggest the possibility of keying selection to tense features of a stem. However, this idea rests on a pervasive overinterpretation of morphological terms. Although series are conventionally assigned morphosyntactic labels, such as 'past', 'aorist', 'perfect', etc., the forms in a series often share a common base rather than a set of grammatical properties. In Russian, the past and present series both contain nonfinite as well as finite members. The past series in Table 4.14 contains the infinitive and past participle; the extension of the present series in Table 5.1 adds the present participle. Hence the familiar designations 'past' or 'present' participle register the fact that these forms are based on the same stems that underlie the past and present paradigms, and do not reflect tense features that could regulate the distribution of the stems.

4.3.3 Contrastive distribution

In classical WP terms, series are FORM CLASSES, defined in terms of patterns of mutual implication rather than in terms of common morphosyntactic features or shared derivations. The same type of analogical deduction that allows speakers to predict new forms of a paradigm from an encountered form applies within a larger inflectional series. The predictive value of series is further enhanced by the fact that members of different series often occur in distributionally-matched 'minimal pairs'. In Russian, the contrast between nearly any pair of forms from the present and past series identifies class. The contrast between the present and past indicative forms is particularly useful, given that contrasting pairs have overlapping distributions. For example, a syntactic context that contains a 3pl nominative subject defines a 'diagnostic frame' since any pair of past and present indicative forms of a given verb that can occur in construction with this subject identify the class of the verb.

The more intricate an inflection class system is, the more useful these types of diagnostic pairs and contexts are. Estonian conjugations contain at least three minimally contrasting pairs that identify class. The system is organized along

---

[23] Though as Timberlake (2004: 98) notes, even regular verbs have contrasting present and past stems. For example, the past stem of DELAT', *dela*, ends in a vowel, whereas the present stem, *delaj*, ends in a glide that triggers palatalization in Table 4.13.

TABLE 4.16   Conjugational classes and series in Estonian (Viks 1992: 52)

	I ('Weakening')	II ('Strengthening')	III ('Invariant')	
Infinitive	õppida	hüpata	elada	'tarbida
Supine	õppima	hüppama	elama	'tarbima
Pres Indic (1sg)	õpin	hüppan	elan	'tarbin
	'to study'	'to jump'	'to live'	'to consume'

TABLE 4.17   Members of conjugational series in Estonian (Viks 1992; Blevins 2007)

Series	Diagnostic minimal pairs				Additional forms
Infinitive	Infinitive	2pl Imp	—	Past Prtl	(Gerund, Jussive)
Present	—	2sg Imp	Pres Indic	—	(Pres Cond)
Supine	Supine	—	Past Indic	Pres Prtl	(Evidential)

two dimensions into three conjugations and four series. The conjugations are distinguished by characteristic stem alternations across the series, rather than by patterns of affixal variation. The first (or 'weakening') conjugation is based on a strong stem in the infinitive and supine series and a weak stem in the present series. The second (or 'strengthening') conjugation is weak in the infinitive series and strong in the present and supine series. The 'third' conjugation contains non-alternating verbs. These verbs may be based either on a 'short' (Q1) stem, as in the case of ELAMA, or on an overlong (Q3) stem, as in the case of TARBIDA.[24] It is the fact that the stems of overlong third conjugation verbs are of the same Q3 length as the strong stems of alternating verbs that entails that a Q3 form (or a pair of Q3 forms) is not diagnostic of class. The stem patterns that define each conjugation are exhibited in Table 4.16.

The three alternating series are represented by the infinitive, present indicative and supine forms in Table 4.16.[25] Further members of each series are listed in Table 4.17, aligned to highlight matched pairs. The contrastive value of these pairs derives from the fact that stem grade is constant throughout a series. Hence any member of a series identifies the grade of that series and each pair exhibits a grade contrast that at least partially identifies class.

Three salient contrasts are set out in Table 4.18. The contrast between 2sg and 2pl imperatives is perfectly diagnostic. If the 2sg form is weak and the 2pl form is strong, the verb belongs to the first conjugation. If the 2sg form is strong and the 2pl form is weak, the verb belongs to the second conjugation. If both are based on a single stem, the verb belongs to the third conjugation.

The other constrasts are diagnostic except when both members of the pair are Q3. The contrast between present and past indicatives is reminiscent of but less informative than the alternation in Russian. If the present indicative

[24] Since the non-alternating Q3 is not marked othographically in the forms of TARBIDA, it is conventional to mark length by a preceding open quotation mark.

[25] The fourth, Impersonal, series, is always weak in the first and second conjugation.

TABLE 4.18   Diagnostic conjugation contrasts in Estonian (Viks 1992; Blevins 2007)

	Imperative		Indicative		Infinitival	
	2sg	2pl	Pres	Past	Infinitive	Supine
I	õpi	õppige	õpin	õppisin	õppida	õppima
II	hüppa	hüpake	hüppan	hüppasin	hüpata	hüppama
III	ela	elage	elan	elasin	elada	elama
III	'tarbi	'tarbige	'tarbin	'tarbisin	'tarbida	'tarbima

is weak and the past is strong, the verb belongs to the first conjugation. If neither form is Q3, the verb belongs to the third conjugation. If both forms are Q3, the verb may belong either to the second or third conjugation. The final, infinitival, pattern involves forms with complementary rather than overlapping distribution. Infinitival complements in Estonian take one of two forms, the supine (or *ma*-infinitive) and the infinitive (or *da*-infinitive). Although the supine has more of a default status, both forms can be governed, and speakers must know both. If the infinitive of a verb is weak and the supine is strong, the verb belongs to the second declension. If neither form is Q3, the verb belongs to the third declension. Ambiguity arises again if both forms are overlong (Q3), since the verb may belong either to the first or the third conjugation.

Participles from different series and other pairs of forms may also be of use in identifying class. But a consideration of the pairs in Table 4.18 should suffice to show that the lack of morphosyntactic coherence in series is not noise but can be of diagnostic value. The 2sg and 2pl Imperatives have more in common with each other morphosyntactically than they do with members of their inflectional series, and the same is even more true of the infinitive and supine. In both cases, common morphosyntactic properties will determine similar syntagmatic distributions. Yet because the members of these pairs belong to distinct series, the distributional patterns will not be associated with series (or subseries) but will define diagnostic frames in which series-level stem alternations can identify the class of a verb. This diagnostic pattern depends on morphosyntactically similar forms being distributed across series in Estonian, and would be sacrificed if the series were morphosyntactically coherent.

4.4 Pedagogical idealizations

The classical factorization of inflectional systems into principal parts and exemplary paradigms embodies a strong hypothesis about the interdependency of forms in a paradigm. A language whose paradigms consisted entirely of mutually independent forms could not be broken down in this way, since no set of forms smaller than a full paradigm would identify the class of an item. Matthews' observation that predictive relations prevent alternations from becoming too 'numerous' on p. 80 is a traditional formulation of what have come to be known as 'paradigm economy' effects.[26] A 'principal parts and exemplary paradigms' description of a language with weakly interdependent forms would likewise achieve negligible economy and indeed obscure the patterns in the language within a large and unilluminating collection of paradigms that 'multiplied out' the unconstrained co-occurrence possibilities. Hence patterns of mutual implication in a system must be fairly tight in order for classical factorizations to simplify rather than complicate the description of the system. Implicational relations between the forms of a lexeme play a similar role in constraining the size of the principal part inventories required to describe conjugational systems comprising multiple paradigms and series.

At the same time, it is important to recognize that the interpretation of familiar notions such as 'paradigm' and 'principal part' taken over from pedagogical and reference grammars is strongly coloured by the uses to which the notions have been put in descriptive sources. It is usually assumed that inflectional systems can be factored into a discrete number of inflection classes, each represented by the full paradigm of some exemplary member of the class. Principal part inventories are likewise taken to be 'static' in the sense of Finkel and Stump (2007), in that each non-exemplary item of a given class is represented by the same forms or sets of forms, e.g., the nominative singular or first person singular indicative active. The deduction of new forms from exemplary paradigms and principal parts is in turn attributed to the operation of symbolic processes of the kind typically expressed by proportional analogies.

Insofar as these assumptions contribute to the "scientific compactness" so prized by Bloomfield (1933: 238), they play a well-defined role within standard pedagogical and descriptive grammars. But, as with Bloomfieldian notions of 'compactness' and 'concision', these assumptions contribute to the economy and uniformity of a classical WP model when it is interpreted as a template for (usually written) grammatical descriptions. There is no justification for maintaining these kinds of idealizations when, following Robins (1959), classical WP accounts are interpreted as models of the acquisition and use of language by speakers. The contrast between pedagogical and psychological interpretations of WP models is, again, clearly drawn by Hockett (1967):

There would remain this difference: the situation for the student is artificially simplified. He is enabled to operate, in his analogizing, in terms of a neat minimal set of reference paradigms and a fixed point-of-departure set of principal parts. The native user of the language, of course, does not do this. He operates in terms of all sorts of internally stored paradigms, many of them doubtless only partial; and he may first encounter a new basic verb in any of its inflected forms. For the native user, the forms that we have for convenience selected to be our 'principal parts' have no such favored position. They are as likely to be created analogically, as needed, as are any of the other forms. (Hockett 1967: 221)

Unsurprisingly, each of the familiar pedagogical idealizations creates problems for classical WP accounts when these accounts are interpreted as general morpho-logical models. The practice of identifying a single exemplary paradigm for each

---

[26] Paradigm and lexeme economy effects are discussed in more detail in Chapter 7.3.

inflection class of a language, if taken literally, gives rise to the pseudo-problem of selecting 'the' exemplary paradigm for each class. It is of course possible to specify selectional criteria. One could, for example, select the lexeme whose forms had the the highest summed frequency. However, as Hockett (1967) observes in the passage on p. 93 above, the real problem lies in the idealization that speakers must impose a rigid separation of exemplary paradigm and principal part and then find themselves compelled to pick one item as exemplary. Any psychologically plausible WP model would represent classes by families of paradigms that reinforce a pattern. As Hockett once again stresses, there is no reason to assume that the patterns need be represented by full paradigms for each item. Given the suggestive connection between frequency and storage established by Stemberger and MacWhinney (1986) and Bybee (1999, 2010), among others, the split between exemplary and analogized forms is likely to come down to frequency. Exemplary patterns will then be emergent generalizations over partial paradigms, themselves composed of forms that occur above the frequency threshold for storage.

Questions about the number and composition of inflection classes raise analogous issues. Within a pedagogical tradition, there may be broad agreement concerning the approximate number of classes in a language. However, as in the case of agreement regarding the choice of exemplary items, this consensus usually reflects established practices or shared pedagogical goals. Attempts to enumerate the classes of a language confront essentially the same kind of analytic indeterminacy at the paradigm level as attempts to identify 'correct' segmentations at the word level. Just as descriptions of Romance verbs explore the possible space of segmentations into roots, theme vowels and inflections, estimates of the number of declension classes in a language like Estonian vary enormously between sources. At one extreme, Saagpakk (2000) recognizes over 400 types, organized into six classes and Mürk (1997) distributes 260-odd types over eight classes. More conservative estimates are offered by Erelt (2006: 18ff.), who identifies 38 basic 'word types', Viks (1992: 43ff.), who distinguishes 26 nominal 'types', and Erelt et al. (1995: 333), who give twelve basic 'exemplary declensional paradigms'. Karlsson (2006: 476) reports similar variation in descriptions of Finnish.[27]

There is no principled basis for adjudicating between these kinds of divergent estimates because they are merely descriptions at different levels of generality, designed to serve different needs. Again like segmentations, classifications of word forms are not 'more or less correct' in some absolute sense but 'more or less useful' for a particular purpose. The classes are part of a description imposed on a language, not discovered 'in' the language, so that estimates of the number and type of classes can only be evaluated against the intended purposes of the classes. In a grammatical description, prepared for reference or pedagogical purposes, it is clearly useful to adopt a fixed classification scheme. However, this is not a constraint that has any counterpart when classical WP approaches are construed as general morphological models. Native speakers are under no pressure to reach a decision about the precise number of classes in a language, any more than they

---

[27] Finnish declensional patterns and their relevance for measures of inflectional economy are discussed at more length in Chapter 7.3.

are constrained to identify exemplary items. Instead, they are free to analogize over classes and patterns at different levels of specificity in the production or interpretation of novel forms.

The difficulty of motivating the choice of principal parts (or 'leading forms') is the third and most familiar of this group of recalcitrant problems:

One objection to the Priscianic model . . . was that the choice of leading form was inherently arbitrary: the theory creates a problem which it is then unable, or only partly able, to resolve. (Matthews 1972: 74)

The origin of this problem is transparent. For pedagogical purposes, it is clearly useful to draw the most informative cells of a paradigm to the attention of language learners. It is particularly useful to emphasize diagnostic cells that unambiguously identify class. Some theoretical accounts integrate this pedagogical desideratum into a general model of paradigm organization or a morphological acquisition strategy. A consequence of the Paradigm Economy Principle of Carstairs (1983) (discussed in Chapter 7.3) is that every inflection class system will have some maximally allomorphic cell that predicts the variation in the other cells. The Single Base Hypothesis of Albright (2002) likewise constrains the bases available to learners in the course of paradigm acquisition:

The first [hypothesis JPB] is that learners are limited to selecting a single form as the base, and that the base must be a surface form from somewhere within the paradigm. Furthermore, the choice of base is global, meaning that the same slot must serve as the base for all lexical items. (Albright 2002: ix)

However, there is no reason to assume that a single form will always identify the inflectional pattern of an item. And even in systems that contain such a form, there is no guarantee that a speaker will encounter that form first. As Hockett (1967) remarks above "[t]he native user of the language . . . may first encounter a new basic verb in any of its inflected forms". The binary split between principal parts (or cells or bases) and the forms that are deduced from these privileged elements provides a misleadingly idealized description of inflectional systems. Although individual forms vary in informativeness, they vary as a matter of degree, and there are almost always multiple combinations of partially informative forms that identify the other forms of an item.

All of the standard assumptions discussed above are reasonably well motivated in the pedagogical or descriptive contexts in which they arose. The assumptions only become problematic when classical WP accounts are reinterpreted as general morphological models. Those assumptions with natural counterparts in a general model will be susceptible to explicit analysis. In particular, the problem of principal part selection can be subsumed under the more general problem of measuring relative informativeness. This problem can be approached using information-theoretic notions of uncertainty and uncertainty reduction to model the interdependence of paradigm cells, as discussed in Chapter 7. Familiar principal parts will correspond to cells that eliminate all (or nearly all) uncertainty, but they just represent limiting cases. The same formal measures identify cells that reduce uncertainty about a subset of other cells, as well as sets of cells that are collectively diagnostic.

Moreover, just as the classical WP model is defined primarily by implicational relations, and only secondarily by specific units of analysis ('words' and 'paradigms'), the structure of an inflectional system will be modelled by networks of implications, expressed in terms of uncertainty reduction. One type of implication holds between cells and patterns of exponence. A second type holds between pairs (or clusters) of cells.[28] An inflection class in the broad sense is defined by any mutually consistent set of inflectional implications. Standard classes will again be definable as limiting cases, corresponding to maximally specific sets of implications. Reconstructing notions like 'principal part' and 'inflection class' in terms of implicational relations thus preserves the central role of these notions. However, this interpretation jettisons the pedagogical baggage that these notions had acquired and highlights the fact that they are part of a classification scheme and not elements in a language.

Extracting pedagogical idealizations from notions like 'paradigm' and 'inflection class' addresses some reservations about the relevance of these notions to a general model of morphology. Within the Post-Bloomfieldian tradition, there are also avowedly 'atomistic' approaches that entirely reject the classical notion of morphological 'units' consisting of collections of forms. In much the same way that classical models lack counterparts of morphemes, these approaches tend to regard paradigms as 'descriptive artifacts' or 'epihenomena'.[29] Yet this assessment of paradigms is itself largely an artifact of a method of analysis. By reducing words to inventories of stems, exponents and combinatory rules, radically constructivist models disrupt any morphological relations that hold across larger networks of words. To the extent that those relations are preserved at all, they are encapsulated in the system of rules and constraints employed to construct words from smaller parts. Relations between these 'outputs' can only be expressed in terms of relations between their parts or between the derivations that combined them. The claim that paradigms have no "theoretical significance" thus makes a virtue of necessity.

The descriptive cost of this theoretical virtue is described in a preliminary way in this chapter and elaborated in more detail in those that follow.

---

[28] These relations are most familiar as 'rules' that define the formal 'spell-out' of features in the realizational models in Chapter 6. However, as discussed in Chapter 7 the same relations can also be interpreted as constraints that are satisfied (or not, as the case may be) by pairs consisting of paradigm cells and full word forms.

[29] From the perspective adopted by Müller (2002: 113), "the notion of paradigm emerges as an epiphenomenon without theoretical significance".

5

Analogy

Within a classical WP model, words not only function as basic lexical units but also play a pivotal role in what is often termed 'the creative use of language'. The description of principal parts in Hale and Buck (1903), summarized in Section 4.3.2, sets out how the information expressed by exemplary paradigms and principal parts is combined to define novel forms.[1] The special status of an exemplary paradigm lies in the fact that it exhibits general patterns of inflection. A set of principal parts contributes item-specific word forms. Matching the principal parts of an item against cells of an exemplary paradigm establishes a correspondence between principal parts and their counterparts in the exemplary paradigm. New forms are then deduced by generalizing this correspondence analogically to cells whose forms have not been encountered.

In contemporary grammatical models, the relevance of analogy is usually taken to be confined to pedagogical and historical contexts. To the extent that analogy is invoked in synchronic processes, its application is restricted to 'local' generalizations that run counter to more general rule-governed patterns. However, from a classical WP perspective, analogy guides language acquisition, use and development. Although analogy figures in one of the earliest recorded linguistic debates, the analogy vs anomaly controversy of classical antiquity, it is in the Neogrammarian period that analogy is most explicitly associated with creative and productive language use. The role of analogy in the acquisition and use of morphology is forcefully expressed by Paul (1920):

The creative activity of the individual is also very considerable in the domain of word building and even more so in inflection... We see the effect of analogy especially clearly in the grammatical acquisition of inflected forms of a foreign language. One learns a number of paradigms by heart and then memorizes only as many forms of individual words as is necessary to recognize their affiliation to this or that paradigm. Now and then a single form suffices. One forms the remaining forms at the moment that one needs them, in accordance with the paradigm, that is, by analogy.[2] (Paul 1920: 112)

---

[1] Here and below, 'novel forms' refers to unencountered forms, not neologisms.
[2] Sehr bedeutend ist die schöpferische Tätigkeit des Individuums aber auch auf dem Gebiete der Wortbildung und noch mehr auf dem der Flexion... Besonders klar sehen wir die Wirkungen der Analogie bei der grammatischen Aneignung der Flexionsformen einer fremden Sprache. Man lernt eine Anzahl von Paradigmen auswendig und prägt sich dann von den einzelnen Wörtern nur soviel Formen ein, als erforderlich sind, um die Zugehörigkeit zu diesem oder jenem Paradigma zu erkennen. Mitunter genügt dazu eine einzige. Die übrigen Formen bildet man in dem Augenblicke, wo man ihrer bedarf, nach dem Paradigma, d.h. nach Analogie.

Word and Paradigm Morphology. First edition. James P. Blevins

A similar outlook is expressed by Hockett (1967: 221) when he imputes "a net gain in realism" to "the student of the language" who "would now be required to produce new forms in exactly the way the native user of the language produces or recognizes them—by analogy". Matthews (1991) likewise illustrates the process of analogical generalization with reference to the inflection of the Latin nouns DOMINUS 'master' and SERVUS 'slave':

In effect, we are predicting the inflections of *servus* by analogy with those of *dominus*. As Genitive Singular *domini* is to Nominative Singular *dominus*, so *x* (unknown) must be to Nominative Singular *servus*. What then is *x*? Answer: it must be *servi*. In notation, *dominus* : *domini* = *servus* : *servi*. (Matthews 1991: 192f.)

In the continuation of this passage, he echoes Paul's position in attributing the celebrated 'U-shaped learning curve' to the effects of analogy:

Analogy is an important concept in linguistic theory. It plays a major role in morphological change, as we have noted earlier. It also forms a large part of the process by which children learn their native language. One of the most banal and often repeated observations of children's speech concerns the extension of regular inflectional patterns (English *-ed, -s,* and so on) as analogical replacements ... It is hardly surprising that traditional language teaching has made use of the same instinct. (Matthews 1991: 192f.)

Processes of analogical extension are implicit in earlier discussions of the use of partitive singulars to deduce novel forms of Estonian nouns or the use of nominative singulars to determine the novel forms of Russian nouns. Similar principles underlie the use of conjugation tables to exhibit patterns of verb inflection. Verbs in Russian, Estonian and Latin have larger paradigms and larger principal part inventories, but the processes remain the same.

The deduction of forms from exemplary patterns is standardly formalized in terms of what are known as PROPORTIONAL ANALOGIES. The canonical format is a 'four-part analogy' of the form $a : b = c : X$, in which a, b and c are all given, and the analogical step involves 'solving for X'.[3] Matthews' deduction of *servi* in the passage directly above illustrates the form and application of four-part analogies. As this passage clarifies, the apparent simplicity of the traditional formulation rests on tacit assumptions about the terms it contains. The antecedent terms a and b do not represent simple forms, but instantiated cells in an exemplary paradigm, ⟨[NOM,SG], *dominus*⟩ : ⟨[GEN,SG], *domini*⟩ in Matthews' example. The relation between these instantiated cells provides a model for generalizing from a principal part c, here ⟨[NOM,SG], *servus*⟩, to the form X in the corresponding instantiated cell ⟨[GEN,SG], X⟩ in the paradigm of SERVUS. These interpretations are unpacked in (5.1), in which F and G represent feature bundles and ϕ, ϕ', ψ and ψ' represent forms.[4]

---

[3] Although proportional analogies are often associated with Paul (1920), Morpurgo Davies (1978: 46) notes that they appear slightly earlier in the work of Paul's contemporaries.

[4] The antecedents a and b are usually drawn from the same exemplary paradigm, but this reflects a use of four-part analogies rather than a property of the format.

(5.1)   Interpretation of terms in traditional four-part analogy

$$a \quad : \quad b \quad = \quad c \quad : \quad X$$
$$\langle F, \phi \rangle \quad : \quad \langle G, \phi' \rangle \quad = \quad \langle F, \psi \rangle \quad : \quad \langle G, \psi' \rangle$$

Four-part analogies represent the smallest proportional deduction, as at least three known forms are needed to identify a fourth. The exemplary forms a and b exhibit a pattern, which is extended from the principal part c to the unknown form X. Without both a and b, there is no pattern to extend, and without c no base for the extension. A deduction may also specify more than two exemplary forms when any single form matches multiple patterns. Paul (1920: 107) gives triples such as *Tag* : *Tages* : *Tage* = *Arm* : *Armes* : *Arme* to illustrate proportions between case forms of the German nouns 'day' and 'arm'.

As a member of the last generation of linguists to be trained in the Neogrammarian tradition, Bloomfield retained a notion of regular analogy, which he also accorded a central role in the creative use of language:

A grammatical pattern (sentence-type, construction or substitution) is often called an ANALOGY. A regular analogy permits a speaker to utter speech-forms which he has not heard; we say that he utters them ON THE ANALOGY OF similar forms which he has heard. (Bloomfield 1933: 275)

It is only during the Post-Bloomfieldian period that analogy came to be reinterpreted as a minor process governing idiosyncratic deviations from productive patterns based on superficial similarities. Chomsky (1975) contains a blanket dismissal of familiar analogical processes, including "inductive procedures, methods of abstraction, analogy and analogical synthesis, generalization and the like" on the grounds that "the fundamental inadequacy of these suggestions is obscured only by their unclarity" (Chomsky 1975: 31). Chomsky's assessment of analogy, and the motives of those who invoked this notion, become more scathing over time, as objections to "inadequacy" and "unclarity" gave way to charges of outright "misleading" equivocation:

Suppose one were to argue that the knowledge of possible words is derived "by analogy". The explanation is empty until an account is given of this notion. If we attempt to develop a concept of "analogy" that will account for these facts, we will discover that we are building into this notion the rules and principles of sound structure. There is no general notion of "analogy" that applies to these and other cases. Rather, the term is being used, in an extremely misleading way, to refer to the properties of particular subsystems of our knowledge, entirely different properties in different cases. (Chomsky 1988: 26f.)

The idea that analogy amounts at best to an imprecise proxy for generative rules is expressed more directly by Kiparsky (1975: 75) when he claims that "generative phonology argues that at the point where the analogies begin to make the right generalizations, they are indistinguishable from rules". Following a discussion of processes of analogical levelling and extension, Haspelmath (2002: 56) likewise concludes that "the solution of an analogical equation is practically the same as the application of a word-based rule to a novel word". Generalizing this point to express a consensus that spans the Chomskyan tradition and extends to some degree beyond it, Haspelmath (2002: 103) goes on to suggest that "some morphologists have concluded . . . that morphological analogy and morphological rules are really one and the same thing".

5.1 No segmentation without representation?

To make this issue more concrete, let us return to the proportion discussed by Matthews (1991: 192f), repeated in (5.2), with the deduced form in italics.

(5.2)   Analogical deduction of Latin case forms
        dominus : domini = servus : *servi*

It is easy to see why the pattern matching and pattern extension involved in this deduction can be interpreted as tacitly introducing the same elements that would be combined in a rule-based analysis. The analogical principles that yield the solution *servi* implicitly recognize the noun stems *domin* and *serv*, along with the case inflections *-us* and *-i*. Analogical extensions of the Russian noun forms in Table 4.1 likewise operate over the stems and endings isolated and cross-indexed in Table 4.2. Hence in these cases, analogical deductions appear to achieve much the same result that would be obtained if word forms were built by rules that combined lexical stems and inflectional exponents.

Yet there is an essential difference between the STATUS of sub-word forms in analogies and in analyses that build words from smaller parts. A pair of exemplary cells *a* and *b* may consist of a common stem and distinct inflections, as in (5.2). But *a* and *b* may exhibit ANY pattern that can be extended to another pair of forms. Proportional analogies thus apply to cases in which a principled stem-exponent segmentation is difficult to motivate, to cases in which segments do not correspond to general units in a language or in which segments cannot be assigned a consistent morphosyntactic analysis.

This flexibility derives from the morphotactic agnosticism of a classical WP implicational model, which in turn reflects an emphasis on relations rather than on units of analysis. As Morpurgo Davies (1998: 258f.) puts it, proportional analogies "offered an algorithm for a structurally based form of morphological segmentation, without making any claims about the segments in question". Because analogical principles deduce rather than build novel forms, they can exploit any predictive patterns, without attaching grammatical significance to the segmentations that are of predictive value. Distinct proportions that extend different patterns need not even impose consistent segmentations. The structural agnosticism of proportional analogies addresses the concerns expressed by Lounsbury (1953) on p. 4 in cases where "comparison of forms suggests one placement, while another comparison suggests another".

The inflectional systems in preceding sections exhibit a variety of patterns that bring out the differences between deductive analogy and constructive rule application. One correspondence involving Russian participles is stated below:

A convenient way of forming this [present active JPB] participle is by replacing the final [-*t*] of the 3rd pers. pl. by the ending [-*ščij*] (Unbegaun 1957: 169)

The present active participle is formed by replacing the final [-*t*] of the third-person plural of the present tense by the endings [-*ščij*] (Wade 1992: 361)

Another frequently-noted correspondence between present and participial forms holds between the 1pl present and the imperfect passive participle:

A convenient way of forming this [imperfective passive] participle is by adding the adjectival ending [-*yj*] to the 1st pers. pl ... (Unbegaun 1957: 170)

The imperfective passive participle is formed by adding adjectival endings to the first-person plural of an imperfective TRANSITIVE verb ... (Wade 1992: 364)

Like many of the principles stated in descriptive grammars, these correspondences are explicitly 'Priscianic' (Matthews 1972), directly relating two surface word forms. Since the patterns apply across conjugation classes, nearly any verb can define the antecedents for a valid analogy. The proportions in (5.3) use the relation between forms of the exemplary verb GOVORIT' 'speak' as a model for the deduction of the italicized forms of VIDET' 'see'. The correspondence between 3pl forms and present active participles is expressed in (5.3a); the relation between 1pl forms and imperfective passive participles in (5.3b).

(5.3)   Analogical deduction of Russian participles
    a. govorjat : govorjaščij = vidjat : *vidjaščij*
    b. govorim : govorimyj = vidim : *vidimyj*

As with Matthews' original example, these proportions adopt a convenient short-hand that suppresses the features associated with terms. Each term in a proportion is a 'word' in the sense of "a form which may be uttered alone (with meaning)" (Bloomfield 1926: 156). Hence *govorjat* is not a simple form but is implicitly associated with the 3pl cell of the present indicative paradigm of the verb GOVORIT'. The other terms have similar grammatical meanings.

The simple patterns described by the deductions in (5.3) can of course be expressed by word-building rules that combine stems and exponents. However, when we examine the rules we find that they largely mimic analogical deductions in ways that are alien to the normal operation of rule systems.

It might seem that the present active participle forms in (5.3a) could be built by adding a participial ending to the consonant-final "present-future stem" (Wade 1992: 228) that underlies the present conjugational series. On this analysis, the ending -*aščij* would be added to the stems *govor*, *vid* and *smotr* in Table 5.1. But this analysis would fail to apply correctly to the forms *delajuščij*, *iščuščij* and *moguščij*, which contain the vowel *u* (instead of *a*). A general rule-based analysis must then add the consonant-initial ending -*ščij* to vocalic stems WHICH PRESERVE THE VOWEL OF THE 3PL PRESENT FORM. Hence, extending a rule-based description to the patterns in (5.3a) is possible, but only at the cost of recognizing an extra vocalic variant of the "present-future" stem.

TABLE 5.1   Present active participle formation in Russian (Unbegaun 1957: 169f.)

3pl	delajut	iščut	mogut	govorjat	smotrjat	vidjat
	delajuščij	iščuščij	moguščij	govorjavščij	smotrjaščij	vidjaščij

TABLE 5.2   Imperfect passive participle formation in Russian (Unbegaun 1957: 170)

1pl	delaem	iščem	možem	govorim	smotrim	vidim
	delaemyj	iščemyj	možemyj	govorimyj	smotrimyj	vidimyj

A rule-based strategy can, again in principle, be applied to the pattern in Table 5.2 but here the choice of 'stem' is even more problematic. The base for the imperfect passive participle differs from the present-future stem in forms like *možemyj*, which exhibit consonant mutations that distinguish them from the basic stem *mog*. The base also differs from the "infinitive-preterite" stem (Wade 1992: 228) in forms like *iščem*, which contrast with past-infinitive forms based on the unmutated *isk(a)*. The final vowel also varies across verbs, and contrasts with the vowel in the present active participles. In short, there is no form that provides a better base for the imperfect passive participle than "the first-person plural of an imperfective transitive verb" (Wade 1992: 364).

A rule-based analysis can avoid a direct relation between the present forms and participles in Tables 5.1 and 5.2 by positing abstract stems that underlie both pairs of forms. But it is unclear that these stems serve any real purpose other than avoiding a direct relation between word forms. Within a model of morphological analysis that is committed to constructing words from smaller units, the avoidance of word-level correspondences may be regarded as a goal worth pursuing for its own sake. However, this strategy has a range of consequences for a rule-based account. As discussed above, one immediate effect is the expansion of the stem inventory and/or an increase in affixal ambiguity.

More subversive is the effect on the INTERPRETATION of these components. A rule-based analysis of *delaemyj* must either treat *delaem* as realizing 1pl in some contexts and as an uninflected stem in others, or it must assign this context-dependent interpretation to a subsequence that includes at least *-em*. Parallel remarks apply to forms like *delajuščij*. Each of the choices available to a rule-based analysis represents a retreat from a model in which forms are assigned stable segmentations into recurrent units with fixed grammatical interpretations. Instead, the use of stem allomorphy and affixal ambiguity in rule-based account introduces, to paraphrase Morpurgo Davies (1998: 258f.), 'a structurally based form of morphological segmentation, without making any CONTEXT-INDEPENDENT claims about the segments in question'.

In sum, to the extent that "analogies . . . are indistinguishable from rules" (Kiparsky 1975: 75), this merely reflects the fact that generative rule systems are powerful enough to mimic the effects of proportional analogies. Reencoding analogies by rules that invoke stem allomorphy and affixal ambiguity does not of course show that the original analogies tacitly incorporate "the rules and principles of sound structures" (Chomsky 1988: 26). Instead, this analysis illustrates how morphotactically agnostic proportions can be recast in terms of rules if there are no constraints on the abstractness or ambiguity of units.

5.2 Morphomic stem syncretism

Part of the explanation for the contemporary neglect of analogy lies in the selective coverage of theoretical studies. Since Bloomfield's time, the goal of comprehensive or even broad coverage has receded to the point that linguistic theories are justified in ignoring analogical patterns that challenge their analytical assumptions. This serves to reinforce the impression that such patterns are infrequent or marginal and somehow fall outside 'core grammar'. For a more accurate assessment of the prevalence and status of these types of patterns one can, however, turn to linguistic traditions that retain a commitment to broad coverage. One pattern that has attracted philological, pedagogical and theoretical attention concerns the 'supine' stem in Latin. Gildersleeve and Lodge (1895: 71) provides a standard description of the relation between the supine, the past passive participle and future active participle:

From the Supine stem as obtained by dropping final -m of the Supine, form
a. PERF. PART. PASSIVE by adding -*s*.
b. FUT. PART. ACTIVE by adding -*rus* (preceding *u* being lengthened to *ū*).

The regularity of this pattern is illustrated in Table 5.3, which isolates the supine stem in forms of the exemplary Latin verbs from Table 4.12.

As Matthews (1972) notes, this analysis is formulated, in almost identical terms, in the grammar of Priscian:

Priscian's rule would actually derive the Nominative Singular Masculine . . . by the addition of *rus* to the *u:* form of the 'Supine' and would moreover be limited to verbs in which the 'Supine' is not deficient . . . (Matthews 1972: 85)

Matthews's own statements of this pattern differ only in treating *r* as a stem formative rather than as part of the future active participle ending:

TABLE 5.3   Analysis of Latin supine stems (Gildersleeve and Lodge 1895)

Verb	Supine	Past Pass Prtl	Fut Act Prtl	Gloss
AMŌ	amātu-m	amātu-s	amātū-rus	'to love'
MONEŌ	monitu-m	monitu-s	monitū-rus	'to advise'
TEGŌ	tēctu-m	tēctu-s	tēctū-rus	'to cover'
CAPIŌ	captu-m	captu-s	captū-rus	'to take'
AUDIŌ	audītu-m	audītu-s	audītū-rus	'to hear'

The stem of the Future Participle is derived from the stem of the Past Participle by the suffixation of *u:r* [orthographic *ūr* JPB]. (Matthews 1972: 86)

There are a few exceptions; but, in general, if the stem of the Past Participle is *x*, no matter how irregular it may be, that of the Future Participle is *x* with *-ūr-* added. (Matthews 1991: 200)

These formulations determine the segmentations in Table 5.4, which depart from those in Table 5.3 in assigning uniform participial endings in *-us*.

The theoretical interest in this pattern resides in the fact that the common stem in the supine series does not make any consistent morphosyntactic contribution to the forms it underlies. The challenge that this poses for a model of morphemic analysis is set out clearly as early as Matthews (1965):

But in *monitūrus*, etc. the case is not so simple. Preceding the segment *ūr* (which can clearly be assigned to FU [the Future Active Participle JPB]) one finds precisely those segments which in *monitus*, etc. were assigned to PA [the Past Passive Participle JPB]: each form, apparently, includes the allomorph of a morpheme which is absent from its syntactic analysis! (Matthews 1965: 143)

The supine stem represents a complex case of recurrent but non-redundant structure. Like the simpler Russian and Estonian patterns in Chapter 4.1, separating out the stem from the forms in which it occurs leads to 'overextraction', the isolation of a recurrent 'unit of form' that has no fixed meaning or function in isolation. The difficulties raised by overextraction cannot be overcome by further division. Analyses like those in Table 5.5 merely push the problem down a level. As Matthews (1972: 83) notes, "*ūr* could be handled as a quite unproblematic allomorph of Future Participle". "But", as he then asks, "what morpheme would the *t* or *s* [in *lāpsūra* JPB] then belong to?".

TABLE 5.4   Forms based on the supine stem (Matthews 1991: 200)

Verb	Supine	Past Pass Prtl	Fut Act Prtl	Gloss
AMŌ	amāt-um	amāt-us	amātūr-us	'to love'
MONEŌ	monit-um	monit-us	monitūr-us	'to advise'
TEGŌ	tēct-um	tēct-us	tēctūr-us	'to cover'
CAPIŌ	capt-um	capt-us	captūr-us	'to take'
AUDIŌ	audīt-um	audīt-us	audītūr-us	'to hear'

TABLE 5.5   Morphomic structure of Latin *monitus* and *monitūrus*

	Root	Theme Vowel	?	Fut	Masc Nom Sg
Past Pass Prtl	mon	i	t	—	us
Fut Act Prtl				ūr	

In short, the supine stem cannot be associated with properties that either make a consistent contribution to the meaning of the forms in which it occurs or determine its distribution in those forms—rather than in other forms—of an item. Recurrent 'units of form' that cannot be associated with consistent 'units of meaning' have come to be known as MORPHOMES. The term originates with Aronoff (1994), who initially applies it to 'purely morphological' functions that mediate between morphosyntactic properties and phonological form:

Let us call the level of such purely morphological functions MORPHOMIC and the functions themselves MORPHOMES. What is novel about this level, and what warrants giving it a special name, is that it embodies an empirical claim: the mapping from morphosyntax to phonological realization is not direct but rather passes through an intermediate level. (Aronoff 1994: 25)

In the continuation of this passage, Aronoff acknowledges that an intermediary level is only motivated in cases where the mapping between morphosyntax and phonology is indirect. Hence, although "all . . . mappings technically involve morphomes", whether direct or indirect, "it is morphomes like F$_{en}$ [which maps Perfect and Passive onto the same participial form in English JPB] that truly earn their name" (25). In his subsequent description of Latin conjugational stems, Aronoff (1994) construes 'morphomic' as 'non-morphemic', and even as "abstract and unmotivated morphological machinery":

On the other hand, unlike morphosyntactic entities, they do not directly reflect the semantic or syntactic system. Instead they are morphomes, part of the abstract and unmotivated morphological machinery of the language. In this respect, stems are much closer to theme vowels than to more orthodox affixal markers of morphosyntactic properties. (Aronoff 1994: 58)

From a Post-Bloomfieldian standpoint, a negative characterization of 'morphomes' is entirely apt. If morphemic relations can be taken to be normative, morphomic patterns will seem like noise. But from a classical WP point of view, classifying morphomes as "part of the abstract and unmotivated morphological machinery of the language" concedes too much. Categorizing patterns as 'non-morphemic' is informative only if morphemic patterns do, in fact, enjoy some privileged status. Not only is this far from established, but, as discussed in Chapter 2.4.1, it is unclear that contemporary notions of 'morpheme' are of any classificatory value. Even in their heyday, morphemic models never represented more than an extreme and programmatic approach to morphological analysis. Hence the justification for singling out morphomic patterns must rest on a positive characterization of their function or distribution.

An obvious candidate is their predictive value. The systematic character of morphomic patterns makes one member in a morphomic relation a reliable predictor of another. This is precisely the role that morphomic patterns play in classical and pedagogical grammars. Moreover, this practical conception can be extended naturally to a more general theoretical position. If one takes predictability to be the fundamental relation that binds together the elements of a morphological system, then morphomic patterns can be interpreted in terms of predictive relations and morphomes defined as 'recurrent units of predictive value'. Morphemic relations, where they exist, can be construed as limiting cases in which the predictive value of a pattern derives from or is enhanced by a stable feature-form correspondence. Morphomic patterns are then of interest not because they fail to exhibit this simple feature-form correspondence but because they provide a pure expression of predictive relations.

5.2.1 Priscianic deduction

Indeed, if we return to classical and philological treatments of morphomic patterns, we find that they are not characterized as 'units of pure form', but as something more akin to 'units of predictive value'. This perspective is fully explicit in Matthews (1972), in which the reference to "knowledge" of form variation anticipates the information-theoretic proposals in Chapter 7:

What one is saying . . . is that the Future Participle formation is 'parasitic', in a sense on the Past Participle formation: if one 'knows' the latter then one can use this 'knowledge' to derive the former. (Matthews 1972: 86)

Strikingly, when Maiden (2005) summarizes Aronoff's analysis, he formulates it in implicational terms that are largely absent from Aronoff (1994):[5]

The third ['supine'] stem constitutes an allegedly inviolable distributional regularity—what Aronoff terms a MORPHOME—in that its presence in any one member of the specified, idiosyncratic, set of cells, always implies its presence in all of the other members of the set. (Maiden 2005: 137)

The other cases of 'Priscianic' or 'parasitic' syncretism cited by Matthews (1972, 1991) are likewise described in terms of predictive or implicational patterns. The correspondence between present active infinitives and imperfect subjunctives is again expressed as a predictive relation between surface forms:

For any Verb, however irregular it may be in other respects, the Present Infinitive always predicts the Imperfect Subjunctive. For the Verb 'to flower', *flōrere* → *flōrerem*; for the irregular Verb 'to be', *esse* → *essem*, and so forth without exception. (Matthews 1991: 195)

Although Latin (and Romance) stems have attracted particular theoretical attention, similar patterns are found in other languages with rich stem inventories. Both Whitney (1889) and Macdonnell (1927) describe the formation of the perfect active participle in Sanskrit in morphomic terms, as involving the addition of the possessive suffix to the past passive participle:

---

[5] The main implications that Aronoff considers relate syntactic categories and morphological units, as in, for example, the suggestion that "there is indeed a mutual implication between the complex syntactic category Perfect Active and the perfect stem type" (Aronoff 1994: 55f.).

TABLE 5.6   Morphomic structure of Sanskrit
kṛtá and *kṛtávat* (Whitney 1885: 21)

	Root	Past Pass	Poss
Past Pass Prtl	kṛ	tá	—
Perf Act Prtl			vat

From the past passive participle, of whatever formation, is made, by adding the possessive suffix *vant*, a secondary derivative having the meaning and construction of a perfect active participle: for example *tát kṛtávān* 'having done that'; *tám nigīrṇavān* 'having swallowed him down'. Its inflection is like that of other derivatives made with this suffix . . .; its feminine ends in *vatī*; its accent remains on the participle. (Whitney 1889: 344).

By adding the possessive suffix *vat* to the past pass. part., a new form of very common occurrence is made, which has the value of a PERFECT ACTIVE participle;—e.g. *kṛ-tá*, 'done': *kṛtá-vat*, 'having done'. It is generally used as a finite verb, the copula being omitted . . . (Macdonnell 1927: 136).

The participles in Table 5.6 present the same problem as those in Table 5.5. The past passive participle *kṛtá* can be divided into a root and passive exponent *tá*. Neither the participle nor the exponent preserve past or passive features when they occur within the perfect active participle *kṛtávat*. However, they do reliably PREDICT the form of the perfect active participle.[6]

This predictive relation is naturally expressed by proportional analogies. The proportion in (5.4a) licences the deduction of the Latin imperfect subjunctive *essem* from the present infinitive. Proportion (5.4b) sanctions the deduction of the past passive *monitūrus* 'advise' from the future active participle.

(5.4)   Priscianic analogy in Latin conjugations
   a. flōrere : flōrerem = esse : *essem*
   b. amātus : amātūrus = monitus : *monitūrus*
   c. amātum : amātus : amātūrus = monitum : *monitus* : *monitūrus*

The proportion in (5.4c) likewise expresses the full deductive import of the original generalization in Gildersleeve and Lodge (1895: 71). Given an exemplary item that exhibits the three-way dependency, the supine of a new verb sanctions the deduction of both the past passive and future active participle.

Significantly, these analogies do not require that a common meaning be assigned to shared 'units of form' such as *amāt/monit* or *flōrere/esse*. The value of recurrent elements resides in their predictive force, and it is only the full word forms in (5.4) that must be assigned grammatical features. From a classical WP perspective, segmentations are also principally motivated by their predictive value. The

---

[6] Another morphomic correspondence in Sanskrit holds between indicative verbs and active participles. As Whitney (1889: 246) remarks, "the active participle-stem may be made mechanically from the 3rd pl. indic. by dropping *i*".

proportion in (5.4a) predicts the future active participle form *monitūrus*, irrespective of whether *-r-* is grouped with the stem or ending.

Bases such as *flōrere*, *amāt* and *kṛtá* are all clearly 'morphomic' in the sense of Aronoff (1994). But in this respect they are not fundamentally different from the stems in any other proportional analogy. The exemplary forms and principal parts in a proportional analogy are associated with the features of a paradigm cell (or 'morphosyntactic representation'). However, there is no kind of 'derivational' relation between these features. Instead, they serve solely to locate co-varying forms within exemplary paradigms and to match principal parts against exemplary forms. Because the proportional format imposes no analysis below the word level, it can exploit the predictive value of the stems in (5.4) without creating the problem of assigning grammatical features to them. In other cases it may be possible to associate properties with stems, just as single morphs may sometimes realize a simple property. However, within a classical WP model, morphemic stems are no more normative morphosyntactically than stems that can stand alone as words are normative morphotactically. Both just represent limiting cases whose isolability is of significance only insofar as it enhances predictions about other forms.

5.2.2 Paradigmatic morphomics

Restoring a traditional predictive interpretation of morphomic patterns also clears away much of the unclarity and confusion that has grown up around the term 'morphome' since it was first introduced in Aronoff (1994). The stem syncretisms described by Matthews (1972, 1991) and Maiden (2005) involve not only patterns, but systematic patterns. Isolated non-morphemic formatives, such as the 'cran' and 'sham' morphs in 'cranberry' and 'shamrock', are not morphomes. Pairs of elements with no discernible connection, such as the agentive and comparative *-er* markers in English, are also not morphomes. A morphomic pattern can, in principle, involve words, parts of words, or even sequences of words. But there must be some paradigmatic connection between these elements, at the level of the paradigm, the lexeme or the family.

The domain over which morphomic patterns apply highlights the function they perform in extending predictive deductions beyond individual paradigms or sub-paradigms to larger collections of forms. This function in turn clarifies why reifying this relation creates the impression of "abstract and unmotivated morphological machinery". One member of a pair or cluster of interpredictable elements cannot be assigned any interpretation in isolation. Hence attempts to characterize the morphome in terms of a unit or entry ultimately provide a reductio that supports the initial point of departure, namely that the elements in a morphomic relation make no constant substantive morphosyntactic contribution in all of the contexts in which they occur. Like the 'morphophoneme', which, as Hockett (1987: §7) notes, is a theoretical back formation of morphophonemic alternations, the 'morphome' *qua* unit is a back formation of morphomic patterns, obtained by isolating one term in a relation.

5.2.3 Word-based analogy

From a Post-Bloomfieldian perspective, the challenges raised by the participial patterns in Russian, Latin and Sanskrit might still be regarded as consistent with the view that analogy is relevant to marginal constructions occupying the 'periphery' of a language but that the 'core' remains governed by rules of a more conventional sort. It is also possible to deny that morphomic patterns have any real status in the grammar and reanalyze morphomic patterns as instances of simple homophony. In the case of the Latin third stem pattern, the present stem could be treated as a common base for past passive participles in -*t* and future active participles in -*tūr*. On this analysis, there would be no direct relation involving these participles (or the supine).[7] The correspondence between the present infinitive and the imperfect subjunctive could also be regarded as fortuitous, on the grounds that it does not characterize the (regular) alternation between the short -*re* in the infinitive and the long -*rē* in 1pl imperfect subjective *flōrerēmus* and the corresponding 2pl form *flōrerētis*.[8]

Yet the treatment of putatively morphomic patterns as homophony raises a number of general issues. As discussed in Chapter 8.3, genuine homophony appears to be much less common than previously assumed, and is often an artifact of imprecise descriptions. Although it is not possible to investigate sub-phonemic variation in Latin conjugations, it is at least clear that homophony enjoys no distinguished status as a null hypothesis. Moreover, as Maiden (2005: 169) notes, morphomic conjugational patterns in the modern Romance languages appear to be highly resilient, to the point that "speakers can actually pass up golden opportunities to align allomorphs with morphosyntactic properties . . . in favour of the 'morphomic' distribution". More significantly, the question of whether the -*t* in *amātus* is the 'same element' as the -*t* in *amātūrus* or whether the -*re* in *flōrere* is the 'same' as the -*re* in *flōrerem* betrays a residually derivational perspective. For a morphomic analysis, it is the predictability of form variation that is of central importance; whether the variants can be derived from a common historical source is largely immaterial.

Thus these alternatives highlight a latent ambiguity in the description of morphomic 'units'. The reuse of familiar terms like 'stems' may imply a notion akin to a 'shared derivational base'. However, if morphemes are, as suggested in Section 5.2.1, interpreted as units of predictive value, then stems will merely be interpredictable sequences larger than individual formatives. Derivational relations between stems will play no role in a synchronic description but will instead characterize shared historical origins. This 'abstractive' conception of stems is expressed by the definition offered by Robins (1989).

The term *stem* is often specifically to refer to that part of an inflected word less its inflections; stems may therefore be the same in form as roots, or they may consist of root morphemes together with one or more derivational affixes. (Robins 1989: 244)

---

[7] See Blevins (2003) for discussion of a similar choice in West Germanic.
[8] I am grateful to Hans-Heinrich Lieb for pointing out these alternatives.

The availability of homophony-based alternatives also reflects the simplicity of stem syncretisms in Latin. Although the Latin third stem has become a standard example of a morphomic correspondence, more intricate patterns of this type may play a fundamental role within an inflectional system. As recognized in everything from elementary school textbooks to philological studies, the patterns of basic noun and verb inflection in Estonian are irreducibly analogical. Consider the patterns within grammatical case forms, described first in Chapter 4.2. The proportions in (5.5) use the exemplary noun PUKK 'trestle' and principal parts of LUKK 'lock' to exhibit two class-specific patterns.

(5.5)   Analogical deduction of Estonian case forms
    a. pukki : pukkide = lukku : *lukkude*
    b. pukkide : pukkides = lukkude : *lukkudes*

The proportion in (5.5a) expresses a general correspondence between the strong vowel-final partitive singulars *pukki* and *lukku* and the corresponding genitive plurals *pukkide* and *lukkude*. The proportion in (5.5b) in turn expresses an exceptionless correspondence between the genitive plural and the inessive plural, here *pukkides* and *lukkudes*. These patterns raise precisely the same issues as the relation between 1pl forms and imperfect passive participles in Russian. The form *pukki* functions as the partitive singular in isolation and as a case- and number-neutral base in the genitive plural *pukkide*. The form *pukkide* functions likewise as the genitive plural in isolation and as the case-neutral base in inessive *pukides*. Similar analogical patterns apply to other case forms, determining the tight implicational structure of Estonian declensions.

In the Estonian examples, the segmentations are stable, but the interpretation of segments is context-dependent. There is transparent historical motivation for these patterns if, as generally assumed, the semantic case suffixes derive from postpositions that governed the genitive (Grünthal 2003).[9] Once established, the analogical correspondences remain transparent. But a cascade of analogical correspondences in which the inessive plural contains the form of the genitive plural, which in turn contains the form of the partitive singular, is not conducive to analysis in a rule system that builds complex forms out of individually meaningful parts. The letter of a rule-based system can be preserved by treating forms like *pukki* and *pukkide* as abstract stems that take zero partitive singular and genitive plural markers, respectively. But, like the infamous analysis of English verb morphology in Bloch (1947) this analysis ignores the salient morphological variation that identifies forms, and invests all grammatical meaning in nondiscriminative zeros.

The analogies discussed above are typical in deducing novel words, even though the proportional format applies to units of any size. The privileged role of words

---

[9] One reflex of this development is that adjectival modifiers of the most recently grammaticalized cases—the last four in in Table 4.8—still occur in the genitive. Hence in *vanas raamatus* 'in the/an old book' both the noun *raamatus* and the adjective *vanas* occur in the inessive, whereas in *vana raamatuga* 'without the/an old book' the noun *raamatuga* occurs in the comitative but the adjective *vana* retains the historical genitive.

again reflects the fact that, at least in many languages, "[t]he word is a more stable and solid focus of grammatical relations than the component morpheme by itself" (Robins 1959: 128). Proportional analogies exploit two dimensions of this stability. First, words can be assigned a determinate grammatical interpretation that is unaffected by uncertainty about the interpretation of their parts. Second, the word is usually of greater deductive value than any sub-word unit by itself. The reason for this is that the tightest implicational relations hold between paradigm cells, or between cells realized by forms of a particular shape, and it is words (or larger units) that realize cells.

This point can be illustrated by the deduction of infinitive forms in Estonian. As summarized in Table 4.18, Estonian conjugations can be organized into three basic classes, which are identified by a number of minimally contrastive forms. One diagnostic pair is the 2sg familiar and 2pl formal imperative forms. In the first conjugation, the 2sg is weak and the 2pl is strong. The second conjugation inverts this pattern. In the third conjugation there is no alternation. Since a contrast is required to identify class, the deduction of conjugational forms takes the form of the six-part proportions in (5.6). In each triple, the first form is the 2sg imperative, the second is the 2pl imperative and the third is the infinitive. The proportion in (5.6a) uses exemplary forms of first conjugation ÕPPIMA 'to study' to deduce the infinitive of LEPPIMA 'to accept'. The proportion in (5.6b) uses second conjugation HÜPPAMA 'to jump' to deduce the infinitive of LIPPAMA 'to scamper'. The proportion in (5.6c) uses prosodically light third conjugation ELAMA 'to live' to deduce the infinitive of PILAMA 'to laugh at' and (5.6d) uses prosodically heavy third conjugation TARBIMA 'to consume' to deduce the infinitive of MUUTUMA 'to change'.[10]

(5.6)   Deduction of *da*-infinitive forms in Estonian
   a. õpi : õppige : õppida = lepi : leppige : *leppida*
   b. hüppa : hüpake : hüpata = lippa : lipake : *lipata*
   c. ela : elage : elada = pila : pilage : *pilada*
   d. 'tarbi : 'tarbige : 'tarbida = 'muutu : 'muutuge : *'muutuda*

As in the Estonian declensions in Tables 4.3 and 4.5, the forms in (5.6a) and (5.6b) exhibit quantitative grade alternations (which are marked by the contrast between single and double consonants). Also as in the declensions, first and second conjugation verbs have both strong and weak stems: õpi~õppi in first declension ÕPPIMA and hüpa~hüppa for second conjugation HÜPPA. Given this parallelism, no grammatical meaning can be assigned to strong and weak stems in isolation. Moreover, no deductions can be drawn from these stems without knowing their distribution in the paradigm.

As this example shows, the role of words in proportional analogies derives in part from the fact that contrasting pairs of words (strong and weak in this case) may sanction reliable deductions about other forms of an item that cannot be

---

[10] Recall from Chapter 4.3.3 that Estonian contains two infinitival forms: the supine (or *ma*-infinitive) and the infinitive (or *da*-infinitive). The supine functions as the conventional citation form and is strong in both the first and second conjugations.

deduced from the parts of those words that exhibit the alternation. The same logic underlies the applicability of proportional analogies to other types of word-based alternations in which the alternating parts cannot be classified in isolation. Exchange patterns involve oppositions between segments or suprasegmental properties in which the contrasting elements may express either value of the contrast. As Matthews (1991: 199) notes, the contrast between 3sg indicative and subjunctive verbs in Spanish is marked by a process of "vowel reversal". A first conjugation verb such as COMPRAR 'to buy' has the 3sg indicative form *compra* and the subjunctive *compre*. Second conjugation verbs like COMER 'to come' and third conjugation verbs like VIVIR 'to live' invert this pattern, combining a 3sg indicative *come* or *vive* with a subjunctive *coma* or *viva*. Both patterns provide a basis for analogical extension, as the deduction of the 3sg subjunctive forms *hable* 'speak' and *meta* 'put' in (5.7) show.

(5.7)   Exchange patterns in Spanish (Matthews 1991: 199)
      a. compra : compre = habla : *hable*
      b. come : coma = mete : *meta*

It is possible to divide the forms in (5.7) into stems and theme vowels, but not possible to assign a fixed mood value to either part in isolation. Instead, the opposition between forms in -*a* and -*e* is intrinsically relational, mediated by their place in a larger set of forms. As Matthews (1991: 199) concludes:

In reality, it is not the vowels as such that are important. A form in *e* is Subjunctive only if it belongs, as a whole, to the paradigm of a Verb like COMPRAR. A form in *a* is Subjunctive only if it belongs as a whole to the paradigm of a Verb like COMER or VIVIR. (Matthews 1991: 199)

Further examples of exchange patterns have already been encountered in the paradigms described in previous chapters. The alternation between the partitive singular *pukki* and stem partitive plural *pukke* in Table 4.7 illustrates the most regular exchange pattern in Estonian. The proportion in (5.8a) uses exemplary forms of PUKK 'trestle' to deduce the partitive plural of HEKK 'hedge'. Proportion (5.8b) exhibits the opposite deduction, in which forms of exemplary KUKK 'rooster' identify the partitive plural of LILL 'flower'. As in Spanish conjugations, neither -*e* nor -*i* have number features in isolation. One is plural in paradigms where the other is the theme vowel, and vice versa.

(5.8)   Partititive patterns in Estonian (Erelt *et al.* 1995)
      a. pukki : pukke = hekki : *hekke*
      b. kukke : kukki = lille : *lilli*

5.3 Schematization and foundation

The cases considered above show how proportions can isolate systematic patterns while avoiding problematic or undermotivated morphotactic or morphosyntactic commitments. The transparency and representational neutrality of this format contributes to its role in pedagogical traditions. Yet, as discussed in Chapter 4.4, grammatical devices and principles drawn from pedagogical or reference grammars often carry along idealizations that have no status in a general model of morphology.[11] The directional character of the preceding descriptions and proportions has this artifactual status, reflecting the same kind of pedagogical convention as the selection of exemplary lexemes or principal parts. As Aronoff (1994) observes, there is no formal basis for choosing either the supine or the past passive participle as basic:[12]

It is clear . . . that by judging from form alone, there is no way to choose either one of the supine or the perfect participle as underlying the other or to choose either one as underlying the future participle, since they are the same morphome, identical in all constant aspects of their sound forms . . . In fact, the grammar books are just about evenly divided as to whether they derive the future participle from the perfect participle or the supine. (Aronoff 1994: 38f.)

The parity that Aronoff (1994) describes is, however, only inconvenient for the descriptive or pedagogical grammarian. From the standpoint of the learner or speaker it is clearly DESIRABLE that the forms of a conjugational series should be mutually informative and that deductions of other forms should be, as far as possible, independent of the order in which the forms are encountered.

From a speaker's perspective, it is the generality of a pattern that is most important. Does the relation exhibited by a pair of forms characterize just a single lexeme, a whole inflection class or even a word class? The most systematic attempts to address this issue are developed in the context of analogy-based models, particularly in the work of Kuryłowicz.[13] Anderson's (1992) summary of this tradition bears repeating at length here:

The most extensive attempt in the philological literature to provide a genuinely theoretical understanding of the operation of analogical change is that associated with Kuryłowicz (1949, 1964, and elsewhere), whose goal was to find principles that cover the cases in which analogy could (or could not) operate.

Kuryłowicz's theory is based on the model of proportional analogy, but he makes it abundantly clear that not all proportionals are well formed, even where they involve related

---

[11] As discussed in Chapters 7 and 8, the goal of describing a speaker's knowledge of a language as a symbolic representation of the patterns in the language reflects an even more basic idealization, one that is incorporated in the notion of a 'formal' grammar.

[12] Aronoff (1994) appears to discount the possibility that a longer form, in this case the future active participle, could be the basic member of the series. From an implicational perspective, there is no reason to make this assumption. Longer forms are more informative than shorter forms in cases, like the nominative singular in Estonian, where the longer form retains bits of form that cannot be predicted from the shorter form.

[13] Itkonen (2005) presents an extended discussion of analogy; some of the issues raised in this work are subsequently considered in the papers in Blevins and Blevins (2009). For computational approaches to analogical modelling, see discussions of AM (Skousen 1989, 1992) and TIMBL (Daelemans and Van den Bosch 2005).

terms. Thus, *write* : *writer* = *receive* : *receiver* is valid, but *write* : *receive* = *writer* : *receiver* is "nonsensical as between *write* and *receive* there is not only no grammatical relation but not even a lexical one" (Kuryłowicz 1964: 37). In other words, one side of a proportion must instantiate a relation between two (classes of) forms that is governed by some rule of grammar; the other side represents the extension of this rule to other forms. A proportion relates 'basic' forms to forms "founded" on them, and a relation of foundation $a \rightarrow b$ must exist in order for $a : b = c : d$ to be admissible as a proportion.

> Relations between founding and founded forms play much the same role in Kuryłowicz's system that rules play in a generative grammar, but there are also important differences. Most interestingly, if b is founded on a, this means that the existence of b presupposes the existence of a, rather than that b is constructed by starting with a and adding something. Thus, the stem of a paradigm is founded on the various fully inflected forms, rather than *vice versa*. Kuryłowicz regards the grammar as a set of relations among full surface forms (much as de Saussure did: see Anderson 1985), rather than a set of rules specifying the construction of complex forms from simple components. (Anderson 1992: 369)

A 'complex system' perspective is implicit in the conception that Anderson attributes to Kuryłowicz. A relation of foundation between a and b that "means that the existence of b presupposes the existence of a" is an abstractive implication over a network of forms. But proposing that antecedents of a proportional analogy must stand in a "relation of foundation" or instantiate a "rule of grammar" just states a formal prerequisite for valid analogies, without specifying an effective procedure for validation. What is missing is a notion of 'informativeness' that measures how reliably one element identifies another. Yet informativeness is precisely what remains implicit in the classical model.

The same fundamental issue recurs in a different guise in the problem of selecting principal parts. Within the descriptive traditions that grew up around individual languages and language families, there was often a consensus regarding the number of classes in a language and the choice of diagnostic forms. But there was again no procedure for selecting diagnostic forms or for determining the informativeness of single forms or sets of forms. Although the problem was posed in a way that reflected irrelevant pedagogical biases, the difficulties that arose in principal part analyses reflected a genuine shortcoming in classical models, which had no means of measuring informativeness.

In both of these cases what is missing is a strategy for making explicit the "knowledge" that Matthews (1972) appeals to in the quotation on p. 106. Of all of the kinds of morphological knowledge, two varieties are particularly relevant to the validation of analogies and the selection of principal parts. The first kind of knowledge concerns 'unconditioned' dependencies between cells. Knowing that the present infinitive form of a Latin verb is X implies that the imperfect subjunctive is Xm. Similarly, knowing that a genitive singular of an Estonian noun is X entails that the nominative plural is Xd. The implication is not dependent on variation in the shape of X. A second kind of knowledge concerns conditioned dependencies. For example, feminine nouns in German can follow four of the plural patterns in Table 4.10. But feminine nouns ending in schwa almost always follow pattern P2 and have a plural in *-n*. Knowing the nominative singular form of a Russian noun is likewise reasonably informative about the accusative singular. But knowing that the nominative singular ends in *-a* identifies a second declension noun and sanctions an even more reliable deduction of an accusative singular in *-u*.

The 'knowledge' involved in these deductions concerns the reduction in uncertainty about one form based on acquaintance with another form. The reduction of uncertainty can, in turn, be modelled directly by information-theoretic notions. The conditional entropy between one cell and another measures how much uncertainty is left in the second if one knows the form of the first. Specific conditional entropy applies to conditioned dependencies. Mutual information between cells likewise gives a symmetrical measure of informativeness. Recasting proportional analogies in information-theoretic terms thus provides a means of calculating the soundness of a putative "relation of foundation". This formal reconstruction of classical WP analyses also allows for the generalization and schematization of proportions. One can determine the reliability of deductions between cells, between cells with particular patterns of affixation, between cells with particular patterns of stem allomorphy, combinations of affixes and stems, etc. As in standard proportions, patterns are motivated by their predictive value and carry no larger commitment.

More generally, a description of a speaker's knowledge of morphological patterns in terms of discriminative learning and information-theoretic measures can incorporate the dependencies exhibited by proportional analogies without endorsing the four-part format in which these patterns are conventionally expressed. A formalization of classical WP models in terms of notions of uncertainty and uncertainty reduction is outlined in Chapters 7 and 8. However, before considering this approach, it will be instructive to review the realizational tradition, which represents the first attempt to incorporate insights from classical models into a framework of morphological analysis.

Part II
Contemporary WP models

6

Realizational models

The exemplar-based structure of a classical WP model led, in short, to an impasse. Interdependencies were exhibited by the forms of exemplary items, or encapsulated in 'inflection classes' that these items were taken to represent. Individual correspondences were described in terms of analogical patterns. Neither strategy provided a general representation of implicational dependencies. Hence, at the point where Hockett (1954) sought to return the model to the attention of the theoretical community, there was no version of the model that was formulated independently of the description of a specific language.

Robins (1959) presents a sketch of the general architecture of a WP model and a description of some patterns that seem amenable to analysis in WP terms, but no explicit formalization of any of the patterns. The first formalizations were outlined shortly afterwards, in Chomsky (1965) and Matthews (1965). But following "the Decade of the Morpheme" (Hockett 1987: 81), the main focus of linguistic research shifted elsewhere and an extended presentation of a modern WP model did not appear until Matthews (1972), followed by an independent WP model in the axiomatic grammar format in Lieb (1976).[1]

6.1 The inflectional component of a WP grammar

In the half century since the initial formalizations, a range of approaches have been developed, which, in different ways and to varying degrees, develop the insights of a classical WP model. The most familiar group of models consists of what are usually termed 'realizational' approaches. The realization rules that give these approaches their name are essentially interpretive counterparts of the processes of an 'Item and Process' model. As described in Chapter 2.3, an IP process $\mathbb{P}$ can be thought of as applying to an 'input' pair $\langle B, X \rangle$, consisting of a property bundle B and a form X. The 'output' of the process is a pair $\langle f(B), o(X) \rangle$, in which $f(B)$ is the result of applying the feature-changing function f to B and $o(X)$ is the result of applying the operation o to X. In contrast, when a realizational rule of EXPONENCE $\mathbb{R}$ applies to $\langle B, X \rangle$, it preserves the properties in B, and just applies an operation to X. The difference between these rule types is illustrated by the contrast between the 'feature-changing' process in (6.1a) and the 'interpretive' exponence rule in (6.1b).

---

[1] Lieb's model again falls entirely outside the realizational tradition, as reflected in the use of non-realizational processes to cover both word formation and inflection in Lieb (2013), supplanting the 'paradigm bases' previously used to arrive at paradigms.

Word and Paradigm Morphology. First edition. James P. Blevins
© James P. Blevins 2016. First published 2016 by Oxford University Press

(6.1) Processes vs exponence rules
    a. $\mathbb{P}(\langle \mathcal{B}, X \rangle) = \langle f(\mathcal{B}), o(X) \rangle$
    b. $\mathbb{R}(\langle \mathcal{B}, X \rangle) = o(X)$

The structure of the rule in (6.1a) isolates the components that Anderson (1992) references in his description of 'A-Morphous Morphology' (AMM):

Within the general typology of Hockett 1954, which continues to be referred to in the literature, this is an 'Item and Process' model of word structure, though, especially in its treatment of inflection, it could also be called a "Word and Paradigm" view (Anderson 1992: 72)

The affinity with classical WP models reflects the fact that the property bundle $\mathcal{B}$ typically represents the features that define a paradigm cell. It is the use of the operation $o(X)$ in (6.1b) that expresses an IP conception of word structure, in which form variation is described in terms of phonological operations.

Anderson's description of AMM in the quotation above also summarizes the properties that distinguish realizational approaches as a class from the IA and IP models reviewed in Chapter 2. By retaining an operational treatment of word structure, realizational approaches preserve the advantages that IP models enjoy over IA accounts in the analysis of non-affixal patterns. Moreover, by embedding operations within interpretive rules that do not modify property bundles, realizational models permit multiple rules to apply to the same bundle. Different rules may then 'spell out' overlapping features by distinct operations in the realization of a form. This flexibility allows realizational rules to describe the variable relations between 'units of meaning' and 'units of form' that challenge the underlying morphemic conception of an IP or IA model.

Yet as implictly acknowledged in Anderson's description, the combination of an 'IP model of word structure' with a 'WP view of inflection' conveys advantages for the analysis of specific types of phenomena. From the inception of the realizational tradition, it has been understood that interpretive rules are particularly well adapted to the description of inflectional systems. The descriptive success of these rules derives largely from the fact that inflectional systems can be idealized in terms of an essentially closed and uniform feature space. This space can thus be modelled by sets of property bundles whose composition is determined by the distinctive features of a language. Applied to a set of independently-specified property bundles, interpretive rules can then define the feature combinations that have distinctive formal realization in a language.

The extension of an interpretive approach to derivational patterns is far from straightforward, given that the derivational family of an item is much more variable and much less predictable. Even within the domain of inflection, the advantages of a flexible spell-out relation depend on assumptions about the granularity and function of units of form and units of meaning. Realizational models relax a morphemic form-meaning correspondence to a weaker, many-many relation. But they retain the assumption that the global relation between systems of contrasts at the level of meaning and the level form are mediated by relations between individual meaning contrasts and form contrasts.

To clarify this point, consider the example of two expressions, x and y, that differ minimally in form and in meaning. The expression x is associated with a property F_x and form Φ_x that contrast with the property F_y and form Φ_y associated with y. A morphemic model will establish morphemes that link the associated units of form and meaning, F_x with Φ_x and F_y with Φ_y. A realizational model will likewise treat the units of form Φ_x and Φ_y as the 'spell-outs' of corresponding properties F_x and F_y. As noted in Section 6.3.2, the innocuous-seeming linkage defined by a realizational model has a range of implications, including characteristic patterns of 'overgeneralization'. These effects do not arise in models, such as the learning-based discriminative models outlined in Chapter 8.3, which do not invariably reduce the relation between SYSTEMS of contrasts at the level of meaning and the level of form to relations between INDIVIDUAL contrasts at the level of meaning and form.

A wide range of strategies and devices have been proposed within realizational approaches to accommodate derivational formations, to 'block' overgeneralization, and to describe other classes of patterns that resist description in terms of interpretive rules. The fragmentation created by these often incompatible extensions is compounded by other factors, including the lack of a common rule format for exponence rules, chronic disagreement about the status of rules of 'referral', etc. Variation in the degree of formalization introduces a further dimension of variation. The models outlined in Matthews (1991) and Aronoff (1994) are among the purest expositions of realization-based analyses, though the simplicity of these analyses is often achieved by leaving execution details open. At the other extreme, analyses formulated within models of Paradigm Function Morphology (PFM) of Stump (2001) are highly formalized.[2] However, this degree of formalization often comes at the cost of obscuring the intuitive content of an analysis. Models of Network Morphology (NM; Corbett and Fraser 1993; Brown and Hippisley 2012), have likewise been specified in sufficient detail to permit computational implementation. Yet this formalization carries a commitment to an inheritance-based view of generalizations and a particular knowledge-representation system.

The fragmentation of realizational approaches has also inhibited the development of a secondary literature of the kind that facilitated collaboration within the Post-Bloomfieldian tradition. In part, this fragmentation is due to the fact that realizational approaches—unlike morphemic models—were not consciously developed by a single cohesive community. To the extent that the various realizational approaches are defined less by shared assumptions than by a shared morphemic adversary, it may even be misleading to treat them as instantiations of a common framework in the sense of Chapter 1.3.2.

These factors present challenges for a summary of the realizational tradition, and it is unlikely that any summary will satisfy proponents of individual approaches. The limited goal of the present chapter is just to provide an overview of the realizational tradition that highlights the principal benefits of basing morphological analyses on realization relations. This objective is in many ways orthogonal to the aims of the individual approaches, each of which explores a different idiosyncratic

---

[2] As were the analyses in the initial monograph-length study of Matthews (1972).

path through the space of extensions to a basic realizational conception. To avoid potential misunderstandings and allay concerns about misrepresentation, it is perhaps worth emphasizing that the chapter will, insofar as possible, attempt to isolate the core intuitions underlying realizational approaches and focus primarily on maximally general notions of 'exponence rules', 'referral rules', 'rule ordering', 'rule blocks', etc. Section 6.4 rounds out this overview with a concise summary of distinctive aspects of some currently influential realizational models. Otherwise, formalism-specific variants are discussed only where this serves some larger expositional goal.

6.2 Realization rules

The first formalizations of a modern WP model were proposed, more or less simultaneously, in Chomsky (1965) and Matthews (1965). Both accounts proceeded from the observation that the inflectional features that were distinctive for a given word or inflection class could be specified independently of their formal realization. In brief and programmatic remarks about the German declensional system, Chomsky (1965) notes that "the traditional paradigmatic treatment" could be reconstructed by a model that 'interprets' features:

In short, the theory of syntactic features developed earlier can incorporate the traditional paradigmatic treatment directly. The system of paradigms is simply described as a system of features, one (or perhaps some hierarchical configuration) corresponding to each of the dimensions that define the system of paradigms. Interpretive phonological rules, some quite specific, some of considerable generality, then operate on the phonological matrix of the lexical entry, giving, finally, a phonetic matrix. (Chomsky 1965: 172)

A similar approach is outlined in greater detail in Matthews (1965) in his analysis of the inflectional component of a WP model:

The present paper is intended to supply a part of this formulation. It is restricted to inflectional problems alone: to be more precise, it deals with that subsection of the grammar (we will call it the INFLECTIONAL COMPONENT) which assigns a realization, or various alternative realizations, to each grammatical word. (Matthews 1965: 142)

The central insight expressed in these passages is that a flexible relation between features and forms can be defined by purely interpretive rules that 'spell-out' or 'realize' features associated with a paradigm cell or feature bundle.

6.2.1 Sequential and cumulative exponence in Finnish

A simple illustration may help to give an initial sense of the components of a realizational account and the way in which they interact. Consider the case forms in the partial paradigm of the Finnish noun TALO 'house' in Table 6.1.

TABLE 6.1   Partial paradigm of Finnish TALO 'house'
(Karlsson 1999: 249)

	Sg	Plu
Nominative	talo	talot
Genitive	talon	talojen
Partitive	taloa	taloja

$$\begin{bmatrix} N \\ talo \end{bmatrix}$$

FIGURE 6.1   Partial stem entry for TALO

A: $\begin{bmatrix} PLU \\ X \end{bmatrix} \rightarrow X + i$ $\begin{bmatrix} PLU \\ NOM \\ X \end{bmatrix} \rightarrow X + t$

B: $\begin{bmatrix} PART \\ X \end{bmatrix} \rightarrow X + a$ $\begin{bmatrix} GEN \\ X \end{bmatrix} \rightarrow X + n$ $\begin{bmatrix} PLU \\ GEN \\ X \end{bmatrix} \rightarrow X + en$

FIGURE 6.2   Plural and grammatical case realization rules

These forms are all based on a stem form, *talo*. The partial entry in Figure 6.1 specifies this stem, along with the word class of TALO. Entries can also include additional stem forms, or 'intrinsic' features, such as inflection class.

The inflections that follow the stem are introduced by the rules in Figure 6.2, organized into ordered 'blocks' A and B. The first block, A, contains rules introducing a number-neutral plural marker *-i* (realized as *-j* intervocalically), and a nominative plural marker *-t*. The rules in the second block, B, introduce a partitive marker *-a*, a genitive marker *-n* and a genitive plural marker *-en*. The observation that the plural marker occurs closer to the stem than the case endings is expressed by assigning the plural rule to the first block, A.

The application of these rules is illustrated in Figure 6.3. The partial feature bundles represent the inflectional properties that distinguish the six grammatical forms. The row below the bundles identifies the lexical stem, *talo*, from the entry in Figure 6.1. The bottom rows then exhibit the effect of the rules in 'blocks' A and B, or indicate, via a gap, that no rule has applied. Although nominative and singular features define a distinctive paradigm cell in Figure 6.3, there are no rules that realize these features in Figure 6.2. Hence the realization of the nominative singular cell preserves the form of the lexical stem. In the absence of a singular rule, the genitive and partitive singular are also based on the basic stem. In contrast, the genitive and partitive plural cells both trigger the application of the plural rule in block A, defining a plural base for the genitive plural and partitive rules in block B. The realization of these simple forms illustrates two core functions of rule blocks. As noted above, the sequential ordering of blocks A and B ensures that the plural marker is realized closer to the stem than the genitive or partitive plural markers. In addition, the rules within a block are assumed to be ordered with respect to specificity.

	$\begin{bmatrix} \text{sg} \\ \text{NOM} \end{bmatrix}$	$\begin{bmatrix} \text{sg} \\ \text{GEN} \end{bmatrix}$	$\begin{bmatrix} \text{sg} \\ \text{PART} \end{bmatrix}$	$\begin{bmatrix} \text{PLU} \\ \text{NOM} \end{bmatrix}$	$\begin{bmatrix} \text{PLU} \\ \text{GEN} \end{bmatrix}$	$\begin{bmatrix} \text{PLU} \\ \text{PART} \end{bmatrix}$
Stem	talo	talo	talo	talo	talo	talo
A				talot	taloi	taloi
B		talon	taloa		talojen	taloja

FIGURE 6.3   Spell-out of grammatical case forms of TALO

This type of 'disjunctive rule ordering' convention (Anderson 1986) regulates rule competition in both blocks. In block A, the rule introducing the nominative plural ending -*t* takes priority over the rule introducing the simple plural ending -*i*; in block B, it is the rule introducing the genitive plural ending -*en* that takes priority over the rule introducing the genitive ending -*n*. The various realizational models build on this foundation in characteristic ways, usually by adding further rule types or more elaborate principles to govern rule interaction. The following subsections will now survey this variation. More detailed discussions can be found in the monograph-length presentations of Matthews (1972), Anderson (1992), Aronoff (1994) and Stump (2001).

6.2.2 Rules of exponence

Following Zwicky (1985), it is conventional to divide realization rules into two basic types: rules of EXPONENCE, which spell features out by forms, and rules of REFERRAL, which relate the realization of distinct feature spell-outs. The rules in Figure 6.2, illustrate the flexibility of exponence rules. As the partitive rule illustrates, a realizational model can express a biunique correlation between the interpretation of a single feature, here partitive case, and the realization of a minimal form unit, here -*a*. Yet the partitive case feature remains associated with the full word forms *taloa* and *taloja*, not with the exponent -*a* alone. Moreover, the one-to-one relation between the case feature and the case marker that 'spells it out' is not normative, but merely a limiting case.

Because exponence rules interpret features rather than 'cancel' or 'consume' them, they can describe feature-form mismatches in both directions: 'fusional' patterns in which there are more features than forms, and 'fissional' patterns in which there are more forms than features. The nominative and genitive plural rules in Figure 6.2 illustrate a fusional pattern, which Matthews (1972: 67) terms CUMU-LATIVE EXPONENCE. In this example, it is multiple features (case and number) that are 'cumulatively' associated with single form units. The converse mismatch, which Matthews (1972: 93) terms EXTENDED EXPONENCE, is not exhibited by a single exponence rule but by a set of exponence rules that realize partially overlapping feature bundles. Extended exponence is exhibited by the Latin form *re:ksisti:* 'you had ruled' in Figure 2.3 and by the Ancient Greek form *elelýkete* 'you had unfastened', in Figures 3.1 and 3.2. The rules that Matthews (1991: 177) proposes to describe *elelýkete* are summarised below.

$$\begin{bmatrix} \text{V} \\ \text{2ND} \\ \text{PLUR} \\ \text{ACT} \\ \text{PAST} \\ \text{PERF} \\ \text{INDIC} \\ \text{ly:} \end{bmatrix}$$

FIGURE 6.4   Root form and 2nd plural active paradigm cell of Greek LYO 'unfasten'

$$\begin{bmatrix} \text{PERF} \\ \text{XV:} \end{bmatrix} \rightarrow \text{XV}$$

FIGURE 6.5   Perfective 'shortening' rule

$$\begin{bmatrix} \text{PERF} \\ \text{CX} \end{bmatrix} \rightarrow \text{Ce} + \text{CX}$$

FIGURE 6.6   Perfective reduplication rule

The analysis starts from the structure in Figure 6.4, which combines the features of the '2nd person plural past perfective indicative active' paradigm cell with the root form *ly:* of the verb LYO 'unfasten'. This structure does not represent the root entry of LYO, which would only contain whatever intrinsic features are taken to characterize uninflected roots, but instead contains the features of the paradigm cell that is realized by the surface word form *elelýkete*. This surface form is obtained by applying exponence rules that interpret the features in Figure 6.4 by successively modifying the root form.[3]

To illustrate extended exponence, it will suffice to review the feature overlap in the rules that define the perfective active stem *lelyk*.[4] The shortening rule in Figure 6.5 applies first. This rule realizes perfective aspect by reducing a long root vowel, shortening *ly:* to *ly*. The reduplication rule in Figure 6.6 then repeats the initial stem consonant, obtaining *lely* from *ly*. The rule in Figure 6.7 applies next, defining the perfective active stem *lelyk* by suffixing -*k* to *lely*.

Figure 6.8 summarizes the ordering of exponence rules, the overlapping features that they realize, and the cumulative effects of their application. Different rule orders would yield the same output in this case, provided that the shortening rule precedes the suffixation of -*k*. But it is only the effect on the shape of the input form that constrains the order of rule application. Since exponence rules

---

[3] Matthews (1991) subscripts the category label 'V' to identify word class, rather than including it among the features to be realized, though nothing hinges on whether category labels are included within feature bundles or subscripted to them. To maintain consistency with Matthews's formulations, the phonemic forms in these rules are not placed between slashes. Thus Figure 6.5 relates a form ending in a long vowel, /XV:/, to a form /XV/, which is identical except that it ends in the short counterpart /V/.

[4] Accent placement is suppressed, as it is predictable here (Goodwin 1894: 29).

$$\begin{bmatrix} \text{ACT} \\ \text{PERF} \\ \text{X} \end{bmatrix} \rightarrow \text{X} + \text{k}$$

FIGURE 6.7   Active perfective stem rule

Features	PERFECTIVE	PERFECTIVE	ACTIVE PERFECTIVE
Rule	XV: → XV	CX → Ce + CX	X → X + k
Output	ly	lely	lelyk

FIGURE 6.8   Spell-out of the active perfective stem *lelyk*

are purely interpretive, the features associated with the paradigm cell in Figure 6.4 remain constant through the analysis, irrespective of the order in which rules are applied. It is the fact that spell-out does not alter features that allows each of the rules in figures 6.5–6.7 to realize the same perfective feature. Vowel shortening, reduplication and suffixation of -*k* all have the same status as exponents of the feature perfective, and there is no obvious sense in which any one marker is 'primary' and the others are 'secondary'.

In sum, the feature-form separation permits a degree of flexibility in the way that features and forms are related by exponence rules. Distinctive features may be biuniquely realized, as in Post-Bloomfieldian models. A morphemic pattern is illustrated by the rule in Figure 6.2 that realizes plural features by -*i*. But multiple features may also be realized cumulatively, as illustrated by the rule in Figure 6.2 that realizes nominative and plural features by -*t*. Features may also be present but remain unrealized, as in the case of nominative singular features, which define a cell in Figure 6.3 but are not realized by any rule. Conversely, features may be realized, individually or cumulatively, by multiple rules. This pattern is illustrated by the three rules that realize perfective in Figure 6.8. None of these patterns are unusual or rare, and even more extreme cases of extended exponence are discussed in Harris (2009).

6.2.3 Rules of referral

The descriptive gain achieved by exponence rules is confined to the relation between features and individual forms. Exponence rules define the structure of word forms directly, and characterize the structure of a morphological system indirectly, as derivative of the properties of single forms. Although they are sometimes described as 'extended WP models', realizational approaches do not adopt the complex system perspective of a classical WP model (see Chapter 7), but instead exhibit a simple organization. The feature constraints of a language define a set of distinctive feature bundles, and a set of realization rules determines the formal spell-out of those bundles. The collection of individually well-formed bundle-form pairs constitutes the morphological system. A realizational model makes no assumptions about the interdependency of forms of the kind that underlie the classical factorization of morphological systems into exemplary paradigms and principal parts. Hence a morphological system in which the realization of each cell of a paradigm is fully independent of the realization of every other cell is no less amenable to a realizational analysis than a system in which the choices are systematically interdependent.

In classical WP models, proportional analogies can be used to express implicational dependencies as well as exponence relations because proportions relate feature-form pairs, not single feature bundles and forms. For example, the proportions in (5.4) above, repeated in (6.2), exhibit patterns of 'Priscianic' syncretism that cannot be treated as simple feature spell-out.

(6.2) Priscianic analogy in Latin conjugations
    a. flōrēre : flōrērem = esse : *essem*
    b. amātus : amātūrus = monitus : *monitūrus*

Many, though by no means all, realizational models include rule types that express these kinds of 'Priscianic' or 'parasitic' dependencies. This family of rule types includes the 'parasitic derivations' of Matthews (1972: 185), the 'morphological transformations' of Matthews (1991), the 'takeovers' of Carstairs (1987), and the 'referral' rules of Zwicky (1985) and Stump (1993b, 2001). The rule that Matthews (1991: 194) proposes for (6.2a), repeated in Figure 6.9, illustrates some common properties of this rule type.

This rule plainly does not spell out a feature bundle, but instead relates the spell-outs of two distinct bundles, a present infinitive bundle, which is realized by 'X', and a 1sg imperfect subjunctive bundle, which is realized by 'X+m'. As the distinct features in these bundles show, the correspondence defined by the rule is purely at the level of form. There need be no intrinsic relation between the features in these bundles, since the features serve solely to locate a particular pair of cells in a conjugational paradigm. In the present case, there is no sense in which the features of the present infinitive underlie or contribute to those of the imperfect subjunctive.[5] Yet since the rule in Figure 6.9 relates two exponence rules, it preserves the interpretive character of exponence rules.

On what might seem like the simplest and most obvious interpretation of this rule, it expresses a direct dependency between two paradigm cells, so that the

$$
\begin{bmatrix} \text{PRES} \\ \text{INF} \\ \text{ACT} \\ \text{X} \end{bmatrix} \rightarrow \begin{bmatrix} \text{1ST} \\ \text{sg} \\ \text{IMPF} \\ \text{sbjv} \\ \text{ACT} \\ \text{X + m} \end{bmatrix}
$$

FIGURE 6.9 Latin present infinitive-imperfect subjunctive correspondence

[5] In this respect they contrast with rules in the IP model in Chapter 2.3, in which one form-feature pair is the input to a process that defines a new feature-form pair.

definition of the 1sg imperfect subjunctive form of a verb involves retrieving the present active infinitive form 'X' of that verb and then adding the inflection -*m*. However, this is not a possible interpretation of Figure 6.9 in an orthodox realizational model. Each form is defined independently, and in the course of deriving one form of a verb, other surface forms of that same verb are not available. A realizational model contains stem entries, realization rules, feature inventories and constraints, and, depending on the model, a predefined 'space' of wellformed bundles, possibly organized into abstract paradigms. But these models contain no repository of surface forms that a rule could reference. The surface forms of a language exist only as potential outputs; they are not stored in instantiated paradigms or otherwise 'cached' by a realizational model. The fact that non-basic units have no permanent status again reflects the realizational focus on exponence relations at the level of single forms.

The treatment of whole-word syncretism is similarly constrained in expanded realizational models, which again contain no persistent units larger than the stem. The model of Paradigm Function Morphology (PFM; Stump 2001) provides a clear illustration. An innovative feature of PFM is the role assigned to 'paradigm functions' of the form $PF_{[\sigma]}(\rho)$, where σ represents the features of a paradigm cell and ρ is the root of a lexeme. The value of a paradigm function $PF_{[\sigma]}(\rho)$ is the form that realizes cell σ of a lexeme ρ. Hence it might appear that whole-word referrals could be expressed in terms of paradigm functions. As Stump (1993*b*) suggests, a constraint $PF_{[\sigma_i]}(\rho) = PF_{[\sigma_j]}(\rho)$ would relate the realization of cells σ_i and σ_j of a lexeme ρ:

one might assume that a rule of referral encompasses whole words. On this assumption, the rule of referral determining the form of Macedonian IMPF *padneše* 'you (sg.) fell' would simply fill the 2sg imperfect cell in the paradigm of *padn-* with the form *padneše* 's/he fell' occupying the 3sg imperfect cell in that paradigm. Viewed in this way, the relevant rule of referral could be stated as a restriction on the evaluation of a paradigm function . . . (Stump 1993*b*: 464)

However, the introduction of paradigm functions does not change the fact that PFM, like other realizational models, realizes individual forms, not paradigms or larger collections of forms. In the course of evaluating a paradigm function $PF_{[\sigma_i]}(\rho)$, the value of other paradigm functions, including $PF_{[\sigma_j]}(\rho)$, is undefined. The only way of obtaining a value from $PF_{[\sigma_j]}(\rho)$ is to explicitly evaluate that function in the course of realizing the original paradigm function $PF_{[\sigma_i]}(\rho)$. Consequently, there is no obvious way of incorporating a whole-word conception of referrals without construing them as essentially transderivational devices that invoke a sub-realization to obtain a form.[6]

The 'parasitic derivations' of Matthews (1972) provide the earliest formulation of a referral relation in a realizational model. Parasitic derivations occupy a

---

[6] Though given that inflectional systems are, for all intents and purposes, finite, transderivational referrals do not raise the formal and computational issues discussed by Johnson and Lappin (1999) in connection with transderivational syntactic devices.

relatively minor role, defining a special case in a more general exponence relation. As expressed in the passage below, a derivation is 'parasitic' in the case when a rule *r* realizes a property *p* with reference to a property *x*:

where *r* refers in its reference-component either to *p* itself or to some morphosyntactic property *x* which is substituted for *p* in accordance with a previous rule. (Matthews 1972: 185)

The idea of realizing a property *p* by proxy, i.e., by realizing a "property *x* which is substituted for *p*" is preserved in the subsequent 'morphological transformations' of Matthews (1991). Matthews suggests that these 'transformations' be interpreted as 'metarules', modelled on the metarules of GPSG accounts (Gazdar *et al.* 1985). On this interpretation, the rule in Figure 6.9 expresses a dependency, not between forms, but between exponence rules that define those forms. This dependency has two components. The first is that the present infinitive provides the base for the 1sg imperfect subjunctive and, more generally, for the entire imperfect subjunctive paradigm. The second is that 1sg imperfect subjunctive features are spelled out by -*m*.[7] These components are expressed separately by the referral and exponence rules in Figure 6.10.

The exponence rule is a conventional spell-out rule, which applies in the inflectional rule block 'C'. The referral, which applies in the stem-formation rule blocks 'A' and 'B', has an essentially counterfactual force, allowing an imperfect subjunctive cell to be realized AS IF it contained present infinitive features. This rule must be interpreted counterfactually and cannot be construed as defining a new feature bundle in which present infinitive features are substituted for imperfect subjunctive features. This substitution would yield an ill-formed bundle, since 1sg and imperative features do not co-occur in Latin.

The referral in Figure 6.10 expresses the dependency between imperfect subjunctive and present infinitive cells. What is required next are the rules that realize the infinitive form. These are provided in Figure 6.11.

$$\text{A/B:} \begin{bmatrix} \text{PRES} \\ \text{INF} \\ \text{ACT} \\ \text{X} \end{bmatrix} \rightarrow \begin{bmatrix} \text{IMPF} \\ \text{SBJV} \\ \text{ACT} \\ \text{X} \end{bmatrix} \qquad \text{C:} \begin{bmatrix} \text{1ST} \\ \text{SG} \\ \text{IMPF} \\ \text{SBJV} \\ \text{X} \end{bmatrix} \rightarrow \text{X} + \text{m}$$

FIGURE 6.10   Latin stem referral and 1sg exponence rule

$$\begin{bmatrix} \text{PRES} \\ \text{X} \end{bmatrix} \rightarrow \text{X} + \text{e} \qquad \text{A:} \begin{bmatrix} \text{INF} \\ \text{X} \end{bmatrix} \rightarrow \text{X} + \text{re}$$

FIGURE 6.11   Present theme vowel and infinitive rule

[7] In fact, 1sg is realized by -*m* more generally in active subjunctive and in active perfective paradigms but this refinement does not materially affect the analysis.

$$\begin{bmatrix} \text{1ST} \\ \text{SG} \\ \text{IMP} \\ \text{SBJV} \\ \text{ACT} \\ \text{flōr} \end{bmatrix}$$

FIGURE 6.12   Root form and 1sg imperfect subjunctive cell of FLŌREŌ 'flower'

$\begin{bmatrix} \text{1ST, SG, IMPF, SBJV, ACT} \end{bmatrix}$		$\boxed{\text{PRES, INF, ACT}}$
Stem	flōr	
A	→	flōre
B		flōrēre
C	flōrērem	←

FIGURE 6.13   Priscianic realization of 1sg imperfect subjunctive

The definition of surface word forms from stems in a realizational model inverts the abstractive perspective of a classical WP grammar, in which "the Present stem [is] obtained by dropping *-re* of the Pres. Inf. Active" (Gildersleeve and Lodge 1895: 71). As discussed in Chapter 5.2, this analytical inversion creates difficulties in assigning determinate features to stems and stem formatives. To sidestep these issues, which are orthogonal to the status of referral rules, the first rule in Figure 6.11 just associates the second declension theme vowel *-e* with the feature 'present' (and also suppresses declension class 'features'). The second rule likewise spells out infinitive features by *-re*. The rules in Figures 6.10 and 6.11 can then realize the 1sg imperfective subjunctive cell in Figure 6.12, which contains the root form of FLŌREŌ.

The realization of *flōrērem* is exhibited in Figure 6.13. The process is seeded by the feature bundle and root form from the cell in Figure 6.12. There are no rules that directly realize this bundle in blocks A and B, so the bundle is initially realized by the rules that interpret the boxed features, which are introduced by the referral rule in Figure 6.10. The referred features are realized in block A by the present theme vowel rule, which introduces *-e*, and in block B by the infinitival rule, which adds *-re*. Block C contains the 1sg exponence rule in Figure 6.10, which interprets the original bundle by adding *-m*.

The realization of *flōrērem* illustrates how the form dependency between distinct paradigm cells can be expressed by referral rules. Because this dependency is expressed not by borrowing the infinitive FORM but by applying the RULES that define that form, there is no representation of the fact that the Priscianic base *flōrēre* is itself a surface form. Hence full-word syncretism plays no special role in a realizational model, apart from the fact that surface forms realize a determinate bundle of features associated with a paradigm cell.

Sub-word stem syncretism is therefore amenable to a similar analysis. To express the Priscianic pattern in (6.2b), a realizational model can decompose the

$$
\text{A:} \quad \begin{bmatrix} \text{PAST} \\ \text{PASS} \\ \text{PRTL} \\ \text{X} \end{bmatrix} \quad \rightarrow \quad \begin{bmatrix} \text{FUT} \\ \text{ACT} \\ \text{PRTL} \\ \text{X} \end{bmatrix}
$$

FIGURE 6.14   Latin past passive–future active stem correspondence

$$
\text{A:} \quad \begin{bmatrix} \text{PAST} \\ \text{PASS} \\ \text{PRTL} \\ \text{X} \end{bmatrix} \quad \rightarrow \quad \text{X} + \bar{a}t
$$

FIGURE 6.15   Latin first conjugation past passive participle stem rule

$$
\text{B:} \quad \begin{bmatrix} \text{FUT} \\ \text{ACT} \\ \text{PRTL} \\ \text{X} \end{bmatrix} \quad \rightarrow \quad \text{X} + \bar{u}r
$$

FIGURE 6.16   Latin future active participle stem rule

$$
\begin{bmatrix} \text{NOM} \\ \text{SG} \\ \text{FUT} \\ \text{ACT} \\ \text{PRTL} \\ \text{am} \end{bmatrix}
$$

FIGURE 6.17   Root form and future active participle cell of Latin AMŌ 'love'

correspondence between 'X' and 'X + ūr' into the sub-generalizations expressed by the rules in Figures 6.14–6.16. The rule in Figure 6.14 defines the future active participle stem as dependent on the past passive participle stem. The rule in Figure 6.15 introduces the stem formative for first conjugation verbs. The rule in Figure 6.16 then adds the future active stem formative.

Like previous rules, these rules apply in a fixed order, determined by their assignment to blocks. To ensure that āt is realized before ūr, the rule that identifies stems in Figure 6.14 triggers the application of the stem formation rule in Figure 6.15 before the application of the rule in Figure 6.16. This interaction is illustrated in Figure 6.18. The entry in Figure 6.17 specifies the features of the nominative singular future active participle cell and the root form am. The cell features in Figure 6.18 are initially interpreted by realizing the boxed past passive participle features, in accordance with the referral in Figure 6.14. The past participle stem rule in Figure 6.15 applies in block A, adding the first conjugation stem formative -āt. The future active participle rule in Figure 6.16 applies to the original features in block B, adding -ūr. The resulting stem, amātūr, defines the base for the future active participle paradigm.

$\big[$NOM, SG, FUT, ACT, PRTL$\big]$	PAST, PASS, PRTL
Stem am	
A →	amāt
B amātūr	←

FIGURE 6.18   Priscianic realization of future active participle stem

6.2.4 Referral and directionality

The rules in Figures 6.10 and 6.14 follow Matthews (1991) in treating Priscianic dependencies as directional. This reflects a general view of the difference between symmetrical neutralization and asymmetrical referral. In the case of neutralization, features that are distinctive elsewhere in a system are collapsed, so that there is just one cell realizing the neutralized features.[8] In cases where form identity cannot be treated as neutralization, the single word or stem form is typically identified as the realization of one of the cells in the referral relation. The realization of the other cell or cells is then taken to 'refer to' or be 'parasitic on' this cell. The directional character of parasitic derivations and morphological transformations is shared by the referral rules of Zwicky (1985) and Stump (1993*b*, 2001), and the 'takeovers' of Carstairs (1987).

A challenge that confronts directional accounts is the need to identify the primary and dependent cells in a referral relation. In the case of the present infinitive-imperfect subjunctive pattern in (6.2a), it might seem obvious that the subjunctive is dependent on the infinitive, since the infinitive form defines the base for the subjunctive paradigm. However, given that a realizational account cannot refer directly to the form that realizes a different paradigm cell, the infinitive form must be assembled independently in the spell-out of infinitive and imperfect subjunctive forms. These realizations invoke the same rules, i.e., those in Figure 6.11, which, one can argue, primarily realize the features of the present infinitive, and derivatively realize the imperfect subjunctive.

Yet an argument of this kind is difficult to make for the past passive-future active participial syncretism in (6.2b). As Aronoff (1994: 38) argues, "there is no way to choose either one of the supine or the perfect participle as underlying the other or to choose either one as the future participle". Aronoff's point is illustrated by the arbitrary character of the rules in Figures 6.14 and 6.15. These rules stipulate that the future active participle is dependent on the past passive, and that -*āt* realizes past passive rather than future active features. However, the directionality of this dependency is not only unmotivated, but also has no independent effects. A realizational account that reversed the dependency would have exactly the same empirical coverage.

Cases in which a syncretic form has a shape that would make it appropriate to fill one of the cells in a referral relation are sometimes taken to provide *prima facie*

---

[8] The neutralization of gender contrasts in the plural of German or Russian adjective paradigms provides familiar examples of symmetrical neutralization.

TABLE 6.2   Dual/plural syncretisms in Slovene (Herrity 2000: 49)

	Sg	Dual	Plu	Sg	Dual	Plu
Nom	pótnik	pótnika	pótniki	člověk	člověka	ljudjé
Acc	pótnika	pótnika	pótnike	člověka	člověka	ljudí
Gen	pótnika	**pótnikov**	**pótnikov**	člověka	**ljudí**	ljudí
Dat	pótniku	pótnikoma	pótnikom	člověku	člověkoma	ljudém
Inst	pótnikom	pótnikoma	pótniki	člověkom	člověkoma	ljudmí
Loc	pótniku	**pótnikih**	**pótnikih**	člověku	**ljudéh**	ljudéh

$$\begin{bmatrix} \text{PLU} \\ \text{GEN} \\ \text{X} \end{bmatrix} \rightarrow \text{X} + \text{ov} \qquad \begin{bmatrix} \text{PLU} \\ \text{LOC} \\ \text{X} \end{bmatrix} \rightarrow \text{X} + \text{ih}$$

FIGURE 6.19   First declension genitive and locative plural rules in Slovene

evidence for a directional referral relation. This intuition underlies the notion of directional 'takeovers' proposed by Carstairs (1987):

the realisation of two or more morphosyntactic properties (A and B) in some context by an inflexion which elsewhere realises only one of these properties. In such circumstances we can say that B takes over A (Carstairs 1987: 117)

The Slovene paradigms in Table 6.2, which are discussed by Baerman *et al.* (2005: 175ff.), among others, illustrate some takeover-type patterns. The paradigm of the regular first declension masculine PÓTNIK 'traveller' exhibits the formal identity of the genitive forms *pótnikov* and the locative forms *pótnikih*. In the suppletive paradigm of ČLOVĚK 'person', the syncretic forms *ljudí* and *ljudéh* also pattern with other plural forms, rather than with dual forms.

As with the infinitive-subjunctive syncretism in Latin, one should be alert to the possibility that the directionality in Table 6.2 records the historical origin of these patterns. From a purely synchronic perspective, these paradigms exhibit two patterns. The first is that nouns have a complete set of distinct forms in the plural. In a realizational model, this pattern implies a full set of plural rules, including the genitive and locative rules in Figure 6.19.

The second pattern, marked by the bold forms in Table 6.2 involves the plural and dual syncretism in the genitive and locative. Given that the plural does appear to 'take over' the dual in these paradigms, directional rules that define the duals with reference to the plurals might appear motivated. Yet within a realization-based approach, the directionality in these rules would be completely redundant. The fact that genitive and locative duals are dependent on plurals, rather than vice versa, does not need to be stipulated in referral rules, since it is already expressed by an independent asymmetry in the rule inventory of Slovene. There are rules realizing the genitive and locative plural, but none realizing the duals. Hence referrals need only identify the genitive and locative duals with the corresponding plurals, as in Figure 6.20. In the course of realizing dative and locative duals, the referral

$$\begin{bmatrix} \text{DUAL} \\ \text{GEN} \\ \text{X} \end{bmatrix} \leftrightarrow \begin{bmatrix} \text{PLU} \\ \text{GEN} \\ \text{X} \end{bmatrix} \qquad \begin{bmatrix} \text{DUAL} \\ \text{LOC} \\ \text{X} \end{bmatrix} \leftrightarrow \begin{bmatrix} \text{PLU} \\ \text{LOC} \\ \text{X} \end{bmatrix}$$

FIGURE 6.20   Symmetrical referral rules expressing dual/plural syncretism

rules in Figure 6.20 will introduce plural features, which can be interpreted by the exponence rules in Figure 6.19. The realization of genitive and locative plurals will be unaffected, because the dual features trigger no new rules.

All of the usual realizational stratagems for controlling rule application remain available for regulating rule interactions involving symmetrical referrals. In particular, a fully developed realizational analysis would associate the class-specific rules described in this chapter with 'class features' that control their interaction. Thus the first declension exponence rules in Figure 6.19 and the referral in Figure 6.20 would be assigned a specification such as [DC 1], which would make the rules more 'specific' than any class-neutral rules and allow them to override general or default patterns of exponence in Slovene.

More broadly, the general (or class-specific) asymmetries in rule inventories assumed by realizational accounts eliminate the need for directional referrals. The Latin referrals in Figures 6.10 and 6.14 can be reformulated as symmetrical rules, given the independent assumption that stem formation rules exist for the 'primary' cell in each of these referrals but not for the 'dependent' cell. Directionality seems equally redundant in other types of referral rules, such as the 'bidirectional' referrals described initially by Stump (1993b):

These facts suggest the accusative singular/dative singular referral in Old Icelandic is bidirectional: for nouns in Class A, the DAT sg takes on the form of the ACC sg, while for nouns in Class C, the ACC sg takes on the form of the DAT sg. (Stump 1993b: 469)

The logic of this reduction is the same as in previous cases. A referral analysis assumes that in class A there is a rule realizing the dative singular but no rule realizing the accusative singular, and that in class C there is a rule realizing the accusative singular but no rule realizing the dative singular. Given this difference in the rule inventory of Icelandic, a symmetrical referral that applies in classes A and C will again determine an asymmetrical dependency.

In sum, a rule that identifies the realization of distinct paradigm cells will determine an asymmetrical dependency if, as in the cases considered in this section, only one of those cells is associated with an exponence rule (or with a rule that is more specific than the referral rule). Hence directionality is a redundant and excisable property of referral rules in these types of cases.

6.3 Rule interaction

The preceding summary of realization rules focusses on properties that are shared by all or most realizational models; the elaborations proposed in various extended models are discussed in Section 6.4. The initial description of basic rule types also introduces common organizational aspects of realizational models. In all models, feature bundles, representing the properties of paradigm cells or syntactic preterminals, specify a set of distinctive features. Realization rules spell out these features by successively modifying an initial root or stem form. Exponence rules express direct mappings between features and forms. Referral rules, in those models that incorporate them, function in effect as 'second order' exponence rules, relating multiple spell-outs.

Although realizational models are not normally regarded as derivational in the same sense as transformational accounts, realizational rules apply successively to spell out a bundle. The first rule in the sequence directly applies to a lexical root or stem, and subsequent rules apply in a fixed order, with each rule in the sequence defining the input to the following rule. At each point in the analysis of a complex form, there is usually a number of inflectional 'choices'. These individual choices are expressed by 'competing' exponence rules.

The principles that regulate rule ordering and rule competition define the syntagmatic and paradigmatic dimensions of a realizational model. Rule ordering is imposed by organizing rules into sets, which, following Anderson (1992), are usually termed BLOCKS. An extrinsic order is defined on blocks, so that rules in an 'earlier' block apply before those in a 'later' block. There is some freedom in how blocks are ordered. In Anderson's analyses of Georgian and Potawotami, prefixal blocks are ordered before suffixal blocks, which appears to reflect the linear structure of formatives, proceeding from left-to-right.[9] In contrast, the stem structure assigned to *elelýkete* by Matthews (1991: 178) exhibits a nested organization, corresponding to a block structure in which earlier blocks occur closest to the root. This order can again be reversed so that earlier blocks are more peripheral. The choice between these alternatives raises a number of further questions, which are taken up in Section 6.3.1.

Within each block, the competition between rules is usually resolved by principles that assign priority to the most specific applicable rule. Informally, rules are applicable to a feature bundle that contains all of the features that they spell out, and one rule is more specific than a second rule when it properly contains the features of the second. A notion of rule applicability defined in terms of feature inclusion rather than simple compatibility avoids the need to constrain realization rules through the use of negative or contrasting feature values (of the kind that prevent the 'overapplication' of IP processes).

The role that specificity-based competition plays in constraining the application of general rules embodies a distinctive realizational perspective on the nature of morphological variation. Each realization rule applies to a natural class of feature bundles, where the generality of the class is inversely proportional to the specificity

[9] However, as Olivier Bonami has drawn to my attention (p.c.), Anderson provides no explicit justification for the relative ordering of prefixal and suffixal agreement blocks, and elsewhere orders the suffixal theme vowel block before the prefixal agreement block. So the relation between linear order and block ordering remains somewhat less clear in Anderson (1986, 1992) than in the model of Crysmann and Bonami (2012).

of the rule. Patterns of variation associated with an apparently non-natural class of bundles are generally assumed to reflect the interaction of a general rule with more specific rules. The general rule is applicable in principle to a natural class of bundles. However it is only realized in a subset of these bundles because it is preempted by more specific rules in others.

In sum, realizational models adopt the hypothesis that patterns that characterize non-natural classes reflect the interaction of natural class patterns of varying levels of specificity. Extending this approach to different types of patterns with a non-natural distribution creates challenges for a realizational model. Some familiar challenges are summarized in Sections 6.3.1–6.3.4.

6.3.1 Intrinsic and extrinsic ordering

There are various formulations of specificity-based constraints on rule application, all reflecting a shared intuition that the rule with the most restricted application takes priority when multiple rules are applicable to a given bundle. For the most part, the relevant restrictions are taken to be determined by the feature component of a rule, and not by constraints imposed on the input form. For models that adopt this assumption, relative restrictiveness or specificity can be expressed in terms of standard set- or feature-theoretic notions.

However, many of the rule formats adopted within realizational approaches extend a basic interpretive feature-form mapping. For example, the inflectional Word Formation Rules of Anderson (1992) impose constraints on the shape of an input form as well as on the properties in a feature bundle:

An inflectional Word Formation Rule operates on a pair $\{\mathscr{S}, \mathscr{M}\}$ consisting of a phonologically specified stem $\mathscr{S}$, together with any further lexical specifications associated with that stem; and the Morphosyntactic Representation $\mathscr{M}$ of some (terminal or nonterminal) position in a Phrase Marker which is to be interpreted by (an inflected form of) that stem.

The Structural Description of such an inflectional Word Formation Rule thus includes two sorts of specification: conditions on $\mathscr{S}$ (e.g. the requirement that the rule may only apply to stems of more than two syllables), and conditions on $\mathscr{M}$ (e.g. the specification that the rule applies to Nouns interpreting positions bearing the feature [+ Ergative]). (Anderson 1992: 185)

The "two sorts of specification" included in the structural descriptions of these types of rule will define two separate relative specificity relations, one at the level of features, and the other at the level of 'forms' (possibly including "lexical specifications"). Hence for rules of this type, a specificity-based ordering constraint must either explicitly regulate the interaction of the two dimensions of relative specificity or else classify the form specification as relevant for determining rule applicability but not for determining relative rule priority.

For realization rules that do just interpret properties that are associated with feature bundles, the applicability of a rule can be determined by whether a bundle contains the features specified by a rule. This notion of rule applicability generalizes over nearly all the ways that rules and bundles can be represented formally. On the simplest representational assumption, rules and feature bundles specify sets of features (or feature-value pairs). On these set-based assumptions, a rule is applicable to a bundle whenever the features specified by the rule are a SUBSET of the features in the bundle. Alternatively, rules and bundles can both be interpreted as specifying FEATURE STRUCTURES in the sense defined in feature-based frameworks such as GPSG (Gazdar *et al.* 1985) and PATR-based systems (Shieber 1986). In this case a rule is applicable to a bundle whenever the structure specified by the rule SUBSUMES the structure representing the bundle. It is also possible to interpret rules as specifying sets of features and bundles as constituting structures. In this case, a rule is applicable to a bundle if the features specified by the rule DESCRIBE or are SATISFIED BY the structure, as in model-theoretic feature-based frameworks such as LFG (Kaplan and Bresnan 1982) and HPSG (Pollard and Sag 1994).

Each of these alternatives defines a specificity order on pairs of rules R and S. On a set-based conception, R is more specific than S if the set specified by S is a proper subset of the set specified by R. On a structure-based conception, R is more specific than S if the structure specified by S properly subsumes the structure specified by R. On a description-based conception, the definition of relative specificity depends on the model theory assumed by a framework. In LFG, which allows partially specified structures, R is more specific than S if the most informative structure that satisfies S properly subsumes the most informative structure that satisfies R. In versions of HPSG that do not allow partially specified structures, R can be regarded as more specific than S if the structures that satisfy R are a proper subset of the structures that satisfy S.

Given a set of exponence rules, relative informativeness relations between their associated feature bundles define a partial order that correlates with intuitive notions of relative specificity. The relative priority of any pair of rules can simply be read off their position in the informativeness order. Referral rules will likewise occur at the points in a rule hierarchy dictated by the feature sets specified by the rules. These conceptions of rule and specificity can be formalized to any desired level of precision within a more fully-developed approach. For the most part, the differences between alternatives reflect more general assumptions of a model, and do not themselves have direct empirical consequences. On any of these alternatives, the priority determined by relative informativeness is INTRINSIC in the sense that it reflects the features interpreted by realization rules and does not have to be stipulated or imposed.

In contrast, the relative order in which rules apply cannot be keyed to relative informativeness of the features they interpret, since the properties at different points in a form tend to be at least partially distinct. In forms with comparatively simple morphotactics, these points are described in terms of units such as 'roots', 'stems' and 'terminations'. These units determine a conventional 'head-thorax-abdomen' analysis in terms of lexical roots, derivational stems, and inflectional terminations. The traditional analysis that Matthews (1991) attributes to *elelýkete* is represented by the structure in Figure 6.21.

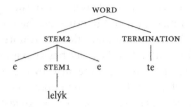

FIGURE 6.21   Traditional stem structure of *elelýkete* (Matthews 1991: 176ff.)

TABLE 6.3   Block stem structures for *elelýkete*

	e	le	lý	k	e	te
Linear	A	B	C	D	E	F
Nested	C	B	A	B	C	D

A realizational model does not assign morphotactic structure to a word form but transfers this organization onto the 'derivational structure' of an analysis. Hence the domains represented in Figure 6.21 correspond to rule blocks, or to sequences of blocks. The precise correspondence depends partly on how order is assigned to blocks, specifically whether it reflects a linear arrangement of exponents or a nested organization. On a linear account, there will be one block for the augment *e-*, a block each for the rules in Figures 6.5, 6.6 and 6.7, which define the perfective active stem *lelyk*, a rule for the past suffix *-e* and a final rule for the termination *-te*. This is a morphotactically consistent view of rule blocks, in which the exponents introduced by the rules in a block occupy a common position (e.g., are suffixal or prefixal) with respect to the input form.

A linear block organization preserves no reflex of the traditional stem structure in the analysis assigned to *elelýkete*, adding exponents from left to right. A nested organization can, however, represent morphotactic domains in terms of blocks. Beginning with the root, which undergoes a perfectivizing shortening rule, a concentric block structure can be defined which represents the traditional domains. The first block contains the reduplicated prefix *le-* and *-k*, the second contains the augment *e-* and suffix *-e*, and the final contains the termination *-te*. These alternatives are set out in Table 6.3.

The paired blocks 'B' and 'C' in the nested structure [[C [B [A] B] C] D] can be interpreted either as containing sets of prefixes and suffixes, or as comprising higher-level blocks containing prefixal and suffixal blocks. Since realization rules assign no morphotactic structure to the forms they spell out, the choice between different strategies for organizing blocks hinges on whether the blocks define domains for realizational principles or constraints. Disjunctive rule ordering is the primary constraint that is taken to apply within blocks. Hence patterns in which the effects of disjunctive ordering appear to span rule blocks provide useful test cases for evaluating different conceptions of block organization. The distribution of verbal agreement markers in Georgian, as described by Anderson (1986, 1992), represents a pattern of exactly this kind.

6.3.2 Rule blocks and disjunctive ordering

The agreement markers that Anderson discusses occur at 'positions' 2 and 11 in the schematic morphotactic structure proposed in Hewitt (1995):

The following are the morphemes that may occur in a Georgian verb-form, though not necessarily simultaneously: 1. Preverb(s), 2. Pronominal Agreement-Prefix, 3. Version-Vowel, 4. Root, 5. Causative Suffix(es), 6. Inceptive/Passive Marker, 7. Thematic Suffix, 8. Perfect/Stative Marker, 9. Imperfect Marker, 10. Mood-Vowel, 11. Pronominal Agreement-Suffix(es). (Hewitt 1995: 117)

The perfect/evidential form *dagixat'avt* 'we have (apparently) painted him/her/them' in Table 6.4 contains formatives in roughly half of the slots identified by Hewitt (1995). Anderson (1986, 1992) suggests that the rules that introduce these formatives are organized into linear blocks, and asserts in particular that the agreement rules in block 2 interact with those in block 11.

The evidence for cross-block rule interaction comes from the distribution of the agreement suffix *-t*. Consider first the future indicative paradigm of XAT'VA 'paint' in Table 6.5, in which the agreement markers are in bold. Table 6.6 shows that *-t* may mark agreement with 1pl and 2pl subjects. Table 6.7 further shows that that *-t* may mark agreement with 2pl objects. However, as Tables 6.5, 6.6, and 6.7 indicate, there are no contexts in this paradigm, or more generally in the conjugational system of standard Georgian, in which *-t* unambiguously marks 1pl subject agreement.

Agreement with 3pl subjects is marked by *-en* in Table 6.5, and by different 3pl markers in the other conjugational series in Georgian. In the Present and Aorist series, verbs do not mark a number contrast for 3p objects. However, paradigms in the Perfect series (along with paradigms of 'indirect' verbs) do exhibit a contrast between 3sg and 3pl indirect object agreement features, as a consequence of an

TABLE 6.4   Block stem structure of *dagixat'avt*

	da	g	i	xat'	av	t
Linear	1	2	3	4	7	11

TABLE 6.5   Future indicative paradigm of XAT'VA 'paint' (Tschenkéli 1958: §31)

Subj	1sg	1pl	Obj 2sg	2pl	3
1sg	—	—	dagxat'av	dagxat'avt	davxat'av
1pl	—	—	dagxat'avt	dagxat'avt	davxat'avt
2sg	damxat'av	dagvxat'av	—	—	daxat'av
2pl	damxat'avt	dagvxat'avt	—	—	daxat'avt
3sg	damxat'avs	dagvxat'avs	dagxat'avs	dagxat'avt	daxat'avs
3pl	damxat'aven	dagvxat'aven	dagxat'aven	dagxat'aven	daxat'aven

TABLE 6.6   1pl and 2pl subject agreement marking by -t

	Subj	1sg	1pl	2sg	2pl
Obj	1sg	—	—	damxat'av	damxat'avt
	2sg	dagxat'av	dagxat'avt	—	—
	3	davxat'av	davxat'avt	daxat'av	daxat'avt

TABLE 6.7   2pl object agreement marking by -t

	Obj	1sg	1pl	2sg	2pl
Subj	1sg	—	—	dagxat'av	dagxat'avt
	2sg	damxat'av	dagvxat'av	—	—
	3sg	damxat'avs	dagvxat'avs	dagxat'avs	dagxat'avt

TABLE 6.8   'Inverted' pluperfect paradigm of XAT'VA 'paint' (Tschenkéli 1958)

Subj	1 sg	1 pl	Iobj 2 sg	2 pl	3 sg	3 pl
1 sg	—	—	dagexat'e	dagexat'et	davexat'e	
1 pl	—	—	dagexat'et	dagexat'et	davexat'et	
2 sg	damexat'e	dagvexat'e	—	—	daexat'e	
2 pl	damexat'et	dagvexat'et	—	—	daexat'et	
3	damexat'a	dagvexat'a	dagexat'a	dagexat'at	daexat'a	daexat'at

inversion alternation that maps logical subjects onto indirect objects and promotes logical objects to surface subjects.[10] The pluperfect paradigm in Table 6.8 exhibits a contrast between 3sg and 3pl object marking, but only in forms with 3rd person subjects. In these forms, -t marks 3pl indirect objects, as well as 1pl and 2pl subjects and 2pl objects.[11]

The aim of Anderson's analysis is to formulate a single 'elsewhere' realization rule that introduces -t in the non-natural environments in which it seems to occur. The analysis incorporates two main claims. The first is that -t is neither a dedicated subject nor object plural marker, but instead "simply a perfectly general marker of the presence of a plural argument" (Anderson 1986: 12). The second claim is that in every plural context where -t fails to occur, it is blocked by some other rule. If we restrict attention to the future paradigm in Table 6.5, the distribution of -t is described in Table 6.9. The dashes again identify cells realized by reflexive forms which do not contain the relevant markers. Cells with no plural features to realize

---

[10] This treatment of inversion is assumed in grammars such as Tschenkéli (1958) and developed more explicitly in Harris (1981, 1984) and Blevins (2015b).

[11] On the assumption that the indirect object is a 'non-canonical' grammatical subject in inversion, Anderson concludes that -t does not mark 3pl objects. However this assumption is independent of the other components of his analysis, and merely introduces a complication into a highly general agreement rule (Anderson 1986: 11).

TABLE 6.9   Occurrence and blocking of -*t*

		Obj	1sg	1pl	2sg	2pl	3
Subj	1sg		—	—	—	-t	—
	1pl		—	—	-t	-t	-t
	2sg		—	Ø	—	—	—
	2pl		-t	-t	—	—	-t
	3sg		—	-s	—	-t	—
	3pl		-en	-en	-en	-en	-en

are also marked by dashes. The remaining cells are indicated by the suffix realized in that cell.

Anderson proposes that the 3pl subject marker -*en* preempts -*t* because the 3rd person plural features realized by the corresponding rule are more specific than the person-neutral plural features realized by the rule that introduces -*t*. This leaves the absence of -*t* in 1pl object forms as the sole remaining gap. As Anderson notes, the occurrence of the 3sg subject suffix -*s* in the realization of 1pl object and 3sg subject features cannot be attributed to competition with -*t*, given that -*t* preempts -*s* in the realization of 2pl object and 3sg subject features. The absence of -*t* also cannot be attributed to any suffixal competition in the unsuffixed form that realizes 1pl object and 2sg subject features.

The solution that Anderson proposes is that the absence of -*t* in forms realizing 1pl object features is due to competition with the 1pl prefix *gv*-:

Clearly the *gv*- rule is more specific than the *t*-rule . . . and thus the operation of the former excludes the latter by disjunctive ordering. (Anderson 1986: 10)

To allow prefixes to block suffixes in Georgian, Anderson proposes the principle in (6.3), which extends a disjunctive ordering condition across blocks:

(6.3)   *"Elsewhere" Principle*: Application of a more specific rule blocks that of a later more general one. (Anderson 1992: 132)

The principle in (6.3) is a highly subversive 'extension' of a disjunctive ordering condition, since it undermines the coherent division between the intrinsic ordering that applies within blocks and the extrinsic ordering that applies across blocks. Moreover, the the descriptive usefulness of this extension depends on a number of stipulations that are independently open to question. For the rules introducing prefixes to take priority over those introducing suffixes, it is critical that the prefixal block precedes the suffixal block. Yet there is no motivation provided for this assumption. However, it is perhaps suggestive that the two sets of agreement markers occur outside the derivational exponents, and show the uniform distribution and interpretation characteristic of inflections. The agreement suffixes are the final element in the template identified by Hewitt (1995), corresponding to the agreement termination -*te* in Figure 6.21. On the left flank, the agreement prefixes follow only the preverb. Hence on almost any stem analysis, the agreement blocks

TABLE 6.10   Block stem structure of *dagixat'avt*

	da	g	i	xat'	av	t
Linear	1	2	3	4	7	11
Nested	A	C	B	A	B	C

a. [... +plural ...]
    /X/ → /X + t/

b. /X/ → /X + t/ in the context of [+Plural]
    (i.e. whenever the feature [+Plural] appears anywhere in $\mathcal{M}$).

FIGURE 6.22   General plural rule in Georgian (Anderson 1986: 12, 1992: 132)

would be peripheral, as in Figure 6.10, outside the blocks that introduce the root, version vowels, thematic suffixes, and other derivational exponents.[12]

In principle, a block structure that mirrored a traditional stem structure could extend the domain of disjunctive ordering in precisely the way required for an analysis that treats -*t* as a general plural marker whose distribution is constrained by competition with agreement prefixes and suffixes. Anderson (1992: 131) alludes to this alternative when he notes that "blocks are (in part) a reconstruction of the traditional notion of POSITION CLASSES in morphological structure" and goes on to acknowledge that the general conception of rule block is flexible enough that "a rule of prefixation and a rule of suffixation could potentially belong to the same disjunctive block". Hence, if one were to assume that -*t* is a general plural marker whose distribution is constrained by competition with more specific prefixes and suffixes, the most natural implementation of an analysis on which *gv*- blocks -*t* would adopt a nested block structure. So, even accepting that prefixes can compete with suffixes provides no support for the claim that disjunctive ordering needs to span rule blocks.

Conversely, there are compelling grounds for questioning both the assumption that -*t* is a general plural marker and the claim that its distribution is due to disjunctive ordering. The argument that Anderson (1986, 1992) develops against a morphemic analysis hinges on the claim that -*t* is introduced by a single rule. The formulations of this rule from Anderson (1986) and Anderson (1992) are repeated in Figure 6.22.

The most obvious problem with these formulations is that neither expresses a realization rule. Instead, both describe a family of rules. As the paradigms in Tables 6.5 and 6.8 show, Georgian verbs may mark the agreement features of subjects and direct or indirect objects. A bundle representing the features of a Georgian verb must likewise represent the agreement features of multiple arguments. In order to spell out the features of such bundles, a realization rule

---

[12] It is immaterial whether the preverb is analyzed as forming a discontinuous stem with the root, as in Figure 6.21, or treated as somehow combining with an inflected form.

TABLE 6.11   Object marking by -*t*

		1sg	2sg	3
Obj	1pl	—	dagvxat'av	dagvxat'avs
	2pl	dagxat'avt	—	dagxat'avt

must in turn specify which of these feature sets it interprets. On the intended interpretation, a specification like '[. . . +plural . . .]' will be satisfied whenever plural features are present in any of the agreement specifications of a bundle. Hence this 'rule' is just a concise expression of a disjunction over the more specified rules that would actually apply in each of the satisfying cases. The later formulation has the same character, where "in the context of [+Plural]" does not specify an exponence relation but describes a class of rules that spell out the [+Plural] features of a subject, object and/or indirect object.

However, even if one were to assume that -*t* could be introduced by a single rule, it is far from clear that the distribution of this marker is attributable to disjunctive ordering. Consider the status of -*t* as a marker of 1pl and 2pl object features. The relevant forms from Table 6.5 are repeated in Table 6.11. The forms in the second row show that -*t* can mark 2pl object features.

The only evidence that -*t* can mark the plurality of 1pl objects is that it is blocked by 1pl *gv*-. And the only evidence that 2pl *gv*- can apply across blocks to constrain the occurrence of suffixal markers is that it blocks -*t*. Outside this loop of mutually-dependent assumptions, there is no evidence that -*t* ever marks the plurality of 1pl objects. In a case like this, it is surely much simpler to assume that -*t* never marks 1pl object agreement, and hence doesn't need to be blocked in the environments where it never occurs. The ultimate motivation for an appeal to blocking here is the claim that -*t* is a general plural marker. But given that the descriptions of the distribution of -*t* in Figure 6.22 describe disjunctions of realization rules in any event, the realization of -*t* as an object marker can be largely restricted to rules specifying 2p objects.

The final pattern that Anderson presents as support for a general plural analysis of -*t* involves the interaction of 3pl subject markers and -*t*:

since [*dagxat'aven*] can refer to either a singular or a plural second person object, we conclude that the *en*-rule introducing the third person plural suffix -*en* belongs to the same disjunctive block as the *s*-rule and the *t*-rule, and in particular that it takes precedence over the *t*-rule within that block. (Anderson 1986: 8)

The implicit claim is that when a rule that spells out subject agreement features takes priority over a rule spelling out object features, the second rule must realize general, argument-neutral features, since there is no principled reason why the subject agreement features of one rule should be disjunctively ordered with respect to the object agreement features of another. This claim might support a general plural analysis of -*t* if rules realizing different argument agreement features did not interact in Georgian. But in fact they do, in both the prefixal and suffixal blocks. The prefixal competition is illustrated by the 2pl form *dagxat'avt* in Table 6.11, where, as Anderson (1986: 6) notes, "we see that instead of the combination of *v*- and *g*- which we might expect, only the *g*- appears". The suffixal competition is illustrated by *dagxat'avt*, again from Table 6.11, where as Anderson (1986: 8) remarks, "the suffix -*t* blocks the otherwise expected appearance of the suffix -*s* marking third person singular subject". In the first case, a 2p object prefix takes priority over a 1p subject prefix, and in the second case a 2pl object suffix takes priority over a 3sg subject. Both patterns involve agreement features of distinct arguments, and neither can be attributed to a specificity-based disjunctive ordering condition.

Various solutions to these challenges have been proposed within the theoretical literature.[13] However, before proceeding to consider some of the general issues raised by the phenomenon of 'slot competition' it is worth recalling that the Georgian patterns summarized above were initially presented as evidence for a blocking analysis, and specifically for an analysis in which disjunctive ordering relations could apply across rule blocks. Even if one accepts the main claims of this analysis, there is no evidence that disjunctive ordering does in fact apply across blocks. As noted above, there also appear to be compelling grounds for rejecting the main claims of this analysis. Moreover, when viewed in terms of blocking, the competition between agreement markers appears chaotic. Far from supporting the role of disjunctive ordering in a realizational analysis, agreement markers in Georgian highlight the limitations of specificity-based strategies for describing paradigm-internal variation.

6.3.3 Generalization and discrimination

From the standpoint of a classical WP model, the challenges that arise in describing Georgian are intrinsic to a strategy that encapsulates the patterns exhibited by a set of forms in a set of rules that apply to a natural class of cells. Unlike morphemic accounts, realizational analyses do not need to impose a biunique correspondence between features and forms. However, if a rule spells out feature specifications in the realization of one cell, it will in general spell out the same specifications when they occur in other cells. For the most part, this is a good thing; it is the mechanism that permits realizational analyses to express consistent patterns of exponence within a system. But if there are deviations from a uniform pattern, the expected rule must somehow be inhibited. In Georgian, the rule realizing 3sg subject features as -*s* does not apply to cells that contain 2pl object features.[14] The rule realizing 1p subject features as *v*- does not apply to cells that contain 2p object features. At the point that these patterns arose in the development of the Georgian verbal system, there may have been principled explanations for the fact that -*t* and *g*- prevailed. But whatever their origins, both patterns are now established in Georgian and are part of what a speaker needs to learn when they acquire the language.

One might ask then why a realizational model would seek to 'derive' this outcome in a synchronic analysis. It is instructive to contrast a realizational account

---

[13] See, for example, the analyses in Carmack (1997) and Stump (2001).

[14] In contrast, the rule realizing 3sg subject features as -*a* DOES apply, before the rule that realizes 2pl object features, as illustrated, e.g., by *dagexat'at* in Figure 6.8.

with the discriminative treatments of these patterns outlined in Chapter 8. To account for the contexts in which the prefixes *v*- and *g*- occur, realizational models introduce a pair of rules, one that spells out 1p subject features by *v*- and a second that spells out 2p object features by *g*-. In cells that contain 1p subject features and 2p object features, the requirements of both rules are met. Given that only *g*- actually occurs in such cases, a realizational model must somehow assign priority to the rule that spells out 2p features. However, Georgian prefixal competition does not fall straightforwardly within the scope of a specificity-based condition, given that 2p object features are in no obvious way more specific than 1p subject features. Solutions to this problem have of course been explored in different realizational frameworks, but it is the logical structure of the challenge that is particularly relevant here. Because they interpret feature specifications, realization rules apply to the natural classes of cells characterized by those specifications. As noted above, patterns of form variation that are associated with a non-natural class of cells are attributed to the interaction of rules, each of which applies to a natural class of cells, but which overlap in a way that creates a distribution over a non-natural class. In a realizational analysis of the paradigm in Table 3.4, the rule that spells out 1p subject features by *v*- is applicable to the natural class of cells with 1p subject features but only applies to those with 3p objects because it is preempted by the rule that spells out 2p object features.

From a discriminative perspective, the problem faced by realizational analyses of slot competition is symptomatic of initial overgeneralization. Speakers of Georgian would be expected to learn from exposure to the patterns in the language that *v*- does not appear in forms that realize 2p object features. The knowledge that such a speaker acquires about the distribution of *v*- is not accurately represented by a rule that introduces *v*- as the realization of 1p subject features everywhere. Within a realizational model, overgeneralization is endemic to the rule format and cannot readily be corrected by adding specifications. For example, the rule introducing *v*- could be revised so that it applies to cells with 1p subject features and 'non-2p' (or 3p) objects. This refinement would have the desired effect for transitive verbs. Yet this solution creates the need for a separate rule to introduce *v*- in the realization of intransitive verbs, which specify no object features that 'compete' for the prefixal slot.

By modelling the attested, non-natural, distribution of agreement markers, a learning-based discriminative approach attempts to avoid the overgeneralization that leads to slot competition. In a realizational analysis, it is natural to associate *g*- with '2p object features' and highly unnatural to associate *g*- with '1p subject features'. Yet within transitive verb paradigms, *g*- is in fact a more reliable cue for 1p subject features than the 1p subject prefix *v*-. Conversely, it would be natural within a realizational analysis to identify the spell-out of '2p object features' as just the prefix *g*-. However, the complementary distribution of 2p object features and *v*- also forms part of the dynamics of the system. A discriminative learning model, like the human learner, will come to recognize that '2p object features' and *v*- exhibit perfect complementarity. But this pattern does not conform to the model of a feature-form spell-out.

Any account must specify the deviations from a fully uniform distribution of agreement markers in Georgian. The cases in which motivated markers fail to occur do not become any more natural if they are attributed to a gerrymandered feature system or to ad hoc extensions of disjunctive ordering. A classical WP analysis also does not make the distribution any more natural. It merely avoids the need for unnatural restrictions by not abstracting an overgeneralized distribution in the first place. An analysis that takes the paradigm in Table 6.5 as an analogical base for proportional analogies would not motivate the presence of -s in a form realizing 3sg features and 2pl object features. The marker v- would likewise not be motivated in forms containing 2p object features. As these examples illustrate, the distributional patterns that can be projected analogically from this paradigm do not invariably correspond to exponence rules. But an analogical analysis has the advantage of avoiding the overgeneralization that is intrinsic to approaches in which rules must apply to natural classes of feature bundles. Consider again the distribution of the marker -s in Table 6.5. A realizational model can fail to generalize altogether and introduce a separate rule for each cell in which -s occurs. However, a more general description must attribute the distribution of -s to the interaction of rules that apply to natural classes of cells. The rules can either treat the distribution in Table 6.5 as the result of a rule blocking a more general rule, as in Anderson's analysis, or as the union of multiple, natural classes of outputs. The first analysis rests on an ad-hoc notion of 'specificity' and the second on a purely expedient classification of occurrences of -s.

Implementing a classical WP analysis in terms of a discriminative learner (as outlined in Chapter 8) again does not make the distribution of prefixes seem more natural or explain why the prefixes have the distribution that they do. However, the brief illustration above suggests how a learning-based account is designed to avoid inducing an overgeneralized distribution and the problems that arise from that distribution. Furthermore, this illustration also suggests how overgeneralization is itself a symptom of a general realizational strategy of isolating single contrasts from within larger systems of contrasts.

This final point can be clarified with reference again to the competition between v- and g-. From a realizational perspective, it may seem that the contrast in meaning between the 1sg subject form *davxat'av* and the 2sg subject form *daxat'av* can be directly associated with the presence or absence of v-, ignoring object features altogether in transitive paradigms. Yet the contrast between *davxat'av* and *dagxat'av* shows that 3p object features facilitate—whereas 2p object features inhibit—the association between 1sg subject features and v-. Hence the overgeneralization expressed by a rule that spells out 1sg subject features as v- results from a strategy of isolating individual form-feature contrasts from the larger system in which those contrasts operate.

6.3.4 Block order and the status of portmanteaux

In a standard realizational model, the organization of rules imposes a clear division of labour. The grouping of rules into blocks permits a description of the sequential structure of a form. A disjunctive ordering condition contributes to an effective procedure for determining which of a set of rules is applicable at a given point in an analysis. While, as noted above, there is no compelling evidence that disjunctive

TABLE 6.12   Partial future paradigm of Swahili TAKA 'to want' (Ashton 1944: 70ff.)

	Positive				Negative		
	IV	III		V	IV	III	
1sg	ni-	ta-	taka		si-	ta-	taka
2sg	u-	ta-	taka	ha-	u-	ta-	taka
3sg	a-	ta-	taka	ha-	a-	ta-	taka
1pl	tu-	ta-	taka	ha-	tu-	ta-	taka
2pl	m-	ta-	taka	ha-	m-	ta-	taka
3pl	wa-	ta-	taka	ha-	wa-	ta-	taka

ordering applies across blocks, other types of disruptive patterns are more robustly attested. Cumulative exponence is the source of one type of block-spanning relation. The cumulative realization of features presents no difficulties at the level of individual rules. The problems arise if some of the features spelled out cumulatively by one rule are spelled out separately, in different blocks, by other rules. The analysis of the Finnish paradigm in Figure 6.2 averts this situation by exploiting the fact that rule blocks need not be morphosyntactically coherent. The rule that realizes nominative and plural features by -*t* can thus be placed in the same block as the rule that realizes plural features by -*i*, rather than in the block that realizes the case features. The more specific nominative plural rule blocks the plural rule and defines the form *talot* 'houses', which remains unmodified in the 'case' rule block.

However, this solution only works because there is no nominative rule in the second block. In other cases, multiple features from a cumulative exponence rule are realized in different blocks. As Stump (1993*c*: 144ff.) shows, the portmanteau marker *si*- in Swahili presents a case of this kind. The agreement features realized in position 'IV' of the positive conjugation in Table 6.12 include a 1sg marker *ni*-. Negative features are realized in position 'V' by the marker *ha*-. Yet in the negative conjugation, 1sg negative features are not realized by the sequence **hani*-, but instead by a single marker *si*-. As Stump (1993*c*) notes, the rule that introduces *si*- must block both the rule introducing *ha*- in block 'V' and the rule introducing *ni*- in block 'IV'.

In formulating an analysis of this pattern, Stump (1993*b*: 144) proposes initially that "*si*- simultaneously occupies both slots". However, he goes on to implement this proposal in terms of a slightly different intuition, by treating *si*- "as the sole member of a portmanteau position class pre-empting slots V and IV". This structure is exhibited schematically in Figure 6.23.[15]

In this structure, the rules introducing *ha*-, *ni*- and *ta* occur, respectively, within the blocks 'V', 'IV' and 'III', whereas the rule introducing *si*- occupies a portmanteau block that spans blocks 'V' and 'IV'. This organization permits the rule introducing

---

[15] Anticipating the 'realizational pair' format in Section 6.4.1, exponence rules are expressed as pairs $\langle F, \Delta \rangle$, specifying the features F they realize and their output Δ.

V	IV	III
⟨[NEG] , ha+X⟩	⟨[2SG], ni+X⟩	⟨[FUT] , ta+X⟩
	⟨[2SG], u+X⟩	
	⟨[3SG], a+X⟩	
	⟨[1PLU], tu+X⟩	
	⟨[2PLU], m+X⟩	
	⟨[3PLU], wa+X⟩	
⟨[1SG, NEG], si+X⟩		

FIGURE 6.23   Portmanteau 'isg negative' rule block in Swahili

A		B
⟨[PLU], X+i⟩	≺	⟨[PART], X+a⟩
⟨[PLU NOM], X+t⟩	≺	⟨[PLU GEN], X+en⟩
	≺	⟨[GEN], X+n⟩

FIGURE 6.24   Total rule ordering in Finnish

si- to block the rules introducing *ha-* and *ni-* in the realization of any feature bundle containing 1sg negative features.

The organization of rules in Figure 6.23 establishes the desired blocking relations. Yet mediating these relations through 'portmanteau blocks' amounts in effect to relaxing the usual assumption that rule blocks must be totally ordered. The idea of a block-spanning portmanteau reinforces the impression that blocks represent an independent level of structure which is associated with sets of rules, much as the 'timing units' of a phonological description are associated with segments. However, blocks need not be treated as objects, but can instead be understood as generalizations over ordering relations among rules. On this conception, a block consists of a set of rules that are (extrinsically) unordered with respect to each other and which all stand in the same ordering relations to rules outside the set. Hence the blocking relations exhibited by markers like *si-* do not necessarily call for a novel type of block, but can instead motivate a reconsideration of the ordering relations that blocks represent.

The rules in a realizational model are implicitly ordered by a strict partial (irreflexive, asymmetric and transitive) precedence order '≺'. The extrinsic order defined over rules must be partial, to permit rules that apply at the same point in an analysis to remain unordered. These extrinsically unordered rules are regulated by a disjunctive ordering condition. The further assumption incorporated in the realizational models of Anderson (1992) and Stump (2001) is that ordering relations among rules partition a rule set into totally ordered subsets. In a rule set that conforms to this description, such as the Finnish rules in Figure 6.24, the rule order is mirrored by the block order.

What portmanteau patterns like the one in Table 6.12 show is that realization rules cannot always be partitioned into totally ordered blocks. Instead, in the partial ordering of realization rules, there may be rules that are unordered with respect to multiple sets of rules, even though the members of those sets are themselves ordered. In the Swahili pattern, exhibited in Figure 6.25, the rule introducing *si-*

'V'		'IV'		'III'
⟨[NEG], ha+X⟩	≺	⟨[1SG], ni+X⟩	≺	⟨[FUT], ta+X⟩
	≺	⟨[2SG], u+X⟩	≺	
	≺	⟨[3SG], a+X⟩	≺	
	≺	⟨[1PL], tu+X⟩	≺	
	≺	⟨[2PL], m+X⟩	≺	
	≺	⟨[3PL], wa+X⟩	≺	
⟨[1SG, NEG], si+X⟩			≺	

FIGURE 6.25   Portmanteau rule ordering in Swahili

is extrinsically unordered (hence disjunctively ordered) with respect to the rule introducing *ha-* and the simple agreement markers.

As Figure 6.25 indicates, a block order can be projected from these partially ordered rules. The order between blocks will just reflect the order between the rules in each block that are not also in the other. Block 'V' will precede block 'IV' because once the shared rule introducing *si-* is disregarded, the remaining rule in 'V' precedes all of the remaining rules in 'IV'. Since both blocks precede the rules in block 'III', the same is true of any rules that span 'V' and 'IV'. These blocks retain their usefulness for indexing rules; here the sole revision involves cross-indexing portmanteaux rules with multiple, overlapping blocks.

As this brief comparison shows, portmanteau rule blocks are an almost exact realizational counterpart of portmanteaux morphs. When the assumption that features and forms were in a biunique correspondence turned out to be false, the Post-Bloomfieldians did not initially revisit their starting assumptions but instead introduced a host of 'special' morphs. When the assumption that rules could be partitioned into totally ordered blocks encountered analogous problems, Stump (1993c, 2001) proposed portmanteau blocks, amongst other types of special blocks. The eventual rejection of special morphs was not due to the discovery of a pattern that could not be assigned a brute-force special-morph analysis. Rather, the Post-Bloomfieldians came to recognize that these extensions merely compensated for the inadequacy of the original conception of 'primary' morphs. Special rule blocks can be seen to have essentially the same compensatory function in realizational models.

6.3.5 Summary

The analyses of Georgian and Swahili discussed above illustrate the main revisions to the 'control structure' of realizational approaches that have been proposed to extend their descriptive scope. As these accounts show, assumptions about intrinsic and extrinsic ordering are highly interdependent, so that revisions of one component tend to impact the other. In the analysis of Georgian proposed by Anderson (1986, 1992), the assumption of a (partially) linear block structure requires an extension of a disjunctive ordering condition. In the analysis of Swahili proposed by Stump (1993c), the blocking relation between agreement markers motivates a revised conception of blocks. Among the more framework-specific revisions are proposals for dissociating block order from exponent serialization, to account for patterns in which common elements occur in different orders (Stump 1993c, 2001; Luís and Spencer 2005).

Before turning next to formalism-specific extensions, it is worth reprising some of the basic points of agreement and disagreement within realizational models. There is broad agreement that rule application is constrained by a disjunctive ordering condition but no consensus about the form of that condition. Most realizational analyses assign rules to blocks, and justify the composition of individual blocks. However, there is rarely any explicit rationale provided for the organization of blocks into a linear (or nested) structure. Some approaches make extensive use of referral rules, while others eschew them altogether. The sole thread that runs through the family of realizational models is the use of exponence rules to relate 'units of meaning' and 'units of form'.

6.4 Alternative and extended formalisms

Even for exponence rules, there are nearly as many formats as there are realizational approaches. For the most part, the differences between formats reflect different ways of organizing the same content. The following discussion thus summarizes the syntactic variation across rule formats then considers more substantive differences between the form and functioning of other rule types.

The information common to all exponence rule formats can be expressed as a triple $\langle B, X, o(X)\rangle$, where B is a bundle of features interpreted by the rule, X is an input form associated with B, and $o(X)$ specifies an operation on X. The different formats simply group these elements in slightly different ways. The format in Matthews (1991) characterizes a rule as a relation between a feature-form pair $\langle B, X\rangle$ and an output form $o(X)$, i.e. as $\langle\langle B, X\rangle, o(X)\rangle$. The formats in Anderson (1992) and Aronoff (1994) represent rules as relations between a bundle B and a 'spell-out pair' $\langle X, o(X)\rangle$, i.e. as $\langle B, \langle X, o(X)\rangle\rangle$. In the format proposed in Stump (2001), X occurs as an index on a rule that maps an input form-bundle pair $\langle X, \sigma\rangle$ onto the output pair $\langle o(X), \sigma\rangle$.

6.4.1 Rules in A-Morphous and Realizational Pair Morphology

The format proposed in A-Morphous Morphology (AMM; Anderson 1992) differs from the format proposed in Matthews (1991) by extracting the stem variable 'X' from the feature bundle of a rule and placing it within a separate spell-out operation under the feature bundle. In this formalism, the Slovene 1st declension genitive plural rule in Figure 6.19 is expressed as in Figure 6.26.

The rule in Figure 6.26 illustrates a pair of other notational conventions adopted by Anderson (1992) in AMM. The first is that AMM just uses juxtaposition to represent concatenation in outputs like 'Xov'. The second is that properties such as plural number and genitive case, and even declension class, are expressed by the binary features +PLU, +GEN, and +DC1, rather than by privative features like PLU and GEN. These binary features explicitly constrain the distribution of some

$$\begin{bmatrix} +\text{PLU} \\ +\text{GEN} \\ +\text{DC1} \end{bmatrix}$$
$$/X/ \rightarrow /Xov/$$

FIGURE 6.26   Slovene genitive plural rule (cf. Anderson 1992)

feature pairs that are implicitly constrained by feature co-occurrence conditions in analyses that use privative features. However, the choice between binary and privative features has no effect on the applicability of exponence rules. Given that spell-out rules are triggered by the PRESENCE of features, conflicting features are not needed to block rule 'overapplication'.

The REALIZATION PAIR format proposed by Aronoff (1994) expresses exactly the same separation of features and operations in a more compact format. The rule in (6.4) again corresponds to the rule in Figure 6.19.

(6.4)   Slovene genitive plural exponence rule (cf. Aronoff 1994)
         $\langle[\text{PLU, GEN, DC1}], (X \rightarrow Xov)\rangle$

The more intricate realization rule format proposed in Paradigm Function Morphology (PFM; Stump 2001) is again intertranslatable, though this is best discussed in the context of the other rule types in PFM in Section 6.4.3.

6.4.2 Separationist morphology and lexical insertion

Recall that in the realizational model outlined by Matthews (1972, 1991), an analysis is 'seeded' by a pair $\langle C, \rho\rangle$, representing a paradigm cell C and a root form ρ. A similar pair provides the input to paradigm functions in PFM. Both approaches adopt a version of the 'Separation Hypothesis' (Beard 1995) in which the distinctive feature bundles associated with paradigm cells are defined independently of any particular syntactic context, and are realized by word forms that are entered as wholes into syntactic representations.

A different conception of the Separation Hypothesis is developed within AMM. On this alternative, word-level feature bundles are associated with the preterminal nodes of a syntactic tree. Realization rules apply to preterminal bundles and spell out the forms that are associated with the terminal nodes of a tree. Since preterminals are not associated with a lexical root form, a separate process must obtain the stem that seeds an analysis. For this, AMM invokes a realizational analogue of the 'lexical insertion' transformation of Chomsky (1965). Anderson (1992) describes the process in the following terms:

"Lexical insertion" involves finding a lexical item consistent with the position to be interpreted—that is, one whose lexical characteristics are not distinct from those of the position in question, and whose subcategorization requirements are met by the containing Phrase Marker. The corresponding phonological form is then "inflected", through the

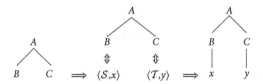

FIGURE 6.27   Lexical insertion in A-Morphous Morphology

operation of inflectional Word Formation Rules, to reflect the morphosyntactic properties
of the position. (Anderson 1992: 132)

The process proceeds in the three stages illustrated in Figure 6.27. In the first
stage, the grammar defines a partial syntactic representation, which terminates in
nodes annotated by the fully specified feature bundles B and C. The spell-out of
these bundles is initiated by selecting stem entries, $\langle S, x \rangle$ and $\langle T, y \rangle$ in Figure 6.27,
from the lexicon. The feature bundles S and T are compared with those of the
bundles B and C, as illustrated in the second tree in Figure 6.27. If the properties
of an entry are 'nondistinct' from those of the corresponding nonterminal, and
appropriate to the syntactic context in which the nonterminal occurs, then the
entry's form is inserted below the bundle. This step is illustrated in the third tree
in Figure 6.27, where the insertion of x and y provides the input to the realization
rules that spell out the features in B and C.

The use of a lexical insertion rule is less of a radical departure than it might
appear. Like realization, lexical insertion is a purely interpretive process. It is,
in effect, just a special, context-sensitive, case of exponence. The nondistinctness check does not modify the properties of a bundle or entry but merely
verifies that there is no conflict and then introduces a stem under a preterminal
node.[16] Moreover, the choice between lexical and syntactic rule application ultimately comes down to whether one regards inflectional properties as being present
'in the lexicon', or 'in the syntax'.[17] This issue represents a free choice within
morphological models, particularly given the difficulty in discerning empirical
differences between a system in which realization rules apply 'late' in the lexicon
and a system in which they apply 'early' in the syntactic component.

6.4.3 Rules in Paradigm Function Morphology

The differences between the rule formats employed by Matthews (1991), Anderson
(1992) and Aronoff (1994) are fairly superficial, and mainly reflect different ways

[16] As noted by Ingria (1990), a nondistinctness check has many of the effects of subsumption
or unification in enforcing feature compatibility within a local domain, though the effects of these
mechanisms diverge over larger domains (Blevins 2011).

[17] The claim that inflectional properties are syntactic (whereas derivational properties are lexical)
is often termed the 'Split Morphology Hypothesis' (Perlmutter 1988). See also Booij 1993, 1996 and
Blevins 2001 for some discussion.

of packaging the same information. In contrast, the rules in PFM differ more substantially. Exponence rules are the most conservative rule type in PFM, since they have the same effect as other spell-out rules. As in earlier formats, *RR* in (6.5) applies to an 'input' form-feature pair and defines an 'output' form.[18] However, unlike previous rules, the rule contains a variable, σ, that explicitly represents the bundle to which the rule applies.

(6.5)   Realization rule format in PFM (Stump 2001: 44)

$$RR_{n,\tau,C}(\langle X, \sigma \rangle) =_{\text{def}} \langle Y', \sigma \rangle$$

Hence $\langle X, \sigma \rangle$ represents the input pair to which *RR* applies, and $\langle Y', \sigma \rangle$ a pair containing the output Y'. As before, 'X' represents a form, whereas 'Y'' represents a CLASS of forms. This class contains 'Y' and all of the forms obtained from 'Y' by "any applicable morphophonological rules" (Stump 2001: 45).[19]

The most distinctive feature of this rule format is the sequence of indices subscripted to *RR*. The block index n identifies the rule block in which the rule occurs, the property set index τ specifies the features that are spelled out by the rule, and the class index C indicates the class of lexemes to which the rule applies. As discussed in Section 6.3, assigning rules to ordered blocks groups together rules that apply at the same point in a structure, and imposes an extrinsic order on rules that apply at different points. The set τ contains the features that are specified in the previous rule types, except for word class and morphological class features, which are segregated in C. The rule in (6.6), which again realizes 1st declension genitive plural nouns in Slovene, shows how information is distributed across pairs and indices.

(6.6)   Slovene case realization rule in PFM

$$RR_{1,\{NUM:plu,CASE:gen\},\{N,I\}}(\langle X, \sigma \rangle) =_{\text{def}} \langle Xov', \sigma \rangle$$

The block index '1' assumes that all nominal inflections are introduced in a single suffixal block. The features {NUM:plu,CASE:gen} are the attribute-value counterparts of the privative and binary features in earlier rule formats. The indices N and I likewise indicate that the rule applies to 1st declension nouns. The variable X again represents the noun stem, and Xov' the result of concatenating -*ov* and applying any morphophonological rules.

Given that the rule in (6.6) achieves much the same effect as simpler types of exponence rules, it is worth identifying the source of additional complexity in PFM. Dividing features among the three indices in (6.6) is the most obvious source. A model that makes use of rule blocks requires some means of assigning rules to blocks and the block index merely annotates that information on the rules

---

[18] As in other realizational models, rules define correspondences between features and forms, so that references to 'input' and 'ouput' structures are a matter of expositional convenience and do not impute any genuine derivational structure.

[19] Although this may appear to be a complication of previous formats, the classes represented by 'Y'' are largely implicit in the phonemic representations in earlier rules.

themselves. The use of separate property set and class indices expresses an intuitive contrast between the 'content' features in τ and the 'context' features in C. However, it ultimately makes no formal difference whether properties are split across two feature sets or pooled in a single set B.

Distributing feature across separate sets and indices in turn complicates the formulation of rule applicability, as illustrated by the 'coherence' conditions in (6.7). The condition in (6.7a) imposes the usual condition on applicability by requiring a bundle σ to contain all of the features in τ.

(6.7) Rule-argument coherence (Stump 2001: 45)
        $RR_{n,\tau,C}(\langle X, \sigma \rangle)$ is defined iff (a) σ is an extension of τ; (b) L-index(X) $\in$ C;
        and (c) σ is a well-formed set of morphosyntactic properties for L-index(X).

The remaining conditions illustrate the kinds of complications that arise from the scattering of feature information in PFM. Both conditions refer to the function, 'L-index', which is described as mapping roots and other forms onto the lexemes with which they are associated. In the passage quoted on p. 63 above, Stump (2001) elucidates the notion of L-indices by suggesting:

lie 'recline' carries a covert index LIE$_1$ (so that L-index(*lie*) = LIE$_1$), while *lie* 'prevaricate' carries a covert index LIE$_2$ (so that L-index(*lie*) = LIE$_2$). (Stump 2001: 43f.)

However, if the value of L-index is a lexeme, then condition (6.7b) will only be satisfied if the class index set C contains lexeme indices. On this interpretation, condition (6.7c) requires that individual lexeme indices must also be typed for properties, much as structures in HPSG accounts are typed. Conditions (6.7b) and (6.7c) would both make more sense if they applied to the word class of the lexeme represented by X. But on this interpretation, it becomes even clearer that condition (6.7b) is only required because word class features have been segregated in C, rather than included in τ. Moreover, although any feature-based approach must specify wellformed combinations of features, this would normally be defined for a word or inflection class as a whole, and not embedded within the definition of a particular rule format.[20]

Even if all of this can be made to work technically, it is unclear why the feature information in an exponence rule should be organized in this way. There are no obvious formal or empirical problems that are addressed by putting some features in τ, others in C and treating yet others as covertly associated by form-to-index functions. Even more fundamentally, it is unclear that different ways of dividing features across sets could have any effect, given that the conditions that apply to particular classes of features can be (and are) defined to look for them in whatever sets they have been assigned to. The main effect of the conditions in (6.7) is to restrict the applicability of exponence rules, and this can be achieved far more transparently if features are pooled in a single set B, as suggested above.

---

[20] A separate technical problem is that 'L-index' cannot be a function, since no actual function can map an ambiguous string to multiple unambiguous lexeme indices.

A rule RR that specifies a consolidated property set $\mathcal{B}$ will be applicable to bundles that extend $\mathcal{B}$. Dependencies between class features and morphosyntactic features (as expressed by (6.7c)) are also completely unaffected by whether the features are in a common set or in separate sets, though the statement of these dependencies can be simplified if they are treated as co-occurrence relations within a single feature bundle (or structure).

By consolidating indices into a single set $\mathcal{B}$ and eliminating multiple references to the input feature bundle σ, it is possible to express exponence rules in PFM in the simpler and more transparent format in (6.8).

(6.8) Simplified realization rule format in PFM
$$RR_{\mathcal{B}}(\langle X, \sigma \rangle) =_{\text{def}} Y'$$

Eliminating multiple references to σ is particularly beneficial, as it builds the interpretive character of realization rules into the format itself, rather than enforcing an interpretive construal of a more general format. A realization rule like (6.6) has the syntax of an IP process, which, as described in Chapter 2.3 and in (6.1a), maps entries onto entries. By convention, the property sets represented by the occurrences of σ are identical, but this convention is only required because there are multiple occurrences of σ. The reason that σ is specified at all in (6.8) is that an analysis in PFM proceeds by passing ⟨bundle, form⟩ pairs between the realization rules invoked by a paradigm function.

Stump (2001) acknowledges that exponence rules do not need to make reference to σ. However, he argues that such reference IS necessary for referral rules and suggests that the inclusion of σ permits a unified rule format:

Given any argument $\langle X, \sigma \rangle$ to which a realization rule applies, the corresponding value $\langle Y', \sigma \rangle$ shares the property set σ. In light of this, one might well ask why the definition of a realization rule ever needs to make explicit reference to the shared property set. As it turns out ... there is a subclass of realization rules—namely rules of referral—whose application yields a value $\langle Y', \sigma \rangle$ such that the form of Y' depends on the specific identity of σ; for this subclass of realization rules, mention of the shared property set σ cannot be suppressed. The need for schematization in the definition of paradigm functions makes it desirable to employ a format for the definition of realization rules which is usable for any such rule (whether or not it is a rule of referral) ... (Stump 2001: 280)

As discussed in Section 6.2.2, exponence and referral rules have different effects. An exponence rule spells out features by forms, whereas a referral rule relates a pair of exponence relations. Referrals cannot be formulated as simple spell-out rules. Exponence rules may be expressed as degenerate cases of referrals, but this does not necessarily express any underlying commonality between the rule types. To the extent that referrals implement the same intuition as the 'morphological transformations' and other devices in Section 6.2.3, they trigger the realization of one set of features in place of another. In a PFM analysis, these sets would correspond to values for the index τ (or $\mathcal{B}$ in the simplified format), not to values for the repeated property σ set, representing cells.

The final issue to consider in this brief summary of PFM rules is the form of paradigm functions and the influence that they exert on realization rules. Paradigm functions are the most innovative feature of PFM, representing a distinctive hypothesis about the organization of morphological systems. The basic conception is set out by Stump (2001) in the following terms:

A paradigm function ... is a kind of function ... [that] applies to a ROOT PAIRING $\langle X, \sigma \rangle$ (where X is the root of a lexeme L and σ is a complete set of morphosyntactic properties for L) to yield the σ-cell $\langle Y, \sigma \rangle$ in L's paradigm. (Stump 2001: 43)

This initial form-based format is exhibited in in (6.9).

(6.9)   Root-based format for paradigm functions (Stump 2001: 43)
        $PF(\langle X, \sigma \rangle) = \langle Y, \sigma \rangle$

In a subsequent revision of PFM, Stewart and Stump (2007) propose the format in (6.10), which maps lexeme-property set pairs onto paradigm cells.

(6.10)   Lexeme-based format (Stewart and Stump 2007)
        $PF(\langle L, \sigma \rangle) = \langle Y, \sigma \rangle$

Perhaps the most original characteristic of PFM concerns the central role of paradigm functions in the control structure of a grammar. Paradigm functions do not directly modify a root X or spell out a cell σ but control the application of the rules that do spell out σ by modifying X. An example that Stump (2001: 53) provides to describe verbal paradigms in Bulgarian is repeated in (6.11).

(6.11)   Where σ is a complete set of morphosyntactic properties for lexemes of category V, $PF(\langle X, \sigma \rangle) =_{def} Nar_D(Nar_C(Nar_B(Nar_A(\langle X, \sigma \rangle))))$.

The paradigm function in (6.11) defines the realization of the paradigm cell σ by invoking the most specific realization rules that apply to σ in the ordered rule blocks A through D. The rule in block A modifies the root X, and the rules in each successive block modify the output of the preceding block.

This example illustrates how paradigm functions explicitly control interactions that are built into the structure of other realizational models. The paradigm function in (6.11) expressly stipulates intrinsic and extrinsic ordering relations that would otherwise be incorporated into the definition of rule applicability. The nesting of rule blocks A through D in (6.11) imposes an intrinsic order that is attributed to a general block order in realizational models that assign rules to sequentially-ordered blocks. The function 'Nar', which picks out the narrowest rule in each of the blocks in (6.11) achieves the effect of a disjunctive ordering condition by imposing a specificity constraint on each block independently. Incorporating these ordering conditions within individual paradigm functions allows for greater flexibility. Within PFM, individual paradigm functions can freely reorder blocks or impose conditions other than relative specificity to regulate the application of rules within a block. Stump (2001, 2005a) argues that this flexibility permits an account of patterns that he attributes to 'reversible' rule blocks. Yet even if rule-specific ordering constraints are useful for the description of exponent reversal, it does not follow that constraints should also be stipulated on a rule-by-rule basis in languages that have a uniform block order and obey a general disjunctive ordering condition.

As this brief summary suggests, much of the complexity of PFM derives from two related design features. The first is the use of maximally uniform rule formats, so that the most complex rule type determines the complexity of the entire class to which it belongs. The second is a maximally local control structure, mostly delegated down to the level of individual rules. This again reflects a uniformity hypothesis, which dictates that if the analysis of any construction requires rule-by-rule stipulation of block and rule ordering constraints, then all analyses should stipulate these constraints at the level of individual rules.

A number of recent works, notably Spencer (2013) and Bonami and Stump (2015), propose substantial revisions to PFM, some of which bear on issues that arise within the 'classic PFM' model formulated in Stump (2001). Once these proposals have been integrated into a new reference model of PFM, it may be possible to evaluate the cumulative effect of the revisions and execution choices and clarify the formal and empirical claims they embody.

6.5 Realization and structure

Viewed as a class, realizational approaches represent a more faithful model of the morphological descriptions assigned by classical WP grammars than of the morphological systems described by these grammars. This interpretation of real-izational models is reinforced particularly by the way that they reify traditional descriptive vocabulary and associate morphotactically unstructured analyses with complex forms. These points are clarified briefly below.

6.5.1 Indexical morphology

The nomenclature of classes and series in a classical grammar serves a primarily descriptive function, providing a frame of reference for the classification of forms and systems. These classes and series are not located in languages per se, but merely define the descriptive lens through which the language is viewed. It is these aspects of the classical WP tradition that realizational approaches model when they reify schemes of classification by means of indexical features. Inflection class features appear initially in the treatment of German declensions in Chomsky (1965: 171) and in the analysis of Latin conjugations in Matthews (1965: 150). Once established, these features came to be assumed in nearly all realizational approaches. A strategy of reencoding classifications by means of indices was subsequently extended to encompass other aspects of a traditional description. The analysis of Georgian case marking proposed in Anderson (1992: 150) expresses conjugational series as 'series indices' of the form [±Series II]. The covert 'lexeme indices' discussed in connection with PFM in Section 6.4.3 are also assumed in many realizational models. At the sub-word level, 'stem indices' are widely adopted in analyses of stem syncretisms (Aronoff 1994; Stump 2001; Baerman *et al.* 2005).

In many of these cases, indexical features drive a realizational analysis by determining the choice of an element from a set of alternatives, triggering the application of a rule, or in some other way explicitly guiding choices that are underdetermined by non-indexical features. In languages where inflection classes are not predictable from grammatical or phonological properties, encoding class membership as a separate morphological 'feature' permits the selection of class-specific exponents. A 'stem indexing' analysis allows rules to select recurrent units of form that do not realize a consistent set of grammatical properties in the different constructions in which they occur. More generally, by cross-referencing cells, entries, rules and other elements, it is possible to select, arrange and manipulate units whose form and distribution is not otherwise predictable from a decomposed representation.

In effect, indexical features serve as the 'glue' of a realizational model, providing a general mechanism for reassembling the words and larger units from the parts distributed across the stem and rule inventories of the model. This use of indexical features fundamentally changes the nature of a realizational model. It is unclear in what meaningful sense exponence rules remain 'interpretive' if they can 'spell out' indexical features that function as assembly instructions. Reassembly is typically the only observable function of these features, given that they rarely if ever seem to participate in grammatical dependencies such as agreement, concord or government.

Hence an approach that 'spells out' indexical features can, as suggested above, be interpreted as providing an explicit model of a system of language description. However, as a model of language structure, it runs the risk of incorporating the error, which Hockett (1967) states below, of confounding its own descriptive apparatus with the intended object of description:

One of the most dangerous traps in any of the more complex branches of science . . . is that of confusing one's machinery of analysis with one's object of analysis. One version of this is pandemic in linguistic theory today: almost all theorists take morphophonemes to be things IN a language rather than merely part of our equipment for the analysis and description OF the language. (Hockett 1967: 221)

The empirical scope of realizational models also reflects the descriptive strengths and weaknesses of traditional grammars. Rules that spell out antecedently-specified features are well equipped to exploit the closed, relatively uniform feature space of an inflectional system. Within this closed space, the features of paradigm cells can be defined independently of the forms that realize them. From the class of an open-class item, it is usually possible to determine the features that are distinctive for that class and predict the number of cells in the paradigm of the item. Apart from irregular items, paradigms are broadly comparable in size and structure within a word or inflection class.

However the fact that realizational models are so finely tuned to the structure of inflectional systems creates difficulties in extending them to other types of patterns. In particular, realizational models are less applicable to the variable structure exhibited by 'families' of derivational forms. Processes that relate items with variable word class, valence or other intrinsic properties usually do not define a finite set of forms within a uniform feature space. From just the word or inflection class of an item, one cannot in general predict the number and type of derivational formations in which it occurs. Given a list of derivational processes active in a language, it is of course possible to assign a uniform family of 'potential' forms to all of the members of a word class. Yet the uniformity achieved is deceptive, because it collapses a critical distinction between those forms that are established in a language and those that are merely possible in principle. The point may be clearer in connection with compounds. Of the many possible noun compounds in a language such as English, only a comparatively small number are established, and a speaker cannot predict the established compounds containing an item from the item itself.

Even in cases where a derivational item is predictable from an item of a different word class, it is far from obvious what useful contribution is made by expressing the correspondence as the spell-out of antecedently specified features. Consider just the simple patterns exhibited by deverbal nouns in English. Nearly all verbs that allow an agentive interpretation have corresponding agentive nominals consisting of the verb stem and an invariant -er ending. Many verbs also have counterpart agent nominals, marked by the productive ending -ing and/or by a variety of other endings (Marchand 1960). In the case of agentive nominals, the meaning expressed is essentially relational: a nominal of the form 'Xer' is interpreted as 'one who Xs'. Yet what 'features' in the bundle associated with an agentive nominal are 'spelled out' as -er? In the case of event nominals, the choice of ending is neither uniform, nor determined by otherwise motivated morphological classes. Instead, the choice is a lexical property of individual items, as argued at length in debates about transformational and lexicalist analyses of derived nominals (Chomsky 1970).

To accommodate derivational patterns, realizational accounts such as AMM and PFM incorporate a class of derivational 'word formation rules'. As specified in the following passage, these rules, like the lexical rules of an IP model, map one feature-form pair onto a different feature-form pair:

Our view is that of Stump (1993a, 1995, 2001): that a morphological expression is headed if and only if it arises through the application of a category-preserving rule of word formation. A category-preserving rule of derivation or compounding is one which allows one or more morphosyntactic properties of a base to persist as properties of its derivative. (Stewart and Stump 2007: 407)

Whatever the merits of this treatment of derivational patterns, the use of entry-to-entry mappings implicitly acknowledges the limits of realizational strategies. As in the initial formulation in Matthews (1965), realization rules in models such as AMM and PFM operate within 'the inflectional component of a WP grammar'. Other types of rules, with a greater or lesser family resemblance to realization rules, apply in other components. Hence, as Anderson (1992) emphasizes in the continuation of the quotation on p. 120 above, models like AMM are defined more by their opposition to procedures of morphemic analysis than by their consistent use of purely realizational strategies:

The principal opposition is to "Item and Arrangement" models; and since the dominant, classical picture of word structure based on the structuralist morphemes is firmly of this sort, it is this distinction that is most important to pursue. (Anderson 1992: 72)

The opposition to the IA "picture of word structure" brings out another parallel between realizational approaches and classical WP descriptions. Strikingly, neither incorporates any model of word structure. It is a familiar criticism of the classical model that it developed no counterpart of morphemes—not even roots (Law 1998: 112)—and that it failed to demarcate any unit between sounds/letters and words. Realizational models exhibit a remarkably similar perspective. As in the passage on p. 122 above, realization rules are "interpretive phonological rules" that "operate on the phonological matrix of the lexical entry, giving, finally, a phonetic matrix" (Chomsky 1965: 172). The rule formats summarized in preceding sections map an input form onto an output form. The application of a rule is not conventionally interpreted as introducing 'boundary' elements or as marking morphotactic structure in any way. Instead, as in an IP model, morphological structure is represented in the 'derivational history' defined by the rules that apply to define a surface form. As a consequence, realizational models not only reject morphemic analysis but also dispense with morphs and with morphotactic structure in general.[21]

6.5.2 Neo-Saussurean realizationalism

As in classical WP grammars (and WP models), the grammatical word remains the primary locus of meaning. Yet realizational models are also theoretical hybrids, reflecting the influence of the Bloomfieldian tradition in their treatment of roots or stems as basic units of lexical form. This conception departs from classical approaches, in which the word is the basic unit of lexical form, and exponents, or inflectional exponents at any rate, are regarded as abstractions over whole words. Although the implicational approaches in Chapter 7 provide the most faithful models of the classical WP conception, realizational models can also be interpreted in a more 'abstractive' way (Blevins 2006b).

One way of reinterpreting realizational models is to construe them as automata rather than as grammars. Formal language theory defines a correspondence between classes of rewrite grammars, which 'output' symbols or sequences of symbols, and classes of automata, which 'input' symbols or sequences. Like most morphological models, the realizational formalisms summarized in this chapter are conventionally represented as grammars. On this interpretation, a realization-

---

[21] Though see Spencer (2012) for a morph-based realizational perspective.

based model assembles forms by applying operations to lexical roots or stems that 'spell out' specified features, as discussed above. The same class of approaches can also be construed as automata. On this interpretation, a realization-based model accepts (or rejects) forms, depending on whether they satisfy the feature–form associations expressed by spell-out rules. As with formal grammars and automata, the language (the set of surface feature-form pairs) 'generated' by a real-izational grammar will be the same as the language 'accepted' by the corresponding automaton.

Despite their extensional equivalence, the two interpretations differ in ways that bear on a range of formal and empirical issues. The most salient difference concerns the composition of the lexicon. Whereas realizational grammars assume a model of the lexicon consisting mainly of root or stem entries, realizational automata are compatible with a classical WP view on which the lexicon consists primarily of full word entries. On this interpretation, realization rules function as 'word admissibility conditions' that constrain the compatibility of particular features and form variations in the feature-form pairing associated with a word entry. Hence interpreting realization-based models as automata suggests a rap-prochement with the implicational models in Chapter 7, in which words are basic morphotactic as well as morphosyntactic units. In addition, applying realization rules a to word-based lexicon permits a form-based treatment of referral rules, which can be interpreted as directly relating all or part of the form of multiple paradigm cells.

An automaton-based interpretation of realizational models is also compatible with the model-theoretic perspective of constraint-based approaches to syntax. The feature specifications that determine the applicability of a realization rule can be interpreted formally as a partial description of the feature bundles associated with word entries. The operation performed by a rule is then interpreted as a partial description of a class of forms. An operation of the form $/X \rightarrow X\omega/$ is not interpreted as 'constructing' an output form $/X\omega/$ by concatenating the string ω to a base X, but as 'admitting' a form that is analyzable as a sequence $X\omega$. A word form is admissible if there is an assignment of forms to variables (like 'X') on which it satisfies all of the applicable realization rules. This shift in orientation offers a slightly different perspective on morphophonemic processes that often remain implicit in realization-based models. To express the standard claim that the forms of the regular past participle ending in English [t], [d] and [ɪd] "are variants of ONE formative, not separate formatives", Matthews (1991: 145f.) posits "a single morphological process" that introduces a "basic form" or "basic allomorph". In the models of Anderson (1992) or Aronoff (1994), the 'basic form' is represented by the corresponding phoneme, here /d/. Yet the morphological analyses defined by these models are either abstract or incomplete, as they fail to specify the 'back-end' morphophonemic processes that define surface forms. On a word admissibility interpretation, the phonemes in realization rules can be taken to be descriptions that are satisfied by surface forms in a word-based lexicon. This treatment of morphophonemics subsumes the types of morphological metageneralizations discussed by Stump (2001: §6.2) within the kind of model-theoretic approach to phonology set out in Bach and Wheeler (1983).

To those accustomed to thinking of formal grammars as admissibility conditions, the main effect of adopting an automaton-based interpretation might be that the objects admitted by these conditions are the words of a word-based lexicon, though this shift in perspective has other potential consequences. Applying admissibility conditions to a word-based lexicon should reduce the role of 'indexical' features, since it is no longer necessary to reassemble words from parts that have been dispersed across stem and rule inventories. It is of course to be expected that some problems that arise on a grammar interpretation of a realizational model will recur in a different form on an automaton interpretation. In particular, any challenges that derive from the realizational focus on individual forms rather than systems will have counterparts on grammar and automaton interpretations. To clarify how these kinds of challenges can be met by approaches that incorporate a complex system perspective, the following chapter now turns to the family of implicational WP models.

7

Implicational models

An implicational perspective spans the western grammatical tradition, as one of the first conceptions to be articulated and one of the last to be formalized. Classical advocates of 'analogy' saw morphological systems as exhibiting a kind of 'organized complexity' (Weaver 1948), emerging from regular patterns of accidence and co-occurrence. Proponents of 'anomaly' viewed the irregularity and randomness of morphological systems as exhibiting 'disorganized complexity'. Both conceptions were incorporated in a qualified form in what became the classical WP model. A high degree of system-level congruence was associated with inflectional patterns, while irregularity and variation were treated as characteristic of lexical inventories and, to the extent that they were distinguished, patterns of word-formation. The organized complexity of inflectional systems lent itself to economical factorization. A collection of exemplary items enumerated the distinctive patterns of inflection in a language, while a set of diagnostic forms associated each non-exemplary item with one of the patterns. The disorganized complexity exhibited by the word stock of a language and word formation processes were then listed in grammars and dictionaries.

The classical WP model survives in this exemplar-based form until the present day, remaining, as Hockett remarks in the passage on p. 5 "the traditional framework for the discussion of Latin, Greek, Sanskrit, and a good many more modern familiar languages". The cornerstone of this framework is a conception of organized complexity that derives from the observation "that one inflection tends to predict another" (Matthews 1991: 197). The role of interdependencies underlies the conception of an integrated morphological SYSTEM that is more than a collection of individual forms and patterns. The notion that the words assigned to inflectional paradigms and classes "are themselves the parts within a complex whole" (Matthews 1991: 204) clearly anticipates the characterization of organized complexity as arising from "a sizable number of factors which are interrelated into an organic whole" (Weaver 1948: 539).

Although a complex system perspective is implicit in the descriptive practices of classical grammars, the underlying conception is never explicitly formalized in this tradition. Interdependencies are exhibited by the forms of exemplary items, or encapsulated in the classes represented by these items. Within the philological traditions that grew up around individual languages and language families, there was often a consensus regarding the implicational structure of a language, as reflected in the number of classes recognized in a language and the choice of diag-nostic forms. But this type of consensus largely reflected convergent descriptive or pedagogical goals. Classical WP models never developed strategies for abstracting implicational dependencies from the forms that exhibit them. There are likewise no

Word and Paradigm Morphology. First edition. James P. Blevins
© James P. Blevins 2016. First published 2016 by Oxford University Press

procedures for selecting diagnostic forms, individuating classes, or for measuring the informativeness of forms. This shortcoming encouraged the view that the problem of selecting principal parts was intrinsic to, or possibly even recalcitrant within, classical models. The same issue recurs in a different guise in the problem of distinguishing valid from spurious analogies. Both relations depend on a notion of 'informativeness' that measures how reliably one element identifies another.

7.1 Variation as uncertainty

Although informativeness remains implicit in the classical WP model, this ultimately reflects the purposes for which the model was initially developed. An explicit formalization of the classical WP model can be founded on two basic assumptions. The first is that variation within a system corresponds to uncertainty. The second is that implicational structure within the system corresponds to uncertainty reduction. The various notions of 'informativeness' mentioned above likewise represent different types of uncertainty reduction. The role of uncertainty is also reflected in the selection of units and structures. As discussed in Chapters 3 and 4, neither words nor paradigms have a privileged status *a priori* in a classical WP model. The abstraction of word-sized units and their assignment to larger paradigmatic structures is justified by the reduction in uncertainty that this achieves in a grammatical analysis.

There is an obvious trade-off between the determinacy and the generalizability of a unit. At the level of utterances, many of the ambiguities that arise at lower levels are resolved, as Bloomfield (1914) remarks. Yet a grammatical analysis that merely classifies utterances is universally regarded as too coarse-grained, obscuring regular associations between smaller recurrent units of form and meaning. An analysis into phonemes suffers from the opposite problem, disrupting associations between larger units and properties. Differing assessments of the trade-off between determinacy and generalizability lead approaches to select different units between utterances and phonemes.

As discussed in Chapter 4.1, the choice of segmentally minimal units within initial models of morphemic analysis is motivated by the goal of maximizing "scientific compactness". In contrast, the selection of word-sized units in the classical WP tradition reflects a conception of economy based on the minimization of indeterminacy and the efficient characterization of patterns, rather than on the avoidance of redundancy. A central claim of classical WP models is that words exhibit a morphosyntactic and morphotactic stability that contributes to maximally general descriptions of regularities within a system.

Robins (1959) provides a traditional statement of this position on p. 6 above when he claims that "the word is a more stable and solid focus of grammatical relations than the component morpheme by itself". In uncertainty-based terms, the uncertainty that arises in associating grammatical properties with a word is on average less than the cumulative uncertainty that arises in assigning properties to its parts. The association between words and paradigm cells (or other property sets) 'anchors' a form within a grammatical system, facilitating implicational deductions that further constrain uncertainty within the system.[1] The conception of a morphological system as a structured network of individually stable units determines a notion of economy which corresponds to the characterization of "morphological simplicity" in Bochner (1993: 2) "as conformity with patterns of the grammar, rather than as brevity".

In sum, the status of words in implicational models ultimately reflects the claim that word-sized units minimize uncertainty along both dimensions of a grammatical analysis. Along the syntagmatic axis, words are minimal in the sense that any disassembly into smaller units creates greater uncertainty. Along the paradigmatic axis, words are the minimal units that participate in uncertainty-reducing implicational relations. These dimensions of uncertainty are elaborated in Sections 7.1.1 and 7.1.2 and formalized in Section 7.2.

7.1.1 Syntagmatic uncertainty

The relationship between unit size and grammatical uncertainty guides the discussion of examples in previous chapters, so a brief summary of some of the relevant patterns will suffice here. Consider first the Georgian verb paradigm in Table 6.5, repeated below in Table 7.1, with just plural suffixes in bold.

At the word level, 16 of the 18 forms in Table 7.1 can be associated with a unique cell. In some forms, it is the presence of agreement markers that is distinctive, while in others it is the absence of markers that is contrastive, as Anderson (1992) remarks in the passage on p. 56 above. A form with no prefix can only encode a 3p object. Forms encoding 1sg objects are marked by *m-*, those encoding 1pl objects are marked by *gv-* and those encoding 2p objects are marked by *g-*. A form with no suffixal marker can only encode a singular subject, since all forms encoding 3pl subjects are marked by *-en* and all forms encoding 1pl or 2pl subjects are marked by *-t*. The most extreme example of distinctive absence is provided by *daxat'av*,

TABLE 7.1   Future indicative paradigm of XAT'VA 'paint' (Tschenkéli 1958: §31)

Subj	1sg	1pl	Obj 2sg	2pl	3
1sg	—	—	dagxat'av	dagxat'avt	davxat'av
1pl	—	—	dagxat'avt	dagxat'avt	davxat'avt
2sg	damxat'av	dagvxat'av	—	—	daxat'av
2pl	damxat'avt	dagvxat'avt	—	—	daxat'avt
3sg	damxat'avs	dagvxat'avs	dagxat'avs	dagxat'avt	daxat'avs
3pl	damxat'aven	dagvxat'aven	dagxat'aven	dagxat'aven	daxat'aven

[1] An abstract paradigm 'cell' corresponds to a set of distinctive properties for a given word or inflection class, and the paradigm itself consists of a set of cells associated with an item. The forms that express these properties are described as 'realizations' of the cell—in the traditional sense of 'formal expressions', not in the more recent sense of 'outputs of spell-out rules'. An 'instantiated paradigm' consists of a set of cell-form pairs. The intended sense of cells, paradigms and realizations should be clear from context.

TABLE 7.2   Contrasts marked by *-t*

	Context	Contrast	Example
i	2p object	pl vs sg	*dagxat'avt* vs *dagxat'av*
ii	2p subject	pl vs sg	*damxat'avt* vs *damxat'av*
iii	1p subject	pl vs sg	*davxat'avt* vs *davxat'av*

in which the lack of prefixal and suffixal markers unambiguously encodes a 2sg subject and a 3p object.

The two ambiguous forms, *dagxat'aven* and *dagxat'avt*, both occur in the sub-paradigm with 2p objects. Ambiguity arises in this part of the paradigm in Table 7.1 due to the fact that 2p *g-* occupies the prefixal agreement position, leaving only the suffixal slot to encode the number of the object and the person and number of the subject. Thus *dagxat'aven* realizes the two cells with a 3pl subject, while *dagxat'avt* realizes four of the remaining cells with 2p objects.

In sum, the markers in Table 7.1 define 18 distinct word forms, distributed over 22 paradigm cells. Significantly, the word-level ambiguity in this paradigm cannot be resolved by decomposing forms into sub-word units, even in cases where the units can themselves be assigned unambiguous analyses. In the case of *dagxat'aven*, the prefix *g-* unambiguously marks 2p object features and the suffix *-en* 3pl subject features. However, the use of *-en* to mark 3pl subject features prevents the marking of object number. In cases where sub-word units are also ambiguous, decomposition can lead to an analytical conundrum.

Unlike the unambiguous *-en*, the plural suffix *-t* in *dagxat'avt* marks a contrast between plural and singular in the three 'contexts' in Table 7.2. Contrasts (i) and (ii) share 2p features but differ in grammatical relation, whereas (ii) and (iii) share a common grammatical relation but differ in person. Contrasts (i) and (iii) differ both in person and grammatical relation. Hence, there are essentially three options available for a model that seeks to assign a feature analysis to *-t*. One analysis would introduce separate analyses for each of the contexts in Table 7.2, a second would subsume (i) and (ii) under a general 2p marker, and a third would subsume (ii) and (iii) under a general subject marker.

No coherent analysis could subsume just (i) and (iii), given the contrast in person and grammatical relation. Yet the cell in Table 7.1 that specifies a 2pl object and a 1pl subject is occupied by *dagxat'avt*, which is marked by a single occurrence of *-t*. A model that associates properties with sub-word units must determine 'which *-t*' marks this form. But there is no basis for choosing either (i) or (iii), and no plausible means of consolidating them into a single marker.

This is the conundrum that Anderson (1992) attempts to evade by proposing a 'general plural' analysis on which there is a single *-t* marker. However, as noted in Chapter 6.3.2, the analysis that Anderson formulates does not state a rule so much as describe a disjunctive set of rules. A different strategy is pursued by Stump (2001: 70), who consolidates (ii) and (iii) into a common marker $-t_1$ and represents (i) by a separate marker $-t_2$, which is restricted so that it "appears only in the context of singular subject agreement". At one level, this is a fairly unprincipled

TABLE 7.3   Representative case forms of PUKK 'trestle'

Grammatical Cases			Semantic Cases		
	Sg	Plu		Sg	Plu
Nom	pukk	pukid	Ines	pukis	pukkides
Gen	puki	pukkide	Ades	pukil	pukkidel
Part	pukki	pukkisid	Abes	pukita	pukkideta

stipulation; one could just as well consolidate (i) and (ii) into a common 2p marker $-t_1$, and associate (iii) with a marker $-t_2$ that is restricted so that it 'appears only in the context of singular object agreement'. At a more basic level, this analysis represents a tacit acknowledgment that the distribution of $-t$ cannot be specified in terms of a single set of agreement properties. Instead, as suggested in Chapter 6.3.3 and elaborated in Chapter 8.3, markers function in the context of larger systems of property-form contrasts.

Although the analyses proposed by Anderson (1992) and Stump (2001) are couched in a realizational idiom, they confront a version of the general 'overextraction' problem that arises in Post-Bloomfieldian approaches. The association of properties with individual markers tends to increase uncertainty by disassembling words into parts that are more ambiguous and/or more resistant to analysis than the wholes from which they are obtained. This uncertainty is not inherent to the language itself. Instead, it is symptomatic of analyses that apportion properties to units of form that do not function as signs, but as markers that serve to discriminate larger meaningful units. The issues that these analyses create are largely independent of whether the analyses are formulated in terms of morphemes or realization rules.

The uncertainty that arises in associating grammatical properties with inflectional markers is not a peculiarity of Georgian, which exhibits a pseudo-agglutinative structure that is nearly as favourable as possible to decomposition. The uncertainty created by disassembling more fusional patterns is even greater, as discussed in previous chapters. Consider the forms of the Estonian noun PUKK 'trestle' in Table 7.3, repeated from Tables 4.7 and 4.8.

The forms in each of these columns are fully discriminable and, with the exception of *pukki* (which realizes the short illative singular as well as the partitive singular), they can all be assigned a single grammatical analysis. However, the attempt to associate grammatical properties with sub-word units of form only increases uncertainty. In the singular grammatical cases, the units *pukk*, *puk*, and *-i* combine to express the three case contrasts. However, none of these units can be assigned grammatical properties in isolation that 'add up' to the properties of the word forms. The same pattern recurs in the plural grammatical cases. The forms *puki* and *pukki* combine with *-d*, *-de* and *-sid* to express a three-way contrast. But isolating the bases creates ambiguity between their uses as case forms in the singular and as case- and number-neutral stems in the plural. The same pattern recurs yet again in the semantic cases, where the bases are ambiguous between genitive forms and case-neutral 'oblique' stems.

TABLE 7.4   Priscianic syncretism in Latin

	AMŌ 'to love'	MONEŌ 'to advise'	TEGŌ 'to cover'
Infinitive	amāre	monēre	tegere
Supine	amātum	monitum	tēctum
Past Pass Prtl	amātus	monitus	tēctus
Fut Act Prtl	amātūrus	monitūrus	tēctūrus

Stem syncretisms in Latin conjugations exhibit a similar pattern, differing only in that the recurrent stems function as bound forms and never occur in isolation. The forms in Table 7.4 (repeated from Tables 4.12 and 5.3) contrast the present stem, which occurs in the infinitive, with the supine stem which occurs in the supine, past and future participles. As in previous examples, the full word forms can be associated with determinate grammatical properties. However, as discussed at length by Matthews (1972), Aronoff (1994) and Maiden (2005), syncretic stems in Romance cannot be assigned a determinate analysis in isolation. The supine stems in Table 7.4 can either be assigned different features in each context in which they occur, or they can be treated as grammatically indeterminate or 'underspecified' in those contexts.

In each of these examples, disassembling a word into smaller recurrent parts disrupts an initially stable association between form and grammatical properties, increasing ambiguity and uncertainty. The locus of the uncertainty depends on general characteristics of the language. In Georgian, disassembly isolates agreement markers that cannot be assigned a determinate analysis. In Estonian and Latin, the analysis of words into recurrent partials creates classes of grammatically indeterminate stems. In Latin, the disassembly of fusional forms creates further indeterminacy in the division of stems and inflectional endings. Technical strategies can be devised to manage ambiguity, and policies can be imposed to guide segmentation, as discussed in Spencer (2012). But these proposals all serve as correctives, addressing challenges that arise when, as Matthews (1972: 74) remarks in connection with principal parts, "the theory creates a problem which it is then unable, or only partly able, to resolve".

7.1.2 From word to paradigm

The patterns summarized in Section 7.1.1 illustrate one type of evidence that underpins the classical WP view that associating grammatical properties with word forms creates less uncertainty than associating properties with sub-word units. This does not of course entail that classical WP descriptions treat words as unanalyzable wholes or deny the significance of sub-word units. Rather, as mentioned earlier, these models treat sub-word variation as exhibiting contrasts that discriminate between larger meaningful units. This perspective is clearly expressed in Matthew's summary of Priscian's treatment of Latin stem syncretism (cited on p. 103 and repeated below). As Matthews notes, an inflected form of the future active participle (the nominative singular masculine) is obtained by replacing the -*m* ending of the supine by the ending -*rus*. This analysis does not assign any grammatical properties to *-rus* or *-m*, or explicitly classify *-r* either as a stem formative or inflectional exponent:[2]

Priscian's rule would actually derive the Nominative Singular Masculine . . . by the addition of *rus* to the *u:* form of the 'Supine' and would moreover be limited to verbs in which the 'Supine' is not deficient . . . (Matthews 1972: 85)

From a classical WP perspective, sub-word units may serve discriminative roles without functioning as signs. In the example considered above, the contrast between *-m* and *-rus* distinguishes the supine and nominative singular masculine form of the future active participle within the lexeme of AMŌ. At the same time, the contrast between *-tum* and *-re* distinguishes the supine from the infinitive of AMŌ. The contrast between *amā-* and *moni-* likewise distinguishes the supines (and other members of the supine series) of AMŌ and MONEŌ. In each case, sub-word variation distinguishes pairs of words that can be assigned stable grammatical properties. But the grammatical difference between those words is not assigned to the variants that distinguish them.

From a contemporary perspective, it might seem that the stability of a word-based description incurs a significant cost. In a Post-Bloomfieldian model, the association of properties with sub-word units is designed in part to facilitate the interpretation of novel forms. Although a particular form may be unfamiliar, it can be understood by combining the properties of previously-encountered parts. But if meaning resides wholly at the word level, how do speakers avoid the need to learn the meaning of each word individually?

The answer offered by proponents of classical WP models is that the relation between word forms and the properties of paradigm cells is constrained in various ways by the larger grammatical system in which they are embedded. Robins's quote from p. 67, repeated below, provides a concise statement of the classical WP position:

In many ways, and quite apart from any phonological markers, the word is a unique entity in grammar, and not just a stage in the progression 'from morpheme to utterance'. As a grammatical element the word is unique in its relative fixity of internal morphemic structure, its focal status in relation to syntactically relevant categories, and, in inflected words, the stability of its paradigms. All of these factors make it a strong basis for grammatical description, both morphological and syntactic. The assumption of a simple ascent in order of size from single morpheme to complete sentence, ignoring or blurring the distinction of morphological structuring and syntactic structuring, achieves its apparent simplicity at the cost of neglecting or distorting patent structural features of languages. (Robins 1959: 137)

As Robins notes, the structuralist morpheme is embedded in a general uniformitarian model. At each level of linguistic analysis, minimal units are combined to form the minimal units of the next highest level. Moreover, fundamentally similar combinatoric operations apply across the levels. In contrast, a traditional WP model assumes that, as units increase in size in a grammatical analysis, the

---

[2] This analysis is repeated by Gildersleeve and Lodge (1895) on p. 103 above.

domains over which relations apply to those units scale up as well. At the scale of phoneme-sized units, alternations such as assimilation or dissimilation apply largely to adjacent segments and even suprasegmental patterns tend to operate over a contiguous domain. The paradigmatic pressures that are taken to determine the adaptive dispersion of vowel inventories (Liljencrants and Lindblom 1972) likewise repel elements that are similar along some dimension in a perceptual space. The domains relevant to word-sized units are larger and the relations are more complex, due in part to the role that words play as the primary point of entry for grammatical meaning. Along the syntagmatic axis, collocation relations may hold between non-adjacent words. Paradigmatic relations likewise operate over large sets of words, from inflectional paradigms, to lexemes and derivational families.

It is the affiliation with these larger sets of forms that principally constrains uncertainty in the association between individual word forms and grammatical properties. For each cell in a paradigm, there is uncertainty about which inflectional variant realizes the cell. This uncertainty correlates with the amount of allomorphy exhibited by the realization and the distribution of allomorphic patterns. For each form, there is likewise uncertainty that correlates with the number of cells that it realizes. For a simple illustration, consider the Russian noun paradigms in Table 7.5 (repeated from Table 4.1 on p. 72 above).

These forms exhibit the many-many associations between cells and exponence patterns that characterize languages with inflection classes. The majority of cells are realized by at least two different patterns across different classes, as shown in Table 7.6. Conversely, the majority of exponents realize multiple cells. This is shown in Table 7.7, in which the exponents all happen to be suffixes that follow an inflectionally invariant stem form 'X'.

Nevertheless, each paradigm cell has a single realization in Table 7.5. The generality of this pattern underpins the use of tables to exhibit paradigms (and

TABLE 7.5   Inanimate 'soft stem' declensions in Russian (Timberlake 2004)

	I (Masculine)		II (Feminine)		III (Feminine)	
	Sg	Pl	Sg	Pl	Sg	Pl
Nom	slovar'	slovari	nedelja	nedeli	tetrad'	tetradi
Gen	slovarja	slovarej	nedeli	nedel'	tetradi	tetradej
Dat	slovarju	slovarjam	nedele	nedeljam	tetradi	tetradjam
Acc	slovar'	slovari	nedelju	nedeli	tetrad'	tetradi
Inst	slovarëm	slovarjami	nedelej	nedeljami	tetradju	tetradjami
Loc	slovare	slovarjax	nedele	nedeljax	tetradi	tetradjax
	'dictionary'		'week'		'notebook'	

TABLE 7.6   Cell-exponent ambiguity in Table 7.5

	Nom	Gen	Dat	Acc	Inst	Loc
Sg	2	2	3	2	3	2
Plu	1	2	1	2	1	1

TABLE 7.7   Exponent-cell ambiguity in Table 7.5

Exponent	X*i*	X	X*u*	X*a*	X*e*	X*ej*
Cells	5	3	3	2	2	2

Exponent	X*ëm*	X*am*	X*ami*	X*ax*
Cells	1	1	1	1

the definition of paradigm FUNCTIONS in Stump (2001)). More strikingly, nearly every form of first declension SLOVAR' 'dictionary' receives a single analysis. The sole exceptions are the syncretic accusative and nominative forms, which reflect a general pattern for inanimate nouns in Slavic.[3]

The contribution that paradigms make to reducing uncertainty is exhibited by the contrast between the relatively stable form–property associations in Table 7.5 and the variation displayed in Tables 7.6 and 7.7. In isolation, most of the forms of SLOVAR' are potentially ambiguous. This ambiguity cannot be resolved by disassembling these forms, since it derives ultimately from the fact that recurrent inflectional endings are associated with different cells across classes. It is instead the structure provided by the paradigmatic affiliations of these classes of interdependent forms that effectively constrains variation.

The disambiguating function of paradigms also clarifies where realizational approaches depart from classical WP models. In a WP model, locating words within a larger set of interdependent forms constrains the association between the words and grammatical properties. Class membership is not a property of forms, but is EXHIBITED by patterns of associations between properties and forms.[4] By encoding class membership by means of class 'features', Matthews (1965) explicitly represents the organization that remains implicit in the 'exemplary paradigm and principal parts' formulation of a classical grammar. Yet this strategy collapses the paradigmatic structure of a classical WP model. The implicational structure exhibited by classes is reduced to an essentially neo-Bloomfieldian relation of 'selection' that governs the compatibility of the stems and exponents modified or introduced by realization rules.

7.2 Information-theoretic WP

A formalization of the classical WP model must make explicit the structure that remains implicit in an 'exemplary paradigm and principal parts' description

---

[3] The increase in ambiguity in the second and third declensions is attributable to other general syncretisms. The paradigm of second declension NEDELA 'week' contains a distinctive accusative singular form but exhibits a syncretism between dative and locative singular and between genitive singular and nominative plural. The paradigm of third declension TETRAD' 'notebook' preserves the syncretisms from the first and second declension and, in addition, collapses the genitive and dative singular forms.

[4] The contrast between specifying class features and exhibiting class affiliation is reminiscent of the distinction between *Sagen* and *Zeigen* in Wittgenstein (1921).

while clarifying the uncertainty-reducing role of the insight "that one inflection tends to predict another" (Matthews 1991:197). As discussed in Chapters 4 and 5, the latter insight runs like a leitmotif through the classical WP tradition. The Neogrammarian notion of 'analogy' associated with Paul (1920) rests on the idea that a speaker's knowledge of inflectional patterns can be exploited to reduce uncertainty about the forms of a new item:

One learns a number of paradigms by heart and then memorizes only as many forms of individual words as is necessary to recognize their affiliation to this or that paradigm. Now and then a single form suffices. One forms the remaining forms at the moment that one needs them, in accordance with the paradigm, that is, by analogy. (Paul 1920:112)

Hockett (1967: 221) expresses a similar position in a more contemporary setting when he asserts that a linguist or learner who matches forms against paradigms to deduce novel forms "would now be required to produce new forms in exactly the way the native user of the language produces or recognizes them—by analogy".[5] However, as discussed in Chapter 4.4, Hockett qualifies this endorsement by explicitly rejecting the pedagogical idealization that the forms of a language can be divided into stored exemplars, diagnostic forms and deduced forms:[6]

The native user of the language...operates in terms of all sorts of internally stored paradigms, many of them doubtless only partial; and he may first encounter a new basic verb in any of its inflected forms. For the native user, the forms that we have for convenience selected to be our 'principal parts' have no such favored position. They are as likely to be created analogically, as needed, as are any of the other forms. (Hockett 1967: 221)

Traditional proportional analogies provide a format for expressing deductions sanctioned by the implicational structure of a morphological system. If the system is conceptualized as a network of partially interdependent patterns, somewhat along the lines suggested by Bybee (2010), proportions can be thought of as expressing individual correspondences. Hence a description of the structure of a system can be obtained from sets of mutually compatible proportions, along with sequences of proportions that identify the chains of deductions that originate from a particular morphological choice. The 'paradigm structure conditions' (PSCs) of Wurzel (1984), in which "implicative patterns determine the structure of the paradigms of a language", represent the most explicitly formalized variant of this type of analysis:

Observation of complicated paradigms shows that implicative relations do not only obtain between one basic inflexional form . . . and all the other inflexional forms, but exist through-

---

[5] As mentioned in connection with 'novel forms' in fn. 1 of Chapter 5 above, the term 'new forms' is again interpreted as referring to unencountered forms, not neologisms.

[6] The pedagogical idealization that a single diagnostic form can be identified for each lexical item corresponds to the 'Single Base Hypothesis' of Albright (2002), discussed on p. 95, and to the 'Single Root Hypothesis' assumed in the accounts discussed in Aronoff (2012).

out the whole paradigm: all paradigms (apart from suppletive cases) are structured on the basis of implicative patterns which go beyond the individual word, patterns of varying complexity. (Wurzel 1984: 208)

As discussed in Chapter 4.2, the choice of material implication to represent implicational relations limits the usefulness of PSCs. A formalization of the classical WP model must be able to express exceptionless patterns where they occur. However, a viable formalization must be highly sensitive to the statistical properties of language in order to capture the fact that patterns and predictions typically take the form of tendencies of varying reliability.

Models with these properties were initially developed in processing models in the psycholinguistic literature. Somewhat unexpectedly, the conceptions of uncertainty and uncertainty reduction proposed in these approaches turned out to be equally applicable to the problem of modelling paradigmatic variation and implicational structure. As discussed in Chapter 3.1.1, the point of origin for current formalizations of classical WP models lies in a series of morphological processing studies (Kostić 1991, 1995; Kostić et al. 2003; Moscoso del Prado Martín et al. 2004b) that develop measures of 'morphological information' in terms of ENTROPY (Shannon 1948). By chaining together classical WP conceptions of variation as uncertainty with the information-theoretic treatment of uncertainty as entropy, one arrives at a general characterization of variation as entropy. The greater the variation exhibited by a system (or part of a system), the greater the uncertainty and the higher the entropy. From this point, it is a small step to propose, as Ackerman et al. (2009) do, that the reduction in uncertainty achieved by implicational relations can be modelled in terms of CONDITIONAL ENTROPY.[7] One morphological element—whether a cell or form or some other unit of analysis—is informative about a second element to the extent that knowledge of the first element reduces the amount of uncertainty about the second element measured by its entropy.

There are of course different information-theoretic measures that can be applied to the analysis of morphological systems and different interpretations that can be assigned to those measures, and the measures and interpretations adopted in initial accounts are in many respects provisional. Nevertheless, standard information-theoretic measures have properties that are useful for formalizing classical WP models. Entropy provides a measure of the variation that correlates with the complexity of a system. Entropy reduction provides a good approximation of the notion of 'informativeness' that underpins implicational relations. A similar notion suggests solutions to the longstanding challenges raised by principal part selection and analogy validation.

Sections 7.2.1–7.2.3 now outline an information-theoretic formulation of a classical WP model and clarify how entropy and entropy reduction contribute to a formal treatment of traditional notions of variation and structure.

---

[7] The idea of modelling the structure of morphological systems in terms of entropy had been in circulation before Ackerman et al. (2009) and was proposed the previous year in two independent presentations, Blevins et al. (2008) and Sproat (2008), at the 3rd Workshop on Quantitative Investigations in Theoretical Linguistics in Helsinki.

7.2.1 Implicational relations

Let us first return to the issue of how implicational relations constrain the inflectional uncertainty associated with individual cells, continuing with the example of the Russian noun paradigms in Table 7.5. As shown in Table 7.6, the dative and instrumental singulars exhibit the greatest variation, both with three distinct realizations. In the case of the dative singular, the first declension form *slovarju* ends in *-u*, the second declension form *nedele* ends in *-e* and the third declension form *tetradi* ends in *-i*. The instrumental singular is realized by corresponding forms in *-ëm*, *-ej* and *-ju*. In order to measure the reduction in uncertainty obtained by locating these cells in paradigms, we must determine the amount of uncertainty that would be associated with them in isolation.

A measure of the uncertainty associated with a cell can be defined in terms of the SURPRISAL values of the cell's realizations. Surprisal assigns a measure of information to an 'outcome', in this case the occurrence of a given realization, that is inversely related to its likelihood of occurrence. Let us use '$p(u)$' to represent the probability that the dative singular cell is realized by a form in *-u*. Then I_u, the surprisal value of the dative singular exponent *-u*, can be defined in Figure 7.1 as the negative log of its probability $p(u)$.[8]

This notion of surprisal expresses the intuition that the less likely *-u* is to occur, the more informative it is when it does occur. Surprisal values can be defined for each realization, based on its probability of occurrence. The uncertainty associated with the dative singular cell can then be defined as the sum of the surprisal values of the cell realizations, weighted for frequency. This is the uncertainty value measured by ENTROPY (Shannon 1948).

To apply this measure to a paradigm cell C, let R_C be the set of realizations of C, the set $\{Xu, Xe, Xi\}$, in the case of the dative singular. As in the definition of surprisal, let $p(x)$ represent the probability that the cell C is realized by a realization x. Then $H(C)$, the entropy of C, is defined in Figure 7.2.[9] The entropy of

$$I_u = -\log_2 p(u)$$

FIGURE 7.1   Exponent 'surprisal' (cf. Cover and Thomas 1991, Hale 2001)

$$H(C) = -\sum_{x \in R_C} p(x) \log_2 p(x)$$

FIGURE 7.2   Cell entropy (cf. Shannon 1948)

[8] Hale (2001) applies this notion of 'surprisal' (which he attributes to Attneave (1959:6)) to the syntagmatic task of measuring cognitive load in sentence processing.

[9] Shannon's use of a base 2 logarithm provides an entropy value that measures uncertainty in bits, which is the standard measure of information.

$$H(C_{ds}) = -\tfrac{1}{3}\log_2\left(\tfrac{1}{3}\right) - \tfrac{1}{3}\log_2\left(\tfrac{1}{3}\right) - \tfrac{1}{3}\log_2\left(\tfrac{1}{3}\right)$$
$$= -\log_2\left(\tfrac{1}{3}\right)$$
$$= \log_2(3)$$
$$= 1.59 \text{ bits}$$

FIGURE 7.3   Entropy 'ceiling' for dative singular cell in Russian

a cell increases as a function of the number of outcomes and the uniformity of their distribution. The greatest uncertainty arises when there is a large number of equiprobable outcomes. Uncertainty is reduced when there are fewer 'choices', either because there are either few outcomes in total or because the outcomes have highly skewed distributions. As with surprisal, there is an intuitive correlation between entropy and the number and distribution of alternatives. The larger the choice space and the more evenly distributed the alternatives, the more difficult it is to guess which alternative will occur.

The use of entropy provides a particularly robust estimation of morphological uncertainty. On the one hand, the accuracy of the estimation improves as the accuracy of distributional information obtained from corpora increases. On the other hand, the estimation degrades gracefully as the accuracy of distributional information decreases, so that the absence of frequency information does not produce no estimation, but instead a worst-case estimation. As a consequence, an 'entropy ceiling' can be estimated from a grammar, word list or other descriptive source that identifies an inventory of morphological variants but provides little or no information about their distribution.

For example, an entropy ceiling for the dative singular cell, C_{ds}, can be defined from a standard reference grammar. For the sake of illustration, let us assume that the forms -u, -e and -i are the only dative singular exponents in Russian.[10] In the absence of frequency information, let us also assume that the endings are evenly distributed, so that each occurs one-third of the time. Under these conditions, the probability values '$p(x)$' in Figure 7.2 effectively 'cancel out' in Figure 7.3. As a result, the entropy of the dative singular cell, $H(C_{ds})$, reduces to $\log_2(n)$, where n is the number of case exponents.[11]

The entropy of approximately 1.6 bits represents the worst case uncertainty measure for a cell that can be realized by three exponence patterns. Adding information about the frequency of these alternatives will tend to introduce a distributional bias that reduces entropy. This is again an intuitive effect, since the more unbalanced the distribution of alternatives is, the easier it is to guess the more frequent alternatives. But even in the absence of frequency information, entropy defines a useful uncertainty ceiling for a cell.

Classical WP models constrain the uncertainty associated with individual cells by locating those cells in paradigms that exhibit patterns of interdependent choices.

---

[10] See Timberlake (2004: §3.6) for a more detailed discussion of case allomorphy.

[11] The final step in this reduction exploits the general correspondence between the negative and reciprocal of a log, i.e, for any base b, $\log_b\left(\tfrac{1}{x}\right) = -\log_b(x)$.

$$H(C_2|C_1) = - \sum_{x \in R_{C_1}} \sum_{y \in R_{C_2}} p(x,y) \log_2 p(y|x)$$

FIGURE 7.4   Conditional entropy (cf. Cover and Thomas 1991: 16)

The uncertainty-reducing effect of paradigmatic affiliation can again be expressed in information-theoretic terms, as the CONDITIONAL ENTROPY of a cell C_2 given a known cell C_1. Conditional entropy measures the amount of uncertainty that remains associated with C_2 if C_1 is already known.

Conditional entropy is standardly defined, as in Figure 7.4, in terms of $p(y|x)$, the conditional probability of a realization y of C_2 given a realization x of C_1. The conditional probability of y given x, $p(y|x)$, is in turn defined as $\frac{p(x,y)}{p(x)}$, the joint probability of x and y divided by the probability of x.

Just as entropy corresponds to the frequency-weighted sum of surprisal values, conditional entropy can be thought of as the weighted sum of conditional probabilities. This correspondence again reflects a simple intuition. Continuing with the paradigms in Table 7.5, there will be three basic relations between the realization of the dative singular cell and the realization of other cells. If a cell exhibits no inflectional variation, the same realization will co-occur with each of the three dative singular realizations and therefore be of no value in predicting which of the three occurs in a given paradigm or inflection class. At the other extreme, a cell that exhibits the same three-way contrast as the dative singular cell will be maximally useful in predicting the dative singular realization. Between these extremes lie cells that exhibit variation that partially overlaps with the variation shown by the dative singular.

The paradigms in Table 7.5 illustrate these three types of covariation. The nominative, dative, instrumental and locative plurals exhibit no variation, the instrumental singular exhibits congruent variation, and the remaining cells exhibit overlapping variation. Each pattern is represented by a block of rows in Table 7.8. The first block indicates that the instrumental plural realization *-ami* co-occurs one-third of the time with each of the dative singular realizations *-u*, *-e* and *-i*. Hence the joint probability, $p(-ami, x) = 1/3$ for each dative singular realization x, and $p(-ami)$, the summed probability of *-ami*, is 1.

The second block of rows indicates that the genitive singular realization *-a* co-occurs with the dative singular realization *-u*, while *-i* co-occurs with the other realizations. The final block indicates that the three instrumental singular realizations each co-occur with a single dative singular realization. The conditional probabilities defined in Table 7.8 in turn determine the conditional entropy of the corresponding cells. The conditional entropy of the dative singular given the instrumental plural, $H(C_{ds}|C_{ip})$, is defined in Figure 7.5. The intuitive observation that an invariant cell is a poor predictor of inflectional variants is reflected in the fact that $H(C_{ds}|C_{ip})$ preserves all of the entropy, 1.59 bits, associated with $H(C_{ds})$ in Figure 7.3.

TABLE 7.8   Invariant, overlapping, and congruent co-occurrence

	-u	-e	-i	Σ	
-ami	$\frac{1}{3}$	$\frac{1}{3}$	$\frac{1}{3}$	1	(Inst Pl)
-a	$\frac{1}{3}$	0	0	$\frac{1}{3}$	(Gen Sg)
-i	0	$\frac{1}{3}$	$\frac{1}{3}$	$\frac{2}{3}$	
-ëm	$\frac{1}{3}$	0	0	$\frac{1}{3}$	(Inst Sg)
-ej	0	$\frac{1}{3}$	0	$\frac{1}{3}$	
-ju	0	0	$\frac{1}{3}$	$\frac{1}{3}$	

$$
\begin{aligned}
H(C_{ds}|C_{ip}) &= -\tfrac{1}{3}\log_2\left(\tfrac{1}{3}/1\right) - \tfrac{1}{3}\log_2\left(\tfrac{1}{3}/1\right) - \tfrac{1}{3}\log_2\left(\tfrac{1}{3}/1\right) \\
&= -\tfrac{1}{3}\log_2\left(\tfrac{1}{3}\right) - \tfrac{1}{3}\log_2\left(\tfrac{1}{3}\right) - \tfrac{1}{3}\log_2\left(\tfrac{1}{3}\right) \\
&= \log_2(3) \\
&= 1.59 \text{ bits}
\end{aligned}
$$

FIGURE 7.5   Conditional entropy of dative singular given instrumental plural

$$
\begin{aligned}
H(C_{ds}|C_{is}) &= -\tfrac{1}{3}\log_2\left(\tfrac{1}{3}/\tfrac{1}{3}\right) - \tfrac{1}{3}\log_2\left(\tfrac{1}{3}/\tfrac{1}{3}\right) - \tfrac{1}{3}\log_2\left(\tfrac{1}{3}/\tfrac{1}{3}\right) \\
&= -\tfrac{1}{3}\log_2(1) - \tfrac{1}{3}\log_2(1) - \tfrac{1}{3}\log_2(1) \\
&= \log_2(1) \\
&= 0 \text{ bits}
\end{aligned}
$$

FIGURE 7.6   Conditional entropy of dative singular given instrumental singular

$$
\begin{aligned}
H(C_{ds}|C_{gs}) &= -\tfrac{1}{3}\log_2\left(\tfrac{1}{3}/\tfrac{1}{3}\right) - \tfrac{1}{3}\log_2\left(\tfrac{1}{3}/\tfrac{2}{3}\right) - \tfrac{1}{3}\log_2\left(\tfrac{1}{3}/\tfrac{2}{3}\right) \\
&= -\tfrac{1}{3}\log_2(1) - \tfrac{2}{3}\log_2\left(\tfrac{1}{2}\right) \\
&= \tfrac{2}{3}\log_2(2) \\
&= 0.67 \text{ bits}
\end{aligned}
$$

FIGURE 7.7   Conditional entropy of dative singular given genitive singular

Figure 7.6 shows how cells that covary are each good predictors of the variation in the other. In this case, the conditional entropy of the dative singular given the instrumental singular, $H(C_{ds}|C_{is})$, eliminates all of the entropy associated with the dative singular. A cell that exhibits partially overlapping covariation will likewise reduce uncertainty by an intermediate amount. Thus the covariation of the dative and genitive singular in Table 7.8 is reflected in Figure 7.7 by the fact that the conditional entropy of the dative singular given the genitive singular, $H(C_{ds}|C_{gs})$, eliminates roughly two thirds of the entropy associated with the dative singular.

7.2.2 The Low Conditional Entropy Conjecture

In the examples considered in Section 7.2.1, it is not absolute entropy values that are of interest, but the relations between values. As more accurate distributional information is incorporated into an analysis, estimations of uncertainty become more precise and increasingly useful for modelling a range of behavioural responses, as discussed in Milin *et al.* (2009*b*). What emerges from the present illustration is the general usefulness of information-theoretic notions for the purposes of representing morphological variation and structure. A standard entropy measure defines an uncertainty-based notion of variation, while conditional entropy measures the reduction in uncertainty that underlies the implicational structure assigned by a classical WP model.

The cells in Table 7.5 with the largest number of realizations exhibit the greatest variation and complexity. In isolation, the entropy of these cells is determined by the number of realizations and their distribution. If, as assumed by Post-Bloomfieldian accounts such as Müller (2004: 191), paradigms were "pure epiphenomena", paradigm affiliation would not be expected to make a significant contribution to constraining the entropy of individual cells. For some cells this is essentially true. Given the invariant realization of the instrumental plural *-ami*, there is no uncertainty to resolve and, conversely, no pattern of covariation that reduces uncertainty about the realization of other cells. The dative and locative plural are similarly autonomous in the declensional system of Russian. In a system where the realization of all cells were mutually independent, it would be fair to describe the organization of forms into paradigms as a taxonomic artifact or matter of descriptive convenience.

Yet, as expressed in Matthew's observation that "one inflection tends to predict another", inflectional systems do typically exhibit a high degree of interdependence. In the Russian system, the dative, instrumental and locative plural cells are atypical, achieving an unambiguous encoding of case and number by providing no information about class. Nearly every other cell in a paradigm is at least partially informative about other cells. In the examples considered above, the genitive singular eliminated roughly two thirds of the uncertainty associated with the dative singular, and knowledge of the instrumental singular was sufficient to identify the dative singular realization.

As discussed in Section 7.1.2, this implicational structure underpins the use of exemplary paradigms, principal parts and analogical extension in a classical grammar. At the same time, the fact that diagnostic features and patterns tend to be specific to individual languages, morphological systems and even inflection classes inhibits cross-linguistic generalization of patterns within the classical WP tradition. Hence it is not until Ackerman and Malouf (2013) that there is a systematic attempt within this tradition to measure the informativeness of implicational structure within a range of languages. Ackerman and Malouf (2013) start by identifying four factors that contribute to paradigmatic uncertainty and complexity. They then classify the declensional systems of 10 genetically unrelated and areally scattered languages in terms of these factors. The results are repeated in Table 7.9. The first column (following the language name) specifies the total number

TABLE 7.9   Entropies for a 10-language sample (Ackerman and Malouf 2013: 443)

Language	Total Cells	Total Real	Max Real	Decl Class	Decl	Entropy Paradigm	Avg Cond
Amele	3	30	14	24	4.585	2.882	1.105
Arapesh	2	41	26	26	4.700	4.071	0.630
Burmeso	12	6	2	2	1.000	1.000	0.000
Fur	12	50	10	19	4.248	2.395	0.517
Greek	8	12	5	8	3.000	1.621	0.644
Kwerba	12	9	4	4	2.000	0.864	0.428
Mazatec	6	356	94	109	6.768	4.920	0.709
Ngiti	16	7	5	10	3.322	1.937	0.484
Nuer	6	12	3	16	4.000	0.864	0.793
Russian	12	14	3	4	2.000	0.911	0.538

of cells in a paradigm. The second column identifies the total number of different (morphologically conditioned) cell realizations. The third column identifies the largest number of realizations of any one cell. The fourth column specifies the number of declension classes defined by the variation in cell realizations.

The last three columns in Table 7.9 calculate entropy measures based on the values in the preceding columns.[12] The first measure represents what Ackerman and Malouf (2013) term "Declensional Entropy", indicating the uncertainty associated with guessing the class of a random noun. The value of this measure depends directly on the number of classes; the more classes there are, the harder it is to guess. The next column measures the "Paradigm Entropy", corresponding to the average uncertainty associated with guessing the realization of a cell of a noun. The more realizations per cell, the higher this value will be. The final column gives the "Average Conditional Entropy", the uncertainty associated with guessing the realization of one cell based on knowing the realization of another, averaged over all pairs of cells.

Since Russian is included in this 10-language sample, we can continue with the earlier illustration and use the values in the final row of Table 7.9 to exemplify each of these measures. Consider the first four columns. As shown in Table 7.5, Russian declensions have 12 cells, defined by the six cases and two numbers. The full declensional system contains a total of 14 case-number realizations, adding four to the 10 listed in Table 7.7. No cell has more than three distinct realizations, and the recognition of four major declension classes accords with the number proposed in Corbett (1991).

From this description of Russian declensions, we can calculate the entropy measures. As in the previous illustration, we are dealing with entropy ceilings here, since the descriptions do not contain information about the relative frequency of cells, realizations or classes. Given a class size of four, and a provisional assumption

---

[12] Unfortunately, Table 3 on p. 443 of Ackerman and Malouf (2013) transposes the labels on the final two columns, so that the "Paradigm (Cell) Entropy" column gives the average conditional entropy and the "Avg Entropy" column gives the paradigm entropy.

of equiprobability, the uncertainty associated with guessing the class of a random noun is $\log_2 (4)$ or 2 bits. The paradigm entropy will be lower, since the most highly allomorphic cell has only three distinct realizations (corresponding to roughly 1.6 bits of uncertainty) and the fact that other cells have even fewer realizations brings the average in Table 7.9 under 1 bit.

As in the earlier illustration, the actual values in Table 7.9 are less important than the relations between values. Of particular interest is the contrast between the last two measures in Table 7.9. In every language of the sample, the uncertainty associated with deducing the realization of a cell was reduced, in some cases significantly, by information about the realization of another cell. This pattern is all the more striking given that the omission of frequency information from this sample not only overestimates the overall uncertainty of a system by excluding distributional biases but also underestimates the potential value of these biases for deducing one form from another.

The limitations due to the lack of frequency information reflect a basic trade-off between the genetic and areal diversity of a language sample and the kinds of information currently available for the languages. Subsequent comparisons based on larger samples with more distribution information may permit more secure estimations of the cross-linguistic variation in entropy values. However, even this initial comparison highlights a number of important points. The most significant is that the reduction in uncertainty in the final three columns correlates with an increase in psychological plausibility.

Guessing the class of an item is irreducibly difficult because this is not the sort of task that a speaker is ever confronted with. This reflects the fact that classes are not IN a language per se but, like 'blocks', 'templates' and similar constructs, form part of the scaffolding of a language description. Class assignment is a meta-task performed by linguists for descriptive and pedagogical purposes. Hence assessments of morphological complexity based on the structure of class systems is principally relevant to the classification of grammatical descriptions, not the languages they are meant to describe. Guessing the realization of a cell on the basis of no prior acquaintance with the item is nearly as unrealistic. As Ackerman and Malouf (2013: 443f.) remark, "native speakers are not confronted with situations where it is necessary to guess declension class membership or the cell for particular word forms of novel lexemes without having encountered some actual word form of that lexeme". Consequently notions of complexity determined by sheer numbers of realization patterns are again largely orthogonal to the factors that are relevant for speakers.

It is the final measure, which estimates the difficulty of deducing novel forms of an item from knowledge of other forms of the item, which is most clearly relevant to the analysis of the paradigmatic complexity of morphological systems. From a classical WP perspective, it is no accident that the average conditional entropy is the measure that is most constrained. It is of course true that speakers are not, in a strict sense, presented with the task of guessing the value of paradigm cells. However, the features associated with cells are a realistic proxy for the grammatical properties that would guide the choice of inflected form in production or partition the interpretative space in comprehension.

7.2.3 Cohesion, diagnosticity and validity

The average conditional entropy between cells provides a particularly transparent measure of the implicational structure that underpins the classical factorization of inflectional systems into exemplary paradigms and principal parts. It is highly suggestive that the effects of this structure are so strong even under the simplest idealization of a paradigmatic system. Moreover, just as the use of more informative data sources will improve the precision of entropy estimations, the use of more refined or, perhaps, more appropriate techniques of analysis may also be expected to contribute to better measures. Refinements may be required in cases where Bonami and Luís (2013, 2014) have argued that paradigm cells do not always correspond to random variables.

The use of different measures may likewise offer more accurate estimations or more transparent perspectives. For example, instead of using conditional entropy to measure remaining uncertainty, one might use techniques to estimate degrees of informativeness. The notion of mutual information in Figure 7.8 provides a measure of the mutual dependence between two variables. As its name suggests, mutual information is a symmetrical measure of the information shared by variables. For a pair of variables X and Y, the relations between their mutual information, entropies and conditional entropies is given in Figure 7.9. If a pair of values are independent, their mutual information will be 0. If they are completely interdependent, their mutual information will be identical to their common entropy value. Between these extremes lie a range of values that are useful for characterizing the proportion of uncertainty that one cell eliminates about another or the cohesiveness of sets of cells.

The proportion of uncertainty that a cell C_1 eliminates about a cell C_2 can be obtained by dividing their mutual information, $I(C_1; C_2)$, by the entropy of C_2, as in Figure 7.10. Dividing $I(C_1; C_2)$ by the entropy of C_1 likewise defines the proportion of uncertainty about C_1 eliminated by knowledge of C_2.

$$I(X; Y) = -\sum_{x,y} p(x, y) \log_2 \frac{p(x, y)}{p(x)p(y)}$$

FIGURE 7.8   Mutual information (Cover and Thomas 1991: 18)

$$I(X; Y) = H(X) - H(X/Y) = H(Y) - H(Y/X)$$

FIGURE 7.9   Mutual information and conditional entropy (Cover and Thomas 1991: 19)

$$R_{C_1C_2} = \frac{I(C_1; C_2)}{H(C_2)} \qquad R_{C_2C_1} = \frac{I(C_1; C_2)}{H(C_1)}$$

FIGURE 7.10   Proportional uncertainty reduction

Comparing the proportional values for all pairs of cells in a paradigm or inflection class will determine a ranking of cell in terms of relative informativeness. This ranking provides one means of identifying the best candidates for principal parts in a system. There is of course no guarantee that any single cell will eliminate all uncertainty in other cells. So if the complete elimination of uncertainty is the criterion for the selection of principal parts, 'principle part cohorts' can be defined as all the sets of forms $C_k \ldots C_m$ such that the conditional value $H(C_j|C_k \ldots C_m)$ approaches zero for all cells C_j in a paradigm, class or system. In either case, the use of information-theoretic measures offers a solution, in principle, to the traditional problem of selecting principal parts:

One objection to the Priscianic model . . . was that the choice of leading form was inherently arbitrary: the theory creates a problem which it is then unable, or only partly able, to resolve (Matthews 1972: 74).

An element of arbitrariness remains, in that the selection of principal parts reflects pedagogical goals that have no clear relevance for the native speaker. The relative informativeness of particular cells or forms can be expected to have behavioural correlates in a speaker's willingness to produce novel forms or the speed or confidence with which they identify forms that are presented to them. But there is no reason to believe that speakers isolate the cells or forms that correspond to principal parts from other, partially informative, elements.

The mutual information between cells or forms also determines a natural measure of system cohesion. The cohesion of a pair of cells C_1 and C_2 correlates with the degree to which they are mutually informative (i.e., the proportion of their cumulative uncertainty that they share). The cumulative uncertainty of C_1 and C_2 is defined by their joint entropy in Figure 7.11. In the limiting case where C_1 and C_2 are independent, their joint entropy is just the sum of their entropies. However, a central assumption of WP models is that morphological systems never consist of independent cells, so the cumulative uncertainty of cells is always less than the sum of their individual uncertainty.

Cohesion is then measured by dividing the mutual information of C_1 and C_2 by their joint entropy, as in Figure 7.12. In the case where C_1 and C_2 are independent, their mutual information and cohesion will approach zero. In the case where C_1 and C_2 are identical or perfectly intercorrelated, their cohesion will approach 1. Averaging this value over the cells in a paradigm, class or system will determine a measure of system cohesion which represents how tightly the cells are integrated into a network of mutual implication.

The traditional problem of 'validating' analogical deductions can also be approached from an uncertainty-based perspective. The validity of a four-part

$$H(C_1, C_2) = - \sum_{x \in R_{C_1}} \sum_{y \in R_{C_2}} p(x, y) \log_2 p(x, y)$$

FIGURE 7.11   Joint entropy (cf. Cover and Thomas 1991: 15)

$$\frac{I(C_1; C_2)}{H(C_1, C_2)}$$

FIGURE 7.12   Cell cohesion

proportion of the form $a : b = c : X$ depends on how well a predicts b (and how reliably a can be matched with c). Predictability can again be formulated in information-theoretic terms, most straightforwardly in terms of conditional entropy. This strategy can be illustrated with reference to the proportions in (7.1). As in traditional formulations, the terms in these proportions represent forms with implicit (but unambiguous) interpretations.

(7.1)   Valid and spurious declensional analogies in Russian
   a. slovarja : slovarju = portfelja : *portfelju*
   b. nedeljami : nedelja ≠ tetradjami : *tetradja*

The antecedent of the proportion in (7.1a) establishes a pattern between the genitive and dative singular forms of SLOVAR' 'dictionary' from Table 7.5. Since both of these forms are unique within the paradigm of SLOVAR', the forms alone suffice to pick out a unique cell–form pair.[13] The pattern in the ancecedent then sanctions the deduction of the dative singular form of the first declension noun PORTFEL' 'briefcase' from its genitive singular form. The spurious proportion in (7.1b) establishes a similar pattern between unambiguous instrumental plural and nominative singular forms of NEDELJA 'week' and uses this relation to deduce an incorrect nominative singular of TETRAD' 'notebook'.

The relationship between the 'a' and 'c' terms are parallel in these proportions: *slovarja* and *portfela* are both genitive singulars and *nedeljami* and *slovarjami* are both instrumental plurals. The contrast between the proportions in (7.1) reflects a difference in the relations between the 'a' and 'b' terms. It is this difference that can be expressed in terms of conditional entropy. Proportional analogies do not normally apply to ALL realizations of a given cell, since patterns of that generality can be specified by two terms. For example, the fact that the nominative plural of an Estonian noun corresponds to the genitive singular plus -d can be expressed by a 'two-part' analogy: any noun whose genitive singular is realized by 'X' has the nominative singular Xd.[14] Hence the pattern established in the antecedent of four-part proportion relates a cell to a specific realization. In the case of (7.1a), the antecedent picks out nouns whose genitive singular conforms to the pattern Xa.

The reduction in the uncertainty of a cell C_2 that is attributable to knowledge of a cell C_1 with a realization r can be measured by the SPECIFIC CONDITIONAL ENTROPY $H(C_2|C_1 = r)$. The reliability of the proportion in (7.1a) correlates with the value of $H(\text{Dat.Sg}|\text{Gen.Sg} = Xa)$. Significantly, this use of specific

---

[13] The use of unambiguous forms to represent cell-form pairs in proportional analogies should not be allowed to create the false impression that they express pure form-based deductions.

[14] Similar remarks apply to the Priscianic patterns in (6.2).

conditional entropy preserves the representational neutrality of traditional proportions (cf. Morpurgo Davies 1978). The relevant subclass of the genitive singular is defined by a pattern, expressed by the inflectional ending -*a*. But the pattern could also include theme vowels, segments from the stem or root, or anything else that is of predictive value. Specific conditional entropy can be calculated from conditional probabilities in the same way as the conditional entropy values in Section 7.2.1. As exhibited in Figure 7.7, knowledge of the genitive singular eliminates roughly two thirds of the uncertainty associated with the dative singular. The remaining uncertainty derives from the fact that a genitive singular in -*i* can be associated with a dative singular in -*e* or -*i*, as shown in Table 7.8. However, since a genitive singular in -*a* only co-occurs with a dative singular in -*u*, knowledge of a genitive singular in -*a* eliminates the uncertainty in the dative singular form in this fragment of the Russian declensional system. Hence the reliability of the proportion (7.1a) is reflected in the fact that the value of $H(\text{Dat.Sg}|\text{Gen.Sg} = Xa)$ approaches 0.

In contrast, since the instrumental plural has a single realization, knowledge of an instrumental plural in -*ami* is the same as knowledge of the instrumental plural. Knowledge of the instrumental plural preserves all of the uncertainty associated with the nominative singular in (7.1b), just as the uncertainty of the dative singular is preserved in Figure 7.5. Hence the spurious nature of the proportion (7.1b) is reflected in the fact that the value of $H(\text{Nom.Sg}|\text{Inst.Pl} = Xami)$ is the same as the value of $H(\text{Nom.Sg})$.

As with principal part selection, the formulation and validation of proportional analogies can be expressed in information-theoretic terms. Proportions can be defined over any stable property–form pairs, so that the role of words can be seen to reflect the traditional claim that words are the most morphosyntactically stable units. The reliability of an analogical deduction is likewise defined with reference to the totality of relevant property–form pairs in a language. To the extent that proportions make reference to words, their validation requires a lexicon containing units that are (at least) word-sized. However, the fact that these traditional notions can be reconstructed in terms of uncertainty reduction does not imply that they have a privileged status in a modern WP model. Again like principal parts or exemplary paradigms, proportions isolate individual deductive patterns within a larger network of mutually interdependent elements. Predictive value is a matter of degree and, as suggested by the average conditional entropy measures of Ackerman and Malouf (2013), most inflectional variants are at least partially informative about other forms of an item. Proportions tend to identify patterns that are of particular relevance or salience for language descriptions, but there is no reason to believe that they are distinguished from other patterns by the speakers of a language.

7.3 Implicational economy

Interpreting implicational relations in terms of uncertainty reduction offers a useful perspective on a range of other traditional issues. Perhaps the most direct implications are for the phenomena subsumed under the rubric of 'economy of inflection' (Plank 1991). Inflectional economy effects are of particular interest to classical WP models for two principal reasons. Since economy effects are defined with reference to the paradigm, they provide a measure of support for the theoretical relevance of paradigms. As Carstairs (1983: 116) puts it, "inflexional paradigms do indeed need to be recognized as central in morphological theory, because it is only by reference to them that we can state an important fact about how inflexions behave". Moreover, from a classical WP standpoint, the economical organization of paradigms provides a type of evidence for the general implicational structure of inflectional systems.

7.3.1 Paradigm economy

The contemporary interest in paradigm economy effects stems largely from the influential discussion in Carstairs (1983), which draws attention to these effects and attributes them to a Paradigm Economy Principle (PEP). Subsequent elaborations of this approach treat economy effects as morphological reflexes of more general synonymy avoidance principles (Carstairs-McCarthy 1991, 1994). However the general conception of economy that underlies this family of proposals is articulated most clearly in the initial formulation of the PEP. In contrast to a classical WP model, the PEP is not concerned with distinctive inflectional patterns in general but with 'inflectional resources', by which Carstairs (1983) means 'affixal resources':

Paradigm economy provides at least a partial answer to a question which, so far as I can discover, has not been asked before—a question about how, in any inflected language, the inflexional resources available in some word-class or part of speech are distributed among members of that word class. (Carstairs 1983: 116)

The distribution of inflectional resources is characterized in terms of upper and lower bounds on the space of possible inflection classes, where these bounds are determined by the number of different affixal strategies available for realizing paradigm cells in a given word class. This can be illustrated by a schematic example. Consider a simple declensional system with two contrastive properties, number and case, two distinct number features, N_1 and N_2 and four case features, C_1, C_2, C_3 and C_4. Since each combination of number and case features defines a paradigm cell, these number and case features define the family of eight-cell paradigms summarized in Table 7.10.

The actual number of realizations for each cell are determined mainly by the size of the nominal lexicon, which is independent of the economy of the inflectional

TABLE 7.10   Schematic paradigm structure

	N_1	N_2
C_1	(N_1,C_1)	(N_2,C_1)
C_2	(N_1,C_2)	(N_2,C_2)
C_3	(N_1,C_3)	(N_2,C_3)
C_4	(N_1,C_4)	(N_2,C_4)

system. Hence to describe inflectional economy one must first isolate patterns of inflectional exponence. For each cell (N_i, C_j), let $\xi(N_i, C_j)$ represent the set of patterns that realize the cell and $|\xi(N_i, C_j)|$ the number of patterns in that set. There will be at least one inflectional pattern associated with every cell, since the existence of the pattern is a precondition for recognizing the cell in the first place. In every class system, there will also be a maximum number of patterns realized by any cell, though there need not be a unique 'maximally allomorphic' cell. Let us call this highest value the CELL SUM and represent it by $\mathcal{H}$.[15] In the singular German patterns in Table 4.9, the value of $\mathcal{H}$ is 3, since there are three patterns of exponence in the genitive. In the partial description of Russian in in Table 7.5, the value of $\mathcal{H}$ is again 3, since the dative and instrumental singular cells both have three realizations.

The space of possible inflection classes can then be defined with reference to the allomorphic variation exhibited by individual cells. It is usually assumed that two inflection classes can be distinguished if they exhibit (morphologically conditioned) allomorphy in any cell. From this assumption, it follows that the cell sum $\mathcal{H}$ defines the minimal number of classes. This minimum just reflects the fact that there must be at least as many classes as there are realizations for the maximally allomorphic cells, since otherwise some class would have multiple realizations for those cells. At the other extreme, the largest space of classes corresponds to the CELL PRODUCT $\mathcal{P}$, i.e., the product of all of the realizations of the individual cells. In the case of the the system in Table 7.10, the cell product is defined as $|\xi(N_1, C_1)| \times |\xi(N_1, C_2)|, \ldots, \times |\xi(N_2, C_4)|$.[16] The cell product defines the largest class system, since it exhaustively enumerates all of the combinations of patterns exhibited by individual cells.

Continuing with the schematic system in Table 7.10, let D represent the system and $\mathcal{C}_D$ be the number of inflection classes in D. The assumptions adopted so far dictate only that the value of $\mathcal{C}_D$ must fall somewhere between the cell sum $\mathcal{H}_D$ and the cell product $\mathcal{P}_D$. However, as Carstairs (1983) remarks, inflection class systems are not normally distributed within this space. Instead, they appear to cluster closely around the cell sum value:

when we apply the traditional notion of 'paradigm', we find that the actual total of paradigms is at or close to the minimum logically possible with the inflexional resources involved, and nowhere approaches the logical maximum. (Carstairs 1983: 127)

To account for this clustering, Carstairs (1983: 127) proposes the PEP as "an absolute constraint on the organization of the inflexional resources for every word-class in every language" which has the effect of "keeping the total of paradigms for any word-class close to the logical minimum". In the schematic terms adopted

---

[15] This value corresponds to the Maximum Realizations count in in Table 7.9.

[16] More generally, in an inflectional system with categories $F, G \ldots, H$ and corresponding features $p, q, \ldots, r$ the cell product will be

$$\prod_{i=1}^{p}\prod_{j=1}^{q}\cdots\prod_{k=1}^{r} |\xi(F_i, G_j \ldots, H_k)|$$

above, the PEP requires that for any word-class system $\mathcal{W}$, the class size, $C_{\mathcal{W}}$ is equal to ('or close to') the cell sum $\mathcal{H}_{\mathcal{W}}$. In principle, the PEP would appear to impose a maximally restrictive constraint on class size, since it effectively requires that each inflectional system must be organized into the smallest possible set of classes. In practice, the restrictiveness of the PEP depends on how close is 'close enough' for compliance and, more fundamentally, on how classes are individuated. One immediate qualification is introduced by the decision to "disregard ... stem alternations" (Carstairs 1983: 120) and restrict the notion of 'inflectional resources' relevant to the PEP to 'affixal exponents'. This exclusion reduces the overall number of inflection classes in languages with distinctive, class-specific stem alternations, and contributes to the goal of bringing the count closer to the logical minimum.

Yet even as a constraint solely on the distribution of affixal resources, the PEP places an extremely tight constraint on the relationship between cells in a paradigm. In a system that conforms to the PEP, each maximally allomorphic cell partitions the system into classes, and every pair of maximally allomorphic cells partitions the system into the same classes. No cell in a paradigm can have realizations that vary independently of the realizations of any maximally allomorphic cell. This means that for every realization of every maximally allomorphic cell there will be a unique realization in every other cell (including other maximally allomorphic cells). This entails that every maximally allomorphic cell is diagnostic of class. Moreover, since every class contains a maximally diagnostic cell, it follows that every class will be identifiable from the realization of a single cell. So a system that conforms to the PEP will realize the pedagogical ideal in which a single principal part suffices to identify class.

There are of course *prima facie* counterexamples to any principle that imposes this kind of tight organization on paradigm structure. As Carstairs acknowledges, traditional descriptions of German noun declensions do not appear to conform to the strictures of the PEP. Table 7.11 lists the exponents that Carstairs isolates from the traditional principal parts of these declensions.[17] Since the smallest class space is defined by the maximally allomorphic cell, the five exponents that realize the non-dative plural in Table 7.11 define a minimum class size of five. This corresponds closely to the number of plural classes recognized in traditional sources such as Duden (2005) (provided again that stem alternations are disregarded in defining classes).

TABLE 7.11 Exponents of principal parts in German (Carstairs 1983: 125)

Nom Sg	Ø
Gen Sg	Ø, -(e)s, -(e)n, -(e)ns
Nom/Acc/Gen Pl	Ø~-e, -¨(e), -er~-¨er, -s, -(e)n

[17] Parentheses and dashes mark alternations treated as phonologically conditioned or stylistic, and exponents of the form '-¨er' indicate an umlauted stem vowel.

TABLE 7.12 Co-occurrence of plural and genitive singular endings in German

		S1		S2	S3
	Plu	Masc	Neut	Masc	Fem
P1	-s	-s	-s	—	Ø
P2	-(e)n	-s	-s	-(e)n	Ø
P3	-e	-s	-s	—	Ø
P4	-er	-s	-s	—	—
P5	Ø	-s	-s	—	Ø

To conform to the PEP, the choice of plural ending must determine the nominative and genitive singular endings. The nominative is trivial, since it is always unmarked. However, the genitive appears to vary independently of the plural. This variation is exhibited in Table 7.12, which plots the co-occurrence of plural and genitive singular endings.[18] These patterns are obtained from Table 4.11 by collapsing pairs of rows that differ solely in stem umlaut, and replacing the exemplary lexemes by plural and genitive endings.

At first glance, this pattern appears fully incompatible with the PEP, since every plural ending except -er in the second column corresponds to two or even three distinct genitive singular endings. Yet on closer inspection the system is in fact almost maximally economical. As Carstairs argues more generally, traditional 'declensions' (and 'conjugations') can be brought into closer conformance with the PEP by restricting attention to genuine inflectional variants, and grouping paradigms into common classes if they differ solely with respect to lexically-conditioned properties. In the specific case of German, Carstairs (1983: 126) observes that "Gender is lexically determined for German nouns; and we can readily combine each of the Feminine-only 'declensions' . . . with some non-Feminine 'declension', just as we traditionally combine Latin Neuters and non-Neuters in Declension II". Returning to the classes defined by the P1, P3 and P5 plural endings in Table 7.12, one can see that they exhibit a general contrast between masculines and neuters, which are marked by -s in the genitive singular, and feminines, which are uninflected in the singular. The distribution of umlauted vowels (suppressed in Table 7.12) is likewise a lexical property of nouns in classes P3 and P5.

The only real challenge to the PEP is posed by class P2. There is, first of all, some artificiality in collapsing what are arguably two synchronically distinct plural strategies. Plurals in -(e)n are the default for 'native' feminine nouns, as well as for feminine nouns formed with productive endings such as -ung and -heit, as discussed in Chapter 4.3.1. The formation of masculine and neuter plurals in -(e)n is much more restricted and cannot be regarded as productive in the modern language. Even within the non-productive subclass, neuters have unambiguous singular forms. So it is just the masculines that show inflectional variation, with weak nouns such as PRINZ following the weak singular pattern S2, and mixed nouns

---

[18] Though omitting -(e)ns, which occurs with a small and declining set of nouns.

TABLE 7.13 Economical class space in German

	P1	P2	P3	P4	P5
Masc	S1	S1 S2	S1	S1	S1
Neut	S1	S1	S1	S1	S1
Fem	S3	S3	S3	—	S3

like STAAT following the strong singular pattern S1. The resulting class space is exhibited in Table 7.13.

Hence by consolidating gender-conditioned variation, one can arrive at a space of six classes, assuming just two P2 subclasses, or seven classes, if productive feminines in -(e)n are distinguished from the masculines and neuters. This exceeds, but is indisputably close to, the minimum of five determined by the patterns of plural exponence. One can in principle bring the system into conformance with the PEP by coercing plurals in -(e)n into a single class and making a "specific exemption" for mixed paradigms, as Carstairs (1983: 127) suggests. This kind of exception is of course very different from the consolidation of lexically-conditioned variation. However it is also true that the evaluation of a general principle like the PEP should not hinge too directly on patterns that even traditional sources regard as mixed or hybridized.

It is arguably more instructive to diagnose the general characteristics of German that allow the PEP to work, or at least to work as well as it does. One pivotal property is the clean dissociation of inflectional and lexical variation. The patterns of plural affixation P1–P5 can reasonably be regarded as inflectional, while affixal variation between the singular patterns S1 and S3 can, as Carstairs argues, be attributed to lexical factors. Hence there is only one case, involving masculines of class P2, in which there is inflectional variation in both the plural and singular. Precisely this case is problematic for the PEP.

Although there may be other divisions of labour that promote economical paradigm organization, the separation of lexical and inflectional variation is less a feature of inflection class systems in general than a symptom of the near-complete loss of singular contrasts in German. Hence one useful test case for the PEP comes from declensional systems that are traditionally described in terms of multiple principal parts. Finnish declensions provide a familiar example. Traditional descriptions often list up to five principal parts (typically the nominative, genitive and partitive singular, along with the partitive plural and a plural 'local' case such as the inessive). Some of these forms identify stem alternations that are disregarded in determining compliance with the PEP, while others identify affixal patterns. As in the paradigm of Estonian PUKK 'trestle' in Table 4.8, local case forms in Finnish have mostly invariant endings. Consequently, the grammatical case exponents in Table 7.14 exhibit nearly all of the inflectional variation that is relevant to the PEP.

Examination of Table 7.14 identifies the partitive singular as the most highly differentiated cell, with three distinct patterns -A, -tA and -ttA. The archiphoneme 'A' ranges over the vowels a and ä, which show harmony with the final stem vowel, so that the three patterns in Table 7.14 have six surface realizations. The partitive

TABLE 7.14   Grammatical case exponents in Finnish (Karlsson 1999)

	Sg	Plu
Nom	Ø	-t
Gen	-n	-den~-tten, -en
Part	-A, -tA, -ttA	-A, -tA

TABLE 7.15   Grammatical case forms in Finnish (Pihel and Pikamäe 1999)

Sg	Plu	Part Sg	Part Plu	Gen Pl	
A	A	asemaa	asemia	asemien	'position' (13) [15]
A	tA	perunaa	perunoita	perunoiden	'potato' (17) [3]
tA	A	lohta	lohia	lohien	'salmon' (33) [24]
tA	tA	leikkuuta	leikkuita	leikkuiden	'haircut' (25) [18]
ttA	tA	huonetta	huoneita	huoneiden	'room' (78) [4]
A	A~tA	karitsaa	karitsoja	karitsojen	
			karitsoita	karitsoiden	'lamb' (15) [6]
A~tA	A	lahtea	lahtia	lahtiin	
		lahta			'bay' (34) [12]

plural is realized by the first two endings, -A and -tA, but these endings are usually described as varying independently of the partitive singular endings. The genitive plural is realized by three endings, but two of these, -den and -tten are regarded as variants.[19] For the grammatical cells of the Finnish declensional system, the cell sum $\mathcal{H}$ is then 3, and the cell product $\mathcal{P}$ is 12 (3 x 2 x 2). The actual variation exhibited by grammatical case forms (according to standard descriptions) is set out in table 7.15.[20]

The first two columns in Table 7.15 plot the co-occurrence of partitive singular and plural exponents, followed in the next two columns by forms of exemplary items. We can with no loss of generality restrict attention to word types with unique partitive singular and plural affixes, exhibited in the first five rows in Table 7.15. These word types define the five classes C_1–C_5 in Table 7.16. A class size of five is closer to the maximum of six defined by the partitive exponents than to the minimum of three dictated by the PEP. But it is still far from the cell product of 12, due to the fact that genitive plural endings do not add any new classes. Instead, variation in the genitive plural largely conforms to the expectations of the PEP in aligning with the partitive plural, with -A implying -en and -tA predicting -den (Karlsson 1999: 92f.).

---

[19] "The ending -den can always be replaced by the ending -tten" (Karlsson 1999: 93).

[20] The numbers in parentheses identify the word type numbers from the authoritative *Nykysuomen sanakirja* 'Dictionary of modern Finnish' (Häkkinen 1990), which are used in Pihel and Pikamäe (1999), and the number in square brackets indicates how many of the 85 word types exhibit that pattern of partitive exponence.

TABLE 7.16 Classes defined by unique partitive exponents

	C1	C2	C3	C4	C5
Part Sg	A	A	tA	tA	tA
Part Pl	A	tA	A	tA	ttA
Gen Pl	en	den	en	den	den

The challenge presented by Finnish is that the partitive plural is itself NOT predictable from the partitive singular. The four logical possibilities defined by the exponents -A, and -tA are illustrated in the first four rows in Table 7.15: singular -A co-occurs with each of the plural endings -A and -tA and the same is true of singular -tA. Since there is no grammatical gender in Finnish, it is not possible to collapse the classes in Table 7.16 into 'macroparadigms' whose internal variation is conditioned by gender differences, as in German. Nor are there any other evident non-inflectional properties that condition the choice of partitive singular realizations. Rather, Finnish simply appears to exhibit an unremarkable pattern of cross-variation. Two of the three realizations of the most highly variable cell, the partitive singular, may each co-occur with one of two partitive plural realizations. The interaction of these choices defines a class space that exceeds the theoretical minimum of 3 determined by the cell sum. This of course does not expand the class space to anything approaching the cell product. Significantly, the variation exhibited by the partitive singular plays no direct role in restricting further expansion of the class space, which is constrained by the coocurrence of partitive and genitive plural realizations.

7.3.2 Descriptive and entropic economy

The absolute adequacy of the PEP is again of less interest here than the factors that allow it to work as well as it does.[21] In the initial formulation of the PEP, cited on p. 186 above, Carstairs (1983: 127) describes it as "an absolute constraint on the organization of the inflexional resources for every word-class in every language" without specifying an explicit constraint that would have this effect. In subsequent elaborations of economy principles, Carstairs-McCarthy (1994: 742) proposes what he terms the 'No Blur Principle' (NBP) "to refer to the corollary of the Principle of Contrast [(Clark 1987)] which flows from the proposal to treat inflection class membership as part of the 'meaning' of an affix". His statement of the NBP principle is repeated below:

Within any set of competing inflectional affixal realizations for the same paradigmatic cell, no more than one can fail to identify inflection class unambiguously. (Carstairs-McCarthy 1994: 742)

---

[21] For some discussion of the status of the PEP, see Nyman (1986, 1988); Carstairs (1988), as well as Carstairs-McCarthy (1991) and other papers in Plank (1991).

Although the NBP is expressed as a constraint on the meaning of individual realizations associated with a paradigm cell, rather than with the number of realizations, it will be violated by the same types of patterns that violate the PEP. In the Finnish example above, neither the partitive singular realization -A nor -tA can be said to "identify inflection class uniquely". This simple pattern is deliberately chosen to isolate the interactions that challenge the PEP and NBP; more complex classes of counterexamples are discussed by Stump (2005b). Yet the structure of these patterns is again of far greater interest than their status as counterexamples to specific economy principles. This reflects the fact that the patterns will contribute to uncertainty given any objective measure of system complexity, whereas the theoretical import of particular cases will depend on the status of a range of auxiliary assumptions regarding the various 'extensions', 'exemptions' and 'codicils' proposed in the economy literature.

The difference between patterns and their theoretical import rests on a basic property of economy principles like the PEP or NBP. The PEP is stated as a "constraint on the organization of . . . inflexional resources" (Carstairs 1983: 127) and the NBP as an inflectional version of a "pragmatic principle assisting the acquisition of vocabulary" (Carstairs-McCarthy 1994: 783). However, both principles are ultimately constraints on the form of morphological DESCRIPTIONS, rather than on the organization or acquisition of the systems themselves. It is the essential reference to inflection classes in these principles that determines their status as constraints on descriptions. By treating classes as "things IN a language rather than merely part of our equipment for the analysis and description OF the language" economy principles are guilty of "confusing one's machinery of analysis with one's object of analysis" (Hockett 1967: 221). Like the 'morphophonemes' discussed by Hockett on p. 158 above, 'inflection classes' form part of a frame of descriptive reference for representing paradigmatic variation; their number and type depends on the goals of the description. This point is often stated explicitly in descriptions of individual languages, which do not, in general, assert that there is some fixed number of classes in a language, but instead assume that the number assigned depends on the level of precision to which the classes are described or the purposes for which they are defined. Thus Karlsson (2006: 476) summarizes the variation in the number of declension classes in Finnish in the following terms:[22]

There is no consensus on how many inflectional classes there are for nominals and verbs. Traditional Finnish lexicography as manifested in *Nykysuomen sanakirja* (Dictionary of modern Finnish, 1951–1961) postulates 82 inflectional classes for nominals, whereas at the other extreme, a generative description such as Wiik (1967) operates with none but a wealth of ordered (morpho)phonological rules. A surface-oriented morphological approach would recognize at least 10 nominal inflectional classes.

The existence of a range of class-size estimates does not in itself preclude the possibility of identifying a 'theoretically correct' estimate within that range. If one

---

[22] A parallel situation obtains in descriptions of Estonian (Blevins 2007, 2008a).

assumes that standard grammars incorporate a degree of redundancy that is useful for reference or pedagogical descriptions, then why could economy principles not be satisfied by compressing this redundant description into a theoretically concise analysis? A Russian grammar might, for purely pedagogical purposes, recognize a redundant fourth declension, but the system could be brought into conformance with the PEP by recognizing masculine and neuter subclasses of a general first declension. However, the appeal to 'subclasses' in this reanalysis exposes the fact that a class count of four is already highly idealized. A split between classes and subclasses may be motivated by descriptive or pedagogical goals, but within a grammar, this relocates rather than reduces the variation in the system. In the absence of practical goals, it is unclear what would motivate the division. Two paradigms that exhibit distinct inflectional patterns in each of their cells would be assigned to distinct classes in any classification. But how many cells must vary? Does one always suffice, or does partial overlap between two paradigms give rise to 'subclasses'? Does it matter if variation involves suppletion or some other form of irregularity? How many items must follow an inflectional pattern in order to constitute a 'class'? Presumably single suppletive items do not form classes. But what then is the item threshold that separates classes from residual suppletive patterns?

The issues raised by these types of questions cannot be resolved merely by stipulating an arbitrarily consistent policy for defining classes, subclasses, item-specific patterns, etc. The challenge for an approach that assigns some objective reality to notions like inflection classes lies in arriving at a principled, task-independent, basis for critical definitions. This challenge is scarcely addressed within the economy literature, which, for the most part, consists of case studies.[23] Studies start from an apparently uneconomical class system, often obtained from a traditional descriptive source, and then outline strategies for bringing the description into conformance with a given economy principle. Both the original and economical descriptions depend on the assumption that a distinction can be drawn between classes and subclasses. The fact that traditional sources may agree on the number of classes in a language does not validate this assumption, insofar as the consensus will again tend to reflect shared descriptive or pedagogical goals within a grammatical tradition.

Like 'principal parts' and 'exemplary paradigms', 'inflection classes' are components of a descriptive framework for exhibiting paradigmatic patterns and variation. Principles that make essential reference to these notions constrain the space of grammatical descriptions, much like the requirement of 'scientific compactness' proposed by Bloomfield (1933: 238) on p. 70 above. As Finkel and Stump (2007, 2009) show, a morphological description can minimize its principal part inventory, or choose the same parts for each member of a word class, but in at least some cases must chose between minimization and uniformity. There are no comparable studies of exemplary paradigm selection, since it is more generally understood that nothing of consequence hinges on the choice of an exemplary item. Yet as with

---

[23] Though see Bochner (1993) for a 'pattern-matching' metric and Sagot and Walther (2013) for a metric based on minimum description length (Rissanen 1978).

inflection class size, there is often a consensus regarding the choice of exemplary items within a grammatical tradition. Economy principles that constrain the size of inflection classes or regulate the relationship between realizations and classes fall squarely within the literature that deals with the metatheory of grammatical descriptions.

As with principal part classifications, the applicability of economy conditions will correlate with objective properties of a language. Information theory again provides a means of measuring these properties. According to the PEP, a fully economical system is one in which the number of realizations associated with the maximally allomorphic cell, i.e., the 'cell sum', determines the number of inflection classes. A fully uneconomical system is one in which the product of all of the cell realizations, i.e., the 'cell product', determines class size. These limiting cases can be characterized directly in terms of paradigm (joint) entropy.[24] Let us first generalize the definition in Figure 7.11 to apply to more than a pair of cells, as in Figure 7.13. Then the entropy of a paradigm with cells $C_1, \ldots, C_n$ can be defined as the joint entropy $H(C_1, \ldots, C_n)$.

Joint entropy values are bounded by the values of their component variables, as specified in Figure 7.14. The minimal value is defined by the variable with the greatest entropy, $\max[H(C_1), \ldots, H(C_n)]$. The maximum value is bounded by the sum of their variables, $H(C_1) + \ldots + H(C_n)$. These boundary values define the limits identified by paradigm economy. In any system, there will be a maximally entropic cell (which need not be unique). If, as in Carstairs (1983) and Ackerman and Malouf (2013), the frequency of realizations is disregarded, the maximally entropic cells will correspond to the maximally allomorphic cells. In a fully economical system, the entropy of a paradigm will then correspond to the entropy of a maximally entropic cell. This cell must eliminate uncertainty about every other cell, since otherwise the system will exhibit independent variation that would make the system uneconomical. In a maximally uneconomical system, the entropy of a paradigm corresponds to the other boundary value, the sum of the entropies of its cells. In this case, cell variation is fully independent, and no cell is informative about any other cell.

$$H(C_1, \ldots, C_n) = - \sum_{x_1 \in R_{C_1}} \ldots \sum_{x_n \in R_{C_n}} p(x_1 \ldots, x_n) \log_2 p(x_1 \ldots, x_n)$$

FIGURE 7.13   Joint entropy of multiple cells

$$\max[H(C_1), \ldots, H(C_n)] \leq H(C_1, \ldots, C_n) \leq H(C_1) + \ldots + H(C_n)$$

FIGURE 7.14   Boundary values for joint entropies

[24] This notion of 'paradigm entropy' measures the cumulative uncertainty associated with the cells of a paradigm, in contrast to the notion of 'paradigm cell entropy' discussed in Section 7.2.2, which measures the average uncertainty associated with individual cells.

An entropy-based PEP could, like the class-based principle, posit that the entropy of a paradigm is "close to the logical minimum" (Carstairs 1983: 127). There would, however, be at least three significant differences. The first and most obvious is that the entropies of cells and paradigms would be determined by the distribution of realizations over cells and would not require references to classes or other descriptive or theoretical constructs. The second is that the calculation of entropies from descriptions or corpora would permit an empirical investigation of how closely the entropy of inflectional systems approach the logical minimum. The third difference brings us back to the issue of the robustness of entropy-based measures, discussed in Section 7.2.1. Given a description of a system that specifies only inventories of inflectional realizations, an entropy ceiling can be estimated for the system. However, as more complete and accurate information about frequencies is added, the measures of system economy will show a corresponding increase in precision.

A general benefit of an entropy-based economy measure is that it provides the basis for a cross-linguistic comparison of inflectional economy. An initial study of this kind is presented in Ackerman and Malouf (2013), summarized in Section 7.2.2, which attempts to isolate the factors that contribute to inflectional economy and measure their influence on system complexity across a 10-language sample. This study represents a break from much of the previous literature on inflectional economy, which is taken up with debates about whether particular *prima facie* counterexamples are genuine violations of a proposed economy condition. The notion of economy that emerges from these debates tends to be binary: either a system is 'economical' because it can be made to conform to a given condition, or it is 'uneconomical' because it exhibits variation that violates the condition. Because these debates operate at the level of grammatical descriptions, languages with familiar and well-established descriptive traditions are somewhat overrepresented. The relative inflectional simplicity of familiar modern European languages also contributes to the fact that, as Ackerman and Malouf (2013) observe, many of the languages that figure in discussions of economy exhibit low entropy:[25]

it is evident that the systems [Carstairs(-McCarthy)] examines all display low entropy: low entropy provides a unifying explanation that is affected by the specific factors such as those arising from cognitive principles. (Ackerman and Malouf 2013: 446)

7.3.3 From exemplars to discriminative contrasts

Let us now summarize the broader issues under consideration here. One conclusion that can be drawn from this discussion is that studies of economy effects from different perspectives lend support to the claims underlying principles like the PEP or NBP. The "tendency" that Carstairs (1983: 127) discerns "towards keeping the total of paradigms for any word class close to the logical minimum" appears to be

---

[25] Ackerman and Malouf (2015) subsequently propose that the NBP is best regarded neither as a design feature of language nor as a part of morphological theory proper, but as a special case that falls under the Low Conditional Entropy Conjecture.

robustly attested in paradigmatic systems. Morover, from a classical WP perspective, this tendency derives from the implicational structure of inflectional systems. Within a modern WP model, this structure can be measured in information-theoretic terms. The correspondence between economy effects and paradigm entropy thus illustrates another dimension of a classical WP model that can be reconstructed in uncertainty-based terms. As with the selection of principal parts and the validation of analogies, a formal reconstruction of economy in terms of uncertainty carries no commitment to the kinds of pedagogical idealizations that usually accompany these notions.

More generally, a reconceptualization of economy effects in terms of uncertainty-reducing interdependencies conforms to the general uncertainty-sensitive perspective of a classical WP model. The importance attached to words in Section 7.1 can be seen to be motivated by the contribution that their morphotactic and morphosyntactic stability makes to reducing uncertainty in the association between properties and forms. At the level of form, the word is a maximally discriminable "perceptual gestalt" (Hockett 1987: 52). At the level of grammatical meaning, the word provides "a more stable and solid focus of grammatical relations than the component morpheme by itself" (Robins 1959: 128). As discussed at greater length in Sections 7.2 and 7.3, the affiliation between words and paradigms also reduces uncertainty, by exploiting the information implicit in the interdependencies between cells in a paradigm.

The selection of words and paradigms in WP models thus serves the goal of minimizing grammatical uncertainty (rather than minimizing unit or inventory size). The core claims that underlie the exemplar-based structure of a classical WP model can be summarized as in (7.2).

(7.2)   a. The uncertainty that arises in associating grammatical properties with word forms is less than (or equal to, in the case of simple forms) the sum of the uncertainty that arises in associating properties with the component morphs of those word forms.

b. The uncertainty associated with the set of cells of a paradigm is less than (or equal to, in the case of single-cell paradigms) the sum of the uncertainty of each of the component cells.

The usefulness of information theory for quantifying the notions of 'uncertainty' and 'uncertainty reduction' is highly suggestive, particularly given that an entropy-based formalization appears to offer solutions to problems that have traditionally been regarded as recalcitrant for the WP model. A formal reconstruction of WP models in terms of uncertainty helps to clarify the fundamental questions raised by the descriptive success of this model. Foremost among these are the issues of how variation at the level of individual forms determines the implicational structure of systems, why inflectional systems exhibit the type of structure and the degree of economy that they do, and even why information theory is a useful tool for measuring this structure. These issues are taken up from a discriminative standpoint in the final chapter.

8

Morphology as an adaptive discriminative system

The first part of this volume summarizes some of the types of interdependencies found in morphological systems and reviews traditional arguments that these patterns are implicational rather than derivational in nature. The second part contrasts realizational and implicational perspectives and outlines strategies for representing implicational patterns in terms of standard information-theoretic measures. Many of the specific proposals remain to be worked out in greater detail, and only part of the space of alternatives can be surveyed here. Nevertheless, the overall perspective appears promising, both on its own terms, and as a reconceptualization of the classical WP model.

With the development of approaches that can model the organizational principles that facilitate the prediction of a full system from a subset of forms, it becomes possible to address deeper questions about the source of morphological patterns and the mechanisms that determine them. The final chapter of this volume explores a number of these issues, including the status of regular and irregular formations, the role of probabilistic patterns, the treatment of meaning, and implications of typological variation for morphological models.

8.1 A 'learning-based' approach

The exploration of these issues is guided by two general hypotheses. The first is that form variation serves a fundamentally discriminative function, so that the function of a morphological exponent is best understood in terms of the forms that it distinguishes in a system, not what discrete meanings or properties it expresses in that system. The second is that the organization of a linguistic system is strongly influenced by its communicative function and by the constraints imposed by the process by which it is transmitted. A communicative perspective helps to clarify the role of irregular formations and other patterns that appear nonfunctional or even dysfunctional when language is regarded as a purely formal system. Taking learning into account likewise provides a positive function for regular patterns and offers a particularly natural interpretation of notions like 'competition' as a dimension of the learning process rather than as a component of the morphological system.

When carried to their logical conclusion, these hypotheses suggest a view of language as a complex adaptive system whose form strongly reflects communicative and learning constraints. Such a system is more aptly described in terms of

Word and Paradigm Morphology. First edition. James P. Blevins dynamic communicative pressures and learning and processing principles than in terms of a deductive formal grammar. This general orientation is designated as a 'learning-based' perspective below, in part to emphasize the parallels with the communicative 'usage-based' tradition (Tomasello 2003), and in part to emphasize the role of a (discriminative) learning model.[1]

The hypotheses that guide a learning-based perspective are to some degree independent of the assumptions that underlie implicational WP approaches and it is possible to embed a WP model within a more conservative view of language. However, by combining a learning-based perspective with a WP approach, it is possible to clarify aspects of WP models that have remained largely unexamined. One cluster of such issues is summarized in (8.1).

(8.1)   a. Why do morphological systems exhibit predictive dependencies?
         b. How can the persistence of irregular formations be reconciled with the prevalence of regular patterns and what can their function be?
         c. Why are notions of uncertainty and uncertainty reduction useful for measuring the variation and structure relevant to speakers?

It has long been known that the descriptive success of classical WP models reflects the interdependency of form variation, i.e., that "one inflection tends to predict another" (Matthews 1991: 197). What is less well understood is why this should be the case. The usefulness of information theory for formalizing the classical WP model raises further questions about the probabilistic character of interdependencies. It is clear that these patterns are predominantly statistical but again less clear why this should be the case (particularly from the perspective of grammatical models based on categorical rule and constraint systems). The stable coexistence of regular and irregular formations in many languages raises a related issue. The models of morphological analysis developed within the formal grammar tradition can accommodate deviations from regular patterns but offer no insight into their function or resilience.

A learning-based approach attributes these patterns to factors that are very different in character from the formal constraints on units, representations or rule systems proposed within theoretical models. From a learning-based perspective, the organization of morphological systems is not anchored in a formal architecture or 'innate language faculty' but emerges mainly from the distributional biases of the forms in the system and the general-purpose learning strategies employed by speakers. Hence the first factor is just the structure of the input that speakers are exposed to. The second factor is the learning strategies that speakers employ when exposed to that input. The interaction of these factors suggests the answers in (8.2) to the questions in (8.1).

---

[1] There are also important points of contact with computational models that use temporal self-organizing maps (Chersi et al. 2014; Pirrelli et al. 2015), with a particular convergence at the level of the error-driven learning rules employed in these models.

(8.2) a. Morphological systems exhibit predictive dependencies because, given
           the Zipfian structure of the input, speakers never encounter all the forms
           of a language and must be able to deduce new forms.
       b. Irregular formations serve two useful communicative functions. As indi-
           vidual expressions, they are well discriminated. As exceptional members
           of larger sets of alternating elements, they emphasize contrasts that are
           less saliently marked in regular patterns.
       c. Uncertainty reduction is relevant to speakers because learning a language
           involves the development of a predictive language model that reduces
           uncertainty about forms and distributions.

From a learning-based standpoint, the predictive dependencies exhibited by
morphological systems are not due to abstract economy principles. Instead, interpredictability serves a very practical purpose; it is a prerequisite for the use and
propagation of language, given the structure of the input that speakers encounter.
Interpredictability is essentially a variety of regularity, and regularity aids generalization. Conversely, irregular forms are highly distinctive and communicatively
useful but a much less reliable basis for extrapolation.

8.2 The Zipfian Paradigm Cell Filling Problem

The claim that predictive dependencies play a pivotal role in language learning
and use may appear counterintuitive at first, particularly for speakers of languages
(like English) that exhibit relatively little inflectional variation. Given the volume of
input to which speakers are normally exposed, it might seem reasonable to expect
that they would encounter all or most of the inflectional variants in a language
learned under naturalistic conditions. However, there is good reason to believe that
this expectation merely reflects the fact that speakers are so adept at extrapolating
from partial exposure that they have no introspective ability to identify the forms
they have directly encountered.

Language corpora, which provide the best available representation of language
input, appear to exhibit a systematic form of data sparsity. The forms (usually
words) of a corpus obey Zipf's law (Zipf 1949), according to which the frequency of
a form is inversely proportional to its rank in the corpus. As corpora (or samples of
corpora) increase in size, they do not gradually enumerate all the inflectional variants of regular items. Instead, they reinforce the rank-size distributions established
in smaller corpora or samples.

The result is sparsely populated inflectional paradigms that collectively exhaust
the inflectional variation exhibited by the inflection and word classes of a language.
The distributional biases in the input thus create a genuine 'stimulus sparsity'
problem for morphological acquisition, since a speaker cannot be assumed to
encounter all of the forms of their language. This problem is in some ways
reminiscent of the 'stimulus poverty' issue that has been debated in the domain
of syntax. However, morphological sparsity appears to be a robust fact about the

observable composition of what is sometimes termed 'primary linguistic data'.[2] Sparsity at the morphological level merely reflects the fact that, as Kurumada *et al.* (2013: 440) note, "Zipfian distributions are ubiquitous across natural language". The initially counterintuitive character of this phenomenon is attributable to their observation that the "consequences [of these distributions] for learning are only beginning to be explored".[3]

The phenomenon itself was recognized by Hockett (1967), who drew a pair of initial consequences. The first was that 'exemplary paradigms' were just as much a pedagogical idealization as 'principal parts'. The second was that a psychologically plausible account must model a speaker's ability to extrapolate from any new form of an item on the basis of sparsely populated paradigms:

in his analogizing... [t]he native user of the language... operates in terms of all sorts of internally stored paradigms, many of them doubtless only partial; and he may first encounter a new basic verb in any of its inflected forms. (Hockett 1967: 221)

Given that patterns of interpredictability permit the extrapolation of a larger system from a subset of forms, these patterns contribute to a solution to the challenge posed by morphological sparsity. Of course interpredictability is just a type of system-level regularity, without which speakers could not reliably predict forms that they had not directly encountered. In a classical WP approach, exemplary paradigms provide the model for the deduction of unencountered forms. In a more psychologically realistic approach, the basis for analogical deductions will be sets of paradigms that exhibit congruent patterns of form variation. These sets correspond to the inflection classes of a classical WP model, with the difference that the component paradigms are partial, so it is the set, rather than any individual paradigm, that collectively exhausts the form variation associated with the class. The idea that the organization of items into inflection classes plays a role in guiding analogical deduction is also consistent with psycholinguistic studies showing that these classes have a direct influence on morphological processing (Milin *et al.* 2009*a*).

Although the assignment of paradigms to classes offers a solution to the problem of extrapolating from partial paradigms, this does not entirely avoid the effects of morphological sparsity, given that class assignment is in general less determinate for partial than for full paradigms. In some cases it may be that systems evolve in such a way that the attested variants of items tend to be of high diagnostic value for class assignment. This would, for example, be true of languages in which highly

---

[2] It does not, e.g., depend on assumptions about the status of 'structure-dependent operations' (Chomsky 1965: 56) or on disputed claims—see, e.g., Sampson (1989), Pullum and Scholtz (2002), and Clark and Lappin (2011)—to the effect that "People attain knowledge of the structure of their language for which NO evidence is available in the data to which they are exposed as children" (Hornstein and Lightfoot 1981: 9).

[3] The ubiquity of Zipfian distributions also helps to account for the prevalence of low conditional entropy, in the sense of Ackerman and Malouf (2013). Since a system will be deduced from the forms that speakers actually encounter, it follows, from a learnability perspective, that those forms will be informative about the deduced system.

frequent nominative singular forms were a reliable guide to declension class. Other more general factors may also facilitate class assignment. One candidate is lexical form neighbourhoods, whose effects have been investigated in a range of psycholinguistic studies (Baayen *et al.* 2006; Gahl *et al.* 2011). In systems where there is a systematic correlation between lexical neighbourhoods and inflection classes, neighbourhood structures could facilitate class assignment. There is suggestive evidence that something of this sort is true in German. The preliminary study reported in Blevins *et al.* (2016*b*) found a strong correlation between similarity in form between items, measured by Levenshtein distance (Levenshtein 1966), and the number of co-filled cells in their paradigms. The more similar two forms were, the more of the same cells were filled in their respective paradigms.

These effects may reflect at least in part the fact that the common patterns of inflection that define inflection classes often correlate with similarities in stem shape or other aspects of form. However, whatever their ultimate origin, such correlations will be of use in assigning items to classes in which the variants collectively provide a basis for the analogical deduction of forms.

8.2.1 Discriminative irregularity

The Zipfian structure of the primary linguistic input suggests a system-external explanation for the prevalence of interdependencies and regular patterns in general. Morphological models do not need to treat implicational structure and regularity as normative. They are merely prerequisites for generalization from the sparse, biased language sample that learners encounter.

A learning-based approach raises similar questions about the system-external motivation for irregular patterns. This is where discriminative learning models offer insight into the perseverance of patterns that are often treated as a kind of functionless residue or outright noise in the linguistic system. Viewed from a discriminative perspective, irregular formations are not noise, but on the contrary, are well-discriminated and, correspondingly, highly informative forms. This is particularly clear in the case of suppletion, though many deviations from regular patterns will tend to enhance the discriminability of forms and aid communicative efficiency. In English, for example, a regular preterite form such as *walked* is much less clearly discriminated from the present/base form *walk* than suppletive *went* is from *go*. Precisely this point is demonstrated in the learning model in Ramscar *et al.* (2013*a*). Indeed, given the existence of a separate participle form *gone* (and the near-obsolescence of the historical source WEND), the suppletive preterite *went* comes as close to the 'one meaning-one form' ideal as any verb form in English.[4] Once established as well-discriminated exponents of specific properties, such irregulars will also function as attractors that enhance the salience of regular contrasts. By highlighting communicative contrasts that are distinctive in a language, irregulars can clarify the oppositions between less well discriminated regulars.

---

[4] This ideal is often described in terms of 'transparency' in models of Natural Morphology (Mayerthaler 1981; Wurzel 1984; Dressler 1987). See also Bybee (1985: 208ff.) for critical discussion.

Recognizing the function that irregulars perform does not justify an inverted classification of regularity on which they are communicatively optimal. Instead, irregulars can be seen to enjoy a kind of 'herd immunity' within a morphological system. Any increase in the salience and discriminability of irregulars is offset by a commensurate reduction in generalizabilty. Given the Zipfian structure of the input, irregulars can only function in a system that is either small enough to be acquired from directly encountered forms, or regular enough to allow speakers to deduce the shape of unencountered forms.

From a learning-based perspective, neither regular nor irregular patterns are normative; they merely serve different, broadly complementary, functions in a system. The coexistence of regular and irregular patterns reflects an opposition between a pair of communicative pressures, one that enhances discriminability and another that promotes generalizability. Different languages can be expected to reach different states of equilibrium between these pressures, leading to different proportions of regular and irregular patterns.

This kind of dynamic view constrasts starkly with approaches that adopt a purely formal notion of 'scientific compactness', 'optimality', 'canonicity', 'language perfection' etc. On all of these accounts, irregularity comes out as a defective property. Models that incorporate a diachronic dimension may be able to trace the sources of these defects and identify the distributional factors (whether measured in terms of type or token frequencies) that contribute to their survival in the face of regularizing pressure. However without taking the communicative function of language into consideration, it is difficult to perceive the function that irregulars serve once they enter a system.

8.2.2 Knowledge and uncertainty

A learning-based perspective also helps to clarify why information-theoretic measures are so useful for modelling morphological systems and for predicting speakers' behavioural responses (Milin *et al.* 2009a,b). Contemporary theoretical models typically describe a morphological system by characterizing an inventory of well-formed morphological units and associated sets of contrastive grammatical properties/structures. In almost all models, the wellformedness of each individual unit is determined independently of other units in the system. The main exception involves cases of the kind discussed in Chapter 6.2.3, where an association between forms is established by 'rules of referral'.

The main extension proposed in information-theoretic approaches involves the integration of information about the DISTRIBUTION of units. Taking type frequency into account provides a principled means of correcting the overrepresentation of restricted patterns in 'one-unit-one-vote' inventories. More generally, frequency information permits an uncertainty-based definition of morphological variation in terms of the distribution of alternatives. Implicational structure then correlates with the reduction of this uncertainty.

The notions of uncertainty and uncertainty reduction measured by this kind of information-theoretic approach have direct reflexes in psycholinguistic models of language learning and processing. Language learning, like learning in other cognitive domains, receives a natural interpretation as a process of uncertainty reduction (Ramscar *et al.* 2013a; Ramscar and Port 2016).[5] Uncertainty reduction is so central to language learning that infants appear to track the RATES of uncertainty reduction associated with information sources:

Given how rapidly infants learn, even in complex environments, we can infer that they are able to access implicit knowledge about their rate of uncertainty reduction and use that knowledge to select to which source(s) of information to attend. (Gerken and Balcomb 2010: 82)

Surprisal-based models of syntactic processing (Hale 2001; Levy 2008) operate with a similar conception of uncertainty reduction, most transparently in models that embody the Entropy Reduction Hypothesis (Hale 2003, 2006).

In sum, language learning and language processing are both usefully construed in terms of uncertainty reduction. Speakers appear to be particularly attentive to features that reduce uncertainty about unencountered input. In processing syntagmatic structures, these are the features that permit speakers to predict unencountered input or accommodate to distributional patterns associated with an interlocutor or larger speech community, etc. In a paradigmatic context, implicational dependencies express information that a speaker can exploit in extrapolating from a partial (and biased) sample of a language.

In contrast, theoretical approaches can be construed as modelling an essentially pedagogical task. These approaches confront the same basic challenge as the lexicographer, who must enumerate the well-formed words (or other units) of a language and exclude the ill-formed units. It is of course true that producing and recognizing acceptable expressions of a language are tasks that a competent speaker is normally expected to be able to perform. Yet the ability to distinguish well-formed from ill-formed expressions is a poor idealization of a speaker's linguistic 'knowledge' and there is no evidence that the acquisition of this knowledge is ever a goal in itself. Instead, the task of discriminating the acceptable expressions of a language appears to be subsumed within the larger and more useful task of determining the distribution and use of the expressions that are in circulation in a language community.

The divergence between inventory- and distribution-based approaches can be seen to reflect more fundamental assumptions about the nature of language. For the most part, the theoretical models developed in the contemporary period have approached languages as systems of discrete categorical inventories. The sound system is idealized as a discrete set of phones, classified as phonemes or allophones, and a similar inventory-based conception is extended to larger morphological and syntactic domains (whether characterized in terms of units or rules). Although there are various ways in which models can be augmented to accomodate statistical patterns, the underlying language system remains categorical, as does the speaker's knowledge of the system.

---

[5] The notion of 'information gain' in machine learning expresses a broadly similar notion (Abu-Mostafa *et al.* 2012).

This conception often incorporates a distinction between the content of a speaker's knowledge (their linguistic 'competence' in the terms of Chomsky 1965) and their use of language (Chomsky's 'performance'). However, studies of phenonomena such as frequency effects have shown that a speaker's command of a language involves detailed knowledge about the frequency of expressions, relative frequencies of component parts and larger collections, patterns of collocation, and other types of contextual information.[6] All of these types of ostensibly 'performance-related' knowledge have a much more clearly established psychological relevance than the factors proposed in connection with economy conditions or scientific compactness. The role that distributional information appears to play in learning and its value for predicting behavioural responses support a conception of the speaker's knowledge in terms of a probabilistic LANGUAGE MODEL rather than a simple inventory.

8.2.3 The discriminative perspective

This general orientation places a learning-based model within a larger tradition that includes overlapping 'emergentist' (Bybee 1985, 2010), 'usage-based' (Tomasello 2003; Diessel 2015) and 'construction-based' (Goldberg 2005; Booij 2010) branches, along with other broadly 'cognitivist' frameworks. In the context of this tradition, a learning-based morphological approach could be described as 'a usage-based approach with a discriminative learning model'.

Sections 8.3 and 8.4 suggest that the classic WP model (as well as the model presented in Bloomfield 1933) are best interpreted in discriminative terms. Thus, for example, the idea that form variation serves to discriminate larger forms, rather than to express individually meaningful contrasts, seems implicit in Matthews's description of the classical WP model:

But there is an alternative method, whose sources lie in the work of the ancient grammarians of Greek and Latin. This is simply to relate words as wholes. (Matthews 1991: 186)

Yet the implications of this perspective remain implicit through the whole WP tradition, as reflected in Robins's various criticisms of the failure of classical models to develop "a theory of the morpheme" (Robins 1997: 31):

It was certainly a weakness in the classical grammarians, and in many later writers who followed their example, that they barely recognized any grammatical unit below the level of the word, and certainly never set out with any rigour the establishment of the morphemes of a language. (Robins 1959: 119)

The point of departure for a discriminative perspective on language is the learning rule of Rescorla and Wagner (1972) and Rescorla (1988). This rule provides the basis for the discriminative models developed over the past decade in a series of papers by Ramscar and associates (Ramscar and Yarlett 2007; Ramscar and Dye

---

[6] See, e.g., the essays in Bybee (2007) and the discussion in Baayen (2010).

2010; Ramscar *et al.* 2010, 2013*a*; Ramscar 2013). The claim that form variation serves a discriminative function is first explicitly stated in Ramscar and Yarlett (2007: 931) and elaborated by Ramscar and Dye (2010) below:

While the approach of Haskell et al. (2003) is broadly comparable to our own, we would suggest that a main function of phonology is to discriminate between semantic alternatives (Ramscar & Dye, 2009; Ramscar & Yarlett, 2007; Ramscar et al., 2010). For this reason, we expect that phonological forms that are more discriminable in any given context will be more useful (i.e., informative) in this regard. Given that the presence or absence of a final sibilant is used to discriminate between the plural and singular forms of most nouns, and that there are conventions that apply to plurals in compounds, we would expect that when the phonological forms of singular nouns are easily distinguished from forms with final sibilants, this will be more informative—both about plurality, and about the conventional status of a given compound—than when they aren't (i.e., *rats* may be a more informative plural form than both *mice* and *houses*). (Ramscar and Dye 2010: 28)

There are also antecedents for a broadly discriminative conception of meaning and communication.[7] However, Ramscar *et al.* (2010) provide the first statement of this perspective in an explicitly discriminative model:

If symbolic communication involves predicting symbols from meanings (and context)—and we have outlined many reasons for assuming that it does—then meaning is something that a speaker elicits in a listener simply by engaging the listener in a game of prediction. In this game, symbols are not used to CONVEY meaning, but rather are used to reduce a listener's uncertainty about a speaker intended message (Shannon, 1948). In order for a listener to predict a speaker, the listener has to activate the same semantic cues to symbolic form as the speaker, such that the listener comes to understand an utterance by THINKING about that utterance in a way that converges on that of the speaker. This proposal has much in common with the idea that language is a form of joint action (see e.g., Altmann & Mirković, 2009; Clark, 1993; Garrod & Pickering, 2009; Gennari & MacDonald, 2009; Pickering & Garrod, 2007; Tanenhaus & Brown-Schmidt, 2008); it differs in that it is explicitly nonreferential. (Ramscar *et al.* 2010: 35)

The conception of communication as a process of cooperative 'uncertainty reduction' also clarifies the relation between a discriminate perspective and the information-theoretic measures discussed in Section 8.2.2. Discriminative learning involves the reduction of uncertainty in the information-theoretic sense. Hence the types of entropy measures discussed in Chapter 7 can be seen as providing a global estimation of the uncertainty encountered by a discriminative learning network. The linkage between entropy measures and discriminative learning emerges

---

[7] "Understanding language in terms of learning—and without underspecified appeals to reference—involves a reassessment of what human communication involves, requiring revised theories of language and its role in culture (Quine, 1960; Tomasello, 1999, 2003; Wittgenstein, 1953; see also Fodor, 2000)." (Ramscar *et al.* 2010: 34)

perhaps most clearly in models that use the Rescorla-Wagner learning equations for comprehension and production.[8]

8.3 Refurbishing the structuralist foundations

Although a learning-based perspective is neutral about unit size, it applies most fruitfully to the units that are well discriminated within a system of contrasts.[9] As discussed in earlier chapters, word-sized units appear to provide an optimal combination of discriminability and predictiveness. Both the determinacy of individual analyses and the implicational structure that they define are disrupted by the disassembly of word-sized forms into smaller units. As in WP models in general, the distinguished status of words within a learning-based approach reflects the striking contrast between how well languages facilitate the deduction of whole systems from subsets of forms and how poorly they facilitate the disassembly and reassembly of individual forms.

To a significant extent, this point is acknowledged by nearly all contemporary approaches. What Hockett (1987) termed 'The Decade of the Morpheme' closed with the acknowledgement in Hockett (1954) that the 'problems of morphemic analysis' articulated in descriptivist studies were not ultimately susceptible to solution in terms that preserved the initial morphemic conception. Morphological models developed within the generative school retained a commitment to 'morphemes' (apart from the brief paradigmatic sketch of Chomsky 1965: §4.2.2) but without solving the problems identified by descriptivist accounts. Instead, these problems became moot as a consequence of essentially terminological shifts, as morphemic models came to operate with notions that had at most a historical connection to the morphemes defined in the models of Harris (1942) and Hockett (1947). The break from any morpheme-as-sign conception is complete when models of Distributed Morphology propose that "a morpheme is an abstract syntactic unit" (Marantz 2013: 905).[10]

From a learning-based perspective, morphemic models are not just technically deficient, but more fundamentally misconceived. The ultimate motivation for the entire morphemic tradition can be seen to rest on the two pillars of Post-Bloomfieldian approaches to the analysis of language in general. These are the assumption that (i) recurrence entails redundancy and (ii) that structure implies decomposed (morphemic) representations. The goal of morphological analysis in

---

[8] For example, in current implementations of Implicit Morphology (Baayen et al. 2011, 2016), the forms abstracted from the speech stream are encoded by networks of n-phone (and n-graph) units, associated to a system of units encoding lexically and grammatically contrastive properties, with connection weights between units estimated from corpora using the Rescorla-Wagner learning equations.

[9] As suggested in Section 8.6 below, it is ultimately contrasts rather than units that are significant in a morphological system from a learning-based perspective (i.e., phonemic contrasts do not imply unitary phonemes). As the contrasts discriminated in a system change as a function of learning, the derivative 'units' are expected to vary too.

[10] See Anderson (2015) and Blevins (2016) for further discussion of the various senses of 'morpheme' proposed or assumed in different traditions.

this tradition involves a distillation of variation into general symbolic statements, schemas or rules that describe the distribution and interpretation of isolable units of form. Descriptions that exhibit recurrent patterns are regarded as deficient on the grounds that they 'miss linguistically significant generalizations' or "fall short of scientific compactness", to again repeat the terms that Bloomfield (1933: 238) uses in the quotation on p. 70 above. A similar intuition underlies the use of inheritance hierarchies and other strategies for providing compact representations of lexical and grammatical patterns.

The first of these assumptions operates with notions of 'identity' and 'redundancy' that are defined primarily in terms of orthographic or phonemic transcriptions. Transcriptions may have been regarded as providing sufficient precision in Bloomfield's time, but their limitations are by now familiar. For a contemporary description that aims to model the variation relevant to human speakers, it is not sufficient that an orthographic or phonemic system fails to distinguish separate occurrences of an element; the item must also be produced and interpreted alike by speakers. The usefulness of phonemic transcriptions for capturing the notion of 'identity' relevant for speakers has been challenged by a range of studies that probe sub-phonemic contrasts. Careful acoustic and psychoacoustic investigation of units ranging in size from words to single-segment affixes have shown that speakers consistently produce and comprehend durational differences and other types of phonetic variation that do not determine phonemic contrasts. At the word level, Gahl (2008) found systematic differences in duration between ostensibly homophonous items such as English *time* and *thyme*. Drager (2011) reported similar variation for English *like* in its different functions. At the segment level, Plag *et al.* (2016) likewise found "significant differences in acoustic duration between some morphemic /s/'s and /z/'s and non-morphemic /s/ and /z/, respectively".

Morphological units exhibit similar contrasts. In the domain of word formation, Davis *et al.* (2002) found differences in duration and fundamental frequency between a word like *captain* and a morphologically unrelated onset word such as *cap*. Of more direct relevance to the issue of "scientific compactness" are studies of inflectional formations. The exploratory study of Baayen *et al.* (2003) found that a sample of speakers produced Dutch nouns with a longer mean duration when they occurred as singulars than when they occurred as the stem of the corresponding plural. In a follow-up study, Kemps *et al.* (2005) tested speakers' sensitivity to prosodic differences, and concluded that "acoustic differences exist between uninflected and inflected forms and that listeners are sensitive to them" (Kemps *et al.* 2005: 441). That is, from the perspective of a Dutch speaker, singular forms like *rat* 'rat' and *geit* 'goat' do NOT recur in the corresponding plurals *ratten* 'rats' and *geiten* 'goats' but instead have a distinctive prosodic profile that speakers are sensitive to. As Kemps *et al.* (2005: 441) note in their conclusion, this effect calls into question a fundamental assumption of combinatoric approaches, namely that complex units are constructed via the assembly of simple units drawn from a fixed 'alphabet':

The prosodic mismatch effect documented in this study has important consequences for our understanding of the morphological structure of complex words. The way words are written in languages such as Dutch and English suggests that they consist of stems and affixes that are strung together as beads on a string. Phonemic transcriptions convey the same impression. Our experiments show that this impression is wrong. Plurals are not just singulars with an additional suffix. The precise acoustic realization of the stem provides crucial information to the listener about the morphological context in which the stem appears.

These sub-phonemic effects demonstrate that it is not sufficient for a morphemic model to solve recalcitrant segmentation and association problems; even success in segmentation and association is no guarantee of a correct analysis. A form like *geiten* can be segmented into a stem *geit* and suffix *-en*, and the stem can be assigned lexical properties while the suffix assigned grammatical properties. However, as Kemps *et al.* (2005) show, it is an error of analysis to identify the plural stem *geit* with the singular form *geit* or to associate plurality solely with the suffix *-en*. The morphotactic split between *geit* and *-en* does not correlate with a division in grammatical meaning between 'caprine' and 'plurality'. Instead, the plural stem is tuned to its morphological environment. From a discriminative learning perspective, this suggests that the function of the affix is not characterizable just in terms of the grammatical meaning that it conveys but also involves the 'stem-tuning' context it provides for learners.

Taken together, the kinds of sub-phonemic effects described above suggest that the analytic assumptions of a morphemic model are motivated by an appeal to a conception of economy founded on imprecise orthographic and phonemic notions of 'identity'. If seemingly recurrent units are not genuinely identical, then there is no redundancy in a description that contains their distributional variants, and consequently no economy is achieved by a description that collapses variants into a single item. In this case, morphemic analyses are merely 'lossy' descriptions that achieve no gain in "scientific compactness".

Parallel remarks apply to 'redundancy-free' models of the lexicon, irrespective of whether the redundancy is eliminated by disassembling forms into separate inventories of minimal bases and exponents or by introducing recurrent forms within an inheritance hierarchy. No economy is achieved by ensuring that "an identical feature . . . is noted only once" (Bloomfield 1933: 238) if the identity is an artifact of an imprecise encoding of contrasts.

8.3.1 Discriminative and categorical variation

A discriminative perspective also clarifies why recurrence at a phonemic level provides an imprecise measure of identity and therefore redundancy. This is not ultimately a deficiency of phonemic analysis but a design feature of such analyses. The hierarchies of linguistic levels inherited from descriptivist approaches are often interpreted as encapsulating all of the variation at each level that is relevant for analyses at the next level up. On this view, the phonetic properties relevant to phonemic analysis are encapsulated in phones, the phonemic properties relevant to morphemic analysis in phonemes, etc.[11]

---

[11] As expressed in the quotation from Bloomer *et al.* (2004: 180) in footnote 5: "each sentence consists of clauses, each clause consists of phrases, each phrase consists of words, each word consists of morphemes and each morpheme consists of phonemes".

However, this conception misconstrues the organization of linguistic levels, which in fact categorize patterns of continuous variation in terms of discrete units. This categorization does not aim to approximate the aggregate properties that distinguish units, but instead to isolate a single dimension of categorical contrast. This objective is explicit in standard definitions of phonemes. A pair of phones ϕ_1 and ϕ_2 are assigned to different phonemes if they are themselves discriminable, and if they suffice to distinguish forms (usually words) with a discriminable difference in meaning. The phonemes of a language isolate contrasts with a high individual functional load, since each phonemic contrast discriminates at least some minimal pair. But there is no principled reason to expect that the contrasts with a high INDIVIDUAL functional load will have a high COLLECTIVE functional load within a system. No contrast at the level of sound patterns, however salient or discriminable it may be, will be phonemic if it is invariably triggered or reinforced by some other contrast. In either case, the co-occurrence of the other contrast will ensure that there are no minimal pairs that are solely distinguished by the original contrast.

In sum, phonemic analyses locate discrete units within a system of categorical contrasts. The notion of 'phonemic identity' does not characterize the general notion of 'perceptual identity' relevant to speakers because it isolates one dimension of discriminable variation within a multi-dimensional space.

Many of the contrasts investigated in studies of sub-phonemic differences are concomitants of some independent source of variation. If these sources are completely outside the phonological or morphological system, the sub-phonemic variation can in principle be treated as externally-conditioned 'micro-variation' exhibited by a single categorical unit. The case for abstracting away from sub-phonemic variation is strongest if the variation is governed by factors such as frequency, syntactic position, lexical neighbourhood density, etc. For example, the observation that forms may have different duration and prosodic properties at the beginning or ends of phrases or clauses does not impinge directly on the phonological or morphological analysis of the forms.

Conversely, the impact of sub-phonemic contrasts is strongest if the contexts that influence variation are paradigmatic or grammatical. In the case of the Dutch stems discussed by Baayen *et al.* (2003) and Kemps *et al.* (2005), the prosodic contrast between *geit* when it occurs as the singular and when it occurs as the stem of the plural *geiten* appears to be conditioned by general prosodic differences between monosyllabic and disyllabic forms. However, the comprehension studies in Kemps *et al.* (2005) clearly indicate that Dutch speakers learn to recognize these differences as marking number contrasts.

Since it is the retention of the conditioning context that makes the prosodic difference sub-phonemic, the loss of this context can create a phonemic opposition within a language. This appears to be the origin of the grade alternations in the Estonian declensions and conjugations in Chapter 4, and the source of similar alternations in other Finnic and Uralic languages. From a discriminative perspective, it is significant that analyses of the evolution of these grade alternations treat the discriminability of stem variation as a prerequisite for the grammaticalization of a sub-phonemic contrast. The account of the origin of Finnic grade in Viitso (2003) is particularly clear on this point:

there are no other known phonetic preconditions for the rise of quantity correlation of long syllables than the phonetic alternation of first syllables depending on the openness vs. closedness of the following unstressed syllable in Finnish . . . In order to develop into a morphophonological gradation, this automatic alternation needed only to be perceived. Only a perceived alternation could be accepted as a linguistic norm and subjected to further polarization and reinterpretation of sound patterns caused by openness vs. closedness of the second syllable of a foot as a function of syllabic accentuation in initial syllables . . . This polarization as a norm caused the quantity alternation of stems in their morphological paradigms so that the stressed syllable was longer before an open syllable and shorter before a closed syllable. This quantity alternation was retained, in principle, also after the former conditioning environments changed. (Viitso 2003: 164f.)

Viitso (2003: 163) illustrates these developments by contrasting "the nominative and genitive forms of the stem for 'bushel', cf. *vakka* : *vakan*" in which "the geminate stop was shortened before a closed second syllable". As in Modern Dutch, prosodic differences conditioned by syllable structure in the Finnic languages must have been discriminable, functional load-bearing contrasts at the point where the conditioning environments were still present (as they are, for the most part in Modern Finnish). Hence an analysis of *vakan* that associated genitive case features solely with the ending -*n* would be as misleading as an analysis of *geiten* that associated plurality exclusively with -*en*.

8.3.2 The logic of discrimination

At a basic level, these types of patterns reinforce Matthew's conclusion that the correspondence between minimal 'sames' of 'form' and 'meaning' envisaged by morphemic models does not appear to exist. At a deeper level, they point to more fundamental problems with associative assumptions that underlie these models. Adopting a discriminative perspective throws the issues into sharp relief. That is, a discriminative analysis requires that the contrasts within a system suffice to distinguish the elements of the system. There is no requirement that particular contrasts in form will be associated with specific features. Nor is there any need for contrasts to partition elements into natural classes.

In the Dutch examples, there is no need to associate the prosodic properties that distinguish stems with determinate number features. It suffices for speakers to know that nouns have two inflected forms, that monosyllabic and disyllabic forms have different prosodic contours and that the weak plural marker -*en* conditions variation in syllable structure in monosyllabic nouns. In Estonian declensions, there is no stable association between stem grade and features. This is illustrated by the grammatical case forms of VAKA 'bushel' in Table 8.1, in which there is no consistent association between features and grade. Neither singular nor plural forms are consistently strong or consistently weak. Nominative and genitive cases are similarly based on different stems in the singular and plural. Partitive case is in fact the only feature that is consistently associated with stem grade. The strong and weak stem grade classes are associated with correspondingly heterogeneous features.

TABLE 8.1 Grammatical
case forms of VAKK 'bushel'

	Sg	Plu
Nom	vakk	vakad
Gen	vaka	vakkade
Part	vakka	vakkasid

The problems that these patterns of 'gestalt exponence' pose for a decompositional analysis are discussed in Chapter 4. What is most important from the present perspective is the parallel between the 'sub-morphemic' variation in Table 8.1 and the sub-phonemic contrasts discussed directly above. The six grammatical case forms of VAKK are effectively discriminated by variation in the form of stems and endings. The fact that these components cannot be associated with stable 'units of meaning' does not impair their discriminative value. The sub-morphemic character of this variation merely precludes an analysis on which their discriminative function is subsumed within a direct contrast-meaning association. The fact that contrasts within a system may effectively discriminate the elements of the system without a stable association between individual contrasts and meanings calls into question the value and status of this association.

8.3.3 Contextual discrimination

Elements that serve principally to discriminate larger forms need not have a single function or meaning in all of the contexts in which they occur, but may perform different discriminative functions in different contexts. The basic distinction between a discriminative and associative interpretation of form variants can be illustrated with reference to the Georgian agreement markers in Table 8.2, repeated from Table 6.5. This paradigm consists of fully discriminated sets of forms with 1p and 3p objects, and a set of partially ambiguous forms with 2p objects. Let us consider each set in turn.

In forms with 1p objects, the contrast between the prefixes *m*- and *gv*- consistently distinguishes singular from plural objects, freeing suffixal variation to mark person and number properties of subjects. The suffix -*t* unambiguously marks the plurality of 2p subjects in the contrasts *damxat'av~damxat'avt* and *dagvxat'av~dagvxat'avt*. The contrast between -*s* and -*en* likewise distinguishes 3sg from 3pl subjects in the pairs *damxat'avs~damxat'aven* and *dagvxat'avs~dagvxat'aven*. In forms with 3p objects, the lack of any formal marking of these objects leaves both agreement positions available, in principle, to mark subject properties. Thus -*t* unambiguously marks the plurality of a 1p subject in the contrast *davxat'av~davxat'avt* and the plurality of a 2p subject in the contrast *daxat'av~daxat'avt*. The alternation between -*s* and -*en* again distinguishes 3sg from 3pl subjects in the pair *daxat'avs~daxat'aven*.

Forms with 2p objects are less well discriminated, due to the fact that they all reserve the prefixal agreement position for the number-neutral object marker *g*-. This leaves only the suffixal position to mark the person features of subjects and the

TABLE 8.2   Future indicative paradigm of ХАТ'VA 'paint' (Tschenkéli 1958: §31)

Subj	1sg	1pl	Obj 2sg	2pl	3
1sg	—	—	dagxat'av	dagxat'avt	davxat'av
1pl	—	—	dagxat'avt	dagxat'avt	davxat'avt
2sg	damxat'av	dagvxat'av	—	—	daxat'av
2pl	damxat'avt	dagvxat'avt	—	—	daxat'avt
3sg	damxat'avs	dagvxat'avs	dagxat'avs	dagxat'avt	daxat'avs
3pl	damxat'aven	dagvxat'aven	dagxat'aven	dagxat'aven	daxat'aven

number features of both subjects and objects. With respect to person, it follows that only subject features that are associated with suffixal markers can be expressed and, hence, that the 1p subject marker -*v* cannot occur in forms with 2p objects. In the domain of number, the result is widespread syncretism. In some cases, the number of subjects is unmarked, in others, the number of objects is unmarked, and in yet others subject and object number is marked ambiguously. Thus in *dagxat'av* the lack of plural marking unambiguously identifies 2sg object and 1sg subject features. As in forms with 1p and 3p objects, the contrast between -*s* and -*en* in the pair *dagxat'avs*~*dagxat'aven* marks an opposition between 3sg and 3pl subjects.

Since all of the remaining forms with 2p objects contain at least one plural argument, the result is widespread ambiguity. The fact that -*en* marks all forms with 3pl subjects leaves no means of marking the contrast between 2sg and 2pl objects, so that both are associated with the form *dagxat'aven*. A parallel conflict is resolved in favour of the marking of object plurality in forms with 3sg subjects. Although both *dagxat'avs* and *dagxat'avt* are associated with 3sg subjects, the use of -*t* to mark the plurality of the 2p object in *dagxat'avt* entails that 3sg subject features remain unmarked in this form. As noted above, the marking of 2p objects by *g*- prevents the use of the prefixal position to mark 1p subject features by *v*-. Hence, in addition to expressing 3sg subject features, the form *dagxat'avt* can be associated with 1pl subject, a 2pl object or both.

In sum, Georgian verbs mark the person and number features of two verbal dependents by means of a pair of agreement slots and sets of four prefixal and three suffixal markers. The fact that both slots may contain either subject or object markers and that some of these markers neutralize number or person features gives rise to two ambiguous forms, *dagxat'avt* and *dagxat'aven*. Variation in agreement markers suffices to distinguish the remaining (nonreflexive) forms of a transitive verb. The relations between agreement features and markers are summarized in Table 8.3. Associations that characterize a majority of cells within a column (with common object features) or a row (with shared subject features) are set in italics. Exceptionless patterns are set in bold.

8.3.4 Learning without overgeneralization

The correspondence between features and markers is relatively transparent in Table 8.3. Yet, as discussed in Chapter 6.3.2, the contrasts that discriminate the

TABLE 8.3 Agreement properties and markers

SUBJ	OBJ					
	1sg	1pl	2sg	2pl	3p	
1sg			g—	g—t	v—	g-
1pl			g—t	g—t	v—t	g-/-t
2sg	m—	gv—			—	—
2pl	m—t	gv—t			—t	-t
3sg	m—s	gv—s	g—s	g—t	—s	-s
3pl	m—en	gv—en	g—en	g—en	—en	-en
	m-	gv-	g-	g-/-t	—	

forms of a transitive verb cannot be disassembled straightforwardly into a set of context-independent form-meaning relations, whether expressed as morphemes or as realization rules. Recall that the sub-paradigm of forms with 1p object features are effectively discriminated, with the prefixal opposition between *m-* and *gv-* distinguishing 1sg from 1pl objects, and the suffixal opposition between Ø, *-t*, *-s* and *-en* distinguishing subjects with 2sg, 2pl, 3sg and 3pl features. In particular, the contrast between 2sg and 2pl object features are unambiguously marked in the pair *damxat'av~dagvxat'av* by the opposition between *m-* and *gv-*. There is no motivation within this sub-paradigm for marking the second of these forms by *-t*, and hence no need for a constraint to 'block' this generalization. On the contrary, marking *dagvxat'av* redundantly by *-t* would have the clearly harmful effect of eliminating the contrast with *dagvxat'avt*, which is associated with 2pl subject features.

It is precisely with the goal of preventing the addition of a redundant *-t* that Anderson (1992: 132) proposes extending a disjunctive ordering condition to apply across rule blocks. As discussed in Chapter 6.3.2, this extension allows 1pl *gv-* to preempt a 'general plural' marker *-t*. The need for such an extension derives from the treatment of *-t* as a single marker introduced by a single realization rule R_t that spells out the intersection of the features associated with *-t* in all of the environments in which it occurs. This is of course an extreme analysis but the problem it raises, capturing context-dependent contrasts by context-independent rules, is endemic to a realizational approach.

Consider next the marking of 1p subject properties in Table 8.3. In forms with (formally unmarked) 3p objects, 1p subjects are marked by the prefix *v-*. In a realizational account, this pattern is expressed by a realization rule R_v that spells out 1p subject features (however represented) by the marker *v-*. Just as the general plural rule R_t introduces *-t* whenever a feature bundle contains a plural feature, R_v introduces *v-* whenever a bundle contains 1p subject features. This rule will have the desired effect in transitive forms with 3p objects, as well as in 'absolute' intransitive paradigms with a single subject argument (Harris 1981: 137f.). However, in transitive forms with 2p objects, R_v does not apply, since the prefixal slot is occupied by the 2p object marker *g-*. As discussed in Chapter 6.3.2, realizational approaches explore a variety of strategies to regulate the 'competition' between the rules introducing *v-* and *g-*.

From a learning-based perspective, invoking a notion of 'rule competition' appears to misconstrue the problem. There is no case in Tables 8.2 and 8.3 in which -t marks object plurality IN THE CONTEXT OF 1P OBJECT FEATURES, and no case in which v- marks 1p subject features IN THE CONTEXT OF 2P OBJECT FEATURES. The rules R_t and R_v 'overapply' in these contexts because they are overly general. Instead of characterizing the sets of cells in which -t and v- actually occur, the rules express context-independent associations between agreement markers and natural classes of cells (i.e., the class with plural features or with 1p subject features). Hence the statement of the rules overgeneralizes the distribution of the markers that they are meant to describe.

The goal of 'resolving' conflicts involving overgeneralized rules seems even more fundamentally misconceived. Most formal accounts of Georgian verb morphology attempt to provide some kind of principled account for the fact that the 2p object marker g- prevails over the 1p subject marker v- in forms with 2p object and 1p subject features. There may, again, be an illuminating historical explanation for this pattern but for a speaker of Modern Georgian, there is no indeterminacy in the resulting synchronic system. All forms with 2p object features are marked by g-, irrespective of the features of the subject. There is no 'competition' for a learner to resolve because v- never occurs with 2p objects. The same is true of the other cases of 'slot competition'. All forms with 3pl subjects are marked by -en, even when this prevents the expression of a contrast between 2sg and 2pl objects. In present paradigms, forms with 3sg subjects and 2pl objects are marked by -t, leaving the 3sg features unmarked.[12]

8.3.5 Pedagogical overextraction

From a learning-based perspective, manoeuvres designed to resolve competition are a symptom of analytic 'overextraction'. Individual contrasts are isolated from the larger system of contrasts in which they function and the 'grammar' serves an essentially remedial role in correcting the original overgeneralization.

Rules that isolate form alternations from the system of contrasts in which they function appear to be a relic of an essentially pedagogical perspective. Such rules are useful for drawing grammatical generalizations to the attention of the language learner in an explicit learning context. But they have no established relevance to psychologically plausible models of language processing or acquisition. Many of the other idealizations of formal grammars discussed above can also be traced to the pedagogical origins of contemporary grammatical traditions. The notion of "scientific compactness" invoked by Bloomfield refers to the length of an orthographic or phonemic description of a pattern or system. A compact description that draws recurrent patterns to the attention to the reader may be of pedagogical value, though this economy has never been shown to have any psychological relevance. The same is true of 'redundancy-free' models of the lexicon, which adopt

---

[12] Though syncretism is unavoidable, since a form with -s instead of -t would neutralize the contrast between 2sg and 2pl objects, as in the forms with 3pl subjects.

an organizational property that is useful for dictionaries, but of no proven relevance to human lexical knowledge.

In sum, a fully regular grammatical description and a redundancy-free lexicon both contribute to the concision of a pedagogical grammar. Yet the economy achieved by a maximally concise grammatical description does not translate into advantages for the speaker or hearer. The problem with a fully irregular language is not that it violates a theoretical economy principle but that the lack of patterns inhibits the generalizations required to learn the language. A perfectly regular language would facilitate generalization but also incur costs in acquisition and processing due to cue competition between similar forms (Ramscar *et al.* 2010; Arnon and Ramscar 2012). For the speaker or learner, there is no 'perfect' (or even perfectly economical) language design, just different trade-offs between communicative strategies. Various structural or social factors (perhaps including some of the factors suggested by Trudgill 2011) may influence the way that different languages resolve these conflicts.

8.4 Discriminative tagmemics

A discriminative learning perspective also suggests a reconceptualization of Bloomfield's model that resolves at least some of the "contradictions" perceived by Harris (1942: 169) in ways that permit a rapprochement with a WP model. One of the reasons that Bloomfield's model "didn't make sense" to Descriptivists such as Hockett (1968: 20) was that it incorporated dimensions of analysis that were difficult to isolate as 'units' within a decompositional approach. However, these dimensions receive a particularly natural interpretation in terms of discriminative contrasts. A general view of language in terms of systems of discriminative contrasts is also compatible with a distributional operationalization of 'meaning' that can address the familiar objection that Bloomfield and his successors 'excluded meaning' from the study of language.

8.4.1 Contrastive arrangements

One of the most obscure aspects of the model set out in Bloomfield (1933) is the notion of grammatical "arrangements" of linguistic forms. This notion is explicated in the passage cited on p. 21, repeated in its entirety below:

The meaningful arrangements of forms in a language constitute its grammar. In general, there seem to be four ways of arranging linguistic forms. (1) ORDER is the succession in which the constituents of a complex form are spoken . . . (2) MODULATION is the use of phonemes which do not appear in any morpheme, but only in grammatical arrangements of morphemes . . . (3) PHONETIC MODIFICATION is a change in the primary phonemes of a form . . . (4) SELECTION of forms contributes a factor of meaning because different forms in what is otherwise the same grammatical arrangement, will result in different meanings. (Bloomfield 1933: 163f.)

The challenge that arrangements presented to Bloomfield's successors was that they represented ABSTRACTIONS over forms rather than PARTS of forms. Extracting individual dimensions of variation from the networks of oppositions in which they operate appeared to create "contradictions" or "make no sense". However, from a discriminative perspective, it is the attempt to isolate these dimensions of variation and associate them with context-independent properties that is senseless, because it disrupts the system in which they function. As Bloomfield states in the passage cited on p. 22 above (and below), "features of grammatical arrangemement" or "taxemes" are individually sub-meaningful contrasts that collectively characterize the meaningful units in a system:

A simple feature of grammatical arrangement is a GRAMMATICAL FEATURE or TAXEME. A taxeme is in grammar what a phoneme is in the lexicon—namely, the smallest unit of form. Like a phoneme, a taxeme, taken by itself, in the abstract, is meaningless. Just as combinations of phonemes or, less commonly, single phonemes, occur as actual lexical signals (phonetic forms), so combinations of taxemes, or, quite frequently, single taxemes, occur as conventional grammatical arrangements, TACTIC FORMS. (Bloomfield 1933:166)

Bloomfield's successors were comfortable with the idea of sub-meaningful units of lexical form, i.e., phonemes. Yet the notion of a sub-meaningful unit of grammatical form seemed enigmatic. The central problem derives from the fact that their strategy of atomizing systems into 'units' of form and meaning was ASSOCIATIVE. Minimal units at each level were associated with discrete units at the other level. However, there was no recurrent 'unit of meaning' that could be associated with individually sub-meaningful contrasts and, hence, no way to describe the way that they collectively characterize meaningful units.

A discriminative perspective resolves this problem by cancelling the assumption that individual contrasts are individually meaningful. Instead, as Bloomfield proposes, taxemes represent the minimal discriminable contrasts that define variation within a system of forms. Combinations of taxemes DISCRIMINATE forms that can be assigned functions and meanings. But the individual dimensions of variation are sub-meaningful because contrasts between meaningful forms are not mediated by associations with 'units of meaning'.

In sum, the form classes defined by individual taxemes characterize one dimension of variation in a grammatical system. Reconceptualizing these units in discriminative terms suggests an interpretation of the Bloomfieldian treatment of form variation that is broadly compatible with a WP approach.

8.4.2 Distribution and meaning

Yet given that the treatment of meaning is often regarded as the primary deficiency of the Bloomfieldian (and Descriptivist) model, any rehabilitation of this model must also address semantic concerns. A discriminative perspective again suggests a reinterpretation of earlier proposals. The distributional approach to meaning explored by Harris (1954) is particularly amenable to a discriminative construal on which same-different semantic contrasts are grounded in distributional variation rather than speaker judgments. The meaningful expressions in a language can likewise be discriminated by contextual vectors, which can be automatically obtained from corpora by distributional semantic models such as Marelli and Baroni (2015).

Significantly, these models address the concerns originally expressed by Bloomfield, along with the criticisms provoked by his cautious approach to the study of meaning. These criticisms incorporate two main claims and a number of auxiliary assumptions. The first claim is that Bloomfieldian analyses provided purely formal descriptions that took no account of meaning. The second was that the behaviourist orientation of the Bloomfieldians led them to dismiss 'mentalist' conceptions of meaning out of hand. The linkage between these points is clearly articulated in the familiar remarks by Firth:

Certain leading linguists especially in America find it possible to exclude the study of what they call 'meaning' from scientific linguistics, but only by deliberately excluding anything in the nature of mind, thought, idea, concept. 'Mentalism' is taboo. (Firth 1951: 82)

Implicit in this criticism is the assumption that the study of 'meaning' is inextricably bound up with 'concepts' and other 'mentalistic' notions. Accompanying this assumption is the idea that there is a fundamental opposition between distributional analysis and semantic analysis, and that even the identification of units is expected to make some appeal to meaning. These assumptions are explicit in Carroll's survey of Descriptivist contemporaries:

A general characteristic of the methodology of descriptive linguistics, as practiced by many American linguists today, is the effort to analyse linguistic structure without reference to meaning. It is thought possible in theory that one could identify the phonemes and morphemes of a language purely on the basis of their distribution, that is, by noting the linguistic environment in which they occur. (Carroll 1953: 31f.)

There is no shortage of passages from Descriptivist works, which, particularly when lifted out of context, can be construed as endorsing an extreme distributionalist position and/or as adopting a doctrinaire view of the role of meaning. In formulating a 'set of postulates', Bloch (1948) entertains the possibility of establishing phonemic analysis on a purely distributional basis:

Theoretically it would be possible to arrive at the phonemic system of a dialect entirely on the basis of phonetics and distribution, without any appeal to meaning—provided that in the utterance of the dialect not all possible combinations of phonemes actually occurred. (Bloch 1948: 5, fn.8)

A more strident view of the primacy of distributional criteria is expressed in the approach to grammatical analysis outlined in Harris (1951):

The main research of descriptive linguistics, and the only relation which will be accepted as relevant in the present survey, is the distribution or arrangement within the flow of speech of some parts or features relative to others. (Harris 1951: 5)

Yet even the positions expressed in these passages are less radical than they may appear in isolation. In the continuation of the footnote quoted above, Bloch (1948) places his distributional approach in the context of the "non-semantic" tradition of phonemic analysis he associates with Daniel Jones:

An important point to notice is that the phoneme is essentially a phonetic conception. The fact that certain sounds are used in a language for distinguishing the meanings of words doesn't enter into the definition of a phoneme. It would indeed be possible to group the sounds of a language into phonemes without knowing the meaning of any words. (Jones 1929: 44)

The elaboration of Harris's model of grammatical analysis likewise makes it clear that his goal was not to repudiate meaning but to operationalize it, at least partially, in terms that were susceptible to analysis using established methods:

If we know that *life* and *rife* are not entirely repetitions of each other, we will then discover that they differ in distribution (and hence in 'meaning'). It may be presumed that any two morphemes A and B having different meanings also differ somewhere in their distribution: there are some environments in which one occurs and the other does not. (Harris 1951: 7, fn.4)

Like the decompositional models of morphemic analysis discussed in Chapter 2.2 and Section 8.4.1, genuinely 'meaning-free' models of grammatical analysis cannot be traced back to Bloomfield's own work but stem from the elaborations of his successors. This development is noted in the quotation on p. 24 above, where Matthews (1991: 148) observes that "the origin of . . . Bloomfieldian constituency analysis . . . was what remained of Bloomfield's model when, first, grammatical arrangement is reduced to selection and order and, secondly, all reference to meaning is taken out". The central role assigned to meaning in the Bloomfieldian model is stated explicitly in the immediate continuation of the passage on p. 216 above, which goes on to state that "A phonetic form with its meaning is a linguistic form; a tactic form with its meaning is a GRAMMATICAL FORM" (p. 166; emphasis in original).

The types of meanings that Bloomfield proposes, 'sememes' and 'episememes', function essentially as placeholders in his system. This does not reflect a hostility towards the study of meaning or even agnosticism about its importance but instead an assessment that "[t]he statement of meanings is . . . the weak point in language-study and will remain so until human knowledge advances very far beyond its present state" (Bloomfield 1933: 140). The consideration of "mentalistic psychology" in Bloomfield (1933: §9.4) likewise does not treat 'mentalism' as 'taboo', but disputes the usefulness of accounts that "define the meaning of a linguistic form as the characteristic mental event that occurs in every speaker and hearer in connection with the utterance or hearing of the linguistic form" (Bloomfield 1933: 142).[13] Far from excluding meaning, the Bloomfieldian model makes essential reference to meaning, but is forced to acknowledge the limitations of techniques for analyzing meaning.

It is thus misleading to describe Bloomfield as hostile to meaning or to the study of meaning. His caution was grounded in reservations about approaches that sought to study meaning without providing techniques for OPERATIONALIZING meaning.[14] Since operationalization has not been a prominent focus of most subsequent approaches, it is not addressed by accounts that analyze meaning in terms of paraphrases, frames, model-theoretic interpretations, etc.

Instead it is in the context of the distributional model of Harris (1951, 1954) that a general attempt to address Bloomfield's concerns takes shape. What has come to be known as the 'Distributional Hypothesis' links meanings to patterns of occurrence by proposing that linguistic items with similar distributions will have similar meanings. The basic idea, in one form or another, is attributed to a range of sources, including Weaver (1955) and (ironically) Firth (1957), among others. But the hypothesis is particularly compatible with the general distributional methodology developed by Harris.

In effect, this perspective cancels the presupposition that any model can be 'purely distributional', or that distributional analysis is generally incompatible with meaning analysis, given that distributional contrasts will correlate with meaning contrasts. Current models of distributional (or vector) semantics have been most extensively developed in the domain of natural language processing. However, there have also been studies that explore the relevance of the Distributional Hypothesis to learning (McDonald and Ramscar 2001) and others that develop sophisticated models of morphological meaning (Lazaridou *et al.* 2013; Marelli and Baroni 2015). A distribution operationalization of meaning not only addresses Bloomfield's methodological qualms but provides an observable correlate of meaning that can be acquired by a discriminative learning model based on the primary linguistic data available to a speaker.

8.4.3 Form and distribution

Given the clear 'atomistic' tendencies in Bloomfield's own work, it is not entirely plausible to claim him as a precursor of contemporary WP approaches. Nevertheless, the analysis of form into sub-meaningful contrasts and the imposition of operational criteria on the analysis of meaning determine a strikingly convergent perspective. The morphological variation exhibited by a system can be described in terms of contrasts within and across the two observable dimensions of variation in a system, form and distribution classes.

---

[13] Bloomfield's scepticism about the value of Firth's "mind, thought, idea, concept" is echoed in the recent review of categorization by Ramscar and Port (2015).

[14] For more detailed discussions of Bloomfield's perspective on meaning, see Hall (1987), Matthews (1993) and Fought (1999).

Despite the importance imputed to semantics in the Post-Bloomfieldian tradition, grammatical analysis remains as independent of issues of semantic 'content' as it was during Bloomfield's time. The main semantic component of grammatical analysis is the 'same–different' discrimination invoked to distinguish phonemes from allophones. The specific 'meanings' assigned to a pair of words play no role in determining the phonemic structure of a language; all that matters is that speakers can determine whether they are the same or different. Any more fine-grained meanings required for the analysis of a grammatical system can again be expressed in terms of distributional vectors.

Grammatical features, properties and categories can likewise be interpreted as proxies for form classes, distribution classes or some combination of the two. In this way, morphological terminology that misleadingly implies an associated semantics can be reduced to robustly observable dimensions of form variation. The overloading of grammatical terms is often most pronounced in the classification of verb forms in terms of 'tense' features that imply a temporal interpretation, and 'mood' and 'aspectual' features that imply meanings connected to notions like factivity, perfectivity, etc. The nomenclature for nouns can be less semantically loaded, as reflected by descriptions of the German case system that eschew Latinate terms in favour of a simple enumeration of forms into *erster/zweiter/dritter/vierter Fall* 'first/second/third/fourth case'. But these categories are all essentially taxonomic; to the extent that the labels have any function at all it is as mnemonics for the meanings conventionally associated with a form or even with the most salient use of that form.[15] Particularly in realizational models, the labels may have no semantic effect but merely encode form contrasts that are 'spelled out' by realization rules, in the process subverting the basic feature-form 'separation' (cf. Beard 1995).[16]

8.5 Morphological typology

One of the most salient aspects of morphological systems is the degree to which they appear to vary across languages. This variation has been interpreted as presenting a fundamental challenge to any unified morphological model (Matthews 1972: 156) or even as evidence that morphology is somehow "unnatural" (Aronoff 1998: 413). However, a framework of analysis that focuses more on implicational relations and discriminative contrasts between units than on the units themselves suggests a basis for a general morphological model that can accommodate the range of attested variation across languages.

---

[15] See Ramscar and Port (2015) for discussion of the problems that arise on a view of categorization on which features are taken to associate items with categories.

[16] The mnemonic character of feature labels is largely a symptom of the fact that they, like most of the classificatory apparatus of modern linguistics, are simply inherited from earlier, mainly classical, traditions. One solution involves clarifying the correspondence between features and observable form and distribution classes, as proposed in Blevins *et al.* (2016a). Alternatively the implicit semantics can be specified, for example, by tracing definitional paths for labels that make their semantics explicit, as proposed in the domain of tense and aspect by Lieb (2005) and Viguier (2013).

8.5.1 Typological and theoretical overfit

The shift from a unit-based to a relation-based perspective helps to reduce the risk of fitting a morphological model too closely to specific patterns of form variation. This problem arises in a particularly acute form in the essentially procrustean procedures of morphemic analysis discussed in Chapter 2. The realizational WP tradition initiated by Matthews (1972) has compiled a catalogue of patterns that defy description in morphemic terms. As critiques of morphemic analysis, these studies are highly effective and leave no doubt that in at least some languages, the hypothesized "matching between minimal 'sames' of 'form' (morphs) and 'meaning' (morphemes) ... does not exist" (Matthews 1972: 124). However, this tradition has been somewhat less successful in formulating a cohesive alternative conception of morphological organization above the implementation level. Demonstrating that a morphemic correspondence cannot be established in all languages does not entail that the correspondence must be incidental in those where it does appear to hold, or that non-morphemic morphotactic units play no grammatical role. Realizational approaches have also tended to treat the identification of 'non-morphemic' patterns as an end in itself and have been more inclined to classify these patterns as 'residue' or 'noise' than to try to determine their function.

There are multiple reasons for the lack of a unifying set of organizational principles within realizational approaches. In the empirical domain, the disunity derives in part from the fact that these accounts often focus on patterns that are recalcitrant for morphemic models and recalcitrant patterns tend not to comprise a coherent class. From an institutional standpoint, it is relevant that proponents of realizational models form less of an integrated school or community than the Bloomfieldians or their successors. Hence there is a greater diversity of perspectives represented in the realizational WP tradition. These views range from scepticism regarding any claims to universality (Matthews 1972), to theory-specific claims about formal universals (Stump 2001) or default inheritance mechanisms (Brown and Hippisley 2012), to the endorsement of an essentially diachronic perspective (Anderson 1992) and even to assertions that morphology is a "pathology of language" (Aronoff 1994: 413).

The possibility that typological variation may determine a variety of models, each optimized for specific patterns, is taken most seriously by Matthews:

Finally, it has become clear at least that different languages raise quite different problems in morphological analysis. It is therefore possible that they also require quite different sorts of description. (Matthews 1972: 156)

From this standpoint, there is no principled reason to expect a 'one size fits all' model of morphology. Instead, the best description of cross-linguistic variation may be provided by a theory that makes available a range of different models, each tuned to particular types of patterns or languages. There may be 'formal universals' (in the sense of Chomsky 1965) that characterize the class of models defined by a morphological theory. But the search for more substantive universal principles or constraints, of the kind represented by morphemic biuniqueness, may turn out to be futile or even misconceived.

The Pāṇinian Determinism Hypothesis proposed by Stump (2001: 23) provides a clear example of the type of theory-internal constraint formulated within the realizational WP tradition. This hypothesis specifies that "[c]ompetition among members of the same rule block is in all cases resolved by Pāṇini's principle", which requires that rules within a block must either be incompatible or ranked by relative specificity. Although this hypothesis constrains the strategies for determining rule priority within a block, the restrictions it imposes also depend on the degree of freedom in the determination of rule blocks, rule compatibility and relative specificity. If none of these components are independently fixed, it is possible to regulate nearly any alternation by appealing to a 'specificity'-based principle. Because the hypothesis presupposes all of these components, its relevance is also limited to a narrowly circumscribed set of approaches. In particular, the hypothesis does not generalize in any straightforward way to classical WP models or even to realization-based models without rule blocks. From a learning-based perspective, it is also unexpected that a model would be highly sensitive to the relative specificity of rules and utterly insensitive to distributional information.

On a traditional understanding of the term, an 'explanation' for recurrent patterns and variation in and across morphological systems must lie outside those systems. A standard locus of explanatory factors is the diachronic domain, and a diachronic perspective on morphological variation is taken up by Anderson (1992). Echoing the approach to sound systems proposed by Baudouin de Courtenay (1895), Anderson suggests that morphological patterns are determined by the possible pathways of evolutionary development:[17]

Especially in the domain of morphology, where much that we find is the product of historical change operating on originally non-morphological material, it is important to recognize that what we find is the product not only of what is possible, but also of what can come into being. (Anderson 1992: 372)

This view not only offers an explanation of the space of morphological patterns and systems in terms of possible developmental trajectories, but also accounts for distributional regularities within that space. The prevalence of a particular morphological pattern will correlate not with the 'markedness' of the pattern in some abstract system-internal sense, but with the number of different pathways of change that can produce the pattern and the frequency of these pathways. Hence the recurrence of morphemic patterns need not reflect anything about the organization of morphological systems. Instead, this generalization (if, indeed, it is one) can be attributed to the way that new morphology tends to arise. If morphologization involves the prosodic reanalysis of formerly free elements as bound formatives, then the meaning and features of the original element may remain associated with the newly bound formative.

---

[17] As proposed in greater detail in the domain of sound patterns in the context of the model of Evolutionary Phonology by Blevins (2004, 2006a, 2014).

There can be no reasonable doubt that any genuine explanations for morphological patterns or systems must lie outside those systems and that diachronic accounts provide the most secure basis for a predictive, explanatory model. There are, however, two fundamental limitations of this perspective. The first is that the space of possible 'next moves' in a morphological system is much denser and less predictable than in sound systems. This difference is strikingly reflected in the fact that morphological change is not sufficiently constrained to serve as the basis for language reconstruction using the comparative method. Although cognate morphology, particularly irregular patterns, plays an important role in establishing genetic affiliation, there is no morphological counterpart of regular sound change.[18] It may be that emerging simulation-based methodologies (Sproat 2008) will provide a means of plotting the developmental trajectories of morphological systems, though at the moment diachronic approaches still offer more in the way of promise than results. The second limitation of a historical perspective is that it does not classify the function of the elements in an existing synchronic system, except insofar as it associates them with a potential for change along one or another dimension. It is of course possible that there is nothing more to say about a synchronic system once its origins and developmental history are sufficiently well understood. But standard accounts also assume that the patterns established within a system influence the directions of change, as reflected particularly by processes like morphological levelling and extension, which are taken to enhance system-level congruence. This is another domain in which a discriminative learning approach may offer a useful perspective on how the patterns in one part of a language guide learners' expectations in other parts.

Before considering synchronic factors that may contribute to congruence, it is worth considering the most sceptical view about the status of organizational principles within morphological systems. This is represented by what Aronoff (1998: 413) memorably terms the "disease view of morphology":

Morphology is inherently unnatural. It's a disease, a pathology of language. This fact is demonstrated very simply by the fact that there are languages, though not that many, that manage without it—you don't need morphology—and by the perhaps more widely recognized fact that some languages like West Greenlandic or Navajo have morphology much worse than others do. I think it's clear that the notion of morphologization or grammaticalization is rooted in this disease view of morphology as being inherently unnatural . . . (Aronoff 1998: 413)

On this extreme view, morphology is essentially noise within a communication channel, a pernicious source of cross-linguistic variability and language-internal arbitrariness. The sheer ferocity of Aronoff's assault calls for some explanation. The charge of pathology cannot simply be grounded in the fact that morphology is not universally present (even assuming that it isn't). Plenty of linguistic features

---

[18] Morphological patterns also figure prominently in the mass comparison descriptions promoted by Greenberg (Greenberg 1966, 1987) and in other approaches to language reconstruction and sub-grouping based on surface similarities.

are non-universal, from consonant voicing contrasts to articles, to syntactically distinctive word order variation. In the languages in which these features are present, they tend to carry some functional load; in languages that lack these features, the load is distributed across the available resources. There is no sense in which non-universality implies pathology, either at the level of linguistic features or at the level of whole components.

The real source of pathology must be sought elsewhere. The most plausible source is the non-morphemic (rather than non-universal) nature of much morphological variation. From the observation that morphology cannot be treated as a direct conduit of grammatical meaning, Aronoff seems to conclude that morphology is therefore an unnatural feature of language. This bleak assessment reveals an insidious effect of the Post-Bloomfieldian tradition, for clearly a morphological system in which form variation DID transparently mirror grammatical meaning would not be unnatural or pathological. The suggestion that naturalness is correlated with a morphemic feature-form correspondence is reinforced by the negative characterization of morphomes as 'purely morphological', i.e. non-morphemic, elements, as mentioned in Chapter 5.2. Hence the 'cure' for the morphological disease lies in diagnosing the positive function that morphomic patterns play in a morphological system and understanding how this function relates to morphemic patterns.

8.5.2 The role of prediction

From a classical WP perspective, the observation that morphology does not serve as a simple conduit for grammatical meaning does not entail that it is unnatural. Instead, this reflects the fact that morphology is a channel for broadcasting different kinds of information, including information about the shape of other forms in a system. By focussing solely on one of the factors that can condition morphological variation, Post-Bloomfieldian approaches (and those that have grown up in the shadow of the Post-Bloomfieldian tradition) create a false opposition between meaning-driven and 'functionless' variation.

The challenge for a general model lies in characterizing the role of morphemic and non-morphemic variation within a single system. Given that morphomes, by definition, are not susceptible to morphemic analysis, the only plausible unification is one that identifies the positive role of morphomes within a system and clarifies how morphemes would also function within this kind of system. The implicational structure of a classical WP model provides a suitably flexible relation. As suggested in Chapter 5.2, this flexibility derives from the fact that the units in a classical scheme of analysis are motivated by their PREDICTIVE VALUE, rather than solely by their grammatical content. In the classical tradition, the deduction of 'inflected' (i.e. 'bent') forms from a basic form attached no significance to the sequences that were preserved or substituted in the deduction (Matthews 1994). Among the Neogrammarians, Paul (1920) was similarly agnostic about the status of the segmentations that guided proportional analogies, again as noted by Morpurgo Davies (1998). This structural agnosticism underlies the classical treatment of morphomic patterns in terms of interpredictability rather than interderivability. Cases of morphomic syncretism are intrinsically predictive, because it is their predictive character that makes them morphomic.

The predictive nature of Priscianic formations is emphasized in Matthews (1991). It is this predictive value that accounts for the function, and the perseverance and extension (Maiden 2005) of morphomic patterns:

> For any Verb, however irregular it may be in other respects, the Present Infinitive always PREDICTS the Imperfect Subjunctive. For the Verb 'to flower', *flōrere* → *flōrerem*; for the irregular Verb 'to be', *esse* → *essem*, and so forth without exception. (Matthews 1991: 195, emphasis added)

A syncretic pattern is morphomic when it involves an implicational relation in which the shared 'units of form' do not correspond to shared 'units of meaning'. It is only when the form correspondence is regular enough to sanction reliable predictions that it is recognized as a case of morphomic syncretism rather than fortuitous ambiguity. Hence morphomic patterns are not random "imperfections" that arise in "the mapping between morphosyntax and morphological realization" (Aronoff 1999: 322). Instead, they serve to sanction deductions about the shape of other forms with different grammatical properties.

These deductions exploit the association between forms and paradigm cells. Pure forms in isolation are of limited predictive value. As the format of referral rules makes clear, it is forms under a given interpretation (i.e. cell-form pairs) that sanction useful deductions. The same is implicitly true of proportional analogies, which extend patterns defined by paradigm cells and principal parts, all of which contain forms with an interpretation. A predictive perspective applies equally to the simpler case of exponence rules, in which a set of features predicts a pattern of exponence. Morphemes fit just as neatly within a predictive model. A morpheme merely represents a type of symmetrical exponence relation in which the features predict the exponent and the exponent also predicts the features. Patterns that exhibit a biunique feature–form association are not only of value in identifying aspects of the grammatical meaning and function of a form, but also help to isolate other components of the form that may recur within a paradigm or elsewhere in the morphological system.

Implicational relations define the central predictive function that unites morphemic and morphomic elements in a morphological system. The composition and distribution of units can vary considerably across languages, but in all languages implicational relations provide a level of common organization. Hence these relations provide a more secure basis for a general morphological model than notions like 'derivational' relations, which can be seen as projecting an essentially diachronic relation onto a synchronic description in ways that offer no insight into the functioning of form variation within a system.

8.6 Discriminative abstraction

Assigning priority to relations within a system, rather than to inventories of elements, is more characteristic of 'European Structuralism'. On one reading of

Saussure (1916), the units of a linguistic system are defined in terms of their opposition to other units and have no value outside that system:[19]

Appliqué à l'unité, le principe de différenciation peut se formuler ainsi: LES CARACTÈRES DE L'UNITÉ SE CONFONDENT AVEC L'UNITÉ ELLE-MÊME. Dans la langue, comme dans tout système sémiologique, ce qui distingue un signe, violà tout ce que le constitue. C'est la différence qui fait le caractère, comme elle fait la valeur et l'unité.

Parmi les oppositions qu'elle comprend, il y en a qui sont plus significatives que d'autres; mais unité et fait de grammaire ne sont que des noms différents pour désigner des aspects divers d'un même fait général: le jeu des oppositions linguistiques. (Saussure 1916: 167f., emphasis in original)

This perspective again tends to be implicitly discriminative, as reflected particularly in the claim that units are defined by oppositions with contrasting units ("ce qui distingue un signe, violà tout ce que le constitue"). The primacy of relations is stressed even more explicitly by Hjelmslev (1948) when he asserts in the passage below that "the real units of language are the relata":

the real units of language are not sounds, or written characters, or meanings: the real units of language are the relata which these sounds, characters, and meanings represent. The main thing is not the sounds, characters, and meanings as such, but their mutual relations within the chain of speech and within the paradigms of grammar. These relations make up the system of a language, and it is this interior system which is characteristic of one language as opposed to other languages, whereas the representation by sounds, characters, and meanings is irrelevant to the system and may be changed without affecting the system. (Hjelmslev 1948: 27)

Identifying the unifying properties of morphological systems as the relations between elements helps to clarify why unit-based typologies lead to agnosticism (Matthews 1972), diachrony (Anderson 1992) or despair (Aronoff 1998). A learning-based approach suggests a further refinement in which the primacy of discriminative and implicational relations reflects their role in reducing uncertainty and thereby aiding learning and communication.

As acknowledged at the beginning of this chapter, the reconstruction of the classical WP model developed in previous chapters can be separated from its reconceptualization in terms of a learning-based approach. But that is to say that it is possible to consider HOW a WP model can be applied to the analysis of morphological systems without considering WHY it applies so generally. A

---

[19] Applied to units, the principle of differentiation can be stated in this way: THE CHARACTERISTICS OF THE UNIT BLEND WITH THE UNIT ITSELF. In language, as in any semiological system, whatever distinguishes one sign from the others constitutes it. Difference makes character just as it makes value and the unit.

Some of its oppositions are more significant than others; but units and grammatical facts are only different names for designating diverse aspects of the same general fact: the functioning of linguistic oppositions. (Saussure 1959: 121f.)

discriminative learning perspective offers a cohesive frame of reference in which to interpret the properties of WP models and the systems that they model.

At the system level, the analogical generalizations expressed (explicitly or implicitly) within classical WP models exploit the implicational dependencies exhibited by morphological systems. But these models provide no insight into why the dependencies exist in the first place. Information theory provides measures that are useful for quantifying dependencies in terms of uncertainty and uncertainty reduction. But the applicability of these measures does not clarify why they, like classical models in general, work as well as they do.

At the level of individual analyses, the advantages of WP approaches largely derive from the that fact that what have subsequently been labelled 'abstractive' analyses (Blevins 2006b) can describe the composition and structure of forms that cannot be 'constructed' from their minimal parts (or at least not without the aid of diacritic features that encode 'assembly instructions'). Yet apart from the general observation that word-sized units appear more stable and informative than smaller units, the basis for the descriptive advantages of abstractive analyses of morphological systems remains mostly unexamined.

A discriminative learning approach offers answers to both of these questions. Implicational dependencies exist because they are a precondition for learning from sparse, biased input. The descriptive success of abstractive analyses derives from the fact that the form variation in the systems they are describing serves a discriminative function. These answers raise further questions, many of which are currently under investigation in the literature cited in this chapter. However, by shifting the debate from 'how' to 'why' questions, this perspective holds out the prospect of explanations for the organization of morphological systems, grounded in factors external to those systems.

Bibliography

Abu-Mostafa, Yaser S., Magdon-Ismail, Malik, and Hsuan-Tien, Lin (2012). *Learning from Data: A Short Course*. AMLBook.

Ackerman, Farrell, Blevins, James P., and Malouf, Robert (2009). Parts and wholes: Implicative patterns in inflectional paradigms. In *Analogy in Grammar: Form and Acquisition* (eds. J. P. Blevins and J. Blevins), pp. 54–81. Oxford University Press, Oxford.

Ackerman, Farrell and Malouf, Robert (2013). Morphological organization: The Low Conditional Entropy Conjecture. *Language*, **89**, 429–464.

Ackerman, Farrell and Malouf, Robert (2015). The No Blur Principle effects as an emergent property of language systems. In *Proceedings of the 41st Annual Meeting of the Berkeley Linguistics Society* (eds. A. E. Jurgensen, H. Sande, S. Lamoureux, K. Baclawski, and A. Zerbe), pp. 1–14.

Ackerman, Farrell and Stump, Gregory T. (2004). Paradigms and periphrastic expression: A study in realization-based lexicalism. In *Projecting Syntax* (eds. A. J. Spencer and L. Sadler), pp. 111–158. CSLI, Stanford.

Albright, Adam C. (2002). *The Identification of Bases in Morphological Paradigms*. Ph.D. thesis, UCLA.

Anderson, Stephen R. (1982). Where's morphology? *Linguistic Inquiry*, **13**, 571–612.

Anderson, Stephen R. (1985). *Phonology in the Twentieth Century*. University of Chicago Press, Chicago.

Anderson, Stephen R. (1986). Disjunctive ordering in inflectional morphology. *Natural Language and Linguistic Theory*, **4**, 1–32.

Anderson, Stephen R. (1992). *A-Morphous Morphology*. Cambridge University Press, Cambridge.

Anderson, Stephen R. (2015). The morpheme: Its nature and use. In *The Oxford Handbook of Inflection* (ed. M. Baerman) Chapter 2, pp. 11–34. Oxford University Press.

Arnon, Inbal and Ramscar, Michael (2012). Granularity and the acquisition of grammatical gender: How order-of-acquisition affects what gets learned. *Cognition*, **122**, 292–305.

Aronoff, Mark (1994). *Morphology by Itself: Stems and Inflectional Classes*. MIT Press, Cambridge, MA.

Aronoff, Mark (1998). Isomorphism and monotonicity. In *Morphology and its Relation to Phonology and Syntax* (eds. S. G. Lapointe and D. Brentari), pp. 411–418. CSLI, Stanford.

Aronoff, Mark (1999). Le système malgré lui. In *Fonologia e morfologia dell'italiano e dei dialetti d'Italia* (eds. P. Benincà, A. Mioni, and L. Vanelli), pp. 321–322. Bulzoni, Rome.

Aronoff, Mark (2012). Morphological stems: What William of Ockham really said. *Word Structure*, **5**, 28–51.

Aronson, Howard I. (1990). *Georgian: A Reading Grammar*. Slavica, Columbus, OH.

Ashton, Eric Ormerod (1944). *Swahili Grammar*. Longmans, Green & Co.

Aspillera, Paraluman S. (1981). *Basic Tagalog*. M & L Licudine Enterprises, Manila.

Attneave, Fred (1959). *Applications of Information Theory to Psychology: A Summary of Basic Concepts, Methods and Results*. Holt, Rinehart and Winston, New York.

Austerlitz, Robert (1966). *Finnish Reader and Glossary*. Mouton, The Hague.

Baayen, R. Harald (2010). Demythologizing the word frequency effect: A discriminative learning perspective. *The Mental Lexicon*, 5, 436–461.

Baayen, R. Harald, Feldman, Laurie B., and Schreuder, Robert (2006). Morphological influences on the recognition of monosyllabic monomorphemic words. *Journal of Memory and Language*, 53, 496–512.

Baayen, R. Harald, Hendrix, Peter, and Ramscar, Michael (2013). Sidestepping the combinatorial explosion: Towards a processing model based on discriminative learning. *Language and Speech*, 56, 329–347.

Baayen, R. Harald, Lieber, Rochelle, and Schreuder, Robert (1997). The morphological complexity of simple nouns. *Linguistics*, 35, 861–877.

Baayen, R. Harald, McQueen, James M., Dijkstra, Teun, and Schreuder, Robert (2003). Frequency effects in regular inflectional morphology: Revisiting Dutch plurals. In *Morphological Structure in Language Processing* (eds. R. H. Baayen and R. Schreuder), pp. 355–370. Mouton de Gruyter, Berlin.

Baayen, R. Harald, Milin, Petar, Filipović Đurđević, Dusica, Hendrix, Peter, and Marelli, Marco (2011). An amorphous model for morphological processing in visual comprehension based on naive discriminative learning. *Psychological Review*, 118, 438–481.

Baayen, R. Harald, Piepenbrock, R., and van Rijn, H. (1995). *The CELEX Lexical Database* (Release 2, CD-ROM edn.). Linguistic Data Consortium, University of Pennsylvania, Philadelphia, PA.

Baayen, R. Harald, Shaoul, Cyrus, Willits, Jon, and Ramscar, Michael (2016). Comprehension without segmentation: A proof of concept with naive discrimination learning. *Language, Cognition, and Neuroscience.*, 31(1), 106–128.

Baayen, R. Harald, Wurm, Lee H., and Aycock, Joanna (2008). Lexical dynamics for low-frequency complex words: A regression study across tasks and modalities. *The Mental Lexicon*, 2, 419–463.

Bach, Emmon (1979). Control in Montague Grammar. *Linguistic Inquiry*, 10, 515–531.

Bach, Emmon (1980). In defense of passive. *Linguistics and Philosophy*, 3, 297–341.

Bach, Emmon and Wheeler, Deirdre (1983). Montague Phonology: A first approximation. In *UMOP 7*, pp. 27–45. University of Massachusetts, Amherst.

Baerman, Matthew, Brown, Dunstan, and Corbett, Greville G. (2005). *The Syntax–Morphology Interface: A Study of Syncretism*. Cambridge University Press, Cambridge.

Balling, Laura and Baayen, R. Harald (2012). Probability and surprisal in auditory comprehension of morphologically complex words. *Cognition*, 125, 80–106.

Barić, Eugenija, Lončarić, Mijo, Malić, Dragica, Paveišić, Slavko, Mirko, Peti, Zeče-vić, Vesna, and Znika, Marija (2005). *Hrvatska Gramatika* (4th edn.). Školska kniga, Zagreb.

Baudouin de Courtenay, Jan (1895). *Versuch einer Theorie phonetischer Alter-nationen; ein Kapital aus der Psychophonetic.* Trübner, Strassburg. Reprinted as 'An attempt at a theory of phonetic alternations' in Stankiewicz (1972), 144–212.

Beard, Robert (1995). *Lexeme-Morpheme Base Morphology: A General Theory of Inflection and Word Formation.* SUNY Press, Cambridge.

Bickel, Balthasar (1994). In the vestibule of meaning: Transitivity inversion as a morphological phenomenon. *Studies in Language,* 19(1), 73–127.

Blevins, James P. (2001). Realization-based lexicalism. *Journal of Linguistics,* 37, 355–365.

Blevins, James P. (2003). Stems and paradigms. *Language,* 79(2), 737–767.

Blevins, James P. (2006b). Word-based morphology. *Journal of Linguistics,* 42, 531–573.

Blevins, James P. (2007). Conjugation classes in Estonian. *Linguistica Uralica,* 43(4), 250–267.

Blevins, James P. (2008a). Declension classes in Estonian. *Linguistica Ural-ica,* 44(4), 241–267.

Blevins, James P. (2008b). The post-transformational enterprise. *Journal of Linguis-tics,* 44, 723–742.

Blevins, James P. (2011). Feature-based grammar. In *Nontransformational Syntax* (eds. R. D. Borsley and K. Börjars), pp. 297–324. Oxford University Press, Oxford.

Blevins, James P. (2013). American descriptivism ('structuralism'). In *Oxford Hand-book of the History of Linguistics* (ed. K. Allan), Chapter 18, pp. 419–437. Oxford University Press, Oxford.

Blevins, James P. (2016). The minimal sign. In *The Cambridge Handbook of Mor-phology* (eds. G. T. Stump and A. Hippisley), Chapter 3, pp. 50–69. Cambridge University Press.

Blevins, James P. (2015b). Thematic inversion in Georgian. Ms., University of Cambridge.

Blevins, James P., Ackerman, Farrell, and Malouf, Robert (2008). An information-based measure of morphological information. *3rd Workshop on Quantitative Investigations in Theoretical Linguistics,* Helsinki.

Blevins, James P. and Blevins, Juliette (eds.) (2009). *Analogy in Grammar: Form and Acquisition.* Oxford University Press, Oxford.

Blevins, James P., Booij, Geert, Milin, Petar, and Ramscar, Michael (2016a). Inflec-tion at the morphology-syntax interface. In *Word Knowledge and Word Usage: A Cross-disciplinary Guide to the Mental Lexicon* (eds. V. Pirrelli, I. Plag, and W. U. Dressler), (to appear). De Gruyter, Berlin.

Blevins, James P., Milin, Petar, and Ramscar, Michael (2016b). The Zipfian paradigm cell filling problem. In *Perspectives on Morphological Structure: Data and Analyses* (eds. F. Kiefer, J. P. Blevins, and H. Bartos), (in press). Brill, Leiden.

Blevins, Juliette (2004). *Evolutionary Phonology: The Emergence of Sound Patterns*. Cambridge University Press, Cambridge.

Blevins, Juliette (2006a). A theoretical synopsis of Evolutionary Phonology. *Theoretical Linguistics*, 32, 117–165.

Blevins, Juliette (2014). Evolutionary phonology: A holistic approach to sound change typology. In *Handbook of Historical Phonology* (eds. P. Honeybone and J. Salmons). Oxford University Press, Oxford.

Bloch, Bernard (1947). English verb inflection. *Language*, 23, 399–418. Reprinted in Joos (1957), 243–254.

Bloch, Bernard (1948). A set of postulates for phonemic analysis. *Language*, 24, 3–46.

Bloomer, Aileen, Griffiths, Patrick, and Merrison, Andrew (2004). *Introducing Language in Use*. Routledge, London.

Bloomfield, Leonard (1914). Sentence and word. *Transactions of the American Philological Society*, 45, 65–75. Reprinted in Hockett (1970), 38–46.

Bloomfield, Leonard (1926). A set of postulates for the science of language. *Language*, 2, 153–164. Reprinted in Joos (1957), 26–37.

Bloomfield, Leonard (1929). Review of *Konkordanz Pāṇini-Candra* by Bruno Liebich. *Language*, 5, 267–276. Reprinted in Hockett (1970), 219–226.

Bloomfield, Leonard (1933). *Language*. University of Chicago Press, Chicago.

Bochner, Harry (1993). *Simplicity in Generative Morphology*. Mouton de Gruyter.

Bolinger, Dwight (1979). Meaning and memory. In *Experience Forms: Their Cultural and Individual Place and Function* (eds. G. G. Haydu), pp. 95–112. Mouton, The Hague.

Bonami, Olivier and Boyé, Gilles (2003). Supplétion et classes flexionnelles dans la conjugaison du français. *Langages*, 152, 102–126.

Bonami, Olivier and Boyé, Gilles (2006). Deriving inflectional irregularity. In *Proceedings of the 13th International Conference on Head-Driven Phrase Structure Grammar* (eds. S. Müller), pp. 361–380. CSLI Publications, Paris.

Bonami, Olivier and Boyé, Gilles (2007). Remarques sur les bases de la conjugaison. In *Des sons et des sens* (eds. E. Delais-Roussarie and L. Labrune), pp. 77–90. Hermès Sciences, Paris.

Bonami, Olivier and Luís, Ana (2013). Causes and consequences of complexity in Portuguese verbal paradigms. Paper presented at the 9th Mediterranean Morphology Meeting, Dubrovnik.

Bonami, Olivier and Luís, Ana (2014). Sur la morphologie implicative dans la conjugaison du portugais: Une étude quantitative. In *Morphologie flexionnelle et dialectologie romane. Typologie(s) et modélisation(s)* (ed. J.-L. Léonard), Number 22 in Mémoires de la Société de Linguistique de Paris, pp. 111–151. Peters, Leuven.

Bonami, Olivier and Stump, Gregory T. (2015). Paradigm Function Morphology. In *The Cambridge Handbook of Morphology* (eds. A. Hippisley and G. T. Stump) Chapter 17, pp. 449–481. Cambridge University Press, Cambridge.

Booij, Geert (1993). Against split morphology. In *Yearbook of Morphology 1993* (eds. G. Booij and J. van Marle), pp. 27–49. Kluwer, Dordrecht.

Booij, Geert (1996). Inherent verses contextual inflection and the split morphology hypothesis. In *Yearbook of Morphology 1995* (eds. G. Booij and J. van Marle), pp. 1–16. Kluwer, Dordrecht.

Booij, Geert (1997). Autonomous morphology and paradigmatic relations. In *Yearbook of Morphology 1996* (eds. G. Booij and J. van Marle), pp. 35–53. Kluwer.

Booij, Geert (2010). *Construction Morphology*. Oxford University Press, Oxford.

Brown, Dunstan (1998). Stem indexing and morphonological selection in the Russian verb: A network morphology account. In *Models of Inflection* (eds. F. Ray, A. Ortmann, and T. Parodi), pp. 196–224. Niemeyer, Tübingen.

Brown, Dunstan and Hippisley, Andrew. (2012). *Network Morphology: A Defaults-based Theory of Word Structure*. Cambridge University Press, Cambridge.

Bybee, Joan L. (1985). *Morphology: A Study of the Relation between Meaning and Form*. John Benjamins, Amsterdam.

Bybee, Joan L. (1999). Use impacts morphological representation. *Behavioral and Brain Sciences*, **22**(6), 1016–7.

Bybee, Joan L. (2001). *Phonology and Language Use*. Cambridge University Press, Cambridge.

Bybee, Joan L. (2007). *Frequency of Use and the Organization of Language*. Oxford University Press, Oxford.

Bybee, Joan L. (2010). *Language, Usage and Complexity*. Cambridge University Press, Cambridge.

Bybee, Joan L. and Hopper, Paul J. (eds.) (2001). *Frequency and the Emergence of Linguistic Structure*. Typological Studies in Languages, 45. Benjamins, Amsterdam.

Carmack, Stanford (1997). Blocking in Georgian verb morphology. *Language*, **72**, 314–338.

Carroll, John B. (1953). *The Study of Language: A Survey of Linguistics and Related Disciplines in America*. Harvard University Press, Cambridge, MA.

Carstairs, Andrew (1983). Paradigm economy. *Journal of Linguistics*, **19**, 115–125.

Carstairs, Andrew (1987). *Allomorphy in Inflexion*. Croom Helm, London.

Carstairs, Andrew (1988). Paradigm economy: A reply to Nyman. *Journal of Linguistics*, **24**, 489–499.

Carstairs-McCarthy, Andrew (1991). Inflection classes: Two questions with one answer. In *Paradigms: The Economy of Inflection* (ed. F. Plank), pp. 213–253. Mouton de Gruyter, Berlin.

Carstairs-McCarthy, Andrew (1994). Inflection classes, gender, and the principle of contrast. *Language*, **70**, 737–788.

Chersi, Fabian, Ferro, Marcello, Pezzulo, Giovanni, and Pirrelli, Vito (2014). Topological self-organization and prediction learning support both action and lexical chains in the brain. *Topics in Cognitive Science*, **6**(3), 476–491.

Chomsky, Noam (1965). *Aspects of the Theory of Syntax*. MIT Press, Cambridge, MA.

Chomsky, Noam (1970). Remarks on nominalization. In *Readings in English Transformational Grammar* (eds. R. A. Jacobs and P. S. Rosenbaum), pp. 184–221. Ginn and Company, Waltham. Reprinted in Chomsky (1976), 1–61.

Chomsky, Noam (1975). *The Logical Structure of Linguistic Theory*. University of Chicago Press, Chicago.

Chomsky, Noam (1976). *Studies on Semantics in Generative Grammar*. Mouton, The Hague.

Chomsky, Noam (1988). *Language and Problems of Knowledge: The Managua Lectures*. MIT Press, Cambridge, MA.

Chomsky, Noam and Halle, Morris (1965). Some controversial questions in phonological theory. *Journal of Linguistics*, 1, 97–138.

Chomsky, Noam and Halle, Morris (1968). *The Sound Pattern of English*. Harper & Row, New York.

Clahsen, Harald (1999). Lexical entries and rules of language: A multidisciplinary study of German inflection. *Behavioral and Brain Sciences*, 22, 991–1013.

Clahsen, Harald, Rothweiler, Monika, Woest, Andreas, and Marcus, Gary F. (1992). Regular and irregular inflection in the acquisition of German noun plurals. *Cognition*, 45, 201–249.

Clark, Alexander and Lappin, Shalom (2011). *Linguistic Nativism and the Poverty of the Stimulus*. Wiley-Blackwell.

Clark, Eve V. (1987). The Principle of Contrast: A constraint on language acquisition. In *Mechanisms of Language Acquisition* (ed. B. MacWhinney), pp. 1–33. Erlbaum, Hillsdate, NJ.

Comrie, Bernard (1981). *The Languages of the Soviet Union*. Cambridge University Press, Cambridge.

Corbett, Greville (1991). *Gender*. Cambridge University Press, Cambridge.

Corbett, Greville and Fraser, Norman (1993). Network Morphology: A DATR account of Russian nominal inflection. *Journal of Linguistics*, 29, 113–142.

Cordona, George (1994). Indian linguistics. In *History of Linguistics I: The Eastern Traditions of Linguistics* (ed. L. Guilio), pp. 25–60. Longman, London.

Cover, Thomas M. and Thomas, Joy A. (1991). *Elements of Information Theory*. Wiley-Blackwell.

Crysmann, Berthold and Bonami, Olivier (2012). Establishing order in type-based realizational morphology. In *Proceedings of the 19th International Conference on Head-Driven Phrase Structure Grammar* (ed. S. Müller), pp. 123–143. CSLI Publications.

Curme, George O. (1922). *A Grammar of the German Language*. Macmillan, London.

Curme, George O. (1935). *A Grammar of the English Language*. Heath, Boston.

Daelemans, Walter and Van den Bosch, Antal (2005). *Memory-Based Language Processing*. Cambridge University Press, Cambridge.

Dalrymple, Mary (2001). *Lexical Functional Grammar*. Academic Press.

Davis, Matt, Marslen-Wilson, William D., and Gaskell, M.G. (2002). Leading up the lexical garden-path: Segmentation and ambiguity in spoken word recognition. *Journal of Experimental Psychology: Human Perception & Performance*, 28, 218–244.

de Jong, Nivja H. (2002). *Morphological Families in the Mental Lexicon*. Ph.D. thesis, University of Nijmegen.

Diessel, Holger (2015). Usage-based construction grammar. In *Handbook of Cognitive Linguistics* (ed. E. Dabrowska and D. Divak). Mouton de Gruyter.

Dixon, R. M. W. and Aikhenvald, Alexandra Y. (ed.) (2002). *Word: A Cross-Linguistic Typology*. Cambridge University Press, Cambridge.

Drager, Katie K. (2011). Sociophonetic variation and the lemma. *Journal of Phonetics*, 39, 694–707.

Dressler, Wolfgang U. (1987). *Leitmotifs in Natural Morphology*. John Benjamins, Amsterdam.

Dromi, Esther (1987). *Early Lexical Development*. Cambridge University Press, Cambridge.

Duden (2005). *Grammatik der deutschen Gegenwartsprache*. Dudenverlag, Mannheim.

Elman, Jeffrey L. (1990). Finding structure in time. *Cognitive Science*, 14, 179–211.

Emeneau, Murray B (1988). Bloomfield and Pāṇini. *Language*, 64, 755–760.

Erelt, Mati (eds.) (2003). *Estonian Language*. Estonian Academy Publishers, Tallinn.

Erelt, Mati, Erelt, Tiiu, and Ross, Kristiina (2000). *Eesti keele käsiraamat*. Eesti Keele Sihtasutus, Tallinn.

Erelt, Mati, Kasik, Reet, Metslang, Helle, Rajandi, Henno, Ross, Kristiina, Saari, Henn, Tael, Kaja, and Vare, Silvi (1995). *Eesti Keele Grammatika*. Volume I: Morfoloogia. Eesti Teaduste Akadeemia Eesti Keele Instituut, Tallinn.

Erelt, Tiiu (ed.) (2006). *Eesti keele õigekeelsussõnaraamat ÕS 2006*. Eesti Keele Sihtasutus, Tallinn.

Erelt, Tiiu, Leemets, Tiina, Mäearu, and Raadik, Maire (eds.) (2013). *Eesti keele õigekeelsussõnaraamat ÕS 2013*. Eesti Keele Sihtasutus, Tallinn.

Finkel, Raphael and Stump, Gregory T. (2009). Principal parts and degrees of paradigmatic transparency. In Blevins and Blevins (2009), pp. 13–52.

Finkel, Raphael and Stump, Gregory T. (2007). Principal parts and morphological typology. *Morphology*, 17, 39–75.

Firth, J. R. (1948). Sounds and prosodies. *Transactions of the Philological Society*, 127–152.

Firth, J. R. (1951). General linguistics and descriptive grammar. *Transactions of the Philological Society*, 69–87.

Firth, J. R. (1957). A synopsis of linguistic theory 1930–1955. In *Studies in Linguistic Theory*, pp. 1–32. Philological Society, Oxford.

Ford, Alan, Singh, Rajendra, and Martohardjono, Gita (1997). *Pace Pāṇini*. American University Studies: Series 13, Linguistics. Vol. 34. Peter Lang Verlag, Berlin.

Fought, John (1999). Introduction. In *Leonard Bloomfield: Critical Assessments of Leading Linguists* (ed. J. Fought), Volume 1, pp. 1–26. Routledge.

Fromkin, Victoria, Rodman, Robert, and Hyams, Nina (2010). *An Introduction to Language* (9th edn.). Wadsworth, Boston.

Gahl, Suzanne (2008). "Thyme" and "Time" are not homophones. The effect of lemma frequency on word durations in spontaneous speech. *Language*, 84(3), 474–496.

Gahl, Suzanne, Yao, Yao, and Johnson, Keith (2011). Why reduce? Phonological neighborhood density and phonetic reduction in spontaneous speech. *Journal of Memory and Language*, 66(4), 789–806.

Gazdar, Gerald, Klein, Ewan, Pullum, Geoffrey K., and Sag, Ivan A. (1985). *Generalized Phrase Structure Grammar*. Harvard University Press, Cambridge, MA.

Geertzen, Jeroen, Blevins, James P., and Milin, Petar (2016). The entropy of linguistic unit boundaries. *Italian Journal of Linguistics*, 28(2), 1–24.

Gerken, LouAnn and Balcomb, Francis K. (2010). Three observations about infant generalization and their implications for generalization mechanisms. In *Generalization of Knowledge: Interdisciplinary Perspectives* (eds. M. T. Banach and D. Caccamise), pp. 73–88. Taylor & Francis, New York.

Gildersleeve, B. L. and Lodge, G. (1895). *Gildersleeve's Latin Grammar*. Macmillan & Co., New York. Reprinted by Bolchazy-Carducci Publishers, Inc., 2000.

Gleason, Henry Allan (1955). *An Introduction to Descriptive Linguistics*. Holt, Rinehart and Winston, New York.

Goldberg, Adele (2005). *Constructions at Work: The Nature of Generalization in Language*. Oxford University Press, Oxford.

Goldwater, Sharon, Griffiths, Thomas L., and Johnson, Mark (2009). A Bayesian framework for word segmentation: Exploring the effects of context. *Cognition*, 112, 21–54.

Goodwin, W. W. (1894). *Greek Grammar*. MacMillan, London.

Green, John N. (1997). Spanish. In *The Romance Languages* (eds. M. Harris and N. Vincent), pp. 79–130. Routledge, London.

Greenberg, Joseph H. (1966). *The Languages of Africa* (2nd edn.). Indiana University Press, Bloomington.

Greenberg, Joseph H. (1987). *The Languages of America*. Stanford University Press, Stanford.

Grünthal, Riho (2003). *Finnic Adpositions and Cases in Change*. Société Finno-Ougrienne, Helsinki.

Häkkinen, Kaisa (ed.) (1990). *Nykysuomen Sanakirja: Etymologinen Sanakirja* (6 edn.). WSOY, Helsinki.

Hale, John (2001). A probabilistic Earley parser as a psycholinguistic model. In *Proceedings of the Second Meeting of the North American Chapter of the Asssociation for Computational Linguistics*, pp. 159–166.

Hale, John (2003). The information conveyed by words in sentences. *Journal of Psychological Research*, 32(2), 101–123.

Hale, John (2006). Uncertainty about the rest of the sentence. *Cognitive Science*, 30(4), 643–672.

Hale, William Gardner and Buck, Carl Darling (1903). *A Latin Grammar*. The University of Alabama Press, Tuscaloosa.

Hall, Robert A. Jr. (1987). Bloomfield and semantics. *Historiographia Linguistica*, 14, 155–160.

Halle, Morris (1959). *The Sound Pattern of Russian*. Mouton, The Hague.

Halle, Morris and Marantz, Alec (1993). Distributed Morphology and the pieces of inflection. In *The view from Building 20* (eds. K. Hale and S. J. Keyser), pp. 111–176. MIT Press, Cambridge, MA.

Hamp, Eric, Householder, Fred W., and Austerlitz, Robert (eds.) (1966). *Readings in Linguistics II*. University of Chicago Press, Chicago.

Harris, Alice C. (1981). *Georgian Syntax: A Study in Relational Grammar*. Cambridge University Press, Cambridge.

Harris, Alice C. (1984). Inversion as a rule of universal grammar: Georgian evidence. In *Studies in Relational Grammar 2* (eds. D. M. Perlmutter and C. Rosen), pp. 259–291. University of Chicago Press, Chicago.

Harris, Alice C. (2009). Exuberant exponence in Batsbi. *Natural Language and Linguistic Theory*, **27**, 267–303.

Harris, Zellig S. (1941). Linguistic structure of Hebrew. *Journal of the American Oriental Society*, **61**, 143–167.

Harris, Zellig S. (1942). Morpheme alternants in linguistic analysis. *Language*, **18**, 169–180. Reprinted in Joos (1957), 109–115.

Harris, Zellig S. (1951). *Methods in Structural Linguistics*. University of Chicago Press, Chicago.

Harris, Zellig S. (1954). Distributional structure. *Word*, 10(23), 146–162.

Haspelmath, Martin (1993). *A Grammar of Lezgian*. Mouton, Berlin.

Haspelmath, Martin (1996). Word-class-changing inflection and morphological theory. In *Yearbook of Morphology 1995* (eds. G. Booij and J. van Marle), pp. 43–66. Kluwer, Dordrecht.

Haspelmath, Martin (2002). *Understanding Morphology*. Arnold, London.

Haspelmath, Martin (2011). The indeterminacy of word segmentation and the nature of morphology and syntax. *Folia Linguistica*, **45**(1), 31–80.

Hay, Jennifer (2001). Lexical frequency in morphology: Is everything relative? *Linguistics*, **39**, 1041–1070.

Hay, Jennifer and Baayen, R. Harald (2002). Parsing and productivity. In *Yearbook of Morphology 2001* (eds. G. Booij and J. van Marle), pp. 203–235. Kluwer, Dordrecht.

Hay, Jennifer and Baayen, R. Harald (2006). Shifting paradigms: Gradient structure in morphology. *Trends in Cognitive Sciences*, **9**, 342–348.

Herrity, Peter (2000). *Slovene*. Routledge, London.

Hewitt, B. G. (1995). *Georgian: A Structural Reference Grammar*. London Oriental and African Languages Library. John Benjamins, Amsterdam.

Hjelmslev, Louis (1948). Structural analysis of language. In *Essais linguistiques*, pp. 27–35. Nordisk Sprog- og Kulturforlag.

Hockett, Charles F. (1942). A system of descriptive phonology. *Language*, **18**, 3–21. Reprinted in Joos (1957), 97–108.

Hockett, Charles F. (1947). Problems of morphemic analysis. *Language*, **23**, 321–343. Reprinted in Joos (1957), 229–242.

Hockett, Charles F. (1954). Two models of grammatical description. *Word*, **10**, 210–231. Reprinted in Joos (1957), 386–399.

Hockett, Charles F. (1958). *A Course in Modern Linguistics*. MacMillan, New York.

Hockett, Charles F. (1961). Linguistic elements and their relation. *Language*, **37**, 29–53.

Hockett, Charles F. (1967). The Yawelmani basic verb. *Language*, **43**, 208–222.

Hockett, Charles F. (1968). *The State of the Art*. Mouton, The Hague.

Hockett, Charles F. (ed.) (1970). *A Leonard Bloomfield Anthology*. University of Chicago Press, Chicago.

Hockett, Charles F. (1987). *Refurbishing our Foundations: Elementary Linguistics from an Advanced Point of View*. John Benjamins, Amsterdam.

Hornstein, Norbert and Lightfoot, David (1981). *Explanation in Linguistics.* Longman, London.

Ingria, Robert J. (1990). The limits of unification. In *Proceedings of the 28th Annual Meeting of the Association for Computational Linguistics*, Morristown, NJ, pp. 194–204.

Itkonen, Esa (2005). *Analogy As Structure And Process: Approaches in Linguistics, Cognitive Psychology and Philosophy of Science.* John Benjamins, Amsterdam.

Johnson, David and Lappin, Shalom (1999). *Local Constraints vs Economy.* CSLI, Stanford.

Jones, Daniel (1929). Definition of a phoneme. *Le Maître Phonétique*, 28, 43–44.

Joos, Martin (ed.) (1957). *Readings in Linguistics I.* University of Chicago Press, Chicago.

Kaplan, Ronald M. and Bresnan, Joan (1982). Lexical-functional grammar: A formal system for grammatical representation. In *The Mental Representation of Grammatical Relations* (ed. J. Bresnan), pp. 173–281. MIT Press, Cambridge.

Karlsson, Fred (1999). *Finnish: An Essential Grammar.* Routledge, London.

Karlsson, Fred (2006). Finnish as an agglutinating language. In *Elsevier Encylopedia of Language & Linguistics* (2nd edn.) (ed. K. Brown), pp. 476–480. Elsevier.

Karttunen, Lauri (2003). Computing with realizational morphology. In *Computational Linguistics and Intelligent Text Processing* (ed. A. Gelbukh), Proceedings of CICLing 2003, pp. 203–214. Springer Verlag, Berlin.

Karttunen, Lauri (2006). The insufficiency of paper-and-pencil linguistics: The case of Finnish prosody. In *Intelligent Architectures: Variations on Themes by Ronald M. Kaplan* (eds. M. Butt, M. Dalrymple, and T. Holloway King). CSLI.

Kemps, Rachèl J. J. K., Ernestus, Mirjam, Schreuder, Robert, and Baayen, R. Harald (2005). Prosodic cues for morphological complexity: The case of Dutch plural nouns. *Memory & Cognition*, 33(3), 430–446.

Kiparsky, Paul (1975). What are phonological theories about. In *Testing Linguistic Hypotheses* (eds. D. Cohen and J. R. Wirth). Wiley, New York.

Köpke, Klaus-Michael (1988). Schemas in German plural formation. *Lingua*, 74, 303–335.

Kostić, Aleksandar (1991). Informational approach to processing inflectional morphology: Standard data reconsidered. *Psychological research*, 53, 62–70.

Kostić, Aleksandar (1995). Informational load constraints on processing inflectional morphology. In *Morphological Aspects of Language Processing* (ed. L. B. Feldman), pp. 317–344. Lawrence Erlbaum, Hillsdale, NJ.

Kostić, Aleksandar, Marković, Tanja, and Baucal, Aleksandar (2003). Inflectional morphology and word meaning: Orthogonal or co-implicative domains? In *Morphological Structure in Language Processing* (eds. R. H. Baayen and R. Schreuder), pp. 1–44. Mouton de Gruyter, Berlin.

Kurumada, Chigusa, Meylan, Stephan C., and Frank, Michael C. (2013). Zipfian frequency distributions facilitate word segmentation in context. *Cognition*, 127, 439–453.

Kuryłowicz, Jerzy (1949). La nature des procès dits "analogiques". *Acta Linguistica*, 5, 121–138. Reprinted in Hamp *et al.* (1966), 158–174. [English translation with introduction by Margaret Winters (1995), The nature of the so-called analogical processes, *Diachronica* 12 113–45.].

Kuryłowicz, Jerzy (1964). *The Inflectional Categories of Indo-European.* Carl Winter, Heidelberg.

Laaha, Sabine, Ravind, Dorit, Korecky-Kröll, Katharina, Laaha, Gregor, and Dressler, Wolfgang U. (2006). Early noun plurals in German: regularity, productivity or default? *Journal of Child Language*, 33, 271–302.

Law, Vivien (1998). The *Technē* and grammar in the Roman world. In *Dionysius Thrax and the Technē Grammatikē* (eds. V. Law and I. Sluiter), pp. 111–120. Nodus Publikationen, Münster.

Lazaridou, Angeliki, Marelli, Marco, Zamparelli, Roberto, and Baroni, Marco (2013). Compositional-ly derived representations of morphologically complex words in distributional semantics. In *Proceedings of the 51st Annual Meeting of the Association for Computational Linguistics*, East Stroudsburg, PA, pp. 1517–1526. ACL.

Levelt, W. J. M. (1989). *Speaking: From Intention to Articulation.* MIT Press, Cambridge, MA.

Levenshtein, Vladimir I. (1966). Binary codes capable of correcting deletions, insertions, and reversals. *Soviet Physics Doklady*, 10(8), 707–710.

Levin, Jules F., Haikalis, Peter D., and Forostenko, Anatole A. (1979). *Reading Modern Russian.* Slavica Publishers, Inc, Columbus.

Levy, Roger (2008). Expectation-based syntactic comprehension. *Cognition*, 106, 1126–1177.

Lieb, Hans-Heinrich (1976). Grammars as theories: The case for axiomatic grammar (Part II). *Theoretical Linguistics*, 3, 1–98.

Lieb, Hans-Heinrich (1980). Words as syntactic paradigms. In *Wege zur Universalienforschung. Sprachwissenschaftliche Beiträge zum 60. Geburtstag von Hansjakob Seiler* (eds. G. Brettschneider and C. Lehmann), pp. 115–123. Narr, Tübingen.

Lieb, Hans-Heinrich (1983). *Integrational Linguistics.* Volume 1: General Outline. Benjamins, Amsterdam.

Lieb, Hans-Heinrich (1992). Paradigma und Klassifikation: Explikation des Paradigmenbegriffs. *Zeitschrift für Sprachwissenschaft*, 11, 3–46.

Lieb, Hans-Heinrich (2005). Notions of paradigm in grammar. In *Lexikologie / Lexicology: Ein internationales Handbuch zur Natur und Struktur von Wörtern und Wortschätzen / An international handbook on the nature and structure of words and vocabularies* (eds. D. A. Cruse, F. Hundsnurscher, M. Job, and P. Lutzeier), Volume 2, pp. 1613–1646. de Gruyter.

Lieb, Hans-Heinrich (2013). *Towards a General Theory of Word Formation: The Process Model.* Freie Universität Berlin. Open Access Publication.

Lieber, Rochelle (1992). *Deconstructing Morphology.* University of Chicago Press, Chicago.

Liljencrants, Johan and Lindblom, Bjorn (1972). Numerical simulation of vowel quality systems: The role of perceptual contrast. *Language*, 48, 839–862.

Lounsbury, Floyd (1953). *Oneida Verb Morphology.* Yale University Publications in Anthropology 48. Yale University Press, New Haven. Chapter 1 reprinted in Joos (1957), 379–385.

Luís, Ana and Spencer, Andrew (2005). A paradigm function account of 'mesoclisis' in European Portuguese. In *Yearbook of Morphology 2004* (eds. G. Booij and J. van Marle), pp. 177–228. Springer, Dordrecht.

Lyons, John (1963). *Structural Semantics*. Blackwell, Oxford.

Macdonnell, Arthur A. (1927). *A Sanskrit Grammar for Students* (3rd edn.). Oxford University Press, London.

Maiden, Martin (2005). Morphological autonomy and diachrony. In *Yearbook of Morphology 2004* (eds. G. Booij and J. van Marle), pp. 137–175. Springer, Dordrecht.

Marantz, Alec (2013). No escape from morphemes in morphological processing. *Language and Cognitive Processes*, 28(7), 905–916.

Marchand, Hans (1960). *The Categories and Types of present-day English Word-Formation: A Synchronic-Diachronic Approach*. University of Alabama Press.

Marcus, Gary F., Brinkmann, Ursula, Clahsen, Harald, Wiese, Richard, and Pinker, Steven (1995). German inflection: The exception that proves the rule. *Cognitive Psychology*, **29**, 189–256.

Marelli, Marco and Baroni, Marco (2015). Affixation in semantic space: Modeling morpheme meanings with compositional distributional semantics. *Pscychological Review*, **122**(3), 485–515.

Marslen-Wilson, William and Tyler, Lorraine K. (1980). The temporal structure of spoken language understanding. *Cognition*, **8**, 1–71.

Marslen-Wilson, William D. and Welsh, Alan (1978). Processing interactions and lexical access during word recognition in continuous speech. *Cognitive Psychology*, **10**, 29–63.

Marzi, Claudia, Ferro, Marcello, and Pirrelli, Vito (2014). Morphological structure through lexical parsability. *Lingue e linguaggio*, XIII(2), 263–290.

Matthews, Peter H. (1965). The inflectional component of a word-and-paradigm grammar. *Journal of Linguistics*, 1, 139–171.

Matthews, Peter H. (1972). *Inflectional Morphology: A Theoretical Study Based on Aspects of Latin Verb Conjugation*. Cambridge University Press, Cambridge.

Matthews, Peter H. (1991). *Morphology*. Cambridge University Press, Cambridge.

Matthews, Peter H. (1993). *Grammatical theory in the United States from Bloomfield to Chomsky*. Cambridge University Press, Cambridge.

Matthews, Peter H. (1994). Greek and Latin linguistics. In *History of Linguistics II: Classical and Medieval Linguistics* (ed. L. Guilio), pp. 1–133. Longman, London.

Matthews, Peter H. (2002). What can we conclude? In *Word: A Cross-Linguistic Typology* (eds. R. M. W. Dixon and A. Y. Aikhenvald), pp. 266–281. Oxford University Press, Oxford.

Mayerthaler, Willi (1981). *Morphologische Natürlichkeit*. Akademische Verlagsgesellschaft Athenaion, Wiesbaden.

McDonald, Scott A. and Ramscar, Michael (2001). Testing the distributional hypothesis: The influence of context on judgements of semantic similarity. In *Proceedings of the 23rd Annual Conference of the Cognitive Science Society*, pp. 611–616.

Milin, Petar, Filipović Đurđević, Dušica, and Moscoso del Prado Martín, Fermín (2009a). The simultaneous effects of inflectional paradigms and classes on lexical recognition: Evidence from Serbian. *Journal of Memory and Language*, 60, 50–64.

Milin, Petar, Kuperman, Victor, Kostić, Aleksandar, and Baayen, R. Harald (2009b). Words and paradigms bit by bit: An information-theoretic approach to the processing of inflection and derivation. In Blevins and Blevins (2009), pp. 214–253.

Morpurgo Davies, Anna (1978). Analogy, segmentation and the early Neogrammarians. *Transactions of the Philological Society*, 76, 36–60.

Morpurgo Davies, Anna (1998). *Nineteenth-century linguistics*. Volume IV. Longman.

Moscoso del Prado Martín, Fermín (2003). *Paradigmatic Structures in Morphological Processing: Computational and Cross-linguistic Studies*. Ph.D. thesis, University of Nijmegen.

Moscoso del Prado Martín, Fermín, Bertram, Raymond, Häikiö, Tuomo, Schreuder, Robert, and Baayen, R. Harald (2004a). Morphological family size in a morphologically rich language: The case of Finnish compared to Dutch and Hebrew. *Journal of Experimental Psychology: Learning, Memory and Cognition*, 30, 1271–1278.

Moscoso del Prado Martín, Fermín, Kostić, Aleksandar, and Baayen, R. Harald (2004b). Putting the bits together: An information-theoretical perspective on morphological processing. *Cognition*, 94, 1–18.

Mulder, Komberley, Dijkstra, Teun, Schreuder, Robert, and Baayen, R. Harald (2014). Effects of primary and secondary morphological family size in monolingual and bilingual word processing. *Journal of Memory and Language*, 72, 59–84.

Müller, Gereon (2002). Remarks on nominal inflection in German. In *More than Words: A Festschrift for Dieter Wunderlich* (eds. I. Kaufmann and B. Stiebels), Studia Grammatica 53, pp. 113–146. Akademie Verlag, Berlin.

Müller, Gereon (2004). Inflectional classes and economy. In *Explorations in Nominal Inflection* (eds. G. Müller, L. Gunkel, and G. Zinfounun), pp. 189–228. Mouton de Gruyter, Berlin.

Mürk, Harri William (1997). *A Handbook of Estonian: Nouns, Adjectives and Verbs*. Indiana University Uralic and Altaic Series, v. 163. Indiana University, Bloomington.

Neef, Martin (1998). Reduced syllable plural in German. In *Models of Inflection* (eds. R. Fabri, A. Ortmann, and T. Parodi), pp. 244–265. Niemeyer, Tübingen.

Nida, Eugene A. (1948). The analysis of grammatical constituents. *Language*, 24, 168–177.

Nida, Eugene A. (1949). *Morphology: The Descriptive Analysis of Words*. University of Michigan Press, Ann Arbor.

Norris, Dennis, McQueen, James M., Cutler, Anne, and Butterfield, Sally (1997). The possible-word constraint in the segmentation of continuous speech. *Cognitive Psychology*, 34, 191–243.

Noyer, Rolf (1992). *Features, Positions and Affixes in Autonomous Morphological Structure*. Ph.D. thesis, MIT.

Nyman, Martti (1986). Is the Paradigm Economy Principle relevant?. *Journal of Linguistics*, **23**, 251–267.

Nyman, Martti (1988). Paradigm economy: A rejoinder to Carstairs. *Journal of Linguistics*, **24**, 501–513.

O'Grady, William and Dobrovolsky, Michael (1996). *Contemporary Linguistic Analysis: An Introduction*. Copp Clark Ltd, Toronto.

Paul, Hermann (1920). *Prinzipien der Sprachgeschichte*. Max Niemayer Verlag, Tübingen.

Penke, Martina, Krause, Marion, and Janßen, Ulrike (1999). The representation of inflectional morphology: Evidence from Broca's aphasia. *Brain and Language*, **68**, 225–232.

Perlmutter, David M. (1978). Impersonal passives and the Unaccusative Hypothesis. In *Proceedings of the Fourth Annual Meeting of the Berkeley Linguistics Society*.

Perlmutter, David M. (1988). The split morphology hypothesis: Evidence from Yiddish. In *Theoretical Morphology* (eds. M. Hammond and M. Noonan), pp. 79–100. Academic Press, San Diego.

Pertsova, Katya (2004). Distribution of genitive plural allomorphs in the Russian lexicon and in the internal grammar of native speakers. Master's thesis, UCLA.

Pihel, Kalju and Pikamäe, Arno (eds.) (1999). *Soome-eesti sõnaraamat*. Valgus, Tallinn.

Pike, Kenneth L. (1943). Taxemes and immediate constituents. *Language*, **19**, 65–82.

Pike, Kenneth L. (1967). *Language in Relation to a Unified Theory of Human Behaviour*. Mouton, The Hague.

Pirrelli, Vito, Ferro, Marcello, and Calderone, Basilio (2011). Learning paradigms in time and space. In *Morphological Autonomy: Perspectives from Romance Inflectional Morphology*, pp. 135–157. Oxford University Press.

Pirrelli, Vito, Ferro, Marcello, and Marzi, Claudia (2015). Computational complexity of abstractive morphology. In *Understanding and Measuring Morphological Complexity* (eds. M. Baerman, D. Brown, and G. G. Corbett), pp. 141–166. Oxford University Press, Oxford.

Plag, Ingo (2010). Compound stress assignment by analogy: The constituent family bias. *Zeitschrift für Sprachwissenschaft*, **29**.

Plag, Ingo, Homann, Julia, and Kunter, Gero (2016). Homophony and morphology: The acoustics of word-final S in English. *Journal of Linguistics*, **52**(4), (in press).

Plank, Franz (ed.) (1991). *Paradigms: The Economy of Inflection*. Mouton de Gruyter, Berlin.

Plunkett, Kim and Marchman, Virginia (1993). From rote learning to system building: acquiring verb morphology in children and connectionist nets. *Cognition*, **48**, 21–69.

Pollard, Carl and Sag, Ivan A. (1987). *Information-Based Syntax and Semantics*. CSLI, Stanford.

Pollard, Carl and Sag, Ivan A. (1994). *Head-driven Phrase Structure Grammar*. University of Chicago Press, Stanford.

Pounder, Amanda (2000). *Processes and Paradigms in Word-formation Morphology*. Trends in Linguistics. Mouton de Gruyter, Berlin.

Pullum, Geoffrey K. and Scholtz, Barbara (2002). Empirical assessment of stimulus poverty arguments. *The Linguistic Review*, **19**, 8–50.

Pullum, Geoffrey K. and Zwicky, Arnold (1992). A misconceived approach to morphology. In *The Proceedings of The Tenth West Coast Conference on Formal Linguistics* (ed. D. Bates), pp. 387–398. Stanford Linguistics Association: CSLI.

Ramscar, Michael (2013). Suffixing, prefixing, and the functional order of regularities in meaningful strings. *Psihologija*, **46**(4), 377–396.

Ramscar, Michael and Dye, Melody (2010). Learning language from the input: Why innate constraints can't explain noun compounding. *Cognitive Psychology*, **62**, 1–40.

Ramscar, Michael, Dye, Melody, and McCauley, Stewart M. (2013a). Error and expectation in language learning: The curious absence of *mouses* in adult speech. *Language*, **89**(4), 760–793.

Ramscar, Michael, Hendrix, Peter, Love, Brad, and Baayen, R. Harald (2013b). Learning is not decline: The mental lexicon as a window into cognition across the lifespan. *The Mental Lexicon*, **3**, 450–481.

Ramscar, Michael and Port, Robert F. (2015). Categorization (without categories). In *Handbook of Cognitive Linguistics* (ed. E. Dąbrowska and D. Divak). Mouton de Gruyter, 75–99.

Ramscar, Michael and Port, Robert F. (2016). How spoken languages work in the absence of an inventory of discrete units. *Language Sciences*, **53**, Part A, 58–74.

Ramscar, Michael and Yarlett, Daniel (2007). Linguistic self-correction in the absence of feedback: A new approach to the logical problem of language acquisition. *Cognititive Science*, **31**, 927–960.

Ramscar, Michael, Yarlett, Daniel, Dye, Melody, Denny, Katie, and Thorpe, Kirsten (2010). The effects of feature-label-order and their implications for symbolic learning. *Cognititive Science*, **34**, 909–957.

Rescorla, Robert A. (1988). Pavlovian conditioning: It's not what you think it is. *American Psychologist*, **43**(3), 151–160.

Rescorla, Robert A. and Wagner, Allan R. (1972). A theory of Pavlovian conditioning: Variations in the effectiveness of reinforcement and nonreinforcement. In *Classical Conditioning II* (eds. A. H. Black and W. F. Prokasy), pp. 64–99. Appleton-Century-Crofts, New York.

Rettig, Wolfgang (1972). *Sprachsystem und Sprachnorm in der deutschen Substantivflexion*. Narr, Tübingen.

Rissanen, Jorma (1978). Modeling by shortest data description. *Automatica*, **14**(5), 465–471.

Roark, Brian and Sproat, Richard (2007). *Computational Approaches to Morphology and Syntax*. Oxford University Press.

Robins, Robert H. (1959). In defence of WP. *Transactions of the Philological Society*, **58**, 116–144. Reprinted in *Transactions of the Philological Society* **99**, 2001, 116–144.

Robins, Robert H. (1989). *General Linguistics* (fourth edn.). Longman, London.

Robins, Robert H. (1997). *A Short History of Linguistics*. Longman, London.

Rumelhart, David E. and McClelland, James L. (1986). On learning the past tenses of English verbs. In *Parallel Distributed Processing: Explorations in the*

Microstructures of Cognition (eds. D. E. Rumelhart, J. L. McClelland, and the PDP Research Group), Volume 2, pp. 216–271. MIT Press.

Saagpakk, Paul F. (2000). *Estonian-English Dictionary* (third edn.). Koolibri, Tallinn.

Sackman, Robin (2000). Numeratives in Mandarin Chinese. In *Approaches to the Typology of Word Classes* (eds. P. M. Vogel and B. Comrie), Empirical Approaches to Language Typology 23, pp. 421–477. Mouton de Gruyter, Berlin.

Sadler, Louisa and Spencer, Andrew (1998). Morphology and argument structure. In *Handbook of Morphology* (eds. A. Spencer and A. M. Zwicky), pp. 206–236. Blackwell.

Sagot, Benoît and Walther, Géraldine (2013). Implementing a formal model of inflectional morphology. In *Proceedings of SFCM 2013*, Communications in Computer and Information Science, pp. 115–134. Springer, Berlin.

Sampson, Geoffrey R. (1989). Language acquisition: Growth or learning. *Philosophical Papers*, 203–240.

Sapir, Edward (1921). *Language*. Harcourt Brace, New York.

Saussure, Ferdinand de (1916). *Cours de linguistique générale* (Critical edition edited by Tuillo de Mauro, 2005.). Payot, Paris.

Saussure, Ferdinand de (1959). *Cours de linguistique générale*. Philosophical Press, New York. Translated by Wade Baskin.

Schiering, René, Bickel, Balthasar, and Hildebrandt, Kristine A. (2010). The prosodic word is not universal, but emergent. *Journal of Linguistics*, **46**, 657–709.

Schreuder, Robert and Baayen, R. Harald (1997). How complex simplex words can be. *Journal of Memory and Language*, **37**, 118–139.

Seiler, Hansjakob (1965). On paradigmatic and syntagmatic similarity. *Lingua*, **18**, 35–97.

Shannon, Claude (1948). A mathematical theory of communication. *The Bell System Technical Journal*, **27**, 379–423, 623–656.

Shieber, Stuart M. (1986). *An Introduction to Unification-based Approaches to Grammar*. CSLI, Stanford.

Singh, Rajendra and Starosta, Stanley (2003). *Explorations in Seamless Morphology*. SAGE Publications, London.

Skousen, Royal (1989). *Analogical modeling of language*. Kluwer, Dordrecht.

Skousen, Royal (1992). *Analogy and Structure*. Kluwer, Dordrecht.

Spencer, Andrew J. (1999). Transpositions and argument structure. In *Yearbook of Morphology 1998* (eds. G. Booij and J. van Marle), pp. 73–101. Kluwer, Dordrecht.

Spencer, Andrew J. (2003). Putting some order into morphology: Reflections on Rice (2000) and Stump (2001). *Journal of Linguistics*, **39**, 621–646.

Spencer, Andrew J. (2012). Identifying stems. *Word Structure*, **5**, 88–108.

Spencer, Andrew J. (2013). *Lexical Relatedness: A Paradigm-based Model*. Oxford University Press, Oxford.

Sproat, Richard S. (2008). Morphological evolution. *3rd Workshop on Quantitative Investigations in Theoretical Linguistics*, Helsinki.

Stankiewicz, Edward (ed.) (1972). *Selected Writings of Baudouin de Courtenay*. Indiana University Press, Bloomington.

Steele, Susan (1995). Towards a theory of morphological information. *Language*, 71, 260–309.

Stemberger, Joseph Paul and MacWhinney, Brian (1986). Frequency and the lexical storage of regularly inflected forms. *Memory & Cognition*, 14, 17–26.

Stewart, Tom and Stump, Gregory T. (2007). Paradigm function morphology and the morphology/syntax interface. In *The Oxford Handbook of Linguistic Interfaces* (eds. G. Ramschand and C. Reiss), pp. 383–421. Oxford University Press.

Stump, Gregory T. (1993a). How peculiar is evaluative morphology? *Journal of Linguistics*, 29, 1–36.

Stump, Gregory T. (1993b). On rules of referral. *Language*, 69(3), 449–479.

Stump, Gregory T. (1993c). Position classes and morphological theory. In *Yearbook of Morphology 1992* (eds. G. Booij and J. van Marle), pp. 129–180. Kluwer, Dordrecht.

Stump, Gregory T. (1995). The uniformity of head marking in inflectional morphology. In *Yearbook of Morphology 1994* (ed. G. Booij and J. van Marle), pp. 245–249. Kluwer, Dordrecht.

Stump, Gregory T. (2001). *Inflectional Morphology: A Theory of Paradigm Structure*. Cambridge University Press, Cambridge.

Stump, Gregory T. (2005a). Rules about paradigms. In *Morphology and the Web of Grammar: Essays in Memory of Steven G. Lapointe* (eds. C. O. Orgun and P. Sells), pp. 49–82. CSLI Publications.

Stump, Gregory T. (2005b). Some criticisms of Carstairs-McCarthy's conclusions. *Yearbook of Morphology*, 2, 283–303.

Stump, Gregory T. (2006). Heteroclisis and paradigm linkage. *Language*, 82(2), 279–322.

Su, Xiaoqin (2011). *Reflexivität im Chinesischen. Eine integrative Analyse. Mit zwei Anhängen von Hans-Heinrich Lieb*. Peter Lang Verlag, Frankfurt.

Taft, Marcus (1979). Recognition of affixed words and the word frequency effect. *Memory and Cognition*, 7, 263–272.

Timberlake, Alan (2004). *A Reference Grammar of Russian*. Cambridge University Press, Cambridge.

Tomasello, Michael (2003). *Constructing a Language: A Usage-based Theory of Language Acquisition*. Harvard University Press, Cambridge, MA.

Trudgill, Peter (2011). *Sociolinguistic Typology: Social Determinants of Linguistic Complexity*. Oxford University Press, Oxford.

Tschenkéli, Kita (1958). *Einführung in die georgische Sprache*. Amirani Verlag, Zurich.

Tuldava, Juhan (1994). *Estonian Textbook*. Volume 159, Indiana University Uralic and Altaic Series. Indiana University, Bloomington.

Unbegaun, Boris (1957). *Russian Grammar*. Clarendon Press, Oxford.

van Jaarsveld, Henk J., Coolen, Riet, and Schreuder, Robert (1994). The role of analogy in the interpretation of novel compounds. *Journal of Psychological Research*, 23, 111–137.

Viguier, Marie-Hélène (2013). *Tempussemantik : das französische Tempussystem. Eine integrative Analyse*. Beihefte zur Zeitschrift für romanische Philologie, Band 366. De Gruyter, Berlin.

Viitso, Tiit-Rein (2003). Rise and development of the Estonian language. In *Estonian Language* (ed. M. Erelt), pp. 130–230. Estonian Academy Publishers, Tallinn.

Viks, Ülle (1992). *Väike vormi-sõnastik: Sissejuhatus & grammatika*. Eesti Teaduste Akadeemia Keele ja Kirjanduse Instituut, Tallinn.

Wade, Terrence (1992). *A Comprehensive Russian Grammar*. Blackwell, Oxford.

Weaver, Warren (1948). Science and complexity. *American Scientist*, **36**, 536–544.

Weaver, Warren (1955). Translation. In *Machine Translation of Languages: Fourteen Essays* (eds. W. N. Locke and A. D. Booth), pp. 15–23. MIT Press, Cambridge, MA.

Wells, Rulon S. (1947). Immediate constituents. *Language*, **23**, 81–117.

Whitney, William Dwight (1885). *The Roots, Verb-forms and Primary Derivatives of the Sanskrit Language*. Breitkopf and Härtel, Leipzig. Reproduced as Vol. 30 of the *American Oriental Series*, New Haven: 1946.

Whitney, William Dwight (1889). *Sanskrit Grammar*. Harvard University Press, Cambridge, MA.

Wiese, Richard (1996). *The Phonology of German*. Clarendon Press, Oxford.

Wittgenstein, Ludwig (1921). Logisch-Philosophische Abhandlung. *Annalen der Naturphilosophische*, **XIV**, 185–262.

Wunderlich, Dieter (1999). German noun plural reconsidered. *Behavioral and Brain Sciences*, **22**(6), 1044–1045.

Wurzel, Wolfgang U. (1984). *Studien zur deutschen Lautstruktur*. Akademie-Verlag, Berlin.

Zepeda, Ofelia (1983). *A Papago Grammar*. University of Arizona Press, Tucson.

Zipf, George K. (1949). *Human Behavior and the Principle of Least Effort*. Addison-Wesley, Cambridge, MA.

Zwicky, Arnold M. (1985). How to describe inflection. In *Proceedings of the Eleventh Annual Meeting of the Berkeley Linguistics Society* (eds. M. Niepokuj, M. Van Clay, V. Nikiforidou, and D. Feder), pp. 372–386. Berkeley Linguistics Society, Berkeley.

Index